TRUE
REVEALED ANEW
BY
JESUS

Received Through
JAMES E. PADGETT

Previous Title
MESSAGES FROM JESUS
AND CELESTIALS

Vol. II

First Published 1941
Second Edition 1950
Third Edition 1965

Published by

Church of the New Birth™,SM
Incorporated
Post Office Box 6, Williamsville, N.Y. 14231
Website: www.DivineLove.org

Present Mailing Address

of

Incorporated
Post Office Box 6, Williamsville, N.Y. 14231

The Testimony of James E. Padgett

Mr. J. E. Padgett's religious beliefs were of the orthodox Protestant church before he obtained the Messages .This letter explains his experience and beliefs at the time of receiving these communications. It was written to an orthodox minister of the Protestant faith.

DR. GEORGE H. GILBERT, Ph.D., D.D.,   Dec. 28, 1915.
Dorset, Vermont.

DEAR SIR:

I hope that you will pardon me for writing you as I herein shall, for your evident voluntary interest in a certain subject matter and my involuntary interest in the same, furnish the only excuse. I have read your article, "Christianizing the Bible," in the November issue of the Biblical World, and am much impressed with the same, not only because of its inherent merits but because its demands and suggestions are very similar to those which have been made through me in a way and manner which I can scarcely expect you to give credence to; nevertheless, I shall submit the matter to you recognizing your right to consider what it may say unworthy of your serious attention.

First permit me to state that I am a practical lawyer of 35 years experience, (43 years experience at the time of his decease on Mar. 17, 1923), and as such, not inclined to accept allegations of fact as true without evidencing proof. I was born and reared in an orthodox Protestant church and until quite recently remained orthodox in my beliefs; that a little more than a year ago, upon the suggestion being made to me that I was a psychic, I commenced to receive by way of automatic writing messages from what was said to be messages from the spirit world and since that time I have received nearly * 1500 such messages upon many subjects but mostly as to things of a spiritual and religious nature, not orthodox, and as to the errancy of the Bible.

I have not space to name nor would you probably be interested in the great number of the writers of these messages, but among the writers is Jesus of Nazareth, from whom I have received more than 100 messages I will frankly say that I refused for a long time to believe that these messages came from Jesus because God,** while He had the power as I believed would not engage in doing such a thing. BUT THE EVIDENCE OF THE TRUTH OF THE ORIGIN OF THESE MESSAGES BECAME SO CONVINCING NOT ONLY FROM THE GREAT NUMBER AND POSITIVENESS OF THE WITNESSES, BUT FROM

* Many more messages from Jesus were received up to the year 1923.
** Mr. P. thought as many of the orthodox do; that Jesus is God, or second part of the Trinity. That was before Jesus wrote him and said: "That those who worship him as God commit blasphemy."

THE INHERENT AND UNUSUAL MERITS OF THE CONTENTS OF THE MESSAGES THAT I WAS FORCED TO BELIEVE, AND NOW SAY TO YOU THAT I BELIEVE IN THE TRUTH OF THESE COMMUNICATIONS WITH AS LITTLE DOUBT AS I EVER BELIEVED IN THE TRUTH OF A FACT ESTABLISHED BY THE MOST POSITIVE EVIDENCE IN COURT. I WISH FURTHER TO SAY THAT TO MY OWN CONSCIOUSNESS I DID NO THINKING IN WRITING THE MESSAGES DID NOT KNOW WHAT WAS TO BE WRITTEN NOR WHAT WAS WRITTEN AT THE TIME EXCEPT THE WORD THAT THE PENCIL WAS WRITING.

THE GREAT REVELATION OF THESE MESSAGES FROM JESUS AS HE WROTE IS TO MAKE A REVELATION OF THE TRUTHS OF HIS FATHER. HE ASSERTS THAT THE BIBLE DOES NOT CONTAIN HIS REAL TEACHINGS AS HE DISCLOSED THEM WHILE ON EARTH; THAT MANY THINGS THAT HE SAID ARE NOT THEREIN CONTAINED, AND MANY THINGS THAT ARE ASCRIBED TO HIM THEREIN HE DID NOT SAY AT ALL. AND HE WANTS THE TRUTHS MADE KNOWN TO MANKIND.

AND I MUST SAY THAT MANY OF THESE TRUTHS WHICH HE HAS ALREADY WRITTEN, I NEVER BEFORE HEARD OF, AND I HAVE STUDIED THE BIBLE TO SOME EXTENT. ONE THING IN PARTICULAR IMPRESSED ME AND THAT IS WHAT THE TRUTH IS OF HIS BRINGING "LIFE AND IMMORTALITY TO LIGHT." THE BIBLE DOES NOT STATE IT, AND I HAVE NOT BEEN ABLE TO FIND IN ANY COMMENTARIES ON THE BIBLE AN EXPLANATION OF IT.

Yours truly J. E. Padgett

INTRODUCTION

THE NEW BIRTH

There was a man of the Pharisees, named Nicodemus, a ruler of the Jews: The same came to Jesus by night and said unto him, Rabbi, we know that thou art a teacher come from God: for no man can do these miracles that thou doest except God be with him.

Jesus answered and said unto him, Verily, verily, I say unto thee, Except a man be born again, he cannot see the Kingdom of God.

Nicodemus saith unto him, How can a man be born when he is old? Can he enter the second time into his mother's womb and be born?

Jesus answered, Verily, verily, I say unto you, Except a man be born of water and the Spirit, he cannot enter the Kingdom of God.

That which is born of the flesh is flesh, and that which is born of the Spirit is Spirit.

Marvel not that I said unto thee, Ye must be born again.

John, Chapter III, verses 1-7.

The New Birth is the essence of Jesus' mission. Nowhere else will one find so succinctly and clearly the requirements of the glad tidings of salvation which Jesus received from the Father and proclaimed to mankind. All the promises and prophecies of the Old Testament are here fulfilled.

The meaning of the New Birth, and how it brings salvation to mankind through Jesus the Christ, has never been explained; it is found neither in the Gospel of John, such as it has come down to us, nor in any of the many interpretations of immortality which the fathers of the early church or the spiritual leaders of the later reform sects have sought to inject into the passage.

For the New Birth is not a product of speculation or reasoning coming from the mind; it is an experience of the soul and the fountainhead of that great joy and gladness which constituted the heritage of the early Christians, a heritage now lost to the churches of Christianity. The New Birth resulted in the joyful knowledge that, on leaving this earthly existence, man could look forward with certainty to a life of eternal glory with God.

What, then, is the New Birth? What was this God-given doctrine which Jesus proclaimed, but which has been so long discarded in favor of man-made notions of salvation, to be supposedly achieved through rites and ceremonies? The New Birth is Jesus' revelation to the world that the Divine Love of the Heavenly Father, withdrawn from mankind with the fall of the first parents, had been rebestowed by the Father in His goodness and mercy. Jesus, his soul filled with the Father's Love, was the visible proof of its bestowal.

Our Salvation, then, resides in the Divine Love of the Father. His Love, obtained through earnest longing of the soul and prayer to Him, is not inherent in the soul itself, as some may believe, but it is something added to the soul from the Father in response to individual seeking, and

iv

when obtained in sufficient degree, gives that soul the certainty, knowledge and possession of immortality, eternal life in the Kingdom of God. The soul that seeks the Father's Love may continue to obtain it in increasing abundance throughout all eternity.

That is what Jesus meant by being born of the water and the Spirit. The water is not any symbol of purification, but the "living waters" of God's own essence, His Divine Love, which fills the soul and enables it to live. The Spirit does not come to dwell in the soul of man but, being the instrument of God, has the function of conveying the Father's Love into the soul of whomsoever may seek it in earnest prayer.

The Father's Love, as it continues to permeate the soul, transforms that soul from the image of God, in which it was originally created, into His very essence and nature, and brings it into at-onement with Him. As prayer for His Love continues, the evil desires of the flesh which pollute the soul are in time eliminated and only the Father's Love, Goodness and Mercy abide therein.

This is the real meaning of forgiveness of sin, and in this sense can come only with the New Birth. It is not something that comes miraculously through belief in Jesus' name or trust that God by His mere fiat will overlook the transgressions of His children. And this is confirmed throughout the pages of the Old Testament, in which the children of Israel paid with captivity in Assyria and Babylonia and suffered greatly at the hands of oppressors for creating the conditions leading to such calamities by the accumulation of their sins and backslidings. True, by exercising his will, man can seek forgiveness by trying to tear out of his soul those emotions which are not harmonious with his real nature; and indeed, he should strive to do so. Yet everyone knows how difficult this is. And God's help is available to overcome sin for those who seek it, with a contrite heart and in earnest prayer.

God's forgiveness consists in our turning to Him and seeking His Love, which, on entering the soul, progressively eradicates from it those desires and emotions which are at variance with His Laws. The forgiveness that comes with the New Birth, then, is a positive act of cooperation on the part of man and God. Man must seek it in soulful prayer and God confers it upon man through an active process of eradication.

The New Birth, then, as the transformation of the human soul into the Divine Soul and the consequent purification from sin through the Father's Love, thus qualifies the soul to live throughout all eternity with God in His Celestial Mansions. This is the Love which Jesus manifested in his soul and with which he charged his apostles to love one another at the Last Supper (This is my commandment, *That ye love one another, as I have loved thee,* John XV, 12). It is the Love which he explained to Nicodemus, that master in Israel, and taught men of faith to seek for.

Thus Jesus was born from above; indeed, he was born of the Holy Spirit in the sense that it is the agency through which the Father's Love was poured out in abundance into his soul; and he told Nicodemus that he too and all those of God's children who would obey his teachings, could also be reborn through the Spirit and become at-one with the

Father. This transformation of the soul, this spiritual regeneration, is the New Birth which Jesus taught and which has now been made crystal clear in the TRUE GOSPEL REVEALED ANEW by JESUS and obtained through the mediumship of Mr. James E. Padgett, a Washington lawyer, between the years of 1914 and 1923. These writings, which Jesus himself declares are his "New and Repeated Gospel for all Mankind," brings to light his true teachings of the New Birth and the Father's Love.

D.G.S.

TABLE OF CONTENTS

TABLE OF CONTENTS

TABLE OF CONTENTS

TABLE OF CONTENTS

TABLE OF CONTENTS

TABLE OF CONTENTS

TABLE OF CONTENTS

TABLE OF CONTENTS

TABLE OF CONTENTS

XV

TABLE OF CONTENTS

xvi

TABLE OF CONTENTS

TABLE OF CONTENTS

TABLE OF CONTENTS

TABLE OF CONTENTS

TABLE OF CONTENTS

xxi

TABLE OF CONTENTS

Jesus wants the World to Follow His Teachings.

I am here, *Jesus.*

God is love and they that worship Him in spirit and love will not be forsaken.

I came to tell you that you are very near the kingdom, only believe and pray to the Father and you will soon know the truth, and the truth will make you free. *You were hard hearted and sinful, but now that you are seeking the light I will come to you and help you, only believe and you will soon see the truth of my teachings. Go not in the way of the wicked for their end is punishment and long suffering. Let your love for God and your fellow man increase.

You are not in condition for further writing. I will come to you again when you are stronger. Yes, it is Jesus and I want the world to follow the teachings of my words.

Goodbye and may the Holy Spirit bless you as I do.

Jesus Christ.

Affirming that Jesus Wrote.

I am here. *Helen. (Mr. Padgett's wife)*

Yes, I am here and I love to be with you. (Who last wrote to me?) The Savior of men. He was with you and I was so glad as I feel that you will now believe that I am in the spirit world and in the love of God. He is the Lord who came down from Heaven to save men. Let his love for you, help you to become a more spiritual man. God will bless you in all your doings.

Good night.
Helen.

Affirmation that Jesus wrote through Mr. Padgett.

Yes, I am here **your father.** Yes, it is true. He was with you and you will soon learn much more from him as he says that he will teach you the Truth and the Light and the Way. Love God and keep His commandments. Let your heart be open to the divine teachings of the Master. He will not show you all the love he has for you, but

*Mr. Padgett told me that he had a vision of Jesus many years before he knew he had the mediumistic gift to receive communications from spirits.

He told me that when he saw Jesus at the time he had the vision, that he looked at him with a great love and sympathy as if he wanted him to become a true follower of him.

The first mesages from Jesus are for the purpose of encouraging Mr. Padgett to get into his soul the Divine Love in sufficient abundance so as to change the quality of his brain into that high quality that would enable Jesus to write the high quality of truths or formal messages, that he is so anxious to give to the world. For further explanation, read Foreword, Page X of Preface—Why these earliest personal messages in this Vol. II were not inserted in Vol. I.

will let you feel that he is your loving friend and Saviour. (Why did he come to me?) Because he loves you and believes that you may be of some benefit to the world.

Yes he was the real Jesus of the Bible.

He is not in the Heavens and sitting on the right hand of the Father, but is among all mankind and still teaching them the power of love and truth. He does not need the worship of men, but all that he wants is their love and happiness.

He is not the Saviour of the few but of all who will ask him to help them. Let your love for God increase and you will not be unhappy or cast down.

Good night.

Your father,

John H. Padgett.

Affirmation Jesus wrote.

Give your heart to the Lord and He will bless you as you will soon realize.

He did and he will come to you again soon. He is waiting to tell you of the truths that he is longing to have you know. He is not going to let you feel that he is away up in the heavens far beyond the reach of men, but is with them all the time working and trying to save them from their sins. Let your love for God and His truths keep you from unbelief and doubt. Be a true seeker after the knowledge that is in Christ and you will not be long in doubt as to which is the way to eternal happiness. Keep trying to find the truth. He told me that he would come to you so that you might not doubt any longer, and he is not going to leave you again as he did some years ago when your heart was hard and sinful.

You must believe that he came to you. He is no other than Jesus of the Bible.

I will love and help you at all times.

Your grandmother,

Ann Rollins.

Personal Message to Mr. Padgett.

Jesus is not God, but was sent by the Father to lead men to His favor and love. He is the Way, the Truth and the Life.

I Am Here, *Jesus.*

Be of good cheer for I am with you always. Do not let your heart fear, for the Lord is your keeper and He will be your guide and shield. Only believe and trust in Him and you will soon be born again into the spiritual world of His kingdom. Let me teach you and give you the thoughts that He gave me while on earth. Let me show you that the things of this world are not the things that save the soul from sin and unhappiness. Be a true follower of your God. (The New Birth?) It is the flowing of the Holy Spirit into the soul of a man and the disappearing of all that tended to keep it in a condition of sin and error. It is not the workings of the man's own will but the grace of God. It is the love of God that passes all understanding. You will soon experience the change and then you will be a happy man and fit to lead others to the truths of God. Let your heart be open to the knockings of the Spirit and keep your mind free from thoughts of sin. Be a man who loves his God and his fellow man. Your love is only now of the earthly kind, but it will soon be of the things spiritual.

You must not let the cares of this world keep you from God. Let His Spirit come into your soul. Your will is the thing that determines whether you will become a child of God or not. Unless you are willing to let the Holy Spirit enter into your heart it will not do so. Only the voluntary submission to or acceptance of the Holy Spirit will make the change.

I was the instrument in God's hands of leading men to His favor and love. When I said I am the Way, the Truth and the Life, I meant that through my teachings and example men should be able to find God. I was not God and never claimed to be. The worship of me as a God is blasphemous and I did not teach it. I am a son of God as you are. Do not let the teachings of men lead you to worship me as a God. I am not. The trinity is a mistake of the writers of the Bible. There is no trinity—only one God, the Father. He is one and alone. I am His teacher of truth—the Holy Spirit is His messenger and dispenser of love to mankind. We are only His instruments in bringing man to a union with Him. I am not the equal of my Father— He is the only true God. I came from the spirit world to earth and took the form of man, but I did not become a God—only the son of my Father. You also lived as a spirit in that kingdom, but you took the form of man merely as a son of your Father. You are the same as I am, except as to spiritual development, and you may become as greatly developed as myself; I am the only son when on earth who until then had become vested with the Divine love of God to the extent of being wholly free from sin and error when I lived in the flesh. My life was not a life of earthly pleasure or sin, but was given wholly to my Father's work. I was His only son in that light. He was my Father as I knew Him to be. He is not a spirit of form like myself or yourself.

3

I was born as you were born. I was the son of Mary and Joseph and not born of the Holy Spirit as it is written in the Bible. I was only a human being as regards my birth and physical existence. The account in the New Testament is not true and was written by those who knew not what they wrote. They have done the cause of God's truths much injury. Let not your belief in that error keep you from seeing that my teachings are the truth. Be only a believer of God and His truths and you will soon be in the kingdom. You will soon be able to understand as I understand.

Good night.
Jesus Christ.

I am here—*your father*. Jesus, the one of the Bible. He was with you and you are the one who must feel that you are highly favored. You must believe that it was he. No it was the true Jesus. No imposter could have written as he did. Good night.

Your father,
John H. Padgett.

You were talking to Jesus. I know for I was here, and have talked to him many times. Be of good cheer. You will soon feel the influence of his having been with you.

Your grandmother,
Ann Rollins.

Good night—I love you,

Helen.

You have my blessing. It was the Christ who was talking. He is your friend and Saviour.

Your mother,
Ann R. Padgett.

Divine Love is Reaching Out to Every Man. Mr. Padgett is the Instrument to Receive the Truths.

Christ Jesus is here and wishes to write to you about the love of God and the needs of mankind.

Let your mind be free from all thoughts of evil and sin. The love of God is reaching out for every man so that the meanest will be the object of His care. Do not let the thought that He is only loving the good and righteous lead you to think that you must seek the company of these favored ones only. Let the lost and unhappy be the objects of your efforts to show them the way to the Father.

You will have an opportunity in receiving our messages to teach all mankind the love of God for His children, and that they are the children of His greatest care and love. Be only earnest in your efforts

4

to spread the truths which I shall teach you in my communications, and you will be a successful laborer in the work which the Father has decreed you to do. Give your best endeavors to the spreading of the messages and you will not only save the souls of the blinded and lost, but also will hasten the coming of the kingdom in your own life and heart. Let me come to you often for you are the instrument that I wish to use in "MY NEW OR REPEATED GOSPEL OF GLAD TIDINGS TO THE HUMAN RACE." Be true to the trust that I shall impose in you and let not the cares of the world keep you from spreading my gospel. Come to the love of God in a more enlarged and truthful meaning and you will be my true follower. Let me lead you to the fountainhead of all the truths of God I have in store for humanity.

My own love and power will guide you and keep you in the way of Light and Truth that you may teach to your fellow man. Your own soul must be first purified and then you will be able to show others the power and love that I have for them.

You are not to seek the help of other spirits until I teach you the truths of my Father. He is the only one who has the power to save men from their sins and errors. Be true and earnest in your work, and don't let other things distract your mind or work from the task set before you. The world needs a new awakening, and the infidelity and unbelief of men who think themselves wise but who are foolish as they will ultimately find out, and the material things must not fill their souls much longer or they will suffer more than they can imagine. The material needs of mankind are not the only clouds that must be lifted from their souls.

You are too weak to write more now.

Yes, but I am not able to write more now because you are not in condition.

You must stop writing now.

Jesus Christ.

*Mrs. Helen Padgett's Experience in Leaving Her Body
and Going to the Spirit World.*

I am here, *Helen.* (*Mrs. J. E. Padgett*) *Wife of Mr. J. E. Padgett.*

I am so very happy as you are loving me very much to night, for I can see that your thoughts are with me so much more than of late; so let me continue to feel that you love me so much.

When I realized that the time had come for me to go, I did not fear to do so, but calmly waited and thought that all my sufferings would soon end; and when my spirit left the body I commenced to feel as if I was rising out of it and that I was going upward to the place that

5

I had so often heard my father speak about. But I had scarcely awakened to the fact that my spirit had left the body, before your mother had me in her arms and was trying to tell me that I had nothing to fear or cause me to feel that I was not with those that loved me. She was so beautiful that I hardly realized that it was she, and when I commenced to see that I was no longer in my body, I asked her not to leave me but to take me with her to where she lived. She told me that I could not go there, but that God had prepared a place for me to go to, and that she would accompany me and show me the truth of my future existence. I went with her and she took me to a place that was very beautiful and filled with spirits who had recently passed over. She did not leave me for a long time, and when she did, your father came to me and said "I am Ned's father and want to help you to realize that you are now in the spirit world, and must not let the thoughts of the earth keep you from getting in a condition to learn that all of us are only waiting for the love of God to help us to higher and better things."

Your grandmother soon came to me and told me who she was, and was so beautiful and bright that I scarcely could look at her, for her face was all aglow with what seemed to me to be a heavenly light; and her voice was so sweet and musical that I thought she must be one of God's angels that I had read about in the Bible. She told me of the things that God had perpared for me and He wanted me to love Him and feel that He loved me.

But after awhile I commenced to think that I must be deceived in my sight and hearing and was still on earth, and needed only my body again to know that I was still a mortal. Some time elapsed before I really became conscious that I was a spirit and was not on earth; for when I tried to talk to you, as I did, you would not listen to me and turned away from me as if you did not see or hear me. After a short time your mother and father came to me again, and tried to persuade me that I must not continue in my belief that I was still of the earth, but must believe that I was in spirit life, and needed only the things of the spirit to make me more contented.

So you see, I was so very fortunate in having your dear parents and grandmother welcome me when I passed over. If they had not received me I do not know to what condition of fear and distraction I might have been subjected. No spirit can learn the truth of the change, unless in some way helped by others.

So you see when you come over I will be there to receive you and love you so much that you will never have to go through the period of doubt that I did. Your father is also waiting to receive you, and, in fact, all your spirit band have agreed that when you come, you will have nothing to fear for want of help and love.

6

I first saw my parents after I commenced to believe that I was in the spirit world; and, when I saw them they did not know me, but thought that I was still in the body and that they were still on earth, as they had not yet awakened to the fact that they were in the spirit world. They were very unhappy, and it took considerable talking to make them believe that they were spirits and not mortals. My father was more easily convinced than was my mother, for he commenced sooner to recall that when death comes, the spirit must go to God who gave it. My mother would not believe so soon, for she continued to think that she was with her acquaintances on earth, and that they were not treating her very courteously, for when she spoke to them, they would not answer. But thank God, they both now realize that they are in the spirit world, and that they must learn to love God, if they would be happy.

When I commenced to leave the body there was no pain or suffering, only a feeling that I was rising out of it. No darkness appeared to me, and I saw my body lying there as if it were asleep. I did not try to hold it, but thought that it was merely taking a rest, and that as soon as it felt refreshed I would enter it again and continue to live as before. I did not wait for it to awaken, but continued to arise until, as I told you, your mother clasped me in her arms—she was my own dear mother as well as yours.

I did not know that I was dying, but felt that something unusual was happening; and I was not afraid. As I always in life dreaded death, as you know, the strange thing to me was, that I did not look upon death as dying. It was only a pleasant dreamy feeling, and I only thought that I was going to become absent from my body until it was refreshed. My thoughts were not of death at all. I had been suffering pain, but I thought that I was getting well and the feeling of relief that came over me was the result of my getting better.

As my spirit arose, I thought only of my condition and how soon I would be able to return home and see my friends. No other thoughts came to me—not even my love for God, or the fact that I was not in condition as regards my soul, to meet my Maker, as I had been taught. There was absolutely no fear of what might happen to me, or that I would soon be called upon to account for the sins I had committed. Just before my spirit left my body I was unconscious, but just as soon as the separation commenced I became fully conscious, and knew everything that took place and did not feel at all as if I were in danger or needed the help of anyone.

I did not stay with my body at all, when I commenced to leave it, but continued to rise, as I have told you until your mother met me. So you see death, which I so much feared, was not such a dreadful thing to experience.

7

Yes, when my son came to where my body lay, I returned to it, and saw it taken away and afterwards buried; but I still did not understand what it all meant and only when your grandmother told me that I would no more inhabit it, did I commence to realize that I had left it forever; but even then I had some feeling that she was mistaken, and that in some way I would return to it again and continue to live on earth.

Yes, when I had been in the spirit world a short time, I saw other spirit forms and, even then, I was not in a condition of mind to fully understand that they were spirits and not mortals. The resemblance is very real to one who has never had his spiritual eyes opened; and even though the spirit forms all appear much more beautiful and bright, yet to me they all seemed to be human forms, and I thought that I was not in condition to fully see just what they were. You must let me stop now, for I am tired.

Your own true and loving, Helen.

Mrs. Padgett (Helen) says Mr. P's grandmother will write.

I AM HERE—*Helen*:

I am very happy and so are you as I can see, for you are not worried tonight, but you must not try to write much for our condition is not so good as it might be.

Yes, I think so, or if you feel that you should write a little, let your grandmother write as she is here and wants to say something to you about your love for God and His love for you.

Your own true and loving,

HELEN.

The importance of getting the Divine Love in the soul.

I AM HERE—*Your grandmother*: (Mrs. Ann Rollins).

I wish to tell you more about the things of the spirit for they are the important things that you should know. You are very near the kingdom and if you keep on trying to have more of God's love in your soul you will soon realize the full joy and peace which comes with such possession. Try to let your heart receive more of His love, for He is always ready and waiting to bestow His love upon you as He is the one Lovely Father for you to long for and keep with you in all your thoughts and aspirations. Do not let the worries of life keep you from loving and believing that He wants you to become one with Him in love and grace. He is not only waiting for you to let His love flow into your heart, but He is anxiously knocking at the door of your heart that you may open and let Him enter.

Be true to your best spiritual longings and you will soon feel that you have got that in your soul which will give you perfect peace and happiness. You are only now beginning to learn that you must feel that your Father

8

is so near you that He must become a part of your life and being. When that love has fully taken possession of you, you will know that you are His own true and reconciled son, just as all are who have come into a realization of that love. So do not doubt that you may become such a son of your Father, for I tell you that I know from my own experience and grandeur of living in the favor of His blessing.

Be my own dear boy and do try to reach out and get this love.

You must not let the things of your earth life keep you from the higher things that the Father has prepared to give you. You will soon know as I know, that the only things worth striving after are the things of this spiritual love of the Father. Be more anxious to get this knowledge and it will come to you in all its beauty and convincing force. I so wish that you could see the Holy Spirit's work among men and spirits, for then you would not doubt any more that God is a God of love and not of anger or retribution.

Keep praying, for that is the one great means to receive the love of God. Without prayer men cannot reach the answering ear of the Father's grace. He will hear the penitent only, for he will not accept any one who is not truly and anxiously seeking Him. Man has a will to either accept or reject the love of God, and until he exercises that will in a way to show that he wants that love it will not be given him. No man is ever forced to love God or to let God's love come into his heart.

The love of God cannot be defined, for it passes all understanding, but the result of that love when in the souls of men can be seen and felt in the exceeding beauty in the countenances of men and their wonderful happiness—no fear of death or anything that maketh afraid can possibly exist where that love is. It is not the love that permits any feelings of jealousy or envy to have an entrance, but is so perfect and all soul filling that there cannot possibly be any room for anything but its own great self. I know that the love of God is the only thing that can make man supremely happy while on earth and after he becomes a spirit. My love for Him is such that I love every one of His creatures, be they saints or sinners, and that is the difference that He inspires in all his children, and the love that exists among men and spirits who have not His love for its foundation. Be sure that no man can be perfectly happy without this Divine Love.

You wife is progressing very rapidly in the way to this perfect love, and I think that in a short time she will be with me in my sphere for she will not let anything come between her and her efforts to possess the greatest amount of this love that is possible to obtain.

It is wonderful how her faith has grown since she first became convinced that she must seek the Father's love in order to become one with

9

Him and perfectly happy. You must try to get this faith and progress with her so that when you come over you will go forward together in soul development and conjugal love. She is now in the *third heaven as she has told you and she is almost in a condition of development to leave that sphere and go with your mother to the fifth sphere where her happiness will be so much greater.

She loves you so much that you must feel that she wants you to be with her in all her happiness. She is not the same Helen as when she was on earth, but is so much changed that your mother says her appearance is as different as earth from heaven. She is not only changed in her appearance, but in her temperament and desires for those things which do not tend to retard the progress of the soul.

Let her tell you of her love for you and you must believe what she is telling you, as she surely does. She is not one who is in condition to speak anything else than the truth. Her love for you is so great that I sometimes wonder how it can be, for while we all love you as well as our soulmates, yet she seems to have such intense love for you, that we wonder. We think that her nature is so intense that she cannot do anything in a way that is not the result of her strong and earnest constitution, or rather that is not the result of a power that knows no limitation in effort or force.

But while she loves you so intensely her love for God is not interfered with in the least for just as she gives her whole soul to loving you she devotes it to loving God also; and when you do come over you will find such love in her heart for you as we seldom see in the spirit life for our soulmates.

But you must not think from this that we do not love intensely also, and the love that we all have for our soulmates is very great and deep as I must tell you—but she seems to be almost consumed by this love for you and you must never do anything to hurt her or make her feel that you do not want it or deserve it.

My dear boy we must stop writing now as you are not in condition to write more. So I will say good night and God bless you and keep you in His love and care.　　　　　　　　　　Your loving grandmother.
　　　　　　　　　　　　　　　　　　　　Ann Rollins.
　　　　　　　　Affirming Ann Rollins wrote.
I love you, good night.

Yes she did, and she did not tell you all for she cannot know it all, but I know and I tell you that my love for you is not capable of being told.

Good night, my own dear Ned.　　　　　　　　　　Helen.

Spirit's experience after writing through Mr. Padgett. Obtained the Divine Love and made his progress into the third sphere.

I am here, your old friend G. R.——

Yes it is I, and I am glad to be able to write to you again. I told your

*Later message Mrs. Padgett reached the 3rd Celestial Sphere.

10

wife, that I desired to write and tell you of my progress in spiritual matters, and as you are kind enough to give me the opportunity, I will try to tell you how my eyes were opened to the things of the spirit and my heart to the love of God.

Well, as you know, when I first commenced to write to you, I did not exactly believe in a God or Jesus or his teachings, except as they related to the moral condition of men. When you first commenced to talk to me about these spiritual things, I thought that you were merely telling me the things that you had learned in your church or Sunday school, and that they were only intended for men and women of no capacity to think for themselves, and suited only to receive what the preachers might tell them. So, you see, I was not in a very receptive condition of mind to enable me to believe that what you told me had any foundation in fact or in truth. Jesus, to me, was just the same as any other man who had received large conceptions of the truth; but he was only a mere man in the sense that what he attempted to teach he had learned by study and meditation, or through some worldly source that I did not know of. At any rate, that his teachings were not the result of inspiration, or derived from a source any different from what mankind received other information as to things of nature or of spirit. Well, as you continued to tell me that I was mistaken, and that there is a Source from which all good flows, other than the mere mind or conscience of man, I began to think about the matter, and when I looked around me and saw that your mother and wife, who claimed that they had received this love of God which you insisted was waiting for me to obtain, were so beautiful and happy, while I, and my folks were not very beautiful and not at all happy, I began to inquire the cause, and when you told me that their, I mean your mother's and wife's, condition was due to this love of God, I asked them to tell me about the nature of this love and the way in which they obtained it. And your mother, bless her soul, took great pains to instruct me in these things.

And, when I learned that prayer was the only way to this love and saw you praying for me with all your heart and in great earnestness, I commenced to pray also; but I must confess that my prayers were not accompanied with much faith. But I continued to pray, and every night when you prayed for me and the many others who were with you praying, I tried to exercise all the faith possible—and prayed for more faith. This continued for some time, and one day your grandmother, who is a most wonderful spirit in goodness and beauty, came to me and said, that she was your grandmother and was very much interested in me, on your account as well as on my own, and commenced to unfold to me the great efficacy of prayer, and assured me that if I would only try to believe and pray God to help me believe, He would answer my prayers, and

I would soon find that with my earnest efforts, faith would come to me, and with faith, would come this love into my heart, and with this love would come happiness and joy.

So I listened to her and tried to believe that what she told me must be true, and that she was interested in me and desired only my happiness. I continued to pray, as I said, and one day after I had received some considerable faith, I met Jesus, and he told me of the wonderful things that his Father had prepared for me, if I would only believe and ask Him to give them to me. Jesus was so very beautiful and loving that I could not resist the influence which came over me; and then my faith increased and I prayed with all my heart and soul.

At last, light came to me, and with it such an inflowing of love as I never dreamed could exist, either in the earth or in the spirit world. But it came to me and I felt as if I were a new spirit, and such happiness came as I never experienced before. And then that dear mother of yours came and rejoiced with me; and also, your beautiful wife who had tried so hard to induce me to seek for this love.

Oh, Padgett, I tell you that in all the wide universe of God there is nothing to compare to this love of the Father. Let me say, that in all my life, when only my intellect ruled me, there was nothing to compare with that which came to me with this inflowing of the love.

I am now in the third heaven with many beautiful and happy spirits. Your mother and wife are higher up, and are so beautiful and good that when I am in their company I feel that I will become a much happier man if I will try to follow them. Your father has progressed too, and so has Professor Salyards.

Well, my soul is one now that is filled with this love. My mind is elevated in its thoughts and not inclined to think of those things that are merely intellectual, for, I tell you, that while knowledge of all God's laws and nature's apparent mysteries is desirable, yet, a knowledge of this love of God is far and above compare; and not only more necessary but more desirable. I would not give the feelings that come to me from the possession of this love, for all the sensations of delight that might arise from the discovery of the most stupendous and important law of the workings of nature.

Let this love come first, and then the other acquirements will only help to show the spirit, that God is a God of wisdom and power as well as of love. But as you have read, "Love is the fulfilling of the law"; nothing else is, and the man who has all the knowledge and wisdom without this love is poor indeed.

Jesus is the most wonderful of all the spirits in both love and the knowledge of the Father's attributes. He is the greatest, and knows that the

12

Father's plans to save and redeem mankind are his, and such as he teaches. So you must listen to him and believe.

I am going to try to learn more of his teachings, and, when I do, you shall know what I learn. Jesus appears to me the one altogether lovely— he has no competitor; and no one who sees him, if he has any of this love in his soul, can fail to know that he is the true Jesus of the Bible, and the only perfect son of his Father. I realized this only after this love came to me. It seems that spirits who have not this love do not realize who Jesus is, or how wonderful and glorious he is. This may seem strange to you, but it is a fact. Only when the spirit has an awakening of his soul's love for God, does Jesus appear as their great brother and teacher of this Great Love of the Father.

You must not let the things of the material life lead you to think that you must wait until you come to the spirit world to get this Great Love, for, I tell you, that the man whose soul is opened to the inflowing of this love while on earth, is a much more fortunate man than he who waits until his earthly life ends. If I had only become conscious of this love when on earth, I would have been saved many hours of suffering and unhappiness after I became a spirit. My own experience is so true to what so many undergo, and will undergo, that if I could proclaim to every man on earth the necessity of becoming possessed of this love while on earth, I would do so with all my might and strength.

I can tell you of my experience in passing over, but I do not think it best to do so tonight, as it would take too long and require more strength than you have tonight. Sometime soon I will do so in detail.

I am so glad that I have been redeemed by this Great Love and the teachings of Jesus, and the help of your spirit relatives; and, also by the help of your prayers, that I cannot express the extent of my gladness, **Nothing in all heaven or earth can compare with the feelings of joy that come to a soul when it realizes that it is at-one with the Father in love and power.**

Yes, * they know and are with you every night as you pray. They don't seem to quite understand, though, that you can help them in any way; but still they, in a manner, feel some peculiar sensation as you pray and the others pray with you. Do not stop praying for them.

I tell you that you are a wonderfully blessed man in having such a loving Christian mother and grandmother to pray with and watch over you all your life. If all men had Christian parents to teach and show them the way to this love of God, as they grow from childhood to manhood, many a time of suffering and unhappiness would be avoided, and many a spirit would come into this life with many less sins to atone for.

Your old friend,   ** G. R————.

* Appendix. Old friends of Mr. Padgett in spirit world.
** Whenever initials are given instead of full name is because living relatives might object.

13

Mrs. Helen Padgett describes the method used to communicate her thoughts through Mr. Padgett

I AM HERE—*Helen*: (*Mrs. J. E. Padgett*) *wife of Mr. Padgett.*

Let me tell you that you are only making yourself unhappy trying to learn all about the way that I write to you for you cannot do it as you are not able to see my method and I cannot fully explain it to you. But I will try to do as best I can.

When you take hold of the pencil I exercise all my power to move the pencil so that it will write just what I think, but in order to do that I have to let my thoughts go through your brain. You do not do the thinking but merely let the thoughts pass through your brain, and the movement of the pencil is caused by the exercise of your brain in conjunction with my power which I exercise on the pencil. So you see you do not originate the thought but merely convey it to the hand which I guide in accordance with my thought. You do not have anything more to do with what is written than an electric wire has to do with transmitting a message from the party at the end where the message is given.

Let me explain in another way. When I think a thought I pass it through your brain to your hand and my power to move your hand is brought into action, just as when you think a thought your power to move your hand is brought into action.

My thoughts are not your thoughts; and when I think, your mind catches the thought but does not create the same. So you must believe that I am doing the writing and not you—for I write some thoughts which you could not write if you tried. How do you like that for assurance?

But to be serious you could not write the things that I write without you gave much thought to the different subject matters for some of them are not familar to you as you have often said. Let not the idea that you are writing the things which emanate from what is sometimes called your subconscious mind, for you have no subconscious mind, and the philosophers who teach such an idea are not acquainted with the laws of the mind. The mind is only the spiritual evidence of thoughts that congregate in the brain, but which really are not a part of the material thing which the "wise men" call the subconscious self or mind—there is no such thing, and when they let their explanations of things which they cannot acount for, rest on the assertion that the subconscious mind furnishes these thoughts, they are all wrong.

Only the material brain furnishes thoughts which it puts forth from the observation of the senses, or from the faculties which are brought into action when the reason is made the basis of the thoughts. I am not a very good expounder of these things, but I tried to make it as plain as I could.

14

Yes, I am telling you this from my own observation and understanding of these things. When you receive communications from Mr. Riddle he will be able to explain more fully and more satisfactorily the laws which govern these things, and you must soon let him write.

I am studying the laws of physical and psychical sciences, so that I may be able to assist you in your investigations when you come to search for the true relationship between spirits and mortals and the laws which control these communications. Yes my studies include the investigation of the laws governing clairvoyance and inspirational communications. You will have the opportunity sometime to have an experience in each of these phases, and I want to be in condition to assist you to a degree that will help you in arriving at conclusions which will be correct and which will help others to understand the laws that govern these things.

So you see your wife loves you so much that she is willing to attempt to learn these things which are thought to be only for the masculine minds, in order to help you more clearly understand them.

But while I will do this, I will not cease to try to learn to the fullest those things which will give me a clearer understanding of those spiritual truths that lead closer to God and His love. These are the absolutely necessary--the others are important but not necessary in order that a soul may sooner or later reach the knowledge that makes it one with the Father. The love of God which passes all understanding is the one great thing to learn of and possess.

My home is now so very beautiful that my happiness is more than I can tell you of.

You will be also happy when you come over, for I am filling my home with such beautiful thoughts and so much love that when you come you will wonder how your little wife could possibly have accumulated so much beauty and filled the house with so much love.

Yes, as I receive more of God's love into my soul, my home becomes the more beautiful, only I do not have to be in the home to be able to have this love with me. It is with me all the time and when I am in my home the home becomes a reflection of that love. The home is not beautiful if the love is not there--so you see the home depends upon the existence of the love for its beauty. My soul is the creator of my home, and without the soul being beautiful the home could not be beautiful.

When I leave my home to come to you, the home remains the same, because while my soul is with me, and also the love that makes it beautiful, yet the home retains the reflection, or as you might say, the atmosphere of that love to such a degree, that the beauty of the home is not les-.sened or deteriorated by my temporary absence. So you see the home has a permanency although it depends upon the soul to give it its beauty and loveliness. My home is not yet perfect, but as I grow in God's love then more

15

perfection will come to it--the more love that I have the more beautiful the home.

We all are dependent upon the degree of love in our souls for the appearance of our homes.

Let your endeavor be to get all of this love that you possibly can, and if you succceed in getting as much as I have, you will be one with me and our home will be together. If you do not, I will have to wait until you do before we can live as one together. So do try to get all of God's love that you can. If you will only give your thoughts to the spiritual things and let your soul be open to the inflowing of this love by praying with all your soul longings you can progress just as rapidly as I do. So love enough and want to be with me enough to try with all your heart to get this love. Your own true wife,

HELEN.

Jesus giving Mr. Padgett advice as to prayer and worship. Says he has selected Mr. Padgett for the mission to do his work.

I Am Jesus:

You are my dear brother and I will tell you what I desire you to do at this time.

You must not let the little worries of your business life keep you from giving your thoughts to God in worship and in prayer, and from believing in me and loving me as your friend and teacher; for I am, and wish only to have you do those things which will make you more at-one with the Father and love me more. You must try to let all your thoughts turn to the mission which I have selected you to do, for you I have chosen and you must do my work. **As I am the one that God selected to do His work when I lived on earth, so you are the one that I now select to do my work by giving to the world my messages of truth and love.** I will soon commence to write them and you must preserve them until such time as you shall be in condition to have them published.

I do not want you to think that you are not worthy to do this great work, for you are; otherwise I would not have selected you. and this fact alone should be sufficient to make you not doubt that you are a suitable person for the work.

In my teachings I want to show you that I am only my Father's Son as you are His son, and not to be worshipped as God. He is the only God, and the people who to-day are worshipping me in all parts of the world are not doing what I desire; for they are putting God in the background and making me their object of worship, which is all wrong and which I am so anxious to have cease. They must look upon me only as a son of God and their elder brother who has received from the Father His full love and confidence and which I am bidden to teach to them.

You are not to let anyone tempt you to let your love of God be dis-

16

placed by any love you may have for me, for your love for me must not be of the kind you have for Him—He is the only God and you must worship Him alone—so be careful and make this distinction or you will make an egregious mistake.

I am your own dear brother and teacher and love you with a love that I have for very few of the mortals. Why? because I see that you will become a true follower of me and learn to love God as I love Him; only I do not want you to think that you are now in a condition that leaves you free from sin, or the necessity of praying to the Father with all your heart for an inflowing of His love. You must get all this love that is possible; and that can be gotten only by prayer and faith. So in your prayers have faith, and the time will come when you will become very close to the Father and enjoy His love to a degree that few have so far obtained.

Yes, it is possible, and as I say, it will take place. Only do as I have told you.

Yes, I will help you with all my power and love and you will succeed, only try to believe and you will realize before you come to the spirit world that God is your Father to a degree that will enable you to live very near to Him as I am living. Your faith is now very great as I know, and notwithstanding the fact that at times you have your doubts and get despondent, yet your faith is there, and it will grow in intensity, and become so strong that it will never again be shaken.

You must now let me stop as you are tired and need rest.

Yes, there are many things in my life as written in the Bible which are true, and many that are not true. These I will tell you of when I come to write my formal messages.

So let us stop now—

Your own true friend and teacher.

May God's blessings and mine rest upon you this night.

JESUS.

Affirming Jesus Wrote—by Ann Rollins

Your Grandmother:

Was he not lovely and grand? You certainly are a very favored man and I wonder at the great love that may be yours and promises of the Master.

Yes, I heard what he said, and he knows. You must believe, for he never says what he does not know to be true. You are certainly more blessed than all others. Only think of that promise and the certainty of it.

You are too tired to write more now.

Your loving Grandmother.
ANN ROLLINS

17

I Am Here—*Helen*:

You are too much loved by the Master to ever be unhappy. So let me say good night and that I love you with all my heart and soul.

HELEN.

G. R. Continues his experience in his progress.

I am here, your old friend *G. R———.

I am very happy tonight and I am glad that you are so much better. You had rather a hard time of it, and reminded me somewhat of the suffering that I used to undergo when I was on earth and in Washington. Well you are cured of the indigestion, and your digestive organs will soon be in perfect working order.

The faith that you had in your prayers and the work of the Master! You were actually cured by your faith—the work done was only a means used to impress upon you the fact that God had answered your prayers. I do not see how you could have had such faith as you had at the time, but is is a fact that you had it, and as a consequence, the cure was effective.

When you prayed as you did I was so very much impressed with your faith that I expected to see your prayers answered as they were. Jesus helped you to pray and also helped your faith. He also did the work that you observed through the power which he possesses. It was a revelation to me, I must confess, and caused me to believe more than ever in prayer and faith.

I am now so very happy in my new sphere that I cannot explain to you what that happiness means. I cannot express myself in language sufficiently strong and descriptive that you may comprehend. But this I will say, that my happiness now transcends all conception of what happiness might be when, as a mortal, I sometimes thought of the after life, and the happiness which might be in store for me when I passed over.

I am in the third sphere, but am not contented to remain there, for your mother has told me on many occasions of the far greater happiness existing in the higher spheres, I am now striving and praying for this greater happiness, and I will never be content until I get it. Your wife is in a much higher sphere, and is so very beautiful and so exceedingly happy that I know that where she lives such happiness must exist.

I am also happy because I have my soulmate with me so very often, and her love is so great and pure that it leads me on to higher things, and enables me to seek with so much earnestness the Great Love of the Father, which I now believe is waiting for me if I only will strive to obtain it, and have the faith which all who have obtained a very large degree of this Divine Love tell me of.

Your grandmother is so wonderfully beautiful and filled with this love,

<hr>

* Full name not given because living relatives might object.

18

that her very presence inspires me to believe and seek for the happiness of these higher spheres.

Well, as you want me to tell of some of the laws of the spirit world, I will say that the one great law is that God is love and that he is willing to bestow that love on anyone, spirit or mortal, who asks Him for it. I am not only very happy but I find that my mind is expanding to a great extent by reason of that love that I possess. No man or spirit can possibly be filled with this love, and not have the wisdom that necessarily comes with the love. I am not so much interested in purely mental phenomena as I was before I received this love and believed in a Father of love and truth; but I am, nevertheless, able to understand many things to a far greater degree than I could when I had merely the mental pursuits in mind. I am not yet fully conversant with the laws of communication as I told you I would learn and instruct you in, but I know enough to be able to say that every spirit is trying to communicate with his friends on earth; and why he is not able to is because the mortals are not in that condition of physical rapport that will enable them to receive the communicaitons of the spirit. I do not yet know why one mortal is so susceptible to these influences as to be readily understood and another mortal is not. Some spirits say that the law controlling this matter is not understood by spirits who have been here for a great many years and who have given considerable study on the subject.

But this I do know that when the rapport exists the communications can be made with the exercise of the powers.

But I don't know of any manifestation as satisfactory to both spirit and mortal as the writing such as you are now doing, for we have the opportunity for such a greater extent of communicating and interchanging of thoughts. I am perfectly delighted at the possibilities given me of writing you in this way. So you must believe that I am writing to you, and that all the others of your band are doing the same thing.

Your wife has more power in this regard than any of us, and she does not hesitate by writing you whenever you call for her. She is a wonderful spirit in her grasp of spirit things and in her love for the Father. So you must not let any doubt come into your mind when she writes to you, and tells you of so many wonderful things, and of her love for you. She seems to love you with a love that has no limit or possibility of growing less.

I am now going to tell you of my progress in this love and happiness. When I last wrote you I told you that I had commenced to have faith in the Father, and had received some portion of His love. Well, since then I have been praying and asking God to give me more faith and love; and as I prayed my faith increased, and as my faith increased, more of this love came into my soul, and with it an increased happiness. So I would not stop striving until I realized that my soul was commencing to get such an inflow of this love that it seemed that all things which tended to retard this inflowing were leaving me and only love and goodness were taking possession of me. I am now very far advanced over what I was when you first commenced to talk to me of this love, and I shall through all eternity remember and thank you for what you did for me. I was also fortunate as to have your mother and wife with me very much trying to show me the way to this truth of the New Birth; and then when your grandmother came to me, it seemed as if I could not resist the influence to seek and try to find it.

Lastly, when I had received enough of this spiritual awakening to realize who Jesus was, I gave him my close attention, and as he continued to show me the way to the Father, I commenced to grasp the truth and believe that my salvation depended on my receiving this Great Love and becoming a finer and better man. I tell you that Jesus is the most wonderful of all spirits that I have seen or heard about. He is so filled with love and goodness that there seems no doubt in my mind that he is the son of the Father in the special sense of the term. I mean that he is so much nearer the Father, and has so much and many of His attributes that he is the greatest son in the sense of being more at-one with the Father. We are all sons of the Father; but there is such a difference in our spiritual conditions that the contrast between Jesus and us is so great that we can readily believe that he is the greatest true son, and that his Great Love and knowledge of the qualities of the Father is greater than any Celestial Spirit. I do not mean in the sense that he was created in a different way, physically, from other men. No immaculate conception or birth from the womb of a virgin. I do not believe this dogma, and the Master says that it is not true, for he was truly, so far as his physical being is concerned, the son of a man and woman, as you or I am.

Now, I am also convinced that mankind cannot be saved from their sins unless they follow the way showed them by the Master. No man can save himself, and I wish strongly to emphasize the fact that man is dependent upon God for his salvation from the sins and errors of the natural man. I do not mean that men have not a work to do themselves, for they have. God is willing to save them, if they ask it and acknowledge that without His help they cannot be saved; but unless they do ask and believe, He will not interfere with their conditions. So you see I am not only a believer in God and Jesus, but also in the doctrine that men cannot save themselves.

I thought that man was sufficient unto himself when I was on earth, but now I know that he is not. Man may be comparatively happy and free from what is called sin—that is a violation of God's laws; but that happiness is not the same, nor is man's condition the same, as when he gets this Divine Love from the Father.

I will not speak longer on this subject tonight, but reiterate that when on earth I thought that by my own exertions, I might possibly become Divine, yet now as a spirit, I know that man is not Divine and cannot become so in all eternity unless he receives this Divine Essence which comes to him by the New Birth. Divinity is of God, alone, and only He can bestow it on man. Man, not having this Divinity, cannot create it by his own efforts. So believe what I say and strive to get it, and you will then succeed and become as the redeemed in the Celestial Spheres. With all my love and blessings.

G. R——.

On the Love of Man or Natural Love in Contrast to the Divine Love which is necessary to obtain to give man the highest degree of happiness. I Am Here, Jesus.

I want to write to night on the love of man.

This love is one that is not understood by humanity in its most important particular. I mean that this love is not one that is sufficient to give man the highest degree of happiness which he may obtain in either the mortal life or in the life to come.

This love is of a nature that changes with the change in the ideas and desires of men, and has no stability that will serve to keep him constant in his affections. No man who has only this love can ever be in condition to say that he will continue to have this love for a longer time than the present; and when he thinks that his love can never change, or leave him, he is only giving thought to the wish.

But this love is one that may last for a long time, and sometimes it seems that it can never die or grow less; yet, in its very nature, it has not that constancy which insures its lasting longer than a moment of time.

I do not mean to say anything disparaging of this natural love, for it is undoubtedly the greatest gift that the Father has bestowed upon mankind, and without it, men would be in a very unhappy condition. Yet, it is not the Great Love of the Father which all men may receive, if they will only seek and strive to obtain it by prayer and faith.

This natural love is that which unites men and women in unity while on earth, and enables them to approach nearer to a life of happiness than does any other human quality; but still it has the danger always accompanying it, that sometime, in some way it may cease to exist.

The mother's love is the strongest of all loves given to mortals, and apparently it can never end or grow old, yet a time may come when that love will die or cease to retain all its vitality or beauty. I know it is said that love never dies; but that is not true as regards this natural love:

21

and no man can say that his love of to day will remain his love of a few years hence.

Yet, there is a love that may be called the natural love that will last forever, providing these souls seek and obtain the Divine Love, and that is the love that God has implanted in two souls that he has designed to become one in spirit life. This love is really not two loves, but one and the same love manifested in the two opposite sexes, and which is only a complete one when these two apparently independent souls come together in perfect unity. This is what is commonly called the love of soulmates, and which is that essence of spiritual love which makes the happiness of the two spirits of mortals seemingly complete. Yet this love is not of a divine nature, but merely the highest type of the natural love.

So, when men speak of the love of one mortal for his fellow man, it means merely the love which his human nature is capable of having and giving to another mortal.

I do not wish to be understood as in any way implying that this love is not a great boon and blessing to mankind, for it is, and without it, there would not be the harmony that exists on earth; yet, at this time, hatred and anger seems to have taken its place in the hearts of many men who are now striving to kill and destroy. But this is only for a season; the war will cease and then men will realize more for a long time, that only their love for one another can make the earth a happy and desirable place to live on.

Love, I know it is said, is the fulfilling of the law, but no man can thoroughly understand this until he knows what love is. I do not mean that in order to fulfill every law man must have the Divine Love of the Father, because there are laws that govern the divine existence and laws that govern the human and merely spiritual existence; and the love of the Divine is the fulfillment of the former laws, and the natural love is the fulfillment of the latter laws. So you must see that only as men have the love of the Divine can they fulfill the laws of the divine existence, and so, as they have the natural love only, can they fulfill the natural laws.

But this natural love will not be able to make them one with the Father, as I have before written; and the utmost of its powers and functions is to give them that happiness which they will receive in living the life of a spirit or man unredeemed.

I will not say that man should not cultivate this love for his fellow man, to the greatest possible degree, for he should; and if that should be the only kind of love that he may have, either on earth or in the spirit world, the more of it that he possesses the happier will he be, and the greater will be the happiness of his fellowman and fellow spirit. So when I said, when on earth, that men should love their God and love their fellow men as themselves, I meant that they should do so with all the possibilities of whatever love they might possess.

Yet, if men would only learn, as they can, that there is no necessity for them to have only the natural love, but they should all seek the Greater Love and obtain the corresponding greater happiness and immortality. Men do not realize this, though, and seem to be satisfied with this natural love and the pleasures that ensue from its possession.

I would not have them do anything that would lessen this love or shut their hearts to its influence, when it pure and good; but yet, I cannot help trying to impress upon them the great desirability of having this higher love in their souls.

Yes, I am a lover of all men, and I want them to feel the happiness of the inflowing of the Divine Love, and thereby learn what the love of God means, and what they may have if they will only seek.

This love of the purely natural will not suffice for the temptations that beset men on earth; and, also, will not insure against temptations when they become spirits. I know this, and hence I say it with the positiveness of one who knows—you may say, with authority.

As you are tired I must stop.

With all my blessings and love, I am, Your brother in spirit,

JESUS.

Personal Message to Mr. Padgett from Jesus.

I AM HERE—*Jesus*:

You are my friend and disciple. You are in me and I am in thee, and we are in the Father. You are in me for all eternity.

My kingdom is not of this world and you are not of this world—you are in me as I told my disciples of old. Only believe me and keep my commandments, and I will love you to the end, and the Father will love you.

I mean that you must love all mankind—and try to show them the way to God's love.

I mean that I am my Father's son of truth and righteousness, and as such you must pray the Father in my name, not because I am Jesus, but because I represent all the truth and love of my Father.

Yes, and that is the only way in which men can come to the Father—no other—and when my kingdom is completed only those who have become one with the Father will become a part of it.

Yes, she told you the truth—my kingdom will be composed only of those who believe in my teachings and who have received the Holy Ghost. So do not doubt more. You I have selected and you will be my true disciple and messenger of truth—you have my help and love to the fullest, and no man can take it from you. In all eternity you will be with me.

23

God answers your prayers, because you have faith and are my own disciple. So continue to pray and He will hear you and answer your prayers.

No, only believe and trust Him—He will never forsake you or let you want.

You must love God with all your heart and soul and mind and your neighbor as yourself—this is the great commandment. So observe this and you will be happy and free.

Let your prayers become more fervent and your faith more fully developed—I will help you to know more of your Father's love, and you will soon become a true follower of me.

You must seek and you will know; wait until I give my messages, and then you will know the truth.

Yes, I am the vine and you are the branch—so believe.

What you have written is my thoughts—you did not think any of these thoughts.

So good night and may God bless you as I do now.

JESUS

Mr. Padgett's Mother Writes.

Oh, my dear son—The Master has told you the way to salvation—Only believe.

I am your loving mother.

Spirit's Experience in Progressing from the Third Sphere Into the Celestial Heavens.

I AM HERE, *Your Grandmother (Ann Rollins)* (Celestial Spirit)

Yes, it is I. I want to tell you of my experience in progressing in the spirit life.

Well, when I passed over I was received in the spirit world by your grandfather and my own dear mother who had been in the spirit world for so very many years. She was then living in the seventh sphere and was a most beautiful and happy spirit. Now she is far up in the Celestial Spheres, and occasionally comes to see me and tells me of the great beauty of her home and of the wonderful spirits who inhabit the Spheres where she lives.

She lives in a high sphere of the Celestial Heavens, and is with many of the redeemed spirits who lived on earth many centuries ago. She mentioned some of them who were well known on earth, such as John Wesley and his brother Charles, and Luther and some of his contemporaries who were engaged in the great reforms of those days. Whitfield is one she named, and Bunyan, also. They seemed to have reached this sphere by obtaining the Love that we have written you of. So, when I think that

24

through gradual development and progression of their spiritual being there are these high spheres for me to attain to, I feel that my faith and seeking for the Divine Love have a great deal yet to accomplish in the way of soul development.

Well, shortly after I passed over I progressed to the third sphere and thought that there the very seat of heaven must be, because my happiness was so much greater than I ever anticipated.

Well, when I first entered the spirit world, I confess I was disappointed, because I did not see the Father on his throne and Jesus sitting on his right hand, as I had been taught to believe; but it was not long before I realized that such a belief had no foundation in truth, and that God has no throne, such as the writers of the Bible had declared, but that His Spirit is manifested everywhere and in all places, and is a Spirit that has no form in the sense that I had been taught to believe.

After living in the third sphere for some little time and having received much information from spirits who lived in higher spheres, and having received a great abundance of God's love, I progressed to the fifth sphere and found a wonderful home of beauty and harmony among spirits who had experiences similar to my own, and who had received the Divine Love to a degree which gives us all this great happiness that I tell you of.

In some of the planes of this sphere are many spirits who have not received this Divine Love, but who have attained to wonderful moral and intellectual qualifications; but they were not so happy as were those who had received the Great Love of the Father. They gave their thoughts and works more to things that pertain to moral and intellectual progress than to the soul development in the Divine Love.

It may seem strange to you that these spirits could live in an atmosphere where so much of God's love was manifested by the numerous spirits who had received this Love, and yet, not realize that this Divine Love is the one great thing absolutely necessary for their further progress and greater happiness. But such is the fact, and many of these spirits of the greatest intellectual development are still there pursuing their studies of laws that have to do solely with things that relate to the operations of spiritual laws and the causes of phenomena that astonish both mortals and spirits.

I have wondered many times that they have not had an awakening to the real and grander truths of spirit life, and the causes of the develment of the souls of those with whom they come in contact, and who are so much more beautiful and happier than are these students of merely spiritual laws and causes that produce only astonishing phenomena.

Strange as it may seem to some, intellectual progression is not necessary to soul progression, but with soul progression by obtaining the Divine Love comes a wonderful knowledge of these other things that I speak

25

of. I, as you know, was a person of just ordinary mental acquirements, yet in this spirit world I have left behind me many great minds possessed of wonderful intellectual information. I mean not only as regards the progress of my soul, but also as regards the attainment of knowledge that these men are devoting their time and work to obtain.

Strange, also, it may seem to you, that with soul development in the Divine Love there comes intellectual development, but to us who have experienced this fact it is not strange, because the mind is only an attribute or, as I may say, a quality of the soul, which as the soul develops in the Divine Love the mind must necessarily also develop.

Philosophy is a thing which is merely the conclusions of minds that have given thought and investigation to the subject matter of that philosophy; and when it is determined by the mere mind it is still uncertain and subject to revision and change as the mind may change. The mind, in its development, does not necessarily learn the full and real truths; and in this spirit life among these men of purely great minds that do not possess the Divine Love, there is as much variety of opinion and as many disputes as to what is the truth as there are on earth. The mind of itself cannot always discern the truth, because it is not infallible, even when it is the mind of a spirit and that spirit a highly developed one.

But as the soul develops in the Divine Love this development means that what comes to it as a fact, is a truth, the everlasting truth. The soul does not learn all truths at once, but the truth that it does learn is one that never changes, and lets no revision alter or set it aside. No, truth of the soul's discernment is never shown to be error, and no error ever becomes a part of the soul's discernment of truth. So, you see, the great road to the ascertainment of the realities of God is through and only through the development of the soul by the inflowing of the Divine Love. The eye of the soul is that interior perception which needs not reason from cause and effect to discern and forever establish the truths of God.

So, how very necessary that men and spirits should learn the great fact, that if they would learn the truth of spirit life, they must endeavor to develop the soul's powers of perception by seeking for the inflowing into their souls of the Divine Love.

I could tell you many wonderful things to illustrate these propositions, if I had the time to do so, but I have not now; but sometime I will go more in detail on this subject, and then you will more fully understand what I mean.

Well, after I had lived in this fifth sphere and learned the great and wonderful truths that are taught therein, I progressed to the seventh and there learned what real happiness is, as I thought. No spirit who has not received this Great Love of the Father lives in this sphere, because the mind is, as it were, absorbed by the soul to such a great extent, that without the soul development the mind would have no place of lodgment. I mean that the mind, as such, then becomes so subordinated to the powers and operations of the soul perceptions that it cannot exist as mere mind independent of the soul's development.

In this sphere all is grand and beautiful to an extent that I cannot describe, because you have no possible mental conception with which I can compare such beauty and grandeur.

Our homes are very harmonious and without stain or anything that emanates from things other than the soul's essence and power. No mere intellectual happiness exists, and no spirit who has not this Great Love could possibly be happy there. But yet, while all this happiness exists I was told that happiness is far greater in the Celestial Spheres, and, consequently, I was not satisfied to remain in the seventh sphere, although I could not realize how my happiness could be any greater than it was. Yet, as I say, I was not contented to remain in my home there. And I was also told that there was a way to get into this * Celestial Sphere, and a way so easy that the mere statement of it caused doubt. But I prayed for faith and the Divine Love, and on an occasion my faith brought the Divine Love into my soul in such abundance, and I progressed to the first Celestial Sphere, where I now am.

The Book of Revelation in the Bible, in its most extravagant description of the New Jerusalem, gives no true conception of what the beauty and magnificence of this sphere are; and I will not attempt to describe them, for I cannot. But a man, or spirit either, who has never seen the wonderful beauty of this Sphere, cannot conceive of what its magnificence is.

I am so very happy that it seems to me there can be no greater happiness, and yet, my mother tells me that there is, and that the Divine Love of the higher spheres is so much more intense and filled with so much more of God's Divinity that I cannot have the slightest conception of what it is.

I am now trying to reach these higher spheres, and am told that faith and prayer for the inflowing into my soul of the Divine Love are the only instrumentalities that will enable me to do so. My prayers are constant and my faith is growing, and I realize, that when the Holy Spirit fills me with this Divine Love, as I expect it to do, I shall progress.

So you see, one great element of God's method of making His redeemed happy, is to set before them a higher mark for which they may seek with the assurance that it can be attained.

Well, I have written you quite a letter, and feel that I must stop now, as I need to leave the earth's atmosphere for awhile.

So with all my love and blessings, I am,   Your Grandmother,

ANN ROLLINS.

* Later progressed above the third Celestial Sphere.

Law of compensation is removed from the scope of its operation when the Divine Love fills the soul in sufficient abundance.

I AM HERE, *your own true Helen. Mrs. Padgett.*

You didn't think I could change the announcement of my coming, but you must know that I can do anything to please you, my dear Ned.

Yes you have, and I have been so very happy. Well, sweetheart, I must tell you that I am very happy and am progressing very rapidly. I don't expect to remain in this sphere very much longer, for my love and faith are so great that I feel that I must get closer to God's fountainhead in the Celestial Spheres. Doesn't it seem like some fairy dream? But it is all true, and I am so happy.

I will soon be with you in a long letter, telling you of this Great Love, and how much I love God and you.

No you won't, for you are progressing too. You may not realize it, but it is true, and if you should come over now, you would be surprised to find yourself in a high sphere. Well, I know how you feel, but you must believe that I can see better than you can realize your spiritual condition.

Well that may be so, but when you get this Great Love in your heart in sufficient abundance, and you have much of it now, your sins will be blotted out. This is the law of regeneration; otherwise, the man who continues without this Love, and the man who receives it, would be in the same condition and the New Birth would mean nothing. So do not think that this Great Love is not sufficient to cleanse the soul from the results of the sins of earth life; and, best of all, it cleanses while you are a mortal.

I know that the spiritualists quote and proclaim the law of recompense or compensation, but there is a higher law that nullifies that law; and when love, this Divine Love comes into the soul of a mortal, the law of compensation is removed from the scope of its working, for love is the fulfilling of the law. So do not let that stumbling block make you believe that this Great Love is not sufficient to remove all sin and error and to purify your soul so that you may become fitted to live in the kingdom of the Father and become one with Him.

No, the Love is for the vilest sinner, and no man can by a mere act of restoration fit himself for the inflowing of this Divine Love. It is waiting for the sinner as well as for the saint; and even though your sins be as scarlet they will be made white as wool. I mean that you will not have to wait to make recompense to mortals before this great love can do the cleansing work; else what is the use of having this Great Love provided for man? If he shall first make himself pure what is the necessity for the work of the Holy Spirit?

Only pray for this love and have faith, and you will get it. God is the judge of what a man shall do to render justice and restitution, and when

He says that this Divine Love, with all its cleansing power, is for the sinner who seeks for it by true faith, who has the right to say that the sinner must first do what man may think is justice between himself and his fellow man?

I know whereof I speak, for the experience of many spirits who have been redeemed by this Love, show that they were sinners and had not "paid the last farthing" when they received this Love. God is the judge, not mortals nor spirits.

So, my dear Ned, do not let the idea that you must render to every man that which you think he may be entitled to, keep you from believing in the mercy and Love of the Father.

Oh, how I wish I could be with you a little while in my bodily form, and tell you face to face what this great Love means to you and to me and to all of us.

So sweetheart, believe me when I say that even though you may be a great sinner, yet the Father's love is sufficient to remove all those sins just as soon as you can receive it. Such is the law of this Great Love.

Faith and prayer can open the very heart of the Celestial Spheres, and Love will flow down into your soul as the avalanche of snow that feels the warmth of the sun's bright rays rushes from its mountain heights when winter leaves with its chilling gloom and blasting breath for other climes.

Love is not only warmth, but it is the very burnings of the soul's great storehouse of God's Divine Essence.

I am not only the possessor of this Love to a large degree, but I realize that as I advance to higher spheres there is a greater abundance awaiting to fill my soul with its great undying fires of never ending burnings—but burnings so great and free from everything that makes for unhappiness and discontent.

I must stop now.

So my own dear and precious Ned, love me as I love you and we both will be so very happy that heaven will be with us and in us even while we are writing in the earth surroundings.

Your own, HELEN.

*Helen—Mrs. Padgett, describes her home in * Third Sphere. The importance of seeking for the Divine Love*

I AM HERE, Helen. (Mrs. J. E. Padgett)

I am very happy for I have so much love of God in my heart that I cannot think of any thing that tends to make me unhappy.

Yes, my home is very beautiful and I am perfectly delighted with it. It is made of white marble and is surrounded by lawns and flowers and trees of various kinds. The grass is so very green and the flowers are

* Read Preface on page X, why these earliest messages were not inserted in Vol. I.

so beautiful and variegated. The trees are always in foliage and have such beautiful limbs and leaves. I am most pleased with my home, I mean the building. There are many beautiful pictures on the walls, and the walls are all frescoed and hung with fine coverings, and the floors are inlaid with beautiful mosaics. I have all the splendid furniture that I could possibly wish for, and my library is full of books of all kinds especially of those that tell of God and His love for man. You would be in your element if you could be with me.

I have music, such as you never heard on earth and instruments of various kinds which I am learning to play, and I sing with all my heart and soul as the days go by. I have beds on which I lie down, but I never sleep. We do not need sleep here, we only rest, for sometimes we get tired from our work and are greatly refreshed by lying on the beds and couches which are so comfortable that we do not realize that we are tired after lying down a little while.

Yes I do, and when I sing I think of you and wish that you could hear me as you did when I was with you in the body. I like the "Song that Reached my Heart," it seems to bring me more in rapport with you than any of the others, although "Sing Me to Sleep" is one that I enjoy to sing very much.

Yes we eat fruit and nuts, but do not do so because we are hungry but more because we enjoy the flavors so much; and we drink water, pure and sweet, as it makes us feel so refreshed when we are a little tired. No, our fruit is not of the earthly kind—it is so much more delightful that I am unable to describe it to you. And the nuts are different, also. Yes, the water is purer than what you have and is more refreshing.

No, our instruments are not like those on earth, they are not stringed instruments, but are played by our thoughts of goodness and love. We do not use fingers or lungs, but merely thoughts, and if they are pure and loving, our music is very beautiful and not discordant.

Yes, I am when you are asleep or doing something in the line of your work, then you do not need me and I am free to leave you. You must not think that I am not free to leave you when I am with you, for I am; and I come to you of my own free will; but love compels, and in that particular I am not free and don't want to be. Your love to me is the greatest thing, except God's love, in all the world, and without it I would be very unhappy. You do not know how very necessary your loving me is to my happiness; and you must never cease to love me, for if you do not I will not enjoy my home or the spirit world so much. Yes, I know, but I sometimes fear that you may forget to think of me as I want you to.

Yes it is permanent, and the house and trees and flowers are more real to me than were ever the houses and trees and flowers on earth—they are not shadowy as you may think, but are so very substantial that they never decay or grow old.

Yes, I have one selected for you now, and will make it so beautiful that you will wonder how it was possible for me to do so; there will be so much love in it that there will be no room for anything that is not in harmony with my love, and you will realize that your own Helen loves you with all the love that a soul can have for its mate.

Yes, we will be together in every way and separated only while we are doing some of God's work. You will be with me in all my thoughts and I will be with you in your thoughts. Love will keep us through all eternity.

Yes, we will love our parents and children just as much as on earth, but they will not need our love so much as they will have their own soul-mates to love them. We will visit them and be visited by them, and enjoy their society even more than when on earth. They will love us very much, but the love that makes two souls one will exist only for the soul-mates. God's love will not interfere with that—I mean our love for God. It is of a kind that is different from our love for each other, and is of a more spiritual and holy nature.   .

I am so very much pleased to see that you are getting more of His love in your heart each day, and soon you will do the work that the Master has laid out for you to do.

Yes, I am going to try to progress into the higher planes, and hope to do so as rapidly as is possible, but you may rest assured that no matter what plane I may be in, my love for you will not lessen, and I will not cease to be with you as I now am. The life in the higher spheres without you would not be complete—you are necessary to my complete happiness. God has decreed that two soulmates are intended to make one complete whole, and it 'must, in order to be wholly happy and to fulfill the laws of His love, and live together forever as one.

Yes, I know, because I have asked your grandmother and she has told me. You can progress on earth just as rapidly as I can here if you will let God's love come into your heart as fully and as abundantly as I do; and you can if you will only pray to the Father. He does not require the child of His care to be in the spirit world in order to develop his soul. You have the same soul now that you will have when you come here, and if you let God fill it with His love while you are on earth, why should it not progress as much as it does here? God does not intend to wait until you come over here that He may give you the full enjoyment of His Holy Spirit—it all depends upon you. If you truly and sincerely seek His love you will get it on earth just as easily as you can get it after you have shuffled off the body. The love of God coming into the soul of a man does not depend upon whether he is in the flesh or in the spirit. All souls must answer for the sins done in the body, but it is not necessary that such penalties be paid in the spirit world—you can pay the penalty while on earth. As you sow so shall you reap, but the reaping is not necessarily here.

If you seek earnestly for God's grace and love you can obtain them on earth, and I am informed that when they are obtained on earth the greater will be the progress of the spirit when it comes over. So let me pray you to seek these blessings while you are in your present life, and not wait for them to be given to you after you have entered the spirit world.

Your grandmother says that she had that experience, and when she came here she entered the third heaven, without going through a period of expiation or purification in the lower spheres. She is a wonderfully bright and pure spirit and is very close to God, and has so much of His love in her soul that her countenance really seems an illuminated face. She is in a condition of almost perfect love and peace, though she says that she is striving for a higher plane and a closer at-onement with her Heavenly Father. She is the one who can help you in your spiritual progress more than all others, except Jesus, who is the grandest and most glorious spirit in all the heavens.

Let your thoughts be of a pure and holy kind and you will soon realize that God's love is in your soul to a degree that will make you feel that He is your own near and dear Father. Do not doubt His love or that He can come to you through the Holy Spirit, for that is His messenger of love, and it will never refuse to come into a man's heart and soul where the desire exists to have it come, by earnest sincere prayer for its inflowing.

Be true to yourself, as I have told you, and you will soon be in God's love and favor. Do not let worries or disappointments keep you from seeking His love and believing that He is waiting to enfold you in His arms of mercy and love, for He is not only waiting but wants you to call on Him. Do not let the thought that He is afar up in the heavens cause you to think that He is not always near you anxiously waiting your call.

He is not willing that one of His children should perish, and when they go astray His great Heart of Love yearns for them to return and partake of His bounties and blessings. You must try with all your heart to realize this truth, for it is a truth, and is the greatest truth taught us by Jesus, who is the greatest of all teachers. Make your daily life one of prayer and aspirations, and you will see that what I have told you is not only true, but you can make it a part of yourself. You have only to let your desires turn towards God, and He will meet you more than half way, for He never sleeps or closes His ear to the supplications of His children; and those who have sought Him with an earnest and repentant wish and longing desire of the soul, know that He has always responded to their call.

You are now in the way to obtain these blessings, and I pray that you may continue, for you cannot find true happiness in any other way. This is what Jesus meant when He said, I am the Way, the Truth and the Life. He knew that there was only one way to obtain the Father's love, and that is through the New Birth, which is merely the flowing into the soul of man the Love of God to the extent of eradicating all desires and tastes for things which are not in harmony with God's laws and love.

You must give your thoughts more to this vital consideration of the economy of God's being.

It is not a question of what church you belong to, or what particular faith you may have, or who your preacher may be, or to what duties you owe to the church or to the ceremony of baptism according to the church's dogmas; but whether you have sought God in spirit and in truth and have received His favor and Love.

This is an individual matter, and no man can be saved by the sufferings or progress of another. Each soul is a complete unit when joined with its mate, and the spiritual condition of each soul towards God determines what its place and happiness will be in the spirit world. So do not let the thought that it is necessary to believe in a special church dogma or any ceremony, keep you from seeking the New Birth. This is the fundamental principle that operates in the at-one-ment of man with God, and all other doctrines are merely secondary and need to be believed only as they may lead to a belief in this foundation.

I am writing at the dictation of your grandmother, for she knows, and I, of course, would not be able to write in this way of my own thoughts and experience.

* She says that you must try to get in condition that the Master may write. That which he shall say will show to mankind the everlasting truths of God's kingdom and laws; that she is a mere tyro in the knowledge and ability to explain God's truths that Jesus will teach you. So try to become more spiritual so that you may learn the wonderful teachings of God's love and truth that he will give you.

You must stop writing now as you are tired and so am I.

So love your own true Helen, and pray to God for love and spiritual enlightenment.

HELEN.

The power of love to redeem men from sin and error.

I AM HERE, *Jesus.*

I want to write to-night on the power of Divine Love to redeem men from sin and error.

My Father's love is, as I have written, the only thing in all this universe that can save men from their evil natures and make them at one with Him. This Divine Love I have already explained, and when mankind will read my messages and try to understand the meaning of this Love, it will soon become more at peace with itself and with God.

* Jesus in a message says: Mr. P.'s grandmother is well qualified to write on divine truths.

This Divine Love is the one great power that moves the universe, and without it there would not be that wonderful harmony that exists in the Celestial Heavens of the spirit world; nor would so much happiness exist among the angels who inhabit these spheres.

This Divine Love is also the influence which makes men on earth think and do that which makes for peace and good will among men. It is not possessed by all men, in fact, by comparatively few, yet its influence is felt over nearly the whole earth. Even those who have never heard of my teachings or of my Father, enjoy the benefit of its influence in some kind of belief or faith in an overshadowing spirit of great power and watchfulness. I know that this is true, for I have visited all parts of the earth and have looked into men's hearts and found in them some elements of belief, which evidenced that this Great Love was influencing these unenlightened people. So, notwithstanding the fact that my gospel is not preached to every creature, as I commanded when on earth, yet this Love of the Father is everywhere and all pervading.

Still, it is not received in all that fullness that enables those who feel its influence to realize that God is their Father and they are his children, and may become members of his household in the Celestial Spheres.

No man can receive this Love unless he has faith in the Father's willingness to bestow it upon him, and truly and with earnestness pray for it.

Every man has in him the natural love which will give him great happiness in eternity as a mere spirit and an inhabitant of the spheres lower than the Celestial, even though he refuses to seek for the Divine Love that will make him a divine angel of the Celestial Heavens.

Only this Divine Love can change the natural man into a man having the divine nature in Love that the Father has. I do not mean that man, even though he be filled with this Love to the highest degrees, will ever become a god and equal to the Father in any of his powers or attributes. This cannot be, but this love will make him like the Father in Love and happiness and harmony. This Love has no counterpart in all creation, and comes from the Father alone. It changes not, nor is ever bestowed on anyone who is unworthy, or refuses to seek for it in the only way provided by the Father.

My experience in these Celestial Heavens is, that this Love has the power to change the most hardened sinner into a true child of God, if only through faith and prayer such sinner will seek for it. Let this Love take possession of a man or spirit, and its power to purify and change the heart of that man or spirit never fails.

Your brother and friend,   JESUS.

What Jesus meant when he said "In my Father's house are many mansions." The effect of the Divine Love on the soul to redeem mankind.

I Am Jesus. You are in condition to resume my message tonight.

I am in a condition of love that enables me to know that my Father's love is the only love that can redeem mankind and make it at-one with Him. So you must understand that this Divine Love is a love that has no counterpart in all the universe, and must be received by man in all its fullness, in order for him to attain to the Celestial Spheres, where the Father's fountainhead of love exists. So I say, that no man can become a part of God's divinity until he receives this Divine Love and realizes that he and his Father are one in love and purity.

I will now tell you what this Divine Love means to everyone who has received it. He is in a condition of perfect peace and his happiness is beyond all comparison, and he is not willing that anything or power shall lead him to those things that are not in accord with the Divine Love and God's laws of harmony. He is not only happy, but is away beyond the lower spirits in intellectual development and knowledge of the spiritual things of the Father. I know that no man is able to obtain the great soul perceptions until he has the soul development and is fitted to live in the Celestial Spheres, where only love and harmony exist.

So, do not think if a man merely becomes wonderful in his knowledge in an intellectual sense, he is fitted to live in these higher spheres, for he is not; only the great development of the soul by obtaining into his soul the Divine Love will enable him to live there.

John never said that by me were all things created that were created, and that I, as God, came to earth and became an indweller in the flesh. That is a mistake and an interpolation, for I never was God, neither did I ever create any part of the universe. I was only a spirit of God sent by Him to work out man's salvation and show him the only way to the Heavenly Home that God has in keeping for those who receive the New Birth.

Well, I live in all spheres but my home is in a sphere that is very close to the fountainhead of God's love. It has no name or number. With me in the Celestial Spheres* are all those who have received

* Jesus is higher up in the Celestial Spheres because of having prayed for and obtained the Divine Love in greater abundance than any other Celestial Spirit.

When a spirit obtains a sufficiency of the Divine Love in the soul it leaves the seventh sphere and enters the first Celestial sphere and then progresses to the second Celestial and after this to the third Celestial. Above the third Celestial sphere the spheres are so graduated that no number is used.

The statement by Jesus: "With me in the Celestial spheres are all those who have received the Divine Love," means that the spirits are in one of these Celestial spheres according to the degree they have obtained the Divine Love.

There is no spirit who has obtained the Divine Love in that great abundance that Jesus possesses it. Therefore, no Celestial spirit has yet reached his sphere. But all souls possess this privilege.

this Divine Love to such an extent that they have become entirely purified and at one with the Father. Many are progressing towards that home and will, sooner or later, get there.

Those who fully received this Divine Love through faith and prayer are in the Celestial Spheres, but those who have not yet obtained this love to the degree mentioned, are not. Yes, Paul is, and so are Peter and John and James and several others.

I meant that I would go to the *Celestial Spheres where I now am and prepare these mansions, which I have now done. And it rests with spirits and mortals only to become inhabitants thereof.

Some are, and some are not; the mere fact that these ancient prophets and seers were the mere instruments of God in declaring His purposes and laws, does not mean that they necessarily received this Great Love, so that they are now inhabitants of the Celestial Spheres. Moses and Elias are in the Celestial Spheres and so is John the Baptist; but many great teachers of spiritual things or of future existence are not, because they have not obtained the New Birth.

Well, it will depend on whether you live and believe in such a way as to get this Great Love; if you do, you will not have to wait long years to be with me in the Celestial Spheres. You are now in the right way, and if you will only persevere and let your faith increase and get the Divine Love in sufficient abundance in your soul you will be. And this remember, that I am your special friend and helper and will be, and when you are in doubt or trouble, will keep you from relapsing into a state of unbelief or of carelessness.

If, as you say, he will seek that Divine Love and pray to the Father in faith and believe that the Father will bestow it upon him, he will receive it; and when he receives it in sufficient abundance all sin that he may have committed will be blotted out. No further will he have to pay the penalties of his deeds of sin and error. This is what I came principally to teach mankind. When I said, as you sow so shall you reap, I meant this to be the law of God as applied to the natural man as well as to everything else in nature; but that law is subject to be set aside so far as its operations on the souls of men are concerned, by the soul of man receiving in sufficient abundance, the Divine Love. And when the Great Love of the Father is sought and received by the soul of man in sufficient abundance, the law of compensation is made noneffective and the law of love becomes supreme, and man is relieved from the penalties of his sins.

Yes, I know how men reason about this matter, and that is the great stumbling block that prevents them from receiving this Divine Love and believing that it is efficacious in saving them from paying the penalties of their sins.

*Appendix. Read Vol. I, Pages 125 to 130, Edition 1, *Forgiveness* by Ann Rollins.

Well, you now see what I am trying to do, and I am so well satisfied that you will make a success of your work, that I feel more than ever certain that my messages will be understood and given to the world. So keep up your courage and in a short time all will be in such condition that there will be nothing to interfere with your doing the work as you desire.

Yes, most assuredly, and when you get into the work with all your earnestness and faith, you will see that you will be able to receive the messages just as I intend that you shall receive them.

Let us stop now,

Your own true brother in spirit,

Jesus.

Mrs. Padgett (Helen) describes her home in detail in the Celestial Spheres.

I AM HERE, *Helen.*

Well, I am very happy, and you are happier and feel better.

I am now going to write you about my home, as I promised, and you must not think I am not in condition to write, if I should not be able to describe it as you may think I should; the only reason for my failure will be that I cannot find words to express myself.

Well, my house is a beautiful white one of a substance that you might think of as alabaster, and two stories in height, and rooms on each side of a wide and beautiful hall. The rooms are very large and filled with the most beautiful furniture that you can conceive of. The walls are all hung with satin coverings, and between are lovely pictures. The parlor, as you would call it, is filled with the most exquisite and comfortable couches and chairs, and with beautiful tables and bric-a-brac, and also many pictures of landscapes and fruits and flowers. I don't know who painted them, but they are there and give me much delight, and satisfy to so great an extent my love for paintings and pictures. There are also many little curios that would make the heart of an aesthetic person rejoice and feel glad. My music room has in it instruments of various kinds, and wonderful in sound and construction. I play some of them and also sing in my weak way, as you say on earth; but I enjoy the music more than I can tell you, and so do many spirits who call to see me.

I have other rooms, such as repose rooms, library and room for meditation and prayer. My library is full of books dealing with subjects that are to me now so congenial and necessary, for they tell me of God's love and care for his children. There are also books that deal with the laws of the spirit world and of the other parts of the universe; but these latter I do not read much, for my whole study is so given to the laws pertaining to our own spirit world and its relationship to your world, and the love of God and the love that should exist among mortals and spirits, that I do not find time for these other studies; and, in fact, I have not the inclination.

There are books that you might call fiction, but really are not, for they describe the actual experience of spirits in such a vivid and interesting way, that if they were portrayed in your earthly books you would think it fiction.

Not all the books in my library deal with the higher or more substantial things of this spirit life, for we have our recreation for the mind in the way of variety in reading that you do on earth, and we are the stronger and happier for it. So you see, if you were here, I know that the library would be your place of rest from your work, although I know you like music very much.

We have a dining room also, but we do not need kitchens as nothing is cooked, but everything eaten just as we get it from the trees and vines. We do not eat meat or bread or potatoes or things of that kind. Our food is principally fruits and nuts; and such fruits you never saw and never will until you come with me. The fruits, mostly, are pears and grapes and oranges and pomegranates—of course, not just the same as you know them on earth. I merely use these words of description to give you some idea of what they are like. We have them in great variety and always fresh and ripe. The nuts too, are of many kinds and qualities. None need nut crackers for them to be broken in order to be eaten. There are no cakes or candies or anything of that nature. We do not actually eat these things with our teeth and palate and use intestinal organs, as you do, but we inhale as it were, the delicious flavors and aromas of the fruits; and strange as it may seem to you, we are just as much satisfied, and probably more so than you when you eat them with your physical organs. I cannot more fully explain to you just how this thing is, but, as we say, we eat the fruits and nuts.

We drink pure water, and nothing else; and spirits who say they have wines and other beverages, tell what I have never seen or heard of since I have been in the spirit world. Of course, I do not know every thing and what exists in all parts of this great world of spirits. And this water is so pure and satisfying, that I cannot imagine any spirit would want anything else to drink. But, yet, as I say, I do not know as to this.

We do not actually drink the water for we have not the internal organs that you have in the physical body, but we seem to absorb it in our system in some way that gives all the delight and satisfaction that you enjoy when you drink water.

We often have our "teas", as your fashionable women on earth might say, and very many of our spirit friends attend and help make the gatherings enjoyable and happy ones. Of course the male spirits attend, for I must tell you that in this life there are no clubs or businesses that keep the sexes apart, as in your life. I mean that the two sexes are more together, and enjoy the society of each other to a far greater degree than in your earth life. Of course, I do not mean that these spirits have all found their soulmates, for that is not true; but each enjoys the company of the others as friends and spirits having similar desires and aspirations. My companions are very similar in their love for the Father and in the development of their souls, and in their thoughts and desires for things spiritual. We discuss many questions pertaining to the soul and it progress, and to the love of the Father and to the love of spirits and mortals. While we are joyous and happy beyond compare, yet we do not indulge in frivolities or thoughts that have not a tendency to elevate us to higher things.

We have music and dancing, but our dancing is different from yours. We merely exercise ourselves in graceful and artistic movements without any contact of spirit bodies, or the embracing of each other. Of course, we hold hands as we dance, but no familiarity, as you would say, is indulged in.

Well, I have a room for repose, where after working long and to some extent, feeling tired, I rest on these couches that I tell you of. We do not sleep, but sometimes we go into a kind of dreamy state that gives us much refreshment and vigor. I am now resting from some hard work that I have been doing in your earth plane. I mean that when I am not writing to you, I am resting.

So, you see, we are not enjoying one continuous condition of feeling as that might become monotonous.

I am now trying to help some of the spirits who have recently come over from your city, and who were acquaintances of yours on earth. I will tell you of them when next I write you. I am tired now and must stop.

So with all my love, I am your own true and loving,

Helen.

Corroborates Mrs. Padgett's experience and tells of the happiness of spirits in the Celestial Spheres.

I AM HERE, *Your Grandmother.*

Well, I am exceedingly happy and am glad that you are feeling so much improved.

You had quite a long letter from Helen, and I hope, a very satisfactory one. When she tries she can write a very good letter.

I am, as you know, in the same sphere * with her and your mother; and we are all very much together, though we live in different homes. Helen,

* Grandmother in higher plane of the Celestial Spheres.

of course, is not as far advanced as I am, and neither is your mother, but, nevertheless, we are very congenial and love one another very much. Soon though, I will leave them for a higher sphere, and then they will miss me I know, for they keep telling me so, and say that they will follow soon after, and I believe that they will, for they are wonderful spirits in love and faith; and these two possessions, as you know, are the "open sesame" to things and spheres higher.

Well, my son, as Helen told you of her home, I want to tell you a little bit about the condition of the spirits in this sphere. No spirit who has not **received** this Great Love of the Father is here; or better, all spirits who are here have received and possess this love. Mere intellectual acquirements are not sufficient to fit a spirit for this sphere; and if a spirit ever realizes that the gate is shut to him, it is because he has not this love. And then the great happiness that exists here could not be enjoyed by the mere mind, for the mind is limited in its capacity for happiness. Only the soul can enjoy this great happiness.

I sometimes think that if mortals could be permitted, for one moment only, to realize what this happiness is, they would never let their lives slip by without making the greatest efforts to fit themselves for this great life in the Celestial Spheres.

Our time here is occupied in helping one another to a greater realization of the truths of our Father, and in helping spirits who live on lower planes than we do. I do not, now, very often come to the earth plane to help other spirits or mortals; but, of course, in your case I am so bound by my affections and desires that I am with you quite often, and more so with that darling little daughter of yours; for, as I have told you, I am her guardian angel, and so long as she lives, I will be with her to help and guide.

We are engaged in the study of things that pertain more to the spiritual things of this life, than to studying the things of the other worlds of the universe—these things to us are what might be called the material things; and while a knowledge of them would be very interesting, yet our thoughts are turned to the more important truths of God.

Yes, we all have our libraries and homes, as Helen has told you of, but, of course, there is a great difference in these homes, depending upon the amount of love which the spirit has in his soul. I am now living in a home that is so beautiful, that I could not in the short time that I will write tonight describe it to you; but soon I will in detail, and then you can realize what a home it is.

Well, do not believe everything in the book you have been reading because it is said to be written by spirits, because, even if it is so written, the information given depends upon the condition and knowledge and belief of these spirits. Some may tell the exact truth as they conceive it to be, and yet it may not be the truth.

Well, the explanation is, that the spirits whose communications you read have never learned the truth taught by the Master. They only know what they have learned from what they have read or from what spirits who have not this great knowledge have told them. Any spirit who says that Jesus is not the Great Spirit and Teacher, and the only one of the great teachers who have ever lived on earth, who shows the only and true way to the Father's kingdom, has never learned this way or come under the influence of the Master. So far as that is concerned do not pay any attention to what they say or let their communications influence you; for these communications will not help you spiritually.

There are certain great assembly places in the spirit world where the higher spirits meet and discuss the various plans that they think will benefit mankind, and also the lower spirits; and I believe the Master has attended these meetings and given his advice and encouragement. For you must remember that he is a teacher, not only of the way to God's kingdom, but also of the acquiring of those things that will help and benefit mortals and spirits who have not received this Great Love.

Part of his mission is to make man and spirits happy, even though they may never become inhabitants of the Celestial Spheres. God loves all his creatures, and the Master, as His greatest instrument of love and beneficence, is doing all that he can to make these men and spirits happy; and, as some of these communications say, he has helped in many of these assemblies to do good for all. But, while this is so, yet he is the Father's greatest instrument in showing men the way to the higher life.

Well, that is a question that seems hard to answer; but if these other great teachers will not believe the Master's message as to the only way to the kingdom, they alone know why and will have to bear the consequences.

All spirits are not able to see these great truths any more than mortals are, and the mere fact that they have so much greater opportunities to learn these truths does not seem to persuade them to accept the same.

The higher spheres in which these ancient seers and wise men live are not the Celestial Heavens, but spheres higher up in the spirit world; and no matter how high they may get in these spheres, they will never partake of that Divine Essence or nature of the Father, which we have told you of, unless they seek for and obtain the Divine Love to qualify them to enter the Celestial Heavens. They will always be nothing more than spirits possessed of the natural love which they had on earth, but, of course, more refined and free from sin; yet it is merely natural love and nothing more.

Yes, I have met Paul and Peter and John and James and several others of lesser development. Yes they are all in the Celestial Spheres and very

41

happy, yet they go to the lower spheres to do the work set before them.

No spirit who has not received this New Birth is ever permitted to enter the Celestial Spheres, and, hence, the spirit that you speak of has never seen the home of John, and never will until redeemed by the love of the Father

I do not think these mortals who claim that they left their bodies and entered the Celestial Spheres, ever did so, and I have grave doubt that they ever entered the spiritual spheres above the third.

This is a subject that I will write you more fully about some other time. I must stop now, and you must not write more tonight.

So, with all my love I am your own loving

Grandmother

ANN ROLLINS

Mrs. Padgett's Experience in Trying to Show a Spirit the way to God's Love

I AM HERE, *Helen.*

I want to tell you of my experience in trying to show a spirit the way to God's love, which I had a short time ago.

Well, I talked to this spirit of this love, and told her that the only way to happiness and to the Celestial Kingdom was through prayer and faith, and that all spirits who were inhabitants of those spheres had received this Great Love of the Father only through prayer and faith; and if she wanted to become an inhabitant of these Heavens she must seek for this Love in that way. She said that she was told when on earth that if she only observed rules and regulations of the church, and devoted herself to doing church work and looking after the interest of the church so that it might be sustained and fostered, she would go to heaven just as soon as she had left the earth life, and that that would be all that would be required of her, and that no other seeking or striving after God's love would be necessary to enable her to get into the Heavens where God is and all His angels. I told her that she must now realize that such performance of what she considered to be her duty had not been sufficient to carry her into these Heavens and that she must realize that something more was necessary. But she still persisted that her belief in what she had been taught in the church could not be changed, and that very soon she would become an inhabitant of these higher spheres. So I left her, because I saw that at this time her belief had so fastened itself upon her convictions of these only requisites as she had been taught, that it was useless to try to convince her that she was laboring under an absolutely false belief.

So, I find that in this spirit plane there are many spirits in darkness and bigotry which prevents them from seeing the truth and progressing to the higher spheres. I do not think that mortals when they become spirits have any better opportunity, for sometime at least, to realize and accept these truths than they had when on earth, and the men or women who teach these things have a great sin to answer for, for Jesus said cursed is he who believes and teaches these false doctrines. And I think he must have laid especial emphasis on the teaching as it affected not only the teacher, but many others who had faith in and accepted these teachings as true.

I am so glad that I, when on earth, was never fully convinced of these church dogmas : as I consequently found it so much easier when I came to the spirit world to believe the truths as they are. Of course, I was exceptionally blessed in having your mother and grandmother who are so well versed in these things, to show me the way, and then when Jesus came to me and corroborated what they had said, I could not help from believing.

So you see the importance of learning these truths while on earth, for the greater our comprehension of them as mortals, the more easily will be our progression to the higher things of the spiritual life.

Well, I thought I would tell you of this little incident as it shows you a great and necessary truth, and one which all men should know.

So with all my love I am your own true loving Helen. (Mrs. Padgett)

Assurance that he is Jesus. Refers to a spirit who claims he has lost his soul.

I Am Here. *Jesus.*

I know that what you say is true, but it is I, Jesus, the man who was crucified on Calvary, that comes to you and writes. These persons who will not believe this fact, will some day become convinced.

I am with you as I have told you, because I have work for you to do, and also because I love you very dearly. So you must not doubt me in any way, and if you do not you will soon see from my messages and also from your own spiritual development that I am the Jesus that I represent myself to be. So believe in me and you will be happier and prosper in every way. I want soon to commence my messages again. Yes, you will soon be in condition, and then we will continue our work.

Well, * he was so overshadowed by the results of his confining all his thoughts when on earth, to his mental development that his soul was permitted and compelled to starve, and as he now believes has left him. Of course, he has his soul and only needs an awakening of his spiritual perceptions to realize the fact; but as long as he remains in the mental condition that he is now in he will never find his soul, as he says. The only thing that will get him out of that condition of mind is an opening of his spiritual nature, and then a belief in the love of the Father.

Your grandmother is now endeavoring to bring about his awakening.

* Spirit wrote Mr. P. that he had lost his soul.

43

and she will succeed, for she is a very wise as well as highly developed spirit in her soul qualities.

The spirit is not what you might call a wicked one, only he committed the great error of believing that the mind was everything in existence and as he said, the soul and all spiritual faculties were myths. Many a spirit is in this condition of mind over-shadowing the soul to such a degree, as to cause the soul, so far as the knowledge or belief of the spirit is concerned, to be * lost. He is not one that will find much difficulty in recovering his soul as soon as the soul faculties are awakened.

The unfortunate spirit is one who knows that he has a soul, and that that soul is filled with sin and error, and has no apparent way of becoming cleansed. I know of no spirit more to be pitied, or who needs more the influence and help of both spirits and mortals.

Let me tell you right here that when you help a spirit to find the way to salvation and God's love, you are doing the greatest work that God has given any of his creatures to do--and when that spirit through your help, finds that way and realizes the truth and receives this love, he is forever your most thankful friend and worker in forwarding the interests of your own spiritual being. So when the Bible says, for every soul saved there is a new star added to the crown of one who is the instrument in saving such a soul, it only declares a truth which exists and which never changes. So in your work of helping these poor sinful and darkened spirits you are laying up spiritual jewels, which, when you come over into the spirit world, will form a part of your soul's existence.

Of course, there are no jewels, as such; but they represent great qualities of happiness and love, which the Father will give you. Men do not realize of what momentous importance the saving of a soul is, and what results come to him as such a savior.

I am not going to write more on this subject now as in my other messages I will deal with it.

So I will now say goodnight.

And may the love of the Father be with you and in you this night.

I will give you all my love, and help you to obtain your desires.

Your true brother, JESUS.

Affirming Jesus wrote.

I Am Here. *Helen.* (Mrs. Padgett.)

Well, did not the Master explain what the lost soul means in a way that makes it very plain? I am so glad that you asked him and received the answer that you did.

He is the only Jesus of the Bible and you are right when you say you believe that he is. Let not what men say cause you to doubt this fact, for it is a fact.

* What is a lost soul from Jesus. Edition 1, Vol. 1, Pages 343 to 353.

He is the greatest son of his Father, and when you have him for a friend, you are rich indeed. So my dear Ned continue to believe in him, and listen to his teachings, and follow them.

Well, I love you, as you know, with all my heart and soul, and with a love that increases as the Father's love fills my heart more abundantly, and when I am so filled with more of this love, I will tell you, and you will know that my love for you has increased correspondingly.

So my darling Ned, I must say,

Goodnight,

Your Helen.

Affirming that Jesus writes through Mr. Padgett, and no imposters.
I Am Here—Your *Grandmother*: (Ann Rollins)

Well, I am glad to be with you again as I want to tell you of some truths that you will be benefited by knowing.

You have had more or less doubt pass through your mind as to whether we are really the persons whom we represent ourselves to be, and whether, if your own mind does not produce the thoughts and write, or whether some evil spirit or imposter does not.

I want to tell you now with all the love which I have for you, that everyone of us who writes you is the person he represents himself to be, and no spirit who may seek to impose on you is permitted to write or in any way communicate with you. Our band is sufficiently powerful to prevent any such spirit from intruding himself upon you. Of course, the * unfortunate spirits who write you, we permit to do so, but they are not imposters, but tell you truthfully just who they are.

I know how natural it is for you to doubt this great marvel of spirit communion, and of the truthfulness of our representations, but I assure you that it is all true.

The Master is the one of whom you read in the Bible, and of whom you have heard all your life. The only difference being that he is not God or a part of Him, but a spirit the greatest in all the Celestial Kingdom.

He is not so very different in his desire to do the great work which the Father gave him to do, from what he was on earth, except that he is now more highly developed than when a man traveling the plains and mountains of Palestine.

He is more powerful and knows so many more truths of the Father, but his love is just the same, only greater in degree.

So you must not doubt any longer or you will not develop as you should.

He is the wisest and most filled with the Father's love of all the spirits in the Celestial Spheres.

* Mr. Padgett enabled the unfortunate spirits to visualize the bright ones so that they can receive help. Mr. Padgett gave one evening each week for this purpose.

I know that you love us all, and I believe that you love him also, and when I tell you that his love is greater than that of any of us, I am merely telling you what is true.

I would like to write more to-night, but there are some others here who are very anxious to write you and I will stop.

Your own true and loving *grandmother*. (Ann Rollins)

The result of Mr. Padgett's belief in Jesus writing him.

I AM HERE. *Jesus.*

Well, I am here to tell you of my great gratification in hearing you declare your belief in me again as you did today. This may seem to be a small matter to you, but I tell you it is one of greatest moment, not only to my cause but to you personally, because it puts you in close rapport with me, and helps you get into a condition which enables you to respond with a greater facility to my efforts to convey to you my messages. And also it has a reflex influence on your spiritual condition and tends to increase your faith in what I tell you of the Father's love, and his great mercy and plan for man's redemption.

I am pleased with your declaration and will help you to become more at-one with me in my work.

So let not doubt come into your mind as to my being who and what I represent myself to be, for if there is a truth in all the universe that assertion of mine is a truth. Let your faith increase and your life will be happier and you will become better fitted to inhabit the sphere which I have determined you shall have for your home.

Oh, my dear brother, it is a great consolation to know that you will do my work as I desire it to be done—on earth, and to feel that I can rely upon you to receive *"my Gospel of Truth and Light to mankind."*

Yes, you were correct and I will soon write on this subject at length, and you will see that before me, no man or spirit ever declared the truth of immortality.* You have a right conception of what I meant, and you will sometime realize that that immortality is for you. You and all who believe as you do and *seek for the Divine Essence which alone can bring immortality to man.*

Very soon now I will continue my last message and then we will progress faster in our work.

Well, I will not detain you longer tonight, as there are several present who desire to write.

Well, that is now a part of your ** work, and your band knows that you must do that work. It will not injure your rapport with your band, or cause your power of writing to diminish.

* Vol. I—Page 47, 1st Edition—Immortality by Jesus.

** The work referred to is helping spirits who write through Mr. Padgett, and enable them to visualize the bright spirits who help them in their progress.

So with all my love and the blessings of the Father, I am your own true brother.   JESUS.

Help given to a clergyman of the orthodox church.

Let me write a little. I need your help and believe that you can help me, as I have been told that you have helped others before me.

I am a spirit in darkness in despair. I am a very bad man, but I never knew it until I came to the spirit world, and saw clearly just what kind of character I have. No man really knows his own condition, until he has shuffled off the mortal coil and becomes a transparent spirit; that every inmost thought is apparent, and he becomes, as it were, a mirror of his own true self.

My life was not what the world would call an evil one, and I tried to live, as I thought, correctly in the sight of God and man, but it was all outward appearances only. I mean that I was deceiving myself. My soul was not involved, but merely my intellectual condition as to what was right and wrong. The Beatitudes were not mine—and soul religion was not mine. I was a strict church member and conformed to all the conventions and dogmas of the church so far as their outward appearances are concerned—and was at the same time not of the true soul worship of God. I thought that by observing the dogmas and creeds of my church, I was doing God's will, and that nothing further was necessary. I was baptized and confirmed by the proper dignitaries of the church, and was told that I was a child of God, and was certain of salvation. And when as I grew to manhood and became, as you may be surprised to know, a clergyman, I found a deep consolation in administering the services of the church, and receiving and confirming applicants into membership.

But all this did not bring me true communion and at-onement with the Father, for I had not the love of the Father in my soul. My intellect was all Christian, but my soul was not in unison with the Father's love. How often I thought what a great and satisfying thing it was to be within God's fold. I mean His church, which had been established by Jesus and had come down to us in apostolic succession. But what a mistake! Apostolic succession is of itself a meaningless church government, and no such succession can confer upon any priest or clergyman the power to bestow upon the souls of men the love or mercy of the Father. This I have learned to my sorrow, since I became a spirit.

So I say, let those who think that any priest or bishop can bestow this love of the Father, or can make the soul of man the recipient of this love, awaken to the fact that no such power exists in these church ministers. Only, as I now believe, can God Himself do this great work.

So when I came into this spirit life, and found that I was not in my Father's kingdom, as I had believed, I was sorely disappointed, and in my disappointment commenced to think that the whole of the Bible teach-

47

ings were merely fairy tales, and that God was not, or if He existed, He had deceived His church by having it believe that the members of such church were the specially redeemed children of the Father. I had been in this state of doubt for a long time, and only recently have I commenced to see the truth, and learn that the way to God's love is not through the churches as such, but only through the true and earnest aspirations of the soul; that no mediator is necessary, but that God is waiting and willing to bestow this love upon whomsoever may truly ask it.

No priest or bishop can relieve a soul from sin, or forgive the sinner; and no man can reach the Father's love or favor except through this direct, individual supplication to the Father. The priest may show the way if he knows how, but so few know, for the reason that they not only teach but believe, that all a man has to do is to conform to the church's demands, and that when he does so, God is ready to receive him into His kingdom.

But let all such men know that if they depend alone on such conformity to duty they will be disappointed, as I was. when they come into the world of spirits, where only truth can prevail and where all that is hidden on earth is uncovered here.

Now, I am not to be understood as decrying the churches or the good which they do, for many of their members, notwithstanding the dogmas and creeds, have received this true soul union with the Father—and many preachers have declared truths in their sermons, which have been the means of leading their hearers to a true understanding of the Father's love. What I intend to convey is that the churches in their dogmas and creeds emphasize too much the necessity of conforming to these dogmas and creeds, and neglect to show men the true way to the kingdom.

The only prayers that reach the Father's heart are those which carry the true aspirations of the supplicant to the throne of grace. Men may repeat the written prayers for a whole lifetime, and if the prayers do not express the aspirations and desires of the applicant, they have no more effect than would the repeating of the multiplication table.

And if men will consider for a moment they will see that this must be true,—only the soul of man can receive this Great Love of the Father, and when these written prayers are repeated without the longings of the soul entering into these repetitions, the soul is not open to the inflowing of this Love, and hence man can receive no possible benefit.

So, I say let men learn to know, that religion is a matter purely between God and each individual soul, and no church, or priest or bishop can, because of any claimed warrant existing in it or them, save a man's soul from the sins of life, or make such soul one with the Father. All that such priest or bishop can do is to show the way, if he understands it, and when

48

he does that, he has performed a greater service to mankind than he may realize.

I now see the falsity of my depending on the performance of my duty to my church merely as a duty. I performed my duties, but I starved my soul, not intentionally, but because I thought that the performance of duty was all that was necessary. Some day I hope that men will learn that there is only one way to God, and that through their earnest, personal prayers, with faith.

Well, I have written enough.

I was a clergyman of a church in a western town. My name was W— and I passed over in 1871. I am now learning the way.

I came to you for help, because I saw that you are surrounded by bright and beautiful spirits, who must have this love in their souls to a great degree; and I thought that if I could meet them, and have them tell me of what this love means from their personal experience, I might be benefited.

Well, I have acknowledged the introduction, and I certainly feel myself fortunate in meeting them—they are so beautiful and lovely. I thank you very much, and sometime with the permission of all of you, I will come again and write.

So with my best love, I say

Goodnight,   W———.

Personal—Holy Ghost not God, only an instrumentality of the Father to carry the Divine Love into the soul.

I Am Here—*Jesus*:

Yes, I am, and you will be enabled to fully understand what the * Holy Ghost is, and what meaning should be given to it as you find it referred to in various parts of the Bible. I will say this though; that it is not God. It is merely one of his instrumentalities, used by Him in doing His work for the redemption of mankind.

I will not write any message tonight, but will commence next week, if you are in better condition.

Well, as you believe what I say as to my being a son of God, and not a god, you can easily believe that my coming to you as I do, is not at all contrary to any law of the spirit world. The fact that I have my home in the highest Celestial Heaven does not prevent me from coming to earth to do my work, which has not been carried on by those of earth who should have performed it. I am a spirit of love and sympathy, as well as of great spiritual development; and I desire that all men shall know what the great plan of the Father is for their redemption and happiness.

So, because I am such an exalted spirit as you say, it is no reason that I should not come to you, and communicate with you freely and in a way

* Holy Ghost or Holy Spirit by Jesus. Edition 1. Vol. 1. Pages 72 to 76.

confidentially. I love you as I have told you, and I have selected you to do my work and hence, I am trying to make you one wholly at-one with me.

You must not doubt me just because I come to you so often and speak so familiarly with you, because I hope and expect that in the great future you will be very close to me and with me. I am trying to prepare you for so great a progression in your spiritual condition, that when you come over, you will realize the oneness that I speak of, and be fitted to live near my sphere.

Well, your grandmother is a wonderful spirit in her development, and by the time you come over she will be near me, in my home, and as I believe, will your mother and wife. They are all filled with the Father's love and are receiving it more abundantly all the time. They are now in the first sphere of my kingdom, and will find that their progress will be much more rapid.

So try to believe what I say and do my will, and all will be well with you.

Well, soon you will be free as I told you, and then you can do the work without being interfered with by material things. I know that it is hard for you to lay aside these cares, and I am not disappointed or impatient that you do not, but only believe that the time will soon come when they will trouble you no more.

So as we have written somewhat long to night I will stop now. I will pray for you as I always do.

With all my love and the blessings of the Father.

I am your loving brother, JESUS.

Prof. Salyards—Laws of the Spirit World.

I AM HERE, *Prof. Salyards.*

Well, I am here as I agreed, and will endeavor to write you my thoughts on the subject: *"What may spirits know about the laws of the Spirit World after they have been in that world for a short time."*

As you know, I have been here for a comparatively short time, and while my studies have been to a considerable extent in the study of these laws, yet, I find that I have limited knowledge of the same, and much of my information has been gathered from other spirits who have lived here a great many years and who have devoted their study and investigation to these laws.

Well, I want first to say that no spirit, by the mere fact of having shortly before made his advent to this world, has received any much greater knowledge than he had when on earth.

My knowledge of spiritual laws when on earth was not very extensive, and I found, when I came into the spirit world, that I did not know much more than I did before I came; and such is the experience of every spirit. But, as I continued to investigate these matters, I discovered that my capacity for learning was greatly increased and that my mind was more plastic and received this knowledge more easily than when I was a mortal. This is largely due to the fact that the brain—I mean the mortal brain—is, when compared to what you might call the spirit brain, a thing of much inferior quality, and not so capable of learning the cause and effect of phenomena.

I am now undergoing a course of study that will. I have no doubt, give me wonderful information of these laws, so that ultimately I may become what you mortals might call a learned man.

The first and, to me, the most important law that I have learned is, that man continues to live in the spirit world without his earthly body. This great law, while to you and to many others is well known and is an established fact, yet, to me, was not known, as I had never had any experience in spiritualism and had never given any study to the subject.

When I arrived in the spirit world I learned that this law is one of God's truths, and that it is fixed and will never change, for all will survive the change of so-called death.

The next great law that I learned is, that no man can of his own power make his condition or position in the spirit world just what and where he would have it be. This is another fixed truth, and one, which many spirits even, do not fully comprehend; for they think, or so express themselves, that all they have to do is to exercise a little will power and they can move from certain conditions. But this is not true, for the law controlling this matter never has any exceptions in its operations.

Man or spirit can. in a way, determine what his destiny may be, but when once fixed by this great power of will which God has conferred on man, he cannot by the exercise of that will change that fixed condition until the laws of compensation have been satisfied; and even then the change is not brought about by the exercise of his will, but by the operation of the laws releasing him from memories and recollections which hold him to the conditions that his life has placed him in. So when men think that they, by the exercise of their own will, can release themselves of a condition which they have made for themselves, they are mistaken.

Many spirits here have this idea, and believe that if they only chose to exercise their vaunted will power, they could relieve themselves of their darkened condition and get into happier conditions. But strange, they never try this and the reason therefore is apparent. They could not if they tried, and will not try because they cannot. And yet they think that when they get ready, they will only have to exercise this will and the change will follow. No, this law is as fixed as any law of this great universe of God.

51

Of course, while man or spirit cannot by the exercise of his will change his condition, yet, in order to secure that change, the will has to be exercised, because the help comes from without and which is absolutely necessary to man and which causes the change, and will not come unless man exercises the will in the way of desiring and asking for it.

So let not man think that he is his own savior, because he is not; and if the help did not come from without he would never be saved from the condition which he finds himself in when he enters the spirit world. You hear in your spirit circles and read in the publications about spiritualism that progression is a law of the spirit world. Well that is true; but it does not mean that a spirit by the mere fact of being in the spirit world necessarily progresses, either mentally or spiritually, for this is not true. Many spirits who have been here for years are in no better condition than when they first became spirits.

All progression depends upon the help that comes from outside the mind or soul of man. Of course when this help comes man has to cooperate, but without this help there would be nothing with which to cooperate, and no progress could possibly be made. Many of the spiritualists make this great mistake when they speak or write on this subject. But let them know, that if a man depends upon his own powers, exclusively, he will never progress. And this law does not apply only to the soul's progress, **of which you have heard us** speak so often, but to the progress of **the** mere mind, and also to what might be called the purely moral qualities. My observation and my information from the other spirits that I **have** mentioned, confirmed the truth of what I have said.

Man, of himself, cannot elevate himself either mentally or morally, **and** the sooner he learns that fact, the better for him.

Another law of the spirit world is, that when a spirit once commences to progress, that progress increases in geometrical progression, as we used to say when teaching on earth.

Just as soon as the light breaks into a man's soul or mind, and he commences to see that there is a way for him to reach higher things and make greater expansion of either his mind or soul, he will find that his desire to progress will increase as that progression continues, and with that desire will come help in such abundance that it will be limited only by the desire of the spirit. His will then becomes a great force in his success in progressing and working in conjunction with the help that calls it into operation. It becomes a wonderful thing of power and irresistible force.

This progression may be illustrated by the history of the snowball, which started from the top of a hill covered with snow, as it continues its descent; not only does its velocity increase but it continually enlarges its form and body by the outside snow attaching itself to the ball. So with the mind or soul of a spirit, as it ascends it not only becomes more rapid in its flight, but it meets this outside help that I speak of, which help attaches itself to the spirit and, as it were, becomes a part of it.

So you see the great problem is to make the start; and this principle will apply to mortals as well as to spirits, because, if the start be made on earth, the mere fact of becoming a spirit will not halt or in any way interfere with the progress of the soul of that spirit. Of course this means that a correct start be made. If the start be a false one or based on things other than the truth, instead of progress continuing when the man becomes a spirit, there may have to be a retracing of the way, and a new start made in order to get on the right road.

And this applies to the progress of the mind as well as to the progress of the soul. The mind of a mortal learns many things which seem to that mind to be the truth, and which in its opinion must lead to progress and greater knowledge. But when the earth life gives place to the spirit life, that mind may find that its bases of knowledge were all wrong, and that to continue in the way that it had been moving would lead to increased error, and, consequently, a new start must be made; and frequently, the retracing of that mind over the course that it had followed and the elimination of errors that it had embraced, are sometimes more difficult and takes a longer time to accomplish, than the learning of the truth does after the mind makes its correct start.

So sometimes the mind of great learning, according to the standard of earthly learning, is more harmful and retards more the progress of that man in the ways and acquirements of truth, than does the mind that is, as you might say, a blank—that is without preconceived ideas of what the truth is on a particular subject.

This unfortunate experience exists to a greater extent in matters pertaining to religion than to any other matters, because the ideas and convictions which are taught and possessed of these religious matters affect innumerable more mortals than do ideas and convictions in reference to any other matters.

A spirit who is filled with the erroneous beliefs that may have been taught him from his mortal childhood and fostered and fed upon by him until he becomes a spirit, is of all the inhabitants of this world the most difficult to teach and convince of the truths pertaining to religious matters. It is much easier to teach the agnostic, or even the infidel, of these truths than the hide-bound believer in the dogmas and creeds of the church.

So, I say, let the minds of mortals be opened to the teachings of the truth, and even if they are convinced that what they believe is the truth, yet let not that belief stand in the way of them being able to see the truth when actually presented to them.

Another law is, that not all who know that life in the spirit world is continuous, are certain that continuous life means immortality.

I mean by this, that the mere fact of living as a spirit, does not of itself prove that such spirit is immortal.

This is a subject that spirits discuss as much as do mortals, and it is just as much a question of uncertainty as is the immortality of the soul taught among mortals now and for all ages past.

While men know that the death of the body does not mean the death of the spirit and that such spirit, which is the real man, continues to live with all its qualities of a spiritual nature, yet there has never been any proof presented to man that that spirit will live for all eternity, or, in other words, that it is immortal.

I say this, because I have read the histories and beliefs of most of the civilized, and some not called civilized, nations of the world. And I was not able to find in all my readings that it was ever demonstrated that man is immortal. Of course, many pagan and sacred writers taught this, but their statements were all based on belief and nothing more; and, so I say, immortality has never to mortals become demonstrated as a fact.

In the spirit world, the spirits of not only the lower spheres, but those of the higher intellectual or moral spheres, are still debating the question among themselves. I am informed, that there are some who lived on earth many centuries ago and who have become exceedingly wise and learned in the knowledge of the laws of the universe, and have become so free from the sins and errors of their earth life that they may be called perfect men, and yet they do not know that they are immortal. Many of them think that they are just such men or spirits as were they who were represented by the type of Adam and Eve. They know not that they are any less liable to death than were the ones just mentioned. And hence immortality is a thing which may or may not exist for spirits as well as for mortals.

I know that many of your spiritualist friends on earth claim that the mere fact that spiritualism has demonstrated the continuity of life, establishes the fact of immortality.* But a few moments consideration will show you the falsity of this reasoning.

Change is the law eternal both on earth and in the spirit world, and nothing exists the same for any length of time; and in the succession of these changes, how can it be said that in the future, far or near, changes may not come by which the existence of the spirit—the ego of man—may be ended, and that ego take some other form or enter into some other condition, so that it will not be the same ego—and not the same spirit which is now living as a demonstration of the continuity of life—the mortal life?

And so, many spirits as well as mortals do not know what is necessary

* Read immortality—Edition 1, Volume 1, Pages 47 to 50 from Jesus. Pages 50-53, from Henry Ward Beecher.

to obtain to have the certain knowledge of immortality. But many other spirits know that there is an immortality for spirits who choose to seek that immortality in the way that God in his great wisdom and providence has provided. I will not discuss this phase of immortality now, but will at some later time.

There is another law: Which enables spirits to become by the mere operation of their natural affections and loves pure and free from the consequences and evils of their mortal lives, and again becoming perfect like the first parent before the fall.

This does not mean that the law of compensation does not operate to the fullest and that it does not demand the last farthing. Because such is the exactness in the operation of this law that no spirit is released from its penalties until he has satisfied the law.

As you believe, and as many other mortals believe, a man's punishment for the sins committed by him on earth are inflicted by his conscience and memories. There is no special punishment inflicted by God on any particular man, but the law of punishment operates alike on every man. If the facts that brings that punishment into operation are the same, that punishment will be the same, no matter whether the objects of its infliction be the same or different persons. So you see, it cannot be escaped on any ground of special dispensation so long as the facts which call for its operation exist; and the conscience and memories of the spirit realize these facts.

When a spirit first enters the spirit life it does not necessarily feel the scourging of these memories, and this is the reason that you will so often hear the spirit who has so recently left his mortal life assure his friends or sorrowing relatives, at the public seances, that he is very happy and wouldn't be again in the earth life, and similar assurances.. But after a little while memory commences to work as the soul is awakened, and then never ceases until the penalties are paid. I don't mean that the spirit is, necessarily, continuously in a condition of torment, but substantially that, and relief does not come until these memories cease their awful lashings. Some spirits live here a great number of years before they receive this relief; while others, more quickly obtain it.

The greatest cause which operates to relieve these spirits of these memories, is love. I now mean the natural love; and this love embraces many qualities, such as remorse and sorrow and the desire to make amends for injuries done, etc. Until a spirit's love is awakened none of these feelings come to him. He cannot possibly feel remorse or regret or the desire to atone, until love, no matter how slight, comes into his heart. He may not realize just what the cause of these feelings may be, but it is love just the same.

Well, as these various feelings operate and he acts in accordance with them, a memory here and there will leave him, never to return; and as these memories in turn leave him, the less his sufferings become, and after awhile when they have all left him, he becomes free from the law and it, as to him, becomes extinct. But it must not be understood that this is a work of quick operation, for it may be years long, weary years of suffering, before he becomes thus free and once more a spirit without sin or these memories. This is the way the great law of compensation is satisfied; and it cannot be avoided without the operations of the natural love in its development but all its demands must be met, until sin and error are eradicated by the soul getting in a pure state.

But this gradual release from these penalties does not mean that a spirit is progressing in his journey to the higher and brighter spheres; because even without this torture and torment, he may still remain stationary as to the development of his higher nature, mental and moral; but when he has been relieved of these sufferings, he is in a condition then to start for the progression that I have spoken of.

As you are tired, I will continue the balance of my discourse when I write again.

With all my love I am, Your true friend and professor,

JOSEPH H. SALYARDS.

I AM HERE, *Helen.* (Mrs. Padgett)

Yes, I would be here no matter what happens.

Well, you had quite a discourse from the Professor, and a wonderful one it is. I am glad that he wrote you on the subject as it clears many doubts that you or your friends may have. He has not finished yet, but he saw you were tired and stopped.

Yes, that is what he said, and I am so glad that you realize that he uses your brain as well as your hand. Why Ned, without your brain we could not write at all. So don't think that we merely use your hands, for your brain is the more important of the two.

Your own true and loving, HELEN.

Laws of the Spirit World continued.

I AM HERE, *Professor Salyards.*

Yes, and I am very much pleased that you have, and that you are in such good condition to write to-night. Well, I desire to continue my discourse on the laws of the spirit world as known to many spirits.

The next law is: That no matter how much knowledge of material things and of purely physical laws a man may have acquired on earth, his knowledge is not sufficient to fit him for the higher things of the spirit life.

Many men think that because they have this great knowledge of the material universe that they need not attempt to learn the laws which con-

56

trol the operations of spirit life, or the laws which determine the position and development of that part of man commonly known as the soul.

This is a very great mistake, and all human beings, sooner or later, will realize the necessity of learning these more important laws of the soul development and of the spiritual part of man. I never while on earth attempted to investigate these laws, and, consequently, when I came into the spirit world I was as a new born babe in my understanding of these laws; and so will all humans be who have neglected the investigation and study of these laws, as I did.

I would, therefore, advise every man to give his best endeavor to the study of these laws, and especially that part of them which deals more particularly with the soul's development and progress towards the greatest happiness. These laws are set forth and declared to a very large extent in the New Testament, and in some parts of the old are many suggestions as to what a man should do to save his soul from death; and by this I mean the death that comes with neglect to exercise all the qualities of the soul that a man is capable of exercising when in the mortal life. A man may let his faculties of mind die by neglecting to feed it on proper mental food, and so with the soul. Of course, the soul never dies as far as known, in the sense of absolute destruction and disintegration, but it can get into such a state of inertia or lethargy that so far as it is a part of the activities of man, it may as well be dead.

I don't mean to say that the mere neglect to exercise these soul faculties will cause a man's soul to remain dead forever, for that is not so. Sooner or later, either in the mortal life or in the spirit life, this soul will have an awakening, but that awakening may be delayed for many years, and even centuries, and in its highest sense may never have an awakening. So let men know the importance of studying and applying these spiritual laws to their own selves while mortals, and when they come to be spirits, they will find what a great advantage to their progression and happiness such study and application have proved to be.

There is another law of the spirit world that is of vital importance to those in the mortal life, and one which they can learn, and that is, that no man can of himself, save himself from the penalties of the law of compensation. I have written about this before, but it is of such vast importance and affects all human beings to such an extent, that I feel justified in saying something more on the subject.

This law of compensation is as fixed as any of God's laws, and cannot be avoided under any condition or circumstances, except one, and that is the redemption of a man's soul by the love of the Father entering into it and making it at-one with His own, and like His in all the qualities that partake of the Divine essence.

I know that many men do not believe that there can be any forgiveness of sin, because they say it is impossible to make clean in a moment the soul of a man that has been steeped in everything vile and sinful while living the life of a mortal. Well, this I believe to be true, and I do not think any of our greatest teachers of these highest truths attempt to declare the doctrine of instantaneous cleansing of a vile and sinful soul; at least, that is not the doctrine taught by the greatest of all teachers, the man of Nazareth, whom I sometimes see and converse with; and he, I believe, knows more of the laws governing the salvation of men, than any other or all other teachers combined.

His teaching here is, that while a soul is not instantaneously cleansed by receiving a portion of the Divine Love, as we have heretofore explained it to you, yet the inflowing of such love into the soul of a man starts him into the way of right thinking, and causes him to realize that his soul is open to the influence of this Divine Love.

So mortals as well as spirits may receive this awakening of Divine Grace, to a very large extent, as soon as they realize that this love is the only thing that will remove the penalties of this law of compensation.

I do not believe that immediately the sinner feels this love coming into his soul, he becomes a saint and at once gets rid of his evil nature, for that can hardly be. Such an instantaneous cleansing would scarcely serve the purpose for which the work of this redemptive Love is intended.

Some persons seem to be able to receive more of this love in a short time than do others, and, consequently, their complete redemption is quicker accomplished. But to me, and I have experienced the inflowing of this love and its effect upon my sinful nature, and upon my recollections of the deeds of my earth life which calls into operation this law of compensation, and there does not seem to be any probability of an instantaneous cleansing of the soul, so that a man becomes fitted to live in the Celestial Heavens where the Father's love in all its purity and completeness exists. I know it is taught by many preachers, and it is also the dogma of some churches, that the blood of Jesus cleanses from all sin, and that in the twinkling of an eye; but you must not believe this, for it is not true. The blood of Jesus was spilled many centuries ago and is now become a part of other elements of the natural world, and cannot save anyone. And I go further and say, as Jesus has taught me, that his blood never had any efficacy in saving anyone. He never taught that his blood could do any such thing, or that the shedding of his blood was in any sense, the means of saving a soul. He is not now teaching any such doctrine and is disappointed that those who lead the masses of mankind should teach any such doctrine, because it takes their attention away from the one and vital principle which is necessary to their salvation, **and that is the New Birth, which does not come to a man because the**

58

blood of Jesus was a sacrifice to appease the wrath and requirements of the Father, or because of any * vicarious suffering of Jesus, but solely because this New Birth is apart from all these dogmas, and means merely the flowing into a man's soul and becoming a part of it, of the Divine Love of the Father.

But to return to this law of compensation. No man, by his own exertions, can save himself from the operations of this law, and he, so long as he has this idea of depending on his own powers, will have to pay the penalties. Of course, as he pays these penalties he progresses nearer and nearer to a time and condition when the law will cease to operate upon him, and he will become comparatively happy; but such payment may require long years of suffering and unhappiness.

So, I say, let man know that for every act and deed, and for not doing what he should have done, he will have to answer the law. I do not mean by this repetition to cause men to think that I delight in showing them that they will have to suffer and live in darkness for a time uncertain, for I do not take any pleasure in calling their attention to this great law and the certainty of its operations. Rather I do this to help men to avoid these sufferings and unhappiness by seeking the love of the Father while on earth, because from my observations I believe that it can be found more easily while in the flesh than after a man becomes a spirit.

Another law of the spirit world is that every human being of one sex has in the earth plane, I mean on earth or in the spirit world, one of the opposite sex, who is his soulmate. The importance of this provision of the Father for the happiness of humans and spirits, has never been fully understood by those who have not with certainty met and recognized their soulmates.

I know that on earth men have claimed that certain of the opposite sex were their affinities, and with such claims as an excuse, have done much wrong and sin.

But the soulmate is not an affinity which may be suggested by the passions or desires, but is one provided by the grace and love of the Father to live with the other soulmate through all eternity. Before they took on the form of flesh they were united, and when in accordance with God's plan they separated and became mortals, they became no less soulmates, although they may not recollect their former unity or relationship while living the mortal life. But as certain as God lives, these two soulmates, at some time, after they become spirits, will learn their true relationship to each other, and will, if nothing insurmountable intervenes, come together again in true union and happiness.

The mere fact that a certain man and a certain woman are husband and wife on earth, does not mean that they will live together as husband

* Read Vicarious Atonement—Vol. 1, Edition I—Pages 219 to 230, from St. John, St. Luke, St. Paul and St. Peter.

and wife through all eternity. If they are soulmates, they may, but if they are not, they will certainly separate after they enter the spirit world. That true relationship cannot be hid here, and no mere form of relationship of husband and wife will suffice to keep the persons together.

The great truth of soulmates is one which needs further elucidation and one which I will try hereafter to explain more fully. But now it is sufficient to say that every man born of woman has his soulmate, either on earth or in the spirit world and vice versa.

Well I have written a great deal to-night and you are tired, and so am I, and so I will continue another time the rest of my discourse.

With all my love and best wishes for your happiness and success,

I am, your old professor and friend,

Salyards.

Mr. P.'s Grandmother describes her home in the second celestial sphere.

Well, my darling son, I am so happy to be with you and tell you that I am now in the second Celestial Sphere, where everything is so beautiful, and happiness exists to a degree that I cannot portray to you. I am in my own home and what it is, I can scarcely describe, for you have no words which are adequate to give you an idea of what I may mean in attempting to describe the glories of this sphere.

My home is of a material that you have no faint counterpart of on earth, and it is furnished with everything that is suited to make me happy and more thankful to the Father for His love and kindness.

I am living all alone, but I have many visitors and love is the ruling sentiment among all its inhabitants. No spirit who is not filled with this Divine Love of which I have so often told you can possibly live in this sphere. The spirit who has all the most wonderful intellectual acquirements, and is without this love cannot enter this sphere, nor can the mere natural love of mortals or of spirits fit the spirit for inhabitancy here. Only the Divine Love of the Father can make a spirit so at-one with all the surroundings and atmosphere of love that here exists.

When I left the first sphere I was taken in charge by a most beautiful and glorified spirit and carried from my home in the first sphere up to the entrance of the second sphere where many other beautiful spirits were waiting to give me welcome,—and such a welcome I never thought could be extended to a spirit who is progressing. But I was received with all the love and affection and evidence of joy that the spirits of this sphere have for a spirit who has progressed from the lower one. Oh, I tell you that my happiness was certainly beyond any conception of what I had in the home which I just left.

I thought that the beauty and grandeur of the first sphere could not possibly be surpassed, but when I tell you that comparison cannot be made between the beauty of the two places, it is the best that I can do.

My home was all ready for me and I was carried by a whole host of spirits to it and told that it was for me, and that God had prepared it for my happiness and joy. It certainly is beyond description, and it would be useless for me to try to describe it.

The spirits here are so much more beautiful than those of any other sphere. They are more etherial and their garments are all shining and white—not one little speck reminds one of the earth or the grosser spheres of the spirit world.

And here the music is entirely divine and of such a great variety— all telling of the great love of God, and sung in His praise and adoration. I have not yet seen all the beauties of this sphere, and I may later give you a fuller description of it.

Yes, I met some spirits whom I knew on earth, but not many. Some of the truly Christian men and women who lived and loved and worshipped God, and passed over long before I did.

My own dear mother and father have progressed to this sphere and were ready to receive me; and how glad they were to welcome me and take me to their arms of love.

Well, I must not write more tonight as you are not in condition for extended writing.

So with all my love which is so much greater than when I last wrote you, I am your own true and loving grandmother (Ann Rollins).

Ann Rollins' experience in seeking the Divine Love of God, and in realizing that He is my Father. Describes Jesus' appearance.

I AM HERE, *your Grandmother.* (Ann Rollins)

I am happier than I can tell you. I am living in my home of which I told you a few nights ago, and it is a beautiful home beyond the possibility of description.

Tonight, I want to tell you of my experience in seeking the love of God, and in realizing that He is my Father, who loves me with a Love that knows no shadow of wavering or cessation.

I was not always filled with faith, or believed so implicitly in prayer, but in my early married life, I received the conviction that if I would be happy in life and fitted to receive the blessings which the Bible promised to those who should seek the Lord and his love, I must see the necessity of seeking; and I, with all the earnestness of my nature, commenced seeking for the Father's love, and as a result I found it, and with it a great happiness and peace.

You know what my spiritual condition was in my later years on earth, and how my faith was such that, although I was nearly deaf and blind, yet I was happy and joyful. Well, when I came to the spirit world, I brought that faith and love with me, and I found that it was just as real here as it had been on earth. Of course, in some of my beliefs I was mistaken, such as my belief that Jesus was God, and that his death and blood saved or could save me from sin and damnation; but notwithstanding my mistakes in these particulars, my love for the Father was not interfered with and I continued to live in that love and was happy.

I had not been in the spirit world a great while, before spirits of a higher order than myself came to me and told me many wonderful things of the Father's Kingdom, and that my progress to the higher spheres would depend upon my receiving more of this Divine Love in my soul and becoming more at-one with the Father.

The first time I saw Jesus was after I had been in the third sphere a short while; and when I met him he impressed me as being the most beautiful and loving spirit that I had ever seen, and when he told me that he was Jesus, I, of course, was somewhat surprised, because I had believed that he was sitting in the heavens on the right hand of God, as I had been taught on earth to believe.

And when he saw my surprise he looked on me with a wonderful love and said that I must not further believe that he was God, or even a part of Him, or that he was in the high heavens accepting the worship of men, for he was only a spirit as I was, and was still working among mortals as well as spirits to lead them into the light and the way to the Father's love.

At first, I confess, it was difficult for me to believe this, and I had my doubts; but his manner of talking to me and the wonderful love that he displayed not only for me but for all mankind, soon convinced me that he was the true Jesus and not an imposter. And afterwards, I met many spirits who knew him and had been his followers for many years, and they told me that he was the Jesus of the Bible and I could not do anything else but believe. And now, after my long years of association with him and feeling his ministrations of love and the influence of his greatness, I know that he is the true Jesus, who by his teachings and overwhelming love saves men from their sins, by showing them the way to the Father's kingdom. So my dear son, do not doubt what I tell you now in reference to this matter, or what I have already told you.

Well, it is somewhat difficult to describe his appearance, but I will try, He is of a commanding figure, as you say on earth. His features are regular, and his eyes are of a deep blue, almost a purple blue, with such depths of love in them that under its influence you almost forget to note the color of his eyes. The hair is a beautiful brown, worn long and parted in the middle so that it falls over his shoulders. His nose is straight and somewhat long, with nostrils very refined and showing the artistic elements in his nature. His other features are in keeping with those I have described. He wears a beard quite long and very silky and brown like his hair. His manner is grace itself and modesty personified, and yet in him is the intensity of feeling which can show itself in just indignation when the occasion requires. And yet with all the great beauty of his person and the greater love of his soul showing itself, he is very humble—more so than any spirit I have seen.

I have given you a bare outline of his appearance, and you will never fully realize in your mind's eye just what his appearance is; and only when you come over and meet him will you fully understand the appearance of the most wonderful and beautiful and loving spirit in all God's universe.

Some day this will happen; and you will not have the doubts that I had, and your heart will go out to him from the first moment of your meeting. My dear son, it is a greater privilege than you can appreciate, to be thus prepared to meet your friend and teacher; for he is your friend to a degree that is beyond what I thought he would ever be while you are on earth.

So you see, my experience was a somewhat exceptional one; and one secret of its being so is, that I received very great faith and love of my Father while on earth.

While the teachings of many preachers are that the earth is the only place of probation, and that teaching is not correct, yet if that were believed more, and mankind should prepare their future in view of that belief, many a man when he becomes a spirit would avoid experiences that are very unpleasant and retard his progress in the spirit world. Of course such a belief that the earth is the only place of probation, when the mortal fails to make the preparation, will work him great injury after he becomes a spirit because such a belief is difficult to get rid of, and as long as it lasts the spirit is very apt to believe that his status is fixed forever, and hence he will not progress until he accepts the truth.

So you see, after all, the only belief is a belief in the truth which never changes.

Probation is not confined to the earth life but is with man and spirits alike. In fact it never ends, for each preceding condition of a spirit is nothing more than a probationary condition to what follows. But the great probationary condition, undoubtedly, is that which exists for the mortal while on earth; and if that probation is accepted and made the most of, the spirit of man gains an advantage which is beyond my ability to describe.

Sometimes men do not attempt to take all the advantage of this probation on earth, and come to the spirit world in all their material thoughts and sins, with their souls dead, as Jesus said, and find that in such condition, as spirits, they have a more difficult time to awaken from such condition and progress; and I am informed that some spirits have been in this world for many many years and have not yet had an awakening.

So you must see the importance of taking advantage of the earth probation.

Well, dear son I have written a great deal and must stop now though I should like to write you a much longer time.

So with all my love I will close, and sign myself

Your loving Grandmother.   ANN ROLLINS

Ann Rollins' description of Jesus correct.

I AM HERE, *Jesus.*

Well, I am ready to write more of my discourses, and I want you to prepare for our writing very soon. I think that to-morrow night will suit for the work. Commence about nine o'clock, and then you can write until we finish it.

Yes, very soon the love will come to you in abundance, and you will realize its cleansing effect and will also experience a wonderful peace filling your soul. So to-morrow night we will write.

She was correct, except that she may have overdrawn her description of my beauty and goodness; but she thinks as she' wrote and you must believe what she said.

Well, I love you with all the love of an elder brother who is filled with the Love of the Heavenly Father. This is all that I can say, for it is most comprehensive and leaves nothing to be added.

I will pray with you to night that the Father's love may come to you in great abundance. So with the Love that I mention and my blessings and the Love and blessings of the Father,

I am, Your true friend and brother,   JESUS.

The Real Truth of Life on Earth, and What It Means to Mortals.

I AM HERE, *Jesus.*

You are better to night in your spiritual condition and I will write a formal message.

I desire to write on the subject of, *"The Real Truth of the Life on Earth, and What It Means to Mortals."*

When men come to the knowledge that they are children of the Father and under His care and protection, they will see that they must lead such lives as will fit them to become in union with the Father and be able to partake of His Love which makes them, as it were, a part of Himself. I mean that there are in all men the potentiality of becoming a part of the Divine Essence. But in order for them to partake of this Divinity they must let the Love of the Father, in its highest nature, enter into their souls and make them at-one with Him. No mere love that they had bestowed upon them as creatures of the Father's handiwork will enable them to attain to this exalted condition. The natural love, of itself, is not sufficient, because when that love was bestowed upon them it was merely intended to enable them to live in a good and harmonious way with their fellowmen. It was not the real Love that formed a part of the Divine nature of the Father, and was not intended to make men a part of that nature. So, in order for men to receive this higher Love, they must do the will of the Father while on earth or after they become spirits they will have a more difficult work in receiving the wonderful inflowing of this Divine Love.

The earth is the great plane of probation, and the development of the souls of men depends upon their correct living in accordance with those principles which the Father has established as the means whereby they may receive this condition of Love, which alone can make them at-one with Him.

Merely good deeds are not sufficient. Back of all deeds must be the soul's development, which results only from the possession of this Love. I do not mean by this that deeds do not form a part of this development, for they do; but deeds without the possession of this Love will never make a man the possessor of the one thing needful to ensure his entrance into the Heavenly Kingdom.

Men must love one another, and must, of course, "do unto each other as they would be done by." If this rule of conduct was observed men would be much happier on earth even if they do not possess the Divine Love that I speak of.

No man can of himself become filled with this love, for in only one way will it come into his soul, and that is by prayer to the Father for its inflowing, and faith that He will give it to him who asks earnestly and humbly. I know that some men think that prayer is nothing more than an appeal to their own better selves, but I tell you that this is a wrong belief; and when they realize the truth that prayer ascends to the Father, and is heard by Him and answered, they will understand the great mission and benefit of prayer.

Let men live the most exemplary lives, and yet they will not necessarily become partners of this Great Love, and have the qualities that are necessary to enable them to receive the Great Gift of unison with the Father. I urge all men to live a good moral life, because it has its own reward in the spirit world, and makes them happier as spirit beings in a condition of mere natural love, and will fit them for a life in the spirit world which will bring to them happiness; but not the happiness of those who fit themselves for greater happiness in the Kingdom of Heaven or Celestial Kingdom.

I will not discourage men from seeking the life of a moralist, or of one who tries to follow the truths of conduct which the golden rule imposes, but, on the contrary, emphasize the necessity for such a life.

A good man approaches nearest the image of the Father than any other being can possibly attain to; and his reward in the future life will be that which comes only from living the life of such a man. So, I say, the more a man lives in accordance with these moral precepts, the nearer he will approach the image in which he was created.

But why should men be satisfied with the image when the Real Substance may be theirs by obeying the invitation of the Father? The image may satisfy some who are content with small things, but the aspiring soul wants the Real Substance which the Father offers freely to those who will accept His invitation.

No man can really live a good moral life unless he has as his guide the Love that I have mentioned. I do not believe that any man who knows the difference between the image and the Substance will be satisfied with the former, for if so he is rejecting the greatest happiness that even the Father can bestow upon him.

So let not men be content with trying to live good moral lives, but seek with all their hearts the Love that makes them truly angels of God; and such angels as by reason of the Divinity which such Love brings to them, can feel and realize the certainty that they are immortal.

Immortality is only of God, and anything less than God or His Divine Essence which makes the creature a part of that Divinity, is not immortal.

Adam and Eve or whom they typify were mortals, free from sin and obedient to the Father, and thought that they were immortal; but when the temptation came and they yielded, they realized to their great sorrow that they were not immortal. And so will every spirit of mortal be in the future life where the Divine Love of the Father has not become a part of its existence.

Life on earth is an important part of the great eternity of living, and men should realize this to its fullest meaning, and not think the earth a mere stopping place where the spirit is enfolded in flesh only for the pleasures and gratification of its carnal appetites. This earth life is a fleeting shadow of the spirit life, but an important shadow to the happiness which man may enjoy in the future. It is the most important period of man's whole existence, and the way that such life is lived may determine the whole future life of the man. I don't mean that there is no redemption beyond the grave, for the mercy of the Father continues into the spirit life, but when man fails to accept this mercy, I mean the way in which he may become a Divine child of the Father while in the earth life, he may never accept it in the spirit life.

So many spirits are contented to remain in the happiness of their natural love and refuse to be convinced that there is a greater Love and happiness awaiting them in the Father's Kingdom, which may be theirs, if they will only believe and seek. This I say from my knowledge of the real condition of spirits in the spirit world, and the difficulty which the redeemed spirits have found in their endeavors to convince these spirits who are enjoying the happiness of their natural love that there is a happier and better sphere in which they may live, if they will seek for the Divine Love of the Father.

As I said, when on earth, "strait is the gate and narrow is the way which leads to life eternal and few there be who enter therein." And this saying applies to the spirit world as well as to the material world.

So let me urge upon all men to seek the strait and narrow way, for only by it can men come to the full enjoyment of what the Father has provided for them.

I will now stop, but in closing will say, with all the love and knowledge which I possess: Let men seek this great Divine Love, and in faith they will find it, and forever be one with the immortal Father as He is immortal, and happy beyond all conception.

So I will say with all my love and blessings, and the blessings of the Father, "seek and ye shall find."

Good night. Your loving brother and friend, JESUS.

Comments on the Message Jesus Wrote Mr. P.

I am here, *Your Grandmother.*

What a truthful and important message the Master wrote you, and he knows that what he said is of the most vital importance to mankind. I only wish that all mankind could hear his message, for if that could be, many a thinking and perhaps thoughtless man would turn his thoughts to God and strive to obtain that Great Love, of which the Master wrote so eloquently.

The more I think of the great work that you have been selected to do, the more I am surprised, because, as I conceive it to be, this work is of more importance to mankind than anything that has been attempted since the Master was on earth and unfolded to his disciples and hearers the great truths of His Father.

So try with all your faith and earnestness to get into as high spiritual condition as possible so that you may be able to receive and write the important and heretofore hidden truths which the Master shall disclose to you. He is so much in earnest that these truths shall be given to mankind, that he has done you the greatest honor that could possibly be bestowed upon you.

Your loving Grandmother. Ann Rollins.

What Jesus Means by Immortality.

I am here, Jesus.

I want to tell you what I mean by *immortality,* as you and your friend differed today in your ideas of what it means.

When * Adam, or whom he typified, was told that if he should disobey God and eat of the forbidden fruit he should surely die, the word death meant death of the soul so far as its future progress in that which would insure its receiving the divine essence of the Father's love was involved. It did not mean the physical death or the death of the body, because it is very apparent that after his doom was pronounced, he lived in the flesh a great many years.

But his soul's progression stopped, and it was only after my coming to earth and teaching the doctrine and truth of man being restored to the condition which Adam occupied before his fall, did mankind have the privilege of becoming immortal again--that is, of being permitted and in condition to obtain that soul progress which would enable them to become one with and a part of the Father in His love and affections.

I do not mean that Adam was endowed with this Divine Love when he was created, but that he had that formation of soul potentialities which, if properly exercised, would have brought him in that unison with the Father that would have made his nature divine; and when he disobeyed the commandments of the Father he died, so far as that possibility of obtaining that divine nature is concerned.

As to those who lived on earth between Adam's fall and my revelation of the truth of redemption, they did not receive this nature, or potentiality, and were compelled to live only as mortals and spirits having the natural love. They never were admitted into the Father's heavenly kingdom, but existed merely as spirits having the natural love which was bestowed upon Adam and his race.

Abraham, Isaac and the rest of the persons who are described in the Bible as being children of God, and obedient to his commands, were not partakers of this divine nature, and became so only after my coming to earth and showing the way to its attainment.

When I was sent to earth, God sent me with the truth as to redemption and conferred upon man the privilege of receiving His Divine Essence. No sacrifice or death of mine brought this great boon; but only with my coming came this love and the way to obtain it.

Adam was not created immortal, but had only the potentiality of immortality, and after his death, man ceased to have this potentiality until God sent it to them with my coming to earth.

And when it was said, that as in Adam all men die, so in me were all men

* Adam typified one of the first parents whose names are Aman and Amon. Both these spirits wrote through Mr. Padgett. Their messages will be found on later pages.

68

made alive, it was merely meant, that when Adam fell that which formed a part of his being and made it possible for him to become immortal, was taken from him; that is, as to that potentiality and privilege, he died, and was no more able to attain to the condition of soul that enabled him to become one with the Father, or to partake of His divinity; and in this death remained the condition of mankind until, as I say, I came and brought with me the restored gift of the soul attribute which made it possible for man to again become immortal.

When this gift was bestowed upon man, it was also bestowed upon all those who were then living in the spirit world, but they could obtain it only in the way that was provided for man to obtain it. Understand me, everything that was lost by Adam's fall was restored by my coming with the restored gift; and it embraced every spirit who had ever lived as mortal and every mortal who thereafter lived up to the present time.

My coming, of itself, or the death or sacrifice of me by the Jews, did not restore mankind to the condition that existed in Adam before his fall. I was only a messenger of God sent with that gift, and to teach the truth of its restoration to mankind and to spirits; and when, after my death, I descended into hell, as the Bible says (but which saying does not express the destination of my going, for the true meaning is that I went into the world of spirits), I proclaimed to the spirits the truth of the bestowal of this restored life which had been lost by Adam's disobedience.

All spirits, good and bad, now have this restored potentiality of obtaining the Divine nature that I have spoken of, or immortality. So you see, when Adam died it was the death of the soul quality or potentiality which makes immortality possible.

When the Bible speaks of those men of ancient times who were God's prophets and beloved children and as walking with Him, it merely means that they had obtained such a high developement of their natural love that they could occupy those spheres in the spirit world upon their physical death, which made them mere spirits of mortals, close to the Father and supremely happy. I mean that happiness which does not partake of the divine nature. They were not in the same condition of soul attributes as was Adam before his fall; for they did not have this potentiality, and any interpretation of anything written in the Bible which gives to any man or spirit, at that time, the possibility of receiving the Divine Essence of the Father is erroneous and misleading.

As I have said, my death or sacrifice by blood, as is emphasized in creeds and worship of the churches, did not in the slightest degree work to bring about the restoration of this great favor of God to man. They were merely the results of the conditions of the beliefs of men in the Jewish nation, which would not tolerate my declarations of truth. My death, etc., did not appease any wrath of God towards men, but of His own Great Love for His creatures he bestowed this gift or privilege of the soul, which man had lost by Adam's disobedience.

It was the disobedience of believing that he was not dependent upon God for the soul quality or potentiality that made it possible for him to partake of God's divine nature. The tree of good and evil merely represented the knowledge that God had reserved unto Himself of the existence of that, which if known to Adam, would have subjected him to temptations that would destroy this soul quality of which I have spoken. And when Adam ate of the fruit of this tree, that is when he disobeyed God and sought the knowledge of those things which subjected him to the temptations that might cause him to cease to be all good, God took away the potentiality of Adam becoming one with Him and immortal. It was a direct punishment for disobedience, and the result was that man was left mere man, either as a mortal or as a spirit.

I do not think that it was ever said that if Adam should eat of the tree of life, he would live forever and become as gods, because he was already the recipient of this tree of life in that attribute of his soul which could by its proper development make himself like the gods; and here you must understand that gods could mean only those who possessed this Divine nature of the Father. There was only one God, and all other living beings in the spirit world were merely those who were possessed of the God-like qualities of love and obedience. None were gods. The angels of God were merely the spirits that I have last described.

When it was said that man was made a little lower than the angels, it meant that while these angels had that divine nature perfected to a more or less degree, man had only the potentiality of soul that would enable him to obtain that development which would perfect him so that he could become an angel. But this saying does not apply to any man born after Adam and before my coming with the announcement that God had restored to man this divine attribute which Adam had forfeited.

So you see, the loss of immortality does not mean the death of the physical body, but the death of that quality or potentiality of the soul which enabled man to become like the Father in certain of His divine attributes. And more strictly speaking, the mere possession of the soul of this quality is not immortality, or rather it does not make a man or spirit immortal, but merely gives him such quality of soul and potentiality that by its proper development he may become immortal.

In the future, all men, either as spirits or mortals, will possess that soul quality or potentiality until the great day of judgment shall again take from those who have not, at the time, perfected their souls into the enjoyment of the divine nature, as I have explained. When that

70

day comes, those who are without this divine essence in their souls, will be forever deprived of the privilege of receiving this Great Gift or obtaining of this Divine Essence, or, in other words, of God's Divine Love. And after that time, those spirits who have never acquired this divine nature, will be permitted to live merely as spirits enjoying their natural love, just as Adam after his fall, and all spirits and men who lived between that time and my coming, lived only in their natural love. This is the second death. Adam's was the first, and the great day of judgment will declare the second. And after that never again will man have the opportunity of partaking of this divine Essence of the Father and "becoming as one of the gods."

Men may reason to the utmost of their limited intellects in the way of saying that God would not subject his creatures to this second death and thereby deprive them of this great boon of becoming partakers of His divine nature and the great happiness that comes with it, but such reasoning, or the conclusion reached, will not change the fact. What I tell you is the fact, and many men to their sorrow will, when too late, realize that it is true.

And men will not be justified in complaining of this. The opportunity is now given and will in the future be given to all men and spirits to become the children of the Father in the angelic and divine sense, and if they refuse to do so, they can have no grounds upon which to base the accusation of injustice against the Father or His love.

He will still be their Father, even though they may not accept His Great Gift, and they will from the natural love bestowed upon them be comparatively happy; but they will not partake of His heavenly kingdom. They will be like the guests invited to the marriage feast, who, because of various excuses, declined to attend. While they were not deprived of other food and sustenance, yet the more precious food which the host had provided for them at the feast, they never partook of, and never thereafter had the opportunity to.

Many of my parables in the Bible illustrate this great truth when properly understood. But men in those days did, when I was on earth, and men now harden their hearts and shut their intellects to the truths of these parables and to my teachings.

Of course, ultimately, all these men will be saved from sin and error, and in fact, sin and error will be destroyed entirely, and men and spirits will live comparatively happy; but they will live in death and not in life, so far as the life of the soul with its possibilities of becoming divine, or of enjoying the great happiness which the Divine Love of the Father bestows, is concerned.

So you see, immortality does not pertain to the physical body or to the spiritual body, or to the soul unqualifiedly, but to those qualities

71

of the soul which makes it possible for the soul to become in its nature divine. And immortality does not mean mere continous existence, because every spirit and every soul may live through all eternity in their individualized form. And when it was said in the Bible that I brought immortality and life to light, it did not mean that I showed man merely that they would, as spirits, continue to live forever, but it meant that they would live forever in the Father's Kingdom with natures Divine and not capable of being deprived of the great and true life which obtains only in that Kingdom.

So let you and your friend think over what I have written, and in places where my meaning may not appear plain, I will try by the inspiration of my knowledge and power, to enlighten your souls and intellects. You are both very mediumistic and easy recipients of inspiration, and as your souls seem to be attuned to the truth and as you are seeking earnestly for the truth, I will endeavor with all my powers to inspire you with such intellectual thoughts and spiritual perceptions as will enable you to see these truths in all their nakedness, and face to face, and not as through a glass, darkly.

I must now stop; and give you my blessings, and the blessing of the Father.

Your friend and brother,   JESUS.

*Corroboration Jesus Wrote on * Immortality.*

I am here, *Your Grandmother.*

Well my son, the discourse of the Master is wonderful. Never before has he explained to mortal the real inner truths of immortality and other truths of a kindred nature.

I was somewhat impressed with the earnestness with which he wrote and the great exertion of his thoughts and love that accompanied his writing. You must study the message earnestly, for in it are truths which nowhere else appear that I am aware of. Oh, the great blessings of the Father to his children. How thankful we should be that we live in a time when this Great Gift has been restored to mankind, and we have the privilege of partaking of it.

I will not write more tonight as you are considerably exhausted by your writing.

So, with all my love and best wishes for your welfare, I am your loving
grandmother,   Ann Rollins.

Saleeba, ancient spirit of the sixth sphere, seeking through Mr. P. the way to obtain Divine Love.

Let me write just a little as I need help, and I saw how you helped the

* Appendix.
Also read *Messages on Immortality*, Vol. I, Edition 1, pages 47 to 49, and Henry Ward Beecher, pages 53 to 57.

last * spirit who wrote. It was to me wonderful what a change came to her as you told her of God's love, and when she went with that beautiful spirit who spoke so lovingly to her, I thought that hope is for me too.

So, I know you will help me, as I need it so much, and you seem willing to help us all.

I am a woman who lived a great many years ago in a land that is far distant from your home; and at a time that runs back into the centuries. I was an Egyptian Princess, and lived in the time when your Jesus, that I heard you speak of, was not known to the world. I was taught the philosophy of the ancient Egyptians, and Osiris and Isis were our god and goddess. We worshipped them, but not in love or soul adoration, but in fear and dread. They were not the loving Father, that you say your God is, but the dread things of power and wrath, that called for our obedience through fear of punishment and the tortures of the hells which they were supposed to rule in and torment the spirits of mortals who disobeyed them.

So you see, our souls were not developed with love, but our minds were controlled with fear, and we offered our sacrifices to appease the terrible threatenings of their wrath.

I was naturally a loving woman, and in my life outside of my religious beliefs, I was compassionate and sympathetic. Those who were subject to me in our intercourse of government loved me, and were grateful and obedient subjects; but when it became a question as to our worship and religious duties I sacrificed many of them to satisfy the wrath and demands of our gods. These sacrifices were made at first openly, but so great did they become, and deleterious to the good of the nation in its political aspect, that latterly our sacrifices were made in private, but they were made nevertheless.

Our beliefs were as real and as earnest as are the beliefs of you Christians in your God of love and mercy; and we did the will of our gods with as much belief that we were doing our duty, as do you the will of the Father in the belief that you are doing your duty.

But as I now see, what a difference in the motives and what a difference in the results. Our motives were to appease our angry gods, and thereby prevent their wrath from falling upon us who continued to live, and your motives are to get and be filled with the love and mercy of a Father of love, and to have your souls filled with that which will enable you to live in His presence and become supremely happy.

In the long years that I have lived in the spirit world, I have learned all this intellectually, and many other things that show me the cruelty and degradation of the beliefs that obtained when I was a mortal and

* Appendix. Mr. Padgett had just received a message from a spirit who was in darkness and suffering, and wanted Mr. Padgett to instruct her as to what she should do to progress out of her dark and sad condition.

which resulted in the deaths, physically, of many of my subjects and the death also of their souls.

Love to us, was not a thing divine. Obedience and placating the anger of the gods were the divine things to us.

And now, while I have heard of this love of your Father, and have seen the results of this love upon their appearances, and the apparent happiness of the worshippers of your God, yet I have never understood this Great Love, except in an intellectual way. My soul has never felt the influence of this love and I have never before thought it necessary for me to seek the secret of obtaining the benefit of this love. But I now see that there is something more to it, than the mere knowledge of its existence, which the mind tells me must exist; and so having in my journeys to earth, and hearing of your meetings with the spirits who are seeking this love, or rather a way out of their darkness and sufferings, and having seen the effect of some of their efforts, I came to you to learn the way, if possible, by which I may obtain the soul experience which I have heard you and the beautiful spirits who come to you, speak of.

Of course, my ancient belief still has some influence over me, and I have found that Osiris and Isis are myths; but yet, that negative knowledge has not supplied me with the means by which I can get this love you speak of. While I know that the angry gods do not exist, still there is a void in my soul which I realize has never been filled. So I pray, that if you can help me to the way that will lead to my finding this soul filling love that you speak of, I will be greatly obliged if you will do so, and will follow that way.

In the years since my coming into the spirit world, I have lived in a number of spheres, each one in succession a progressive one. But in none of these spheres which I have lived in, have I found that the inhabitants are possessed of this soul love that I am anxious to obtain. In the higher spheres in which I have lived and in the highest, there is a wonderful development of the mental qualities, and the knowledge possessed by these spirit inhabitants is beyond all conception of mortals; and sin does not exist in these highest spheres and happiness is very great, and the spirits are very beautiful and bright, but in my comparison of the beauty and brightness of these spirits with those who claim this soul development of love, I notice a great difference.

We have our loves and our harmonies, and peace reigns supreme, but yet I am not satisfied, and so with many others who live where I do. But the cause of this dissatisfaction is not revealed to us, and only, as I say, in my visits to the earth plane and hearing of this love, have I become convinced that the great secret of our dissatisfaction may be found among those spirits who claim to have this wonderful love.

So I come to you and ask you to show me the way to learn of it.

Well, I have visited the earth plane many times since I have been a spirit, and occasionally, have conversed with the spirits who claim to have this love, and they have to some degree told me of this love, but I never thought much about it until lately. I was happy in my condition as I have told you of it, and did not think it worth while to inquire into the fact of what this love meant. But somehow, lately, the desire to learn of it has taken possession of me, and hence I come to you because I see others coming to you who say they need help.

I did not go to the others you speak of because I thought that I might get more help by coming to you first. The spirits who are seeking your help say that they can in some way obtain an advantage in coming to you first. I don't know why, but they believe it; and when I saw the effect of their coming to you, I thought it might be so, and hence I came.

I was the daughter of one of the early Pharaohs and my name was Princess Saleeba.

I do not know how to compute the centuries, but I lived before the pyramids were built, so you see I have been in the spirit world a long time.

Not now, but sometime I will come again and write you more in detail a description of the spheres through which I have progressed.

I have called for your mother, and she is so very beautiful. She must have a great amount of this love. She says that she will show me the way to obtain it, and will love me herself,—and take me to the greatest spirit in all the spirit world, in whom I can see this love developed in its greatest perfection. And I am going with her.

So remember my promise to come again for I will come.

So with many thanks and my kindest regards, I will say,—good-night.
* SALEEBA.

Many of the Ancient spirits are not in the Celestial Heavens but are in the sixth sphere possessing merely intellectual and moral development.
I AM HERE. *Jesus.*

No, the spheres in which she (Saleeba) lived are the ones that your grandmother described as being the homes of merely intellectual spirits. In these different spheres are many subspheres, and the different races of mankind naturally congregate with those spirits of their own race— so that while this Egyptian may have lived in these different spheres, it does not follow that she lived in the same subspheres with the spirits of other races, and in all probability she did not. She is a very ancient spirit, but her age as compared with eternity—that which is passed as well as that to follow—is a grain of sand on the seashore to all the rest of the sand. She is old as men consider age, but as we look upon it, she is of the now—and not very old.

* Saleeba was a bright spirit from the highest plane of the sixth sphere.

She will tell you of the spheres in which she lived, but they will not be any different, or any greater than the ones your grandmother described. And she has not progressed above the sixth, and cannot until she receives the Divine Love and essence of the Father.

So, as she describes these spheres to you, keep in mind the fact, that she has never gotten beyond the sixth, as described by your grandmother.

She may have passed through what seems to her many more spheres than the ones described by your grandmother, but all the various stages through which she passed constitute no more than the six lower spheres. She never was in the seventh or passed through it.

So let your mind be settled on this point: No spirit who is without this love has ever gotten beyond the sixth sphere.

The ancient Bible patriarchs and prophets, such as Moses, Abraham, Elisha, and the others, never got beyond the sixth sphere until my coming, when they received the Divine Love—and the fact that they are ancient spirits does not necessarily imply that they are in a very high sphere now.

Your grandmother, for instance, is in a much higher sphere than all of the ancients who have never received the Divine Love.

So the fact that a spirit is ancient, does not, of itself, mean that it is of a very high order of spirit. Many a spirit who passed over comparatively recently is as high in the sixth sphere as are these ancient ones. And many a spirit who came to the spirit world within a short time, your wife for instance, is in a higher sphere than many of these ancient ones, who have been in the spirit life for centuries—yes, centuries upon centuries—and for the reason, that these ancients have only the mental development, which can carry them into the sixth sphere only, while your wife has the soul development which has already carried her to the Celestial Spheres.

So do not think that because a spirit who comes to you may be an ancient spirit, it may be in a high sphere, or can instruct you in those things which will lead you to the Father's kingdom; for it is not true.

The Egyptian who came to you is now seeking this love and she will receive it, and progress higher as she develops her soul, but she will never get higher than the sixth sphere until her soul development fits her for the higher spheres. The mere fact that she has the mental development which enabled her to progress to the sixth sphere will not help her in any degree to progress above it.

As her soul develops she will leave the sixth sphere and inhabit a sphere of soul education which is in unison with her development, and it may be the third only—but this sphere will enable her to make more rapid progress than if she should remain in the sixth, because of the reasons that your grandmother portrayed in her message.

So do not be impressed with the thought, that because a spirit is an ancient one it can help you or instruct you in those things which pertain to your soul development.

Of course, their mental qualities are developed to a high degree, and they can tell you many interesting things about the times in which they lived, and of their experiences in the spirit world; but these things, while interesting, do not help you to attain to the Divine Kingdom. As regards this soul knowledge, they may be mere babes, and totally devoid of all the things necessary for the soul development by obtaining the Divine Love.

I have many things yet to write about, and as we write you will see that I am the true Jesus, and that my knowledge of the Father's kingdom is the greatest possessed by any spirit be he ancient or modern.

I wish that I could write to you every night, but under present earthly conditions I cannot, because it might interfere with your life on earth. But, as I have told you, very soon you will be in the condition, when I will have your services all to myself and my work.

I will not write more tonight, but only say believe, and you will see the glories of the Father and your own salvation and happiness.

Your friend and brother,   J<small>ESUS</small>.

Saleeba's Progress in obtaining the Divine Love.

I A<small>M</small> H<small>ERE</small>. *Saleeba.*

I am in a much happier condition than when I wrote before, and I want to tell you that the love of God in the soul is the cause of my being happier. Your sweet wife was with me a great deal, telling me of this love and showing me the way to seek for it, and I believed her and followed her advice, and as a result, I found a great deal of that love. It is so very great a creator of happiness—and I want more of it.

I am living in the third sphere because I find so much more of that soul love there than in the sixth, and what I want now is that love. So you see I cannot live where this love is not so abundant. When I get more of it I shall go to the sixth and tell the spirits there what a great happiness I have found, and try to persuade them to seek it also and I believe that many will.

I am so glad that I broke into your writing when I did, for if I had not, I would not have learned the way to this love and happiness. I shall always look upon you as my friend and brother, and will do anything in my power to help you.

I have not found any of my race in these soul spheres as yet, but there may be some of them there. But if I can possibly accomplish it, there will be some of them in my sphere very soon.

I have forgotten a great many things in connection with my earth life, but I remember my parents and some of my associates and some portions

77

of my religious beliefs. And sometime I will tell you of these things.

I will also tell you of my experiences in passing through these spheres in my progress to the sixth, where I had to stop progressing. It is strange that I did not find this out until recently, but it is a fact.

No spirit who lives in the sixth sphere is as beautiful as the spirits of the third sphere who have the soul development—and the merely intellectual spirit can never become as beautiful as those having the soul love.

Well, I must stop as I only wanted to let you know that I had not forgotten you.

I will come again soon and tell you what I promised.

So I will say good-night. Your friend and sister,   SALEEBA.

Saleeba progressing and soon will be above the third sphere. She knows that Jesus is the true leader of all the spirits who have the Divine Love.

I AM HERE—*Saleeba*: Ancient Spirit.

Well, I am with you again, and I want to tell you that I am so very happy, as I have progressed so much since I wrote you a short time ago.

I am still in the third sphere, but I am in a higher plane, and with spirits who have the soul development to a very great degree, and in their love I am just so happy that I cannot express to you its extent.

Oh, what a wonderful thing the Divine Love is, and when I consider the long years that I lived as a spirit without knowing anything about this love, I can scarcely express my regret at the unfortunate position in which I lived. I know now that Jesus is the true leader of all the spirits who have this great soul development, and that he can show the way to the Father's kingdom as no other spirit can; and besides, when I come in contact with him, I realize that he has so much of this love himself that what he says must be true.

I will soon progress to a higher sphere, they tell me, and will get love in more abundance, and then in a little while I shall go to my own people and tell them of the wonders and glories of my new found home. What a blessed, happy time I anticipate among these spirits who are now in such ignorance of the only thing that brings this great happiness.

I am not in condition now to tell you of my residence or life on earth as I promised, but sometime I will keep my promise.

You must think kind thoughts of me, and let your love come to me so that I may feel its benefit, for I must tell you that the loving thoughts of a mortal who knows what this Divine Love is, have a wonderful influence on spirits and their advancement in the spirit spheres.

I will not write more tonight.

So with my love and kindest thoughts, I am,

Your sister in Christ,   SALEEBA.

78

Ancient spirit who was for a long time in the sixth sphere now progressing to the Celestial Spheres.

I Am Here. *Saleeba.*

I want to say only a few words that you may know how happy I am, and how much my soul is filled with this Divine Love of which you first told me. Oh, my friend, it is difficult to keep from shouting the fact that I am a redeemed child of the Father, and one who knows that His love is mine, and that I shall live through all eternity, enjoying the happiness which His love and mercy have given me.

I intended to keep my promise and tell you of my life on·earth many thousand years ago, and so I will sometime, but now I am so happy in this great possession that I cannot think of those earthly things in such a way as to relate to you my experience as a mortal. Wait a little while and I will try to describe to you all the things of my earth life that may be of interest to you.

I will go very soon now to my people * and tell them what I have found and urge them to seek for it, and I trust that they will follow my advice. There are many of them that are good and pure spirits, with a natural love in such a state that they are very happy and contented, and yet, when I realize the great difference in the happiness that is theirs and that which may be theirs, I cannot refrain from going to them and telling them of it.

I know that you are glad that I am happy and are interested in my progress, and hence, I love to come and let you know what my condition is.

I will not write more tonight. So believe that I love you as a sister and pray for you and ask the Father to make you happy and fill your soul with His love, and bless you.

Good-night. Your sister,

SALEEBA.

I Am Here, *Saleeba.*

Yes, I only wanted to say that I am very happy, and feel that I must tell you because you first caused me to seek this love and to find the way to my soul's development.

I know that you are not so much interested in me as in some others who write to you, but I further know that no one feels more grateful to you than I do. So you see as I progress I must come and tell you of my happiness.

Yes, that is what I want, and you seem to understand just what is necessary, and I am glad that I can come to you. So my dear brother

* Saleeba was a spirit of the sixth sphere before receiving help through Mr. Padgett causing her to visualize a celestial spirit.

think of me sometimes and pray to the Father to give me more of His Divine Love that makes me at-one with Him.

I will not write more, but will say good-night.

Your sister in Christ, SALEEBA.

Jesus Says—Ann Rollins is a very capable spirit in discussing those things which reveal to men the truths of the Father.

I AM HERE, *Jesus.*

I merely want to tell you to-night that you are so much better in your condition for writing my messages, and for receiving the love of the Father in your soul.

You took my message the other night in a very satisfactory way, and I am pleased with the manner in which you caught my meaning. So very soon we will have another message and a very important one.

I am with you in your hours of lonesomeness trying to help you and comfort you, and lead you to the love of the Father.

To-night, I will not write more, as I desire that another shall write, who will give you a message that will interest you very much.

I mean your grandmother. She is a very capable spirit, in discussing the things pertaining to the spirit. I mean those things which reveal to men the truths of the Father, as she has learned them and understands them; not merely in a mental sense, but in the way of her soul perceptions.

So you will receive much benefit from what she may write, and you will realize that she is a wonderful spirit in the knowledge of all these things that tell of God's love, and of His care and mercy towards mankind.

I will now with my love and blessings and those of the Father say good-night.

Your friend and brother,   JESUS.

Description of the several spheres and the different kinds of spirits inhabiting them. From Ann Rollins.

Well my dear grandson, I am here and desire to write awhile to-night about some things that are true, and show you the workings of God's love among men and spirits.

I have had a great deal of experience, although I have not been in the spirit world a very long time—as we count time, which we do not; but I merely use the expression that you may understand what I mean.

I am, as I told you, in the second Celestial Sphere, where your wife and mother also are. In this sphere all the inhabitants are spirits who have been redeemed by the Divine Love and great mercy of the Father, and by the great gift of * immortality which Jesus wrote you about the other night. (Pages 68 to 72.)

I am now so developed in my soul qualities that I realize that I am a part of the Father's divine nature, and that I have in me those qualities

* Appendix. Read Vol. I, Edition 1, *Immortality by Jesus*—pages 47 to 50.

80

of His nature that make me immortal, and which immortality can never more be taken from me; and what I say applies to all the inhabitants of this sphere.

Of course, you will understand there is yet more Love which we may obtain because our progress in the Divine Love never ceases until we get into the very presence of the Father, and are able to see Him with our soul perceptions.

This phase you cannot possibly understand, as you are now, but when you come to the place where I am you will; and it is even possible for you, in a way, to comprehend it while in the mortal life, but not to the extent that you will when you become a spirit and live in this sphere.

Your mother and wife now have this quality of soul perception, but even among us there is a difference of comprehension of this, and I am told that as I progress higher and receive more of this Love, this soul perception will become clearer and more satisfactory to me. So when you hear us say we are redeemed and have as our possession a part of the Divine Essence of the Father, you must understand that it is a comparative thing, and that we are not perfect—even the Master is not perfect, as God is perfect, so he tells us. But he is progressing in the acquisition of this Love and in the increased power of this soul perception.

Until we reach the first Celestial Spheres we have not a sufficient quantity of this Love to make us partakers of this divine nature of the Father, in that degree so that all the natural loves are absorbed by the Divine Love, for all below that sphere have more or less of the mere natural love, which causes them to retain their worldly affections. I mean those things which tend to retard their progress.

Of course our natural love for our relatives or friends does not leave us even after we reach the Celestial Spheres, but when we become inhabitants of these spheres, we have no interest in the affairs of earth or its government.

The seventh sphere is the one that divides those spirits who have merely intellectual or moral qualities which are developed, as it were, to the highest degree from those spirits who, in addition to mental and moral development, have their souls developed by the Divine Love of the Father.

No spirit who has not this Love can become an inhabitant of the seventh sphere, so that when you hear of any of your spirit friends or acquaintances, or of any other spirits, being in the seventh sphere, you will know that these spirits have received the Divine Love to an extent a little short of that which enables them to enter the first Celestial Sphere and which makes them at-one with the Father, and hence immortal.

The sixth sphere is one where the mental and moral qualities are developed to their greatest extent, and it is not necessary for the spirit to have this soul development to any great extent in order to become an in-

81

habitant of this sphere. In other words it is a sphere which is given more especially to those spirits who have given more thought to the improvement of their minds and their moral qualities than to the development of their souls by obtaining the Divine Love of the Father. This sphere is one of great happiness for these spirits of mental and moral excellence, and it is the highest that they can attain to in their progression in the spirit world.

Of course, these spirits may also receive this greater soul development, for the Divine Love is free and waiting for all of God's children; but my observation has been that when the spirits who find their happiness in purely mental pursuits or in the development of their moral natures, get into this sphere, they seldom become dissatisfied enough with their condition of happiness to desire or seek for a greater one; in fact, the majority of them will not believe that there is any greater happiness that they can attain to, and, hence, the deadening satisfaction which possesses them.

I know it may be a little difficult for you to understand this matter as I have attempted to explain it, but what I have said is true; and in the day of separation these spirits will realize that fact, but then it will be too late to remedy their neglect or want of the soul desire for the soul development, that comes only by the inflowing of the Divine Love into the soul in sufficient abundance, and which is necessary to permit them to become inhabitants of the Celestial kingdom.

Well, when a spirit enters the spirit world its condition of mental, moral or spiritual development determines where it shall first live. In the large majority of cases, the first home of the spirit is the earth plane, and in that there are a number of planes, respectively higher or lower than others. So when the spirit finds itself in the earth plane, it also finds that its condition is not much different from what it was on earth. The same ideas of right and wrong, of beliefs, of affections and of desires obtain.

Sometimes these conditions will last for many years, and again the change will come comparatively soon. This change of condition depends, frequently, upon the friends or relatives when they come over who try to help and instruct them.

If such spirit helpers are themselves developed in the line of intellectual pursuits, they will more naturally endeavor to direct the newly arrived spirit along the same line of thought and aspirations; and so with the morally developed helpers—they will make the questions of morality the important ones for the new spirits to give attention to. And so with the spiritual helpers, or those who have received the Love of the Father in their souls, and to whom such Love is the most important thing in all the spirit world. Naturally they will endeavor to instruct the spirit in matters pertaining to this Love and the increased development of it.

So you see, much depends upon the helpers which the new spirit finds waiting its advent into the spirit world, and the instructions which such spirit helpers give it.

But more will depend upon the condition of the spirit itself. As I have said, when it comes into the spirit world it brings with it all its beliefs, desires and affections, and these respective qualities will, to a more or less extent, influence the directions of its progress. It is much easier to influence a spirit who has had, while on earth, awakened in him a love of God even to a small degree, to pursue the thoughts that will lead him into spiritual ways, than to persuade one who has never had that awakening. And so with the spirit, who while on earth, gave his studies and thoughts to mental pursuits to the exclusion of thoughts relating to God or to religious matters. Such spirits will naturally be attracted to those things which it considers a continuation of its earthly thoughts, or which will enable it to pursue the development of those thoughts; and consequently, they are its treasures which necessarily have the most of its affections, and from these affections will arise its desires which will, unless something greater intervenes, cause it to follow the course of these desires. And the same principles can be applied to every condition of the spirit, mental, moral or spiritual.

Now, to the point of your question.

Such spirit following the natural inclination of its condition, as I have explained, will endeavor to get into that sphere in its progress, where there are afforded the greatest opportunities for the development of the particular phase of its condition which constitutes its chief motive force. And this is in accordance with a spiritual law.

The spirit desiring above all else the development of its mental qualities will naturally seek that sphere where these qualities have the greatest opportunity for such development. And so with the moralist and the spirit of religious thought.

Now, God, in His great wisdom and goodness, has provided these several spheres and made them suited for the purposes of their creation; and all the spirits have the choice as to which they will enter and seek to live in. But, of course, not only one sphere of its kind is provided, but there are several so provided, so that there may be progression on the part of spirits who have these several phases of desires and attractions.

The second, the fourth and the sixth spheres are appropriated for those spirits who have more of the qualifications and desires for advancement in their mental and moral pursuits, or rather for the development of those qualities possessed by them which pertain more to the mental and moral natures.

Of course in their progress from the lowest to the respective higher spheres, that I have mentioned, the spirit must pass through the intervening spheres; but they do not linger in them or seek to make them their homes, or stay in them for their development, because in these intervening spheres the qualities which these spirits are attempting to develop, are not given much attention, and these spirits would not be much benefited by remaining in these spheres. But the fact of passing through these intervening spheres does not indicate, for the contrary is true, that these spirits in so passing, in any degree, receive any additional love or development of their soul qualities. So that a spirit in the third sphere possessing the Divine Love may have more soul development than one who lives in the sixth sphere who has not the Divine Love. And so in contrast to the second, fourth and sixth spheres, that I have named, the third, fifth and seventh spheres are the ones appropriated to and specially prepared for the spirits who are seeking the development of the Divine Love into their souls; and in these spheres, Divine Love is the great thing that is sought for and acquired.

The spirits of these spheres may be just as highly developed in their mental and moral qualities as are those before described; and, frequently, they are more so, for with the soul development in the Divine Love, strange as it may seem to you, comes mental and moral development. But this development of the mind is not the chief thing for which these spirits seek.

Every desire and aspiration with them is subordinated to their great efforts to obtain this Divine Love to the highest degree, and ever and ever are these spirits seeking for it, and they have never become satisfied, in contrast to those who merely seek the mental and natural love development.

As I have said, beyond the sixth sphere, these merely mental or moral seekers cannot progress unless they seek for the Divine Love, and in this sixth sphere the mind's happiness is reached.

And the sixth sphere is a more prolific one of probation, in the sense that many of these spirits are awakened to the necessity of seeking this soul development, than are any of the lower spheres; because after some of these spirits have been there for a long time, they commence to realize this limitation to their mental happiness. And, strange as it may seem to you, they frequently make their first start by calling up the recollections of their childhood days, when they were taught and believed that God loved them, and that His love was the greatest thing in all the world. So you see here illustrated, in a way you probably never have thought of, the saying of Jesus that, "except ye become as little children ye can in no wise enter the Kingdom of Heaven."

But many of these spirits have no childhood recollections of this kind, and then comes the work of the higher spirits who have been redeemed by this Great Love of the Father.

In all this you will see how God recognizes and respects the independent will of His creature. He does not force them to seek His Love, but waits until they, by their own experience, learn that what they once thought was all sufficient for their happiness, is not sufficient; and realizing this insufficiency, they become dissatisfied, and with such dissatisfaction comes the wish to learn the great unknown of desire, which, at last, causes them to feel their dependence upon a source of happiness not emanating from themselves.

And thus, my dear son, in my imperfect way, I have attempted to give you a description of the several spheres and their character and the object of their creation.

You must believe what I have told you, for it is true; and in believing you will see the great advantage in striving to enter the spheres of the soul or the Divine Heavens; for in doing so, you will not only gain your soul's development but also the development of your mental qualities and your moral nature also.

And thus you will understand the great saying of the Bible: "Seek first the Kingdom of God and His righteousness, and all these things shall be added unto you."

Well, I have written you a long letter and must stop. So with all the love of a devoted grandmother, I will say, good night.

ANN ROLLINS.

Why men must receive the Divine Love in order to be admitted to the Kingdom of Heaven or Celestial Kingdom.

I AM HERE, *Jesus.*

I am with you to-night as I heard you longing for me, and have come to comfort and bless you.

My dear brother, you have the love of the Father in your soul to a great extent this night, and I see that you are very happy and feel that the Father is very near you. And I am so glad that your condition is such, for I want to tell you how much the Love of the Father is waiting to bless you and make you at-one with Him and a true child of His affections.

I am now prepared to give you my next formal message, and if you feel that you would like to take it to-night, I will do so.

Well then I will write on the subject: *"Why man must receive this Divine Love in order to be admitted to the Kingdom of Heaven or Celestial Kingdom."*

In that Kingdom there are no spirits who have not received this Love, so that their natures are of the Divine Essence of the Father. I do not mean that any spirit is perfect in this divine nature, but that the spirit has

85

so much of this Divine Love in his soul as to make him in unison with the nature of the Father. There are different degrees of perfection, or rather there are different degrees of possession of this Love by the spirits, and their happiness and glory are dependent upon the amount of Love possessed by them. No spirit though, who is an inhabitant of this Kingdom, is without this Divine Love; and no spirit has in its soul any sin or error that may have been a part of it while in the earth life.

All the spirits know that they are immortal just as the Father is immortal; and this knowledge comes to them only from the possession of this Love which is the Divine Essence that flowed into their souls from the Great Divine Nature of the Father. Should anything in the soul not be in unison with the Soul of the Father, that spirit could not possibly enter into that Kingdom; and as the soul of such spirit remains in such condition of inharmony, it can never be received into the Celestial Kingdom.

I know that among men, and spirits also, it is thought and asserted that the Father is all merciful and all good, and in His great plan for the salvation of men, and for establishing the harmony of His universe, no man or spirit will be excluded from His Heavenly Kingdom; but in this thought mortals and spirits, both, are mistaken; and I am sorry to say that many of them will, when too late, realize this error.

God has certain principles which are fixed and which are necessary for men to know and obey in order for them to become at-one with Him and partake of His Divine nature; and, if they fail to obey the requirements of these principles, they will forever be excluded from that in their souls which will make them like the Father, and admit them to His Kingdom.

They, in such condition or want of the qualifications, even though they were admitted to the Kingdom, would not be happy, for their condition would wholly fail to respond to those things in the Kingdom which give happiness to the true children of the Father; and they, of necessity, would be most unhappy, and heaven would not be a heaven to them. So you see, all spirits in order to inhabit this Kingdom must have the prescribed requirements of soul love and soul development.

As I said when on earth, "He that enters into the sheepfold in any other way than through the gate is a thief and a robber," and no thief or robber is fitted for this Kingdom of Divine Love.

Let man know, that no mercy or love of the Father will be given him to enable him to enter this Kingdom, unless that man seeks this Love and this mercy in the way the Father has ordained that they shall be sought for. No special providence will be extended to any man, and if he comes to the marriage feast without his wedding garment, he will be cast out and not be permitted to enjoy the feast.

Men may reason to the extent of all their reasoning powers to prove that the Father, being a loving and merciful Father, will not cast them out or keep them from entering this Kingdom, because they are all His children and the objects of His love and favor, and that one is as dear to Him as the other, and that He is no respecter of persons, and, therefore, will treat all alike; but I tell them that they are mistaken, and if they wait until the Great Day when the sheep shall be separated from the goats, they will realize to their everlasting exclusion from this Kingdom, that what I say is true.

Of course every spirit ever born is to the Father the object of His care, and He makes no distinction between the spirits and mortals that He has created, and wants every one of them to inhabit His kingdom and partake of those things which He has provided for them, and which are beyond their conception in the greatness of the grandeur and beauty of these things. And He calls to all His creatures to come and partake of these great provisions that He has made for them, and no creature is refused the gift of these things, or heard to ask and not be answered with their bestowal; yet, when that man or spirit who has this great boon, and the way shown by which he can receive these gifts, refuses or neglects to follow that way or to receive these gifts in the way ordained by the Father, then all these Great Gifts are withdrawn from him, and never, after the Great Day of separation, will he have the privilege of receiving them.

And men cannot say that the Father is unjust or unmerciful or unloving because He forever, thereafter, shuts the door to these privileges or the opportunity of receiving them. Men have rejected His Gift and neglected to search His plans for their great happiness, and, consequently, they will have no right to complain, when they, like the foolish virgins, find the door shut against them.

So I say, men must realize the necessity of putting on the wedding garments and of filling their lamps with oil, in order to be admitted into the Kingdom.

I will not herein tell the way in which men must prepare themselves for an entrance into this * Kingdom of the Father, for it would take too long, but I will in a future message explain this fully; but I will say, before closing, that if men will pray to the Father for the inflowing into their souls of His Divine Love, and have faith, they will find themselves on the true way to become inhabitants of * His Kingdom.

As it is late I must stop writing, and with all my love and blessings and the blessings of the Father, will say good night.

Your friend and brother,

JESUS.

* *Way to Celestial Kingdom.* Read Vol. I, Edition 1—Pages 20-25.

Mrs. Padgett Affirms That Jesus Wrote

I am here, *Helen. Wife of Mr. Padgett, Celestial Spirit.*

Well, sweetheart, you had a wonderful and vital message from Jesus, and you must study it, for it lies at the foundation of all the future happiness of men and spirits. Of course you know the way and will follow it, but there are so many men now living and who have lived, who will never see the Kingdom of Heaven or Celestial Kingdom.

I am so glad that I have found this Love which makes me a redeemed spirit, and I am just as glad that you have; and to think, all our band have as well as many of the darkened spirits who have come to you for help. Have you ever thought of the greatness of the work that you are doing, and what the probable result will be to you as well as to them?

Well I am not able to tell you, but the Master says great will be your reward.

Oh, my Ned, what a blessing it is that you have such a wonderful power given you as to be able to do this great work of Love and Salvation.

With all my love and earnest prayers for your happiness, that my soul can utter, I am,   Your own true and loving,

Helen.

Why Men Should Believe He Is the True Jesus, and Why He Writes Through Mr. Padgett.

I am here, *Jesus.*

I want to tell you tonight that you are much better in your spiritual condition and I desire to write a message, and have you take it, if you feel that you are in condition.

Well, I desire to write on the subject of, "Why men should believe that I, who write to you, am the true Jesus of the Bible, and why I write to you."

When I lived on earth men did not believe that I was a God, or that I was anything more than a teacher of God's truths, possessed of wonderful powers, not then so well understood as they are now since men have comprehended to a limited extent the possibility of the spirit forms operating through the material world—that is, the spirits of men and the mortals of the other--have the power to communicate with one another, and that the powers possessed by the spirits, which are almost unlimited, may to a certain extent be conferred upon and exercised by men. This intercommunication and possession of powers and the conferring thereof on men, was not so well understood when I was on earth as they are now

I, by reason of my soul development and my knowledge of spiritual things, was able to exercise these powers to an extent that made the people of my time suppose that I was the only Son of God, possessed of many of His powers and attributes; and as a matter of fact I was possessed of these powers and attributes.   But I was only a mortal when on earth, and only a spirit after I passed from the earth to the spiritual life.

Of course, my development of the soul qualities were such as to enable me to do many things on earth which no other mortal could do, and after I became a spirit to obtain a position in the spirit world that no other spirit had obtained. Yet I am only a spirit, a highly developed one, possessing more knowledge of God's truths and having more soul development than any other spirit.

If I were God or a part of God, I would be something more than the mere spirit that I am, and my position would be such that I could not or would not communicate with you in the manner that I do. But I am only a spirit, having the same form and means of communicating with the mortals of earth that other spirits have, only to a greater degree. I am not doing that which should be surprising to mankind. My home, of course, is in a sphere far above that of the earth sphere, and my condition of development is far greater than that of any other spirit, and I am not of the earth in any particular, yet my powers are correspondingly great and my ability to communicate is in accordance with my powers and knowledge.

If I were God I would not resort to the means of communication that I do now, and it would not be surprising that men would not believe that I would so communicate.   But as I said, not being God there is no reason that I should not communicate through you or any other qualified medium the great truths of my Father and the plan provided by Him for man's salvation.

So men should not think that because I am the Jesus of the Bible, and have for so many years been accepted and worshipped by so large a part of the human race as God, or rather a part of Him, that, therefore, it must not be believed that I, as a spirit, have not the qualifications and powers of other spirits, and because I do so communicate, that I do that which, as God, I should not do.

Well, I must not write more as you are not just in condition.   But I will finish the next time you write, as I very much want men to understand my position with reference to them and to the spirit world.

I am not so much in rapport with you tonight as usual, and you are not in condition to take my meaning.   We will try again, soon.

I want you to pray more to the father and have more faith.   I will come again soon. I will say good night.

Your friend and brother,   JESUS.

Corroboration That Jesus Wrote.

I am here, *Helen.*

Well, sweetheart the Master was disappointed that he could not finish his message, and he seemed to be very anxious to write tonight.   Of course, you could not help the disappointment, but he is so very anxious to continue these messages. I know that you were perfectly willing that he should write, and tried your best to take the messages, but somehow your condition was not just right. Well you will have the opportunity again soon.

No, it was the Master; he was writing and no one else. You will not be imposed upon by anyone claiming to be him; we will not permit such a thing, and you must not doubt.

I want to tell you that you are very much improved in your spiritual condition, and you must pray more and have more faith. We are trying to help you in every way, so pray to the Father and you will soon realize the results of your prayers.

As you must not write more tonight, I will stop. But I must tell you that I love you with all my heart and soul.

x   x   x   x   x   x   x

Well, sweetheart, good night.

Your own true and loving, HELEN.

Her experience in the second Celestial Sphere—can never die again.
Has passed beyond the second death.

I AM HERE, *your grandmother.* (Ann Rollins)

I want to tell you to-night of my experience in my new home, among the redeemed spirits who have entered that Kingdom.

I am living, as I told you, in the second Celestial Sphere, and am surrounded by everything that makes me happy and in unison with the Father. I am also in close attachment with the Master, although he lives in a sphere much higher in the Celestial Heavens, and which, he tells me, is close to the fountainhead of God's Love.

I have with me a great number of spirits who have received the Great Love of the Father in great abundance, and who are so good and beautiful that they are as of the Father. And here I must tell you that all angels in His Kingdom, which is ruled over by Jesus, are the spirits of mortals who once lived on earth, and not what the Old Testament called angels are. I am informed there are beings who never had the experience of living in the flesh. I have never seen any of these angels and I don't know where they live, but Jesus says they are a distinct class of God's creation, and that they live in spheres that are separated from the heavens that he rules in. I have often wished to see some of these angels, but it does not appear that they ever come to our Celestial Heavens.

So when you hear us speak of angels we mean only those who were mortals, and who have been redeemed by the love of the Father and who are living in the higher spheres of our own Celestial Heavens.

Of course I don't know whether these other angels will ever know anything about our Heavens or not, but if they ever should, I doubt that they

90

will ever realize the full meaning of a soul redeemed, because only those who have gone through the experience of living in the flesh and having all the sorrows of mortals and the redemption from their condition of sin and error by the Love of the Father, can ever fully understand what redemption means.

So I believe that no angel without this experience can ever enjoy the happiness that we who become inhabitants of Christ's Kingdom, enjoy. I may be mistaken in this, but this is my belief.

All ministering angels are spirits who once inhabited the physical body, and only such, it seems to me, can have that sympathy and love which fits them to understand and be able to sympathize with the sufferings of humanity. Why, if you will think a moment, you will remember that even Jesus was not fitted to perform his great mission and to declare the Love of the Father, until he had entered into the physical body so that he could understand fully all the frailties and sufferings and longings of mortals.

At any rate, no angel that comes to mortal to minister is other than the spirit of one who has passed through these sufferings and sins of the mortal.

Well, as I have said, I am surrounded by many of these beautiful redeemed spirits, and they are all happy beyond conception by you who live on earth.

I am in a state of perfect happiness myself, and want for nothing that is necessary to make me realize that God is my Father of love and mercy. Yet I desire the progression that will take me to the higher spheres, but not on account of any discontent on my part, but because I am told that there are homes awaiting me and my companions in these higher spheres that are so much more beautiful than those which we now have. And besides, the law of progression is constantly working here, and never are we permitted to cease our longing for the higher life and the greater abundance of the Divine Love that our Father promises us will be ours, if we desire and seek for it. But you must never forget that while we strive to progress, we are never dissatisfied with what our Father has provided for us and what we possess.

My home here is a part of the Celestial Kingdom, and we who live in this sphere are all immortal, in the sense that that word has been explained to you. We are greater in our attributes and qualities than were the first parents at the time of their creation. We can never die again and have passed beyond the second death, as it is written, for our Love is now so abundant that we are all partakers of the Father's divinity to such an extent that it can never be taken from us. No, not in all eternity.

And yet, with all this knowledge and consolation that it brings to us, we still have our love for those who live on earth, who have not yet acquired this Great Gift of the Father; and our work in trying to help mortals is a joy to us and never anything but a labor of love.

I will not tell you at this time how much our interests center in the work that the Master is doing for the salvation of mankind, but only say, that his love for man and his desire for their redemption are greater than they were when he was on earth; and all his followers—all who are in the Celestial Heavens as well as those who are in the spirit spheres—are working in unison with him to accomplish this great work to its fullest extent.

And many mortals are inspired by him and by his spirit followers, to assist in this work and make known to mankind the truths of his teachings and the wonderful Love of the Father which passeth all understanding.

So while the dogmas and teachings of many of the churches are not in accord with the truth, yet the teachers of the spiritual truths of Christ's mission and of the gifts of the Father are now being bestowed upon mankind, and are the causes of many a soul being turned to God's Love and thereby securing their own salvation.

False beliefs and false doctrines as taught in most of the churches do much harm and retard the soul's progress, and keep many souls from the light while on earth as well as in the spirit world, but yet, with all these false teachings are mingled some truths of the soul's qualities for progress, and of the way in which it may find the entrance of God's Love into the soul and into His Kingdom.

I know that many men die with these false beliefs and retain them for a more or less longer time after they become spirits, yet the fact that they have as a part of their beliefs the faith in God's love and in Jesus' teachings, will help them to grasp the real truth and to progress more rapidly after they have gotten rid of these false beliefs.

So while you must pity the followers of most of these orthodox churches because they are living in the security, as they think, of these false ideas, yet you would not be justified in attempting to do anything to abolish these churches in toto, because there is nothing to supply their places, and the truths which they teach would be destroyed and nothing left to serve the soul's interests.

But I tell you that the time is coming when the churches will teach the real truths of God's love and of Jesus' mission and the way to man's salvation; and then humanity will be happier, and the Kingdom of Heaven will exist on earth as it does in our Celestial Heavens. The time is now ripe for these churches to receive these truths, and men's longings for light and happiness will demand that the true gospel be preached, and it will be.

So my dear son, you see the necessity for providing the means by which these great truths may be conveyed to mortals. The Bible is losing its hold on many—not only the students but the common people as well—and the truths which were intended that that book should contain must be brought to the knowledge and consciousness of men and women.

For many years the powers of the spirit world have been making efforts to have these truths communicated to men, but with very indifferent success. Now I believe that I can see before me, as a vision, that many good men and women will develop their psychic powers to such an extent that they can be used as mediums of communication, and they will be so honest and earnest in their work, that men will believe the communications and learn the real truths that the Master is striving to teach.

I must stop now, as I have written a long time and you must rest awhile before you continue to write.

Your loving grandmother.   (Ann Rollins)

On the efforts of the spirits to show men the truths of the Father.

I Am Here, *Jesus.*

I want to add a little to what your grandmother said, *"On the efforts of the spirit world to show men the truths of the Father."*

I know that it will be difficult to make men believe in communications that may come through mediums, and that the churches will antagonize the reception of such communications, but I want to tell you that there will be such power exerted by the spirits of the Kingdom, that no efforts on the part of men or churches will be able to withstand these efforts of the spirits. Just as soon as mortals get in condition to receive these truths, they will be given all the powers necessary, and the truths will come with such force and exactness, that the erroneous beliefs will have to give way and let the truths that I speak of take their places.

I know that it will be difficult to get men and women in the proper condition to receive these communications, but it will be accomplished and that before a great while.

Humanity is now longing for the truth of the Father, and their longings must be satisfied. No longer will form and ceremony and the mere declarations of the churches as to what God has provided for his children and what the churches have provided be sufficient to satisfy. The mind as well as the credulity of men must be considered, and when the teachings of the churches are against reason and the knowledge of spiritual laws which men may learn, these souls which hunger and thirst for God's Love and the way to obtain it must be satisfied.

I know that my Kingdom will be established on earth in a fuller and more truthful way than ever, and men will believe in me with a greater confidence than they ever have—not as a God to be worshipped, but as a brother and friend who is able to show them the way to the love of the Father and to their own salvation and to immortality. So you see the importance of getting good and righteous mediums to convey these great truths.

Mere physical phenomena do not enlighten the soul very much as to its destiny and what road it shall travel to reach God's love; and such phenomena will henceforth become of less importance in bringing men to a knowledge of what awaits them in the spirit life.

I will try to influence many mortals to get in this psychic condition, so that they may receive these truths, and thus do the great work that is necessary for the redemption of men to a greater degree than in the past.

So you must be constant in your work and faith, and after a little while many will engage in the same work.

I must stop now. Your brother and friend,   JESUS.

St. John—On Divine Love. It must not be confounded with the natural love.

I AM HERE, *St. John.*

I felt your call and came. I will tell you of love, as that is what you called me for.

The love that I taught when on earth, is the Love that the Father has prepared for all His children who might seek it. All that is required is that they seek with earnestness and faith, and they will receive it. I know that this Love is frequently confounded with the natural love that God gave to man at his creation, but the two are different and distinct. Every man has this natural love to a more or less extent; and it is a great gift and makes man what he is; but not so many have this other Love, because it is bestowed only in answer to prayer and the real longings of the heart and soul. This is the Divine Love, and this is the Love that makes man a part of the Divinity of the Father, and, consequently, immortal.

God is love—and this is the great truth of His being. But His Love while free for all, yet is not bestowed without the desire of the mortal to receive it. I wish that I had time to-night to more fully explain this Great Love but I have not; and I came to you only because you called me.

No, not to-night, but I will come sometime and write you a long letter on these subjects.

I am supremely happy and am working for humanity, and so directly does the Master. I do more for the advancement of the spirits after they have commenced to enjoy the love of the Father in their souls.

Well, Jesus is the ruling spirit in our Kingdom and His power is supreme. It is, of course, the Kingdom of God; but this Kingdom is being formed by the Master, and to him is given the supreme ruling power, and we are all his followers. He rules by love and ministrations, and not by the hard lines of force and coercion.

Yes, he has many with him in the Celestial Spheres, but they are all subordinate to and obey him, but it is hard to make you understand this. This obedience is the result of love, and the word does not convey the exact meaning intended.

* Well, that was a request made by us in our desire to become of importance, but we did not then understand what His Kingdom would be. We are equal here provided we have the same amount of love—the Divine Love, that alone determines our place and position.

Jesus is the greatest of all, because he has more of this Love than any other spirit, and because he is nearer the Father and knows more of Him and of His attributes. No distinction is made in this Kingdom because of any relationship or personal greatness, but only because of more or less of Divine Love in the soul of the spirit.

I will come to you at times and write you of my knowledge of the truths of the Father, and hope that they may do you and the world some good.

I was not an educated man at that time when on earth, and never was, so far as languages are concerned. I had no knowledge of the philosophy of the great thinkers and writers of that time. All the knowledge I possessed of spiritual matters came to me from the teachings of Jesus and the promptings of the Holy Spirit. I was not a learned man in the earthly sense.

You have my blessings and my love, and I hope that the Holy Spirit may soon fill your soul with the Love of the Father in greater abundance and keep you in its care and keeping.

I will say good night.   St. John.

Jesus affirmed that Beecher wrote the message on "Immortality." It contains the truth.

I Am Here. *Jesus.*

I merely want to say that you are better in your spiritual condition and also physically.

You must not forget to pray to the Father and have faith. I am with you and will help you in all your undertakings and in your soul development, as I promised. So believe what I say and try to throw off all worries from now onward to the time when the occasion for the same will cease.

Yes, the ** message of Mr. Beecher was written by him and it contains the truth with reference to immortality as I have explained to you before. He is a strong and logical reasoner, and I am glad that he wrote on the

---

* St. John, in a message through Mr. P., wrote the following: Saint is not used in the Celestial Heavens. When Saint is used by spirits it is merely used for the purpose of identification.
** Refers to message—Vol. 1, Edition I, page 53—"Immortality" by Henry Ward Beecher.

subject. It may be used in connection with my writings, and will have its effect with a number of persons who thought much of him when on earth.

I want him to be a regular contributor to my cause.

So my dear brother, let your faith in me increase and give all your love to the Father.

I will soon write a message as I suggested last night.

With all my love I am your friend and brother,

JESUS.

Confirmation by St. Andrew that Jesus writes through Mr. P.

I am your friend and brother in Christ and his love. *St. Andrew.*

I came because I am interested in the work which you are called upon to do—and because we all love you and want to see you progress in your soul development and in your capacity for receiving the messages of the Master, which he has selected you, as his disciple, to receive and transmit to the world.

I am the true Andrew of the Bible, and no other and you must believe that I am. I know that you may have doubts as to so many of the disciples of the Master coming to you to write, but you must not be surprised at that fact, for who are more interested in the great work that you are to do than the disciples of the Master, who know that his teachings are the truth, and that mankind needs them at this time, more than at any time in the history of the world.

So let all your doubts disappear and believe that we are with you in all our love and desire that you may be happy, and may have that soul development that will make you one with us and with the Father, the Creator and Preserver of us all.

Well, you must believe in what we say. I know of no way in which you can become more convinced than by our writing to you. Let no man turn away your faith from us, as no man can truthfully say that we are not writing to you, and hence, the testimony of such a man is not of that character as to overcome the positive testimony that you receive from us and all your band that the Master is actually writing to you. No spirit will be permitted to impersonate the Master or any of us. We are of that higher order of spirits that are all powerful, and if any spirit should attempt to impose upon you, we would soon compel such spirit to cease its attempt to deceive you, and leave you in your efforts to seek and learn the truth.

Yes, sooner or later they will disclose their cloven feet.

Well, we expect that you will doubt at times, but we know that after awhile your faith will be so firm that no doubt will ever enter your mind.

Jesus selected you, and because you are not worthy, that must not cause you to doubt that he has made such selection. He knows just what is best,

96

and what your qualifications and possibilities are, and it is not for you to say that you are not worthy or not fitted to the work. Let faith in him and in his love and in his promise be established beyond doubt or questioning.

Yes, you certainly are favored and you should appreciate that fact to its highest conception; for I tell you that you are as much favored in being selected for this work as were any of us when he selected us for his disciples, and I may say to a greater degree, because you are the only one in all the universe that he has chosen to do this great work, and you will find after awhile that it is a work of stupendous importance and involves much labor and exhaustion of both body and mind.

Well, I have written a long letter for my first appearance, and I must stop; and I say as the most important thing to tell you now: Believe, and you shall see the glory of the Father and your own salvation

I will say with all my heart that I am your true friend and brother, and will pray for you with all my love and faith. So good-night—

Your true brother and friend,

St. Andrew, the Apostle.

Confirmation by St. Peter.

I Am Here. *St. Peter.*

I come for the same reasons that Andrew came, and I want to add my testimony to his that you are the true selection of the Master to do his work, and that he is with you very often writing to you and bestowing upon you his love and blessings. You must believe and let not doubt enter your mind or keep you from fully believing that the Master is your friend and brother and is with you in your times of worry and gloom.

I am a spirit, who once, when on earth had great doubts as to the Master's sacred mission, and as to his being the true son of the Father, but these doubts left me when I saw the greatness of his person and the wonderful love of the Father which possessed him. You will remember that I even denied him—that is that I knew him as a mere man—and what anguish and suffering that denial gave me. So you must not doubt or deny him.

I know now beyond all question of doubt that he is the true Master and the true son of God, and the only one in all God's universe that has the Divine Love of the Father to such an extent as makes him almost like the Father in goodness and wisdom. He is your friend and saviour, and even more he is your brother and companion in this great work which he is doing for the salvation of mankind.

I, Peter, tell you this, and I tell you it with all the authority and faith, and more knowledge than I had when I declared him to be the only and true Divine son of God, and you must believe what I say.

97

So let no more doubt or fear that you are not the Master's instrument selected by him and confirmed by his love and grace to do this great work. I, Peter, declare it, and I know what I declare, and say it with all the authority that knowledge gives me.

All the followers of the Master are interested in this work and in you, and we are now forming our band, which shall guide and instruct you in all these truths which only we of the higher heavens know.

I do not mean that we will supersede your present band, but we will work in conjunction with them, and you will receive many messages from us as time goes on, and you will believe that we write them to you.

You have more power of the spirit world being exercised in your behalf than has any other mortal; and with the exercise of this power there will come to you a power that no mortal has ever had since the days when we lived on earth.

So you must have more faith, and to get it you must pray to the Father more and more.

I have written enough for tonight and must stop.

But let me again insist that you pray to the Father and ask for more faith.

I am your brother and friend, ST. PETER THE ROCK.

Confirmation by St. John.

I AM HERE, *St. John,* your friend and brother, and at-one with God and a follower of the Master.

So you must believe what the Master promised you for he will not fail you.

I must not write more tonight, but will stop and say that you have my love and best wishes for your success.

So believe in what we write, and you will realize the results of our promises.

So with my love and blessings, I am your friend and brother.

JOHN THE APOSTLE.

Confirmation by St. James.

Let me add my testimony to what the others have written.

I am also a follower of the Master and was with him in his travels through Palestine, and was with him when he was crucified on the cross, and saw the great manifestations of God and the doom of evil, and the principalities of the air, as St. Paul describes them.

I was a true follower of the Master on earth, and a true one in the spirit world. He is now the Prince of Peace in its truest sense. His love for humanity is so great that we, even though we are his true lovers and very close to him, cannot comprehend it.

So you must believe in him and in the fact that he has chosen you to do his Great Work. Believe and work and you will see the salvation of the Father manifest itself as never before.

You have working with you all the powers of the Kingdom of Jesus and nothing will be able to withstand such powers. And love, the Divine Love of the Father, will enter into many a soul and make it an inhabitant of the Kingdom through this Great Work.

I will not write more tonight but as Peter said he will be with you often in love and sympathy, and will write you of the truths of the Heavenly Kingdom.

So with all my love and blessings, I am your own true brother and friend.

St. James.
an apostle of Jesus.

Confirmation by St. Jerome.

I am also a brother spirit and want to tell you that the wonderful messages that you have received tonight are true, and were written by the spirits professing to write them and that you must not doubt. So believe and you will receive the greatest of all blessings, the Divine Love of the Father.

I will not write more at this time, but will come again and tell you of things no mortal has ever heard of or conceived.

I am your brother and friend,   St. Jerome.
the writer and commentator of the Bible.

Confirmation by St. Anthony.

I am your brother and friend in Christ and in the love of the Father.

I am a man who was a follower of the Master when on earth and a follower of him in the spirit world. I mean in the Heavenly Kingdom, and I am a lover of God and a part of His divinity.

I was not one of his apostles, but I loved him and believed in him, and died in his cause and am now receiving my reward, for I am now, as I say, an inhabitant of his Heavenly Kingdom; and immortality is mine as it will be yours if you continue to believe in him and get the Divine Love of the Father in increased abundance.

So, let me tell you that not every man has bestowed upon him the great favor which the Master has bestowed upon you. No other mortal, at this time, has that great blessing of love and selection that he has given to, and made of you.

The others have told you of this Wonderful Love and power and blessings that have been and will be bestowed upon you.

So I will stop now and say that I am,.

Your brother and friend,

St. Anthony
as the world calls me.

Confirmation by Mrs. P. that Mr. P. is chosen by the Master.

I Am Here, *Helen.* (Mrs. Padgett)

Well, sweetheart, you have received tonight wonderful messages from wonderful spirits and I hardly know what to say.

It almost overwhelms me to see the great spirits of the Kingdom of Jesus come to you and write such messages. It seem to me that they are all interested in your work to such an extent that they feel that every one of them must come to you and bring the Great Love and power which they possess and give it to you.

It is so wonderful and astonishing that I can scarcely conceive that it is true. I did not think that you would ever be so favored in your life on earth, but now I see that you will have a work to do that no other mortal has ever had. And to think, that you are my Ned and a mere man.

So I thank God for His great goodness to you, and also the Master for having chosen you as his disciple to do this great work.

We are praising God and thanking Him for His mercy towards you.

I cannot write more tonight as I want to think of it all.

Only believe and you will see what a wonderful spirit the Master is and how much he loves you.

So sweetheart, I will say good-night.

Your own true loving,

Helen.

Confirmation by St. Stephen that Mr. Padgett is chosen to do the work.

I Am Here. *St. Stephen.*

I am the martyr, and I came to you to tell you that you must believe in us as spirits who once lived on earth and taught the truths of Jesus to men, and who were followers of him and lovers of the Father, and are now inhabitants of His kingdom and immortal.

I died the death portrayed in the Bible and Saul who was my most pernicious persecutor is the same person who afterwards became Paul the Christian. I merely state this fact to identify myself with you, and to show you that I am the same spirit who once died for the faith.

So while I am now a happy spirit and an inhabitant of the Heavenly Kingdom, yet once I was a mortal engaged in teaching the truths of the Master, and suffered the pains and torments which such teachings and such faith brought to many of Jesus' disciples.

But those times are past, and now these truths may be preached and there is none to make afraid; yet opposition will come from the churches and the ecclesiastical brethren who are bound by their beliefs in the creeds of the churches.

But, nevertheless, the truths must be taught, and the Master has chosen you to receive them so that they will be given to the world, and while your task is a glorious one, yet you will find much responsibility and antagonism, and maybe persecution in your private life, because of such teachings. But be firm and stick to these truths, and in the end they will prevail, and mankind will be benefited and will turn to the Love of the Father and pursue the way that the Master will show.

So let not your courage falter or your efforts cease, and you will find a recompense not only in the spirit world but in the world of mortals as well.

I will be one of your band that St. Peter spoke of, and you will find that your power for good will develop wonderfully and in a way that will make the world take heed to the truths that you shall transmit.

You are the chosen one and have with you the powers of the Celestial Kingdom, and the world will not prevail against you or your efforts to show mankind the way to salvation.

So put your trust in the Master and in the Father's love and you will not be forsaken.

I will come to you again and give you some truths of the Father's kingdom that will show the real truths of God's will.

My teachings will be supplemented to those of the Master and in unison with them.

So I must stop now.

I am your brother and friend.

St. Stephen the Martyr.

Confirmation by St. Thomas.

Let your mind be open to the conviction that I and all the others of the disciples of Jesus have and can write to you in testimony of your selection to do the great work that you have been called to do. Never was mortal so favored by the greatest man and most wonderful and powerful spirit that ever lived. I, an apostle, do not see how you could have been selected, and not so great a lover of God as we might expect the mortal to be who should be called to this work. But the Master has chosen you and he knows what is best, and we have no right to pass judgment on his choice. But no matter whether you are worthy or not, you have been chosen and you must do the work.

I know that you will have sustaining you all the power and wisdom of the spirit world that is ruled over by Jesus; and that will be sufficient to insure not only success in your work, but also your own soul's development and salvation.

I wish that I might tell you what a privileged man you are, but I cannot tonight, as I must stop now and let another write.

I am your brother and friend,

St. Thomas the Doubter.

Mr. Padgett asked a question. Answer was given as follows:

Because my faith was failing as it did when I was told that the Master had risen from the dead.

Oh the curse of unbelief!

I say to you above all things,

Believe, believe, and believe.   St. Thomas.

Confirmation by St. Barnabas that Mr. P. is selected by the Master.

Let me supplement what St. Stephen wrote. I am an apostle of the Master and was called Barnabas, the partner of Paul in much of his ministry in extending and making known the truths of the Master throughout Asia and also Judea. I was not only the collaborator with Paul at Jerusalem, but among the circumcised Jews who embraced the faith of Christianity. I am now working with the apostles in trying to help men and spirits understand and believe in these Great Truths.

So you must believe that I am trying to help you in the great work which the Master has decreed and declared you shall perform. We are all with you and will exert all our power and love to forward the cause of righteousness and the redemption of men.

You must acquire the faith which is so necessary to your success. I mean the faith which leaves no room for doubt that the Master has called you, and has, and will give you power and spiritual development that you may do his work as he desires you to do it. Be a true believer and you will not fail.

I will not write more tonight, and will say, may God prosper you and make you like unto Himself in soul qualities and in goodness.

I am your brother and friend.

St. Barnabas, the apostle and a lover of the Master.

Confirmation by A. G. Riddle that the Master and Apostles have Communicated that Mr. P. is Selected to do the work.

I am here. *Your old partner.*

Why, Padgett, such testimony as that would have established in court any fact that you or I might have asserted. Just think a moment. Here are witnesses of the highest character, with the knowledge and opportunity for knowledge that cannot be disputed, and one identifying the other, and all testifying in the most positive way as to that one particular fact.

Who can say that there can be any possibility of mistake? Never in the world has a fact been more conclusively proved, and if you doubt that you have been selected for this great work, I cannot understand the operations of your mind.

Well, my dear boy, to think that in the latter years of your life this great work has come to you! A work that I am informed has never been successfully given to mortal before to do. You certainly are blessed and I am so thankful that it is so, and that you and I were friends on earth.

God moves in mysterious ways His wonders to perform.

So my dear friend, let me congratulate you as you are worthy of congratulations.

I will write soon and tell you more of my opinion of this great surprise when I think more of it.

With all my love, I am your old partner and now your brother in Christ.

A. G. RIDDLE.

Luke Gives His Testimony.

Let me add my testimony also, and you will soon see that any doubt is more than foolishness.

I am St. Luke, the writer of the third gospel, as it is called; but here let me tell you that in that writing are things that I never wrote, and never believed to have any existence. I know that my gospel is considered one of the most authentic of the four, but in it as it is contained in the Bible are many errors—and impossible declarations of the truth as taught by the Master. You must eradicate the errors and retain the truths, and this you will be able to do when you have received the messages from the Master, and the epistles that we, the apostles and disciples, may write.

Your labor will not be an easy one, but you will be given strength and understanding and wisdom sufficient to make your work of showing the truth to mankind a correct and unimpeachable one. I will help you in this particular work with all my love and powers of depicting the true meaning of what may be written you, and will be with you continually when you get ready to compile these messages and other writings which will come to you from the Master and many others of us.

But in order to become perfect in this great work you must acquire abundant faith and a large degree of soul development. These qualifications are very necessary, because spiritual things conveyed must be spiritually received. This we all know now, and we tell it to you for you must know it too.

I must not write more now, and so will say good-night.

Your brother and friend,

ST. LUKE, sometimes called the Doctor and sometimes the learned disciple of the Master.

Confirmation by John Wesley that he heard the Master selected Mr. Padgett.

I AM HERE—a man who lived in the faith of the Christ, and who was a true follower of him, and lover of the Father.

I hesitate to write at the same time with these great spirits who have written you, but yet, I want to give my testimony also to the fact that I have heard the Master say that he has chosen you for the work of delivering his truths to the world.

My dear brother believe this great fact with all your mind and soul, for it is a truth, and one which prefers you before any other mortal.

Jesus, the greatest of all spirits and the one nearest the fountainhead of the Father's love, has declared to us who are close to him, and working to accomplish his great desire for man's salvation, that you he has selected, and that you will do the work and will not fail if you will only have faith.

So make your start in trying to get this faith, and pray to the Father for more of it, and it will be given to you in great abundance. Only the Father can give the faith that will remove mountains and overcome all obstacles.

I must not write more, and say good-night, and sign myself your true brother and co-worker in the cause.

JOHN WESLEY
the Methodist Preacher.

Confirmation by Mr. P's Grandmother, amazed at the great assurance given to Mr. Padgett.

I am your grandmother, and I feel that I must write to you before you stop, for I am so amazed at the great assurances that you have received as to your being called to the great work of the Master, that I cannot let you retire without telling you what a blessed man you are.

I, of course, knew that the Master had chosen you and the writings that you have received do not add one bit to my knowledge, but the thing that surprises me is, that all these exalted spirits should come, one after another, and declare to you the fact that you had been chosen.

Certainly you cannot doubt in view of what this multitude of witnesses have said. I don't quite understand why so many should have come to give you this assurance, unless it be that they wanted you to start into this great work with a faith that admits of no doubt: and to ensure that faith they saw to be necessary, that this great and cumulative testimony should be given you.

My dear son, I feel that you have been blessed above other men now living and that the great favor which has been bestowed on you is one that very few mortals have received.

So I tell you that we all thank God and praise His goodness for what He has done for you.

You must not think that He had nothing to do with this selection, for He is the great Father, and Jesus, the great Son, consulted Him as· has been told me.

Jesus is himself, all powerful and wise and good, but also humble and

104

loving and he is very close to the Father and seeks His advice and guidance as when on earth.

So you see, that our Master, while supreme in this kingdom where the redeemed live, yet he realizes that he needs the help of his Father. This is true and will be true during all eternity.

Well, you are right--but you must not think of your own unworthiness.

So believe.

I think that it will be the most wonderful band of spirits that has ever existed, except that band which watched over and protected Jesus from his birth to his death.

So my dear son, I must stop now and will say that I am your

Own true loving
grandmother,
Ann Rollins.

How Happy She is that Great Spirits have Confirmed Mr. P.'s selection.

I am here. *Helen* (Mrs. Padgett).

Oh, my darling Ned, I cannot tell you how happy I am that all these great spirits should have come to you and testified that you are the chosen of the Master

Of course, I knew it, and you knew it before, but to remove all doubt that you might have, they came, and in such certain terms declared the fact.

I know that you will have the power and love of many spirits to sustain you in your work; and to think of the wonderful messages that you will receive—first those of the Master which will excel all others, and then those of his various apostles and disciples. You will certainly be blessed with wonderful knowledge of the Celestial World.

You must not write more tonight.

Well, the power that will be exerted by that band will surpass any power that has been exerted before, and you will have the protection and sustaining power of spirits that will not permit any undesirable spirits or mortals to interfere with your work.

I am your own true and loving
HELEN.

St. Paul Explains His Thorn in the Flesh, His Experience on the Way to Damascus.
Saul of Tarsus, now Paul of near Damascus.

Well, as you are so longing tonight for love and fellowship with the disciples of the Master, I thought that I would write you just a little to show that all the Master's disciples are in their living spiritual bodies, and I am alive and will never again die.

105

I have written many epistles which are contained in the Bible, and some are nearly correct, and in them you will find my idea of God and of the Master. I never taught that the Master was God, and neither did I teach the doctrine of the vicarious atonement or the sufficiency of Jesus' blood to save a sinner from the sins of his earthly deeds. I never taught that any man's sins would be borne and the penalty for same be paid for by another—and wherever these doctrines are set forth in my epistles, they were not written by me.

I agree with John. God is love. For this means that God is everything that is good and pure and lovely. Love is the fulfilling of the law and love includes everything.

Yes. It (the thorn in the flesh) was my doubt at times that I was called to preach the truth of man's salvation as taught by Jesus. I say I doubted at times that I was called to do such work; for notwithstanding the Bible narrative of my conversion I was not altogether convinced by the vision that I saw. I know now that it was a true vision and that I was called—but when on earth I had doubts at times, and this was my besetting sin.

Well, as to that I am afraid that I will have to disillusion you, for I was never stricken blind or taken to the house of the prophet of God as the Bible says.

My vision though was plain enough, and I heard the voice upbraiding me, and I believed, but at times there would come this doubt that I speak of.

Of course, from my epistles you would never think that I had any doubts, and I purposely abstained from making known my doubts and so called it my besetting sin. But I thank God that I never let that doubt influence me to prevent me from giving the work my call, for if I had I would have undoubtedly relapsed into the persecuting Jew.

As I continued to preach my faith grew stronger and after a while my doubt had left me, and in my latter years I had no doubt.

No, I am not in as high a sphere as is St. John, for I have not that love that he has; but I am in a very high sphere and am the governer of the city in which I live. I am probably as much filled with this love as any of the inhabitants of my city; and consequently, having been a disciple of the Master, they selected me for their governor.

No, Peter is not in the same sphere—he is in a higher one.

Some are higher and some lower. Andrew is in my sphere, but does not live in my city.

I am glad that you called me tonight or rather, the influence of your love, as I am much interested in the work that you have to do for the Master. You will be able to do this work and it will be a great revolutionizing one when it is published.

Well I will be glad to write you at times and will give my present opinion on some of the things I discussed in my epistles.

So as I have written considerable I will say goodnight and stop.

Your friend and brother,   St. Paul of the Bible.

St. John corroborates that Jesus Writes Through Mr. P.

I am the spirit of *St. John.* You called for a spirit of love and I came, because I am such a spirit.

I am the disciple whom Jesus loved and who loved him more than did any of the others.

No, and neither has any spirit in all God's universe. He, Jesus, is the one who loves the Father to a greater degree and has the Father's love above all others.

Yes, I know that he comes to you and tells you the truths of God, and of His love for you and for all mankind.

I feel that he is anxious to have you receive these truths and make them known to mankind, and you will have the power to do so, for he is determined that you shall be his disciple as I was when on earth; and I want to tell you that he loves you very much and is attracted to you beyond his attraction to any other mortal at this time.

You will have a wonderful opportunity to get close to him and to receive the influence of his presence as well as of his love.

So do not fail to do everything in your power to accomplish the task that you have undertaken.

The first great truth is:—God is love, and the second is:—You must be born again. These are the two greatest truths of the Bible. I consider them greater than the commandments to love God and to love your neighbor as yourself.

Yes, I am St. John of the Bible.

I live in a Celestial Sphere which is far above the seventh spiritual sphere. I am with a number of disciples and others who have in their hearts an abundance of God's love. My sphere is not numbered, and it needs no number, for it is near the highest. The Master is higher than anyone else in his home.

I do not live on an island as you say, but my home is in the great city where the redeemed of God live And I am the leader of the city in the teachings of this love and its government. I am working for the good of all its inhabitants as well as for spirits in a lower plane and sometimes for mortals.

I will come to you again sometime and write you some of the truths in my city

Well, I will explain my meaning when I come again, and will say now that the word * which created the universe was not Jesus but God, and He alone. This way gives you an idea of what I meant.

Well, I will say you are very near the Master, and he loves you and I love you also.

So my young brother, I will say goodnight.   St. John of the Bible

Solomon's Position in the Celestial Spheres

Solomon of the Old Testament.

Well, I was visiting the earth plane and happened to see the two last spirits visit you. I thought that I would do so also.

I know Paul and John and converse with them sometimes, but do not live in as high a sphere as do they. Wisdom which I was said to have had in a preeminent degree, is not the equal of love in elevating a spirit in the Father's kingdom; and they are possessed of more of this love than am I. Yet I have great hope that someday I will get this Great Soul filling love to a degree that will enable me to live with them and the others of the followers of the Master. I mean his disciples.

I became a follower of the Master many years ago, and know that he is the only way to the Father—and I mean by that, the way which his teachings show is the only way. It may seem a little surprising to you that I, said to have been such a wise and good man, am not as exalted as are the disciples.   Well, while I lived and died many years before the disciples, and one would suppose that I made more rapid progress than they, yet such is not the fact, because my progress prior to the coming of Jesus was purely intellectual, and after his coming it was a long time before I started on my soul's progression. So you must remember that the fact that a spirit who is called an ancient spirit, does not mean that it is very highly exalted in the spheres—because a spirit prior to Jesus' coming to earth could only make intellectual and soul progress in the natural love and then not higher than the sixth sphere of the spiritual spheres.   But after his coming and rebestowal by God of immortality and the Divine Love on mankind, the ancients had the opportunity to make soul progression which was intended, and would enable them to ascend to the higher Celestial Spheres.

I would like to write more, but you are tired. So l will say goodnight.

Solomon the wise

Refers to John and Paul and Solomon writing

I am here. Helen (Mrs. Padgett).

Well sweetheart, you are tired and must not write much tonight for it will make you feel bad. So when I tell you a few things stop writing.

Well, I see you want to know if the spirits who wrote you last night, I mean the disciples and Solomon, really wrote you. I am glad to say that

* Vol. I, Edition 1, pages 346-347. The true meaning of "In the beginning was the Word."

108

they did. They were whom they represented themselves to be and you must believe.

After he wrote I had a communication with St. John and he told me that you are on the way to the kingdom. He is so loving and so beautiful and seems so filled with love that I really could not help from loving him. But yet he is not so glorious as the Master. None are--he is the one altogether lovely. But St. John is a wonderful spirit and he is interested in your work and will no doubt write you at times.

I did not talk to St. Paul as he left just as soon as he stopped writing, but I will sometime when he comes to you, as he says he will.

Neither did I talk to Solomon, because he departed as soon as he had finished. You may think him a wonderful spirit in appearance, because of the great number of years since he lived on earth. But the years make no difference in appearance. He looks as young as do your own band, though more beautiful and loving. He is not a spirit who has any of his racial appearance, but as I have said, his appearance is caused by the development no matter what race they may have belonged to on earth.

When a spirit who was a negro on earth gets this soul development, he goes into that sphere which his development fits him for, and no distinction is made between spirits on account of what their race may have been on earth. When a spirit who was a negro on earth acquires this soul development the color that distinguished him on earth leaves him and he has the appearance which his soul development gives him. He is no longer a negro but a redeemed spirit and has the color of one.

So you see the color of a mortal on earth does not determine his color in the higher spheres.

In the earth plane the earth color clings to the spirit and sometimes it is intensified. In fact a purely white man may become very dark in that plane, and the negroes become darker. As I have said the condition of the soul determines the appearance.

So the heaven of all races may be the same, provided the individuals of those races obtain this Divine Love in the same degree.

How blinded we are on earth to the fact that all humans are God's children, and all loved by Him just alike, no matter what their color or nationality may be. Well, you must stop now.

So with all my love, I am your own true and loving

HELEN.

The Time Is Now Ripe for the Truths to Be Made Known so that Mankind Can Be Redeemed from the False Beliefs.

I AM HERE. *John the Baptist.*

I come because I want to encourage you to pray more and to believe. The Father's love is waiting for you to fill your soul to its utmost, and the only things required on your part are prayer and faith.

We are all interested in you and want you to get into a condition that will enable you to take the Master's messages as rapidly as possible for the time is now ripe when they should be given to mankind, and started on their work of redeeming men from false beliefs and erroneous doctrines and dogmas. I, John, tell you this, for I can see that men are longing for the truths of God,—such truths as will remove from the teachings of the spiritually guided all superstition and errors. Such truths as will accord with the reasoning of men who are not biased by erroneous beliefs either in matters spiritual or material.

I tell you that these truths will be easier for the mere materialist to receive and understand, than by those who are bound by the beliefs which the creeds and dogmas of the churches have inculcated. And the acceptance of this New Revelation of the truths of God will be by those who have no preconceived ideas of what the nature and relation of man to God, in the spiritual sense, is, rather than by the learned theologian and the simple worshipper at the altars of the churches, who believe whatever may be told them by the priests and preachers.

As I was, at one time, the voice of one crying in the wilderness, I am now the voice of many spirits of God, who know that the Master will teach the truths of his Father, and that these truths must be accepted by mortals on earth, and by spirits in the spirit world in order that they may receive that salvation which the Father has prepared for them, and which, when accepted and realized and possessed, will fit them to become partakers of the happiness and immortality which the Father has promised them.

I have written you in this manner tonight, because I want you to realize more fully and deeply the important work which the Master has selected you to do, and also the necessity of continuing this work at the earliest possible moment.

Well, I have been interested in the great amount of discussion on that point, and how the belief one way or the other has caused those calling themselves Christians to form distinct sects. If they only knew or would know, that it does not make a particle of difference to their soul's salvation, whether Jesus was immersed or sprinkled, they would not let the bitter feeling arise that frequently does in discussing this matter.

But to settle this dispute to the satisfaction of those who may read the book which you may publish and believe in its statements, I will say, that when I baptised Jesus, I went with him into the water and then took the water in my hands and placed it on his head—there was no immersion.

As this water was merely symbolical of the washing away of sin and error, and does not actually accomplish that great necessity, in order for men to become one with God, it did not make any difference whether the recipient of baptism was immersed or sprinkled.

It is strange that many men who profess to have received the forgiveness of their sins and become reconciled to God should let a trifling thing of this kind cause so much strife and bitter disputations.

I will now stop.

Your brother in Christ

JOHN THE BAPTIST

Mr. Padgett must believe in Jesus as a Saviour but not through the vicarious atonement

Go to the Lord, and your strength will be renewed and your soul will receive a wonderful inflowing of the Divine Love, so that you will be able to throw aside all worries and earthly cares, and be in condition to receive the great truths that are awaiting you; for you have as your helper and friend, the greatest spirit in all God's universe.

This I tell you because you need to be sustained and will be as long as you live the life of a mortal.

I am not one who is known in the annals of the church or in the lives of the saints, for I never was a saint on earth and neither am I here, but only a lowly follower of the Master, who to me, is the most wonderful of all God's creatures.

So you must believe that he is your friend and saviour, for he is; and you need not believe in his blood, or his vicarious atonement, or his self sacrifice either. Only believe in the Divine Love and in the further fact that Jesus is the wayshower to all who may seek this great salvation.

I must not write more, for I am not one of the high celestial spirits, as I live in the fifth sphere only, but, nevertheless, I have a very great deal of that love, and a happiness which I cannot tell you of.

So with all my love, I will say goodnight.

Your friend,

JOHN B. CARROLL,
a one time resident of Baltimore, Md.

Nicodemus—On the Importance of the New Birth

A master in Israel, and yet I did not understand this New Birth. How few understood it then, and how few now.

Oh, the long years that have gone by since Jesus told me "that I **must be born again to inherit eternal life**"; and how comparatively seldom this great truth is taught by the churches and the teachers of religious matters.

This truth is at the very foundation of mankind's redemption, and until a man receives this New Birth he cannot possibly enter into the Kingdom of Heaven. Men may claim to have faith in God and believe on Jesus' name and conform to all the essentials and sacraments

111

of the churches, and yet, unless they have this New Birth, their faith and works as Christians are vain.

This I know from my own experience as well as from the teachings of the Master, and I desire to emphasize, with all the powers that I have, that it is the only important requirement to immortality.

The New * Birth means the flowing into the soul of a man the Divine Love of the Father, so that that man becomes, as it were, a part of the Father in His divinity and immortality.

When this truth comes to a man he commences to take on himself the Divine nature of the Father, and all that part of him that may be called the natural nature commences to leave him, and as the Divine Love continues to grow and fill his soul, the natural love and affections for things of the earth will disappear, and as a result he will become at-one with the Father and immortal.

Why don't those who profess to be teachers of Jesus' truths—which are the truths of the Father—and all followers of him, pay more attention to this vital truth?

When you shall have received the messages from the Master, I think you will find this truth of the * New Birth to be the one thing that Jesus will emphasize and reiterate most. It is the most important thing for men not only to hear about and acquiesce in their intellectual beliefs, but also to actually experience.

I wish that I had understood it when on earth as I do now.

He meant as no man could see the wind or tell from whence it came or whither it was going, so no man who received this New Birth could see the operations of the ** Holy Spirit or know whence it came. But this latter expression must be modified, because we all know it comes from the Father; but just how we do not know. The Holy Spirit is as invisible as the wind, and yet it is just as real and existing.

But men need not trouble their intellects to know exactly what this Great Power is, for it is sufficient to know, that which causes the New Birth is the Divine Love of the Father coming into the souls of men.

I must stop as I have written enough for to night.

So let me subscribe myself a brother who has received the New Birth, and a lover and follower of the Master.

NICODEMUS

Gives encouragement to Mr. Padgett—and the wonderful love the Master has for him.

JOHN, *Apostle of Jesus.*

I desire to write a little while and tell you of the wonderful love that the Master has for you in your selection to do his work.

* 1st Edition—Vol. 1, Page 24, second paragraph. Jesus writes: "How to Obtain the New Birth."

** Read "Holy Spirit from Jesus"—Vol. 1, 1st Edition, Page 72.

So I say, he loves you not only because you are his choice for doing his work, but because he wants you to become a very spiritual man having a large soul development, and becoming fitted to enter his kingdom and becoming one of his near and dear followers and brothers in the love of the Father.

I do not know of any mortal who has been so blessed in his earth life. Even we who were called by him when on earth were not so blessed, until we received the Holy Spirit at Pentecost, as you are now doing. You will receive this Great Gift in greater abundance in a short time, and then you will realize what the gift of the Divine Love means to your soul and to your happiness on earth.

So, you are now my brother and a new apostle of the Master, and I know your work will be greater in extent than was the work of any of us when we were trying to spread his teachings while on earth. I hope that God will bless you abundantly and keep you free from all sin and error.

I am with you very frequently, trying to help you to obtain the Divine Love of the Father.

Well, you will receive it, and when you do, as you say, all other things will come to you—I mean all things necessary to carry on the work that has been assigned to you.

So with all my love and blessings, and the assurance that you will soon receive the love in increased abundance and do this Great Work with a faith that will not falter.

I am your brother and friend,

ST. JOHN.

St. John Comments on the Beliefs of the Preacher

And he said, that there is no other salvation than through the blood of Jesus.

How in error he is, and how he will find the truth on his awakening in the spirit life.

Let not your heart be troubled or your faith in the Master be shaken by anything that he or any other man may say.

I was at the meeting and what the preacher said was all right, except that you must believe that only the blood saves from sin. No, he did not say that in so many words, but that was what he intended that his sermon should convey.

I am St. John.

I never said that the blood of Jesus saves from sin, and neither did Jesus or any of his apostles.

Let not the conversation cause you to doubt for a moment what we have written to you.

So I will stop now and will only say further, that we are all with you and want you to believe firmly in what we may write.

113

Yes, I am sorry to say that that is their belief, and what a great mistake they make and how great the awakening will be for them, when they shall learn the truth.   So believe and trust

JOHN.

Importance of prayer so that the soul can be developed and works will follow

I AM HERE, *John, Apostle of Jesus.*

I am the apostle, and you need not try me as your friend said, for no spirit can impersonate me when I am present.

So you must believe me and try to receive what I may write to night, in faith, and you will find that you will be benefited.

I came principally to tell you that I have been listening to the conversation between you two and to the reading of the Sermon on the Mount given to us by the Master in the days of long ago, as you would say.

When that sermon was delivered we were not in a condition of great spiritual development, and we did not understand its inner meanings, and as to its literal meaning we thought it was not intended for the practical affairs of life. People, I know, think that we, at that time, were very spiritually developed and had an understanding of the great truths taught by the Master, which were superior to what men have now, but I tell you that this is a mistake. We were comparatively ignorant men, fishermen by occupation, and had no education above the ordinary working man of that time, and when Jesus called us to become his apostles, we were as much surprised and hesitated as much as you did when the similar mission was declared for you.

Our knowledge came with our faith in the great truths which the Master taught, and from our observation of the great powers which he displayed, and also from the influence of the Great Love that he possessed.   But when mankind think that we easily understood the great truths which he taught, they are mistaken. Only after the descent upon us of the Holy Spirit at Pentecost did we fully come in accord with the Father, or fully appreciate the great truths that the Master had taught.

Of course we learned many things which men of that time did not know, and our souls became developed to a large extent, but not sufficient to bring us to a knowledge of the wonderful meaning of the truths which made men free and brought them in unison with the Father. In your conversation to-night you discussed the relative value of prayer and works, and did not agree with the preacher that works are the great things to develop men into love and bring about great happiness in the world, and that prayer is not of such importance.

Now let me, as a spirit and as a man who worked on earth and prayed on earth, say with an authority that arises from actual experience and knowledge, that comes of observation, that of all the important things on earth for men who are seeking salvation and happiness and development of soul, prayer is the most important, for prayer brings from the Father not only Love and blessings, but the condition of mind and intent that will cause men to do the great works that the preacher admonished men to engage in.

Prayer is the cause of the power being given to men that will enable them to do all the great works which will bring reward to the doer, and happiness and benefit to the one who receives the works.

So you see the results can never be as great as the cause, for the cause, in this instance, not only gives to men this ability to work, but also to love and to develop his soul and to inspire him with all good and true thoughts. Works are desirable, and in some cases necessary, but prayer is absolutely indispensable. So let you and your friend understand and never doubt, that without prayer the works of men would be unavailing to accomplish the great good which even now man performs for his brother.

Pray, and works will follow. Work, and you may do good, but the soul does not benefit, for God is a God that answers prayer through the ministrations of His angels and through the influence of His Holy Spirit, which works on the interior or real part of man.

I will stop now.

With my love to both of you, I am your brother in Christ,

JOHN.

The Blood of Jesus Does Not Save From Sin.

I will say a word also.

I am your own dear grandmother.

I came to tell you that I know now that *"the blood of Jesus does not save from sin."* You will remember how, when on earth I believed this doctrine of error. How I used to talk about the precious blood of Jesus being able to save from all sin, and used to sing with all my heart and belief in the old hymn: "There is a fountain filled with blood" and so forth. Well I know now that that belief is all wrong, and that Jesus is so anxious to have men learn that it is a great error and stumbling block to the soul's progression.

Of course I know that a vast majority of those now living will never believe that this saying of the Bible is erroneous until they come to the spirit world; but if they only could be taught to throw aside this belief and rely entirely on the Divine Love for their salvation while on earth, how much easier their progress would be when they come over.

So you see, that while many say that a belief does not amount to much, yet I tell you that it causes more unhappiness and retards the progress of spirits to a greater extent than any other one thing.

I know that only the Divine Love of the Father saves from sin and makes mortals at-one with Him. So in your work for the Master, you

115

will have to make great efforts to cause people to give up this belief in the blood, and turn to the truth of the New Birth. Many of the orthodox will oppose your efforts and refuse to believe what you may tell them to be the truth, but many will believe and seek this New Birth, and find the peace and happiness of a soul whose sins have been forgiven.

I must not write more tonight.

I will come again soon and tell you more of the result of your work among the unfortunate spirits who seek your help.

So my dear son, I will say good night.

Your loving grandmother,
ANN ROLLINS.

Advice to his people—the Jews.

I AM HERE—*Saul*:

I will say only a word as it is late, and your wife says that I must not write much.

Well, I have not written for a long time, and I desire very much to write you a message regarding some important spiritual truths that I know will be of interest to you; and if you will give me the opportunity, I will come soon and do so.

I am interested in the Jews and I desire to tell them of some truths that may open up their minds to the way to the Celestial Kingdom, and cause them to cease to believe that their old orthodox beliefs in their father Abraham and the God of the Old Testament is all that is necessary to bring them into the presence of the true God.

I realize that it will be difficult to write anything that will convince them of the errors of their beliefs, yet I will try, and pray to the Father to open up their understanding.

The happenings in the countries where war is now raging will have their effect upon the Jews as well as upon the Christians and Pagans, and I desire that they, in their awakening consciousness may have the benefit of the truth. So if you will give me the opportunity I will come soon and write.

I should like to say a few things more, but it is best that I do not tonight, and I will stop.

So with my love and the blessings of God, I will say goodnight.

Your brother in Christ,
SAUL.

Samuel Gives His Experience in the Spirit Heavens and His Progress to the Celestial Kingdom

I AM HERE. Samuel. I am Samuel the Prophet.

I want to tell you that I am in a condition to tell you of my existence here in the spirit world, and what I know about the truths of the doctrines

116

of Jesus as I have learned them since I became possessed of the Divine Love which he brought to earth and to the world of spirits.

I have lived a great many years in this spirit life, more than you may think from the account of my earth life as contained in the Old Testament, for that book does not state correctly the time when I lived as a mortal. Many thousand years have gone by since I lived and performed my work as prophet and teacher on the earth, and I have in all these long years learned many things about the spiritual world, and its conditions and laws.

In the first place, I am not a spirit who was given over to the evils that men are usually possessed of when they become spirits, because when I lived on earth I was very close to the Father in his thoughts and love. I mean the love which He gave to man at that time. This love, while not the Divine Love, yet was a love that was sufficient to make men happy when they possessed it free from sin and error and tried to do the will of the Father as they understood that will. Many men thought that they understood this will, when in reality they only knew that which the laws of Moses taught them to be right in the sight of God. But some men were given a deeper insight into the mind and love of the Father to bless and make men happy in their natural love and consequently were closer to Him, and better understood His will and what was pleasing to Him.

I have since my becoming a spirit learned many truths which I did not understand on earth, and which are necessary to know in order to be able to enjoy this love in its fulness.

I never, though, possessed this Divine Love until after Jesus came to earth and showed men and spirits what this Love meant, and how necessary it was to obtain it in order to become a part of God's Divinity.

I do not now see that I was any more in favor of God, as I then possessed only this natural love, than were many others who had the privilege of receiving from His angels the inspirations which came to them at times, and which made them able to tell the inhabitants of earth what was the purpose of God to have them do.

I was only a man in the sense that I was only possessed of this natural love and hence, could get no higher in the spiritual world than this natural love would enable me to attain.

I am now in a heaven which this Divine Love has opened up to me, and which enables me to enjoy the great happiness which that Love causes all to have, who possess it.

When I lived in the spirit world before obtaining this Divine Love, I was only possessed of that happiness which comes from the natural love, and I knew nothing of the happiness which I now possess. So you see, the spirit which has not this Divine Love can go no higher in the spiritual spheres than it is fitted to occupy by reason of this natural love, and the principal source of happiness is this natural love and the development of the mental faculties. On earth it is possible for a man to obtain this happiness and live in the heaven of the perfect natural man as I did prior to my obtaining this Divine Love.

I was a spirit in the highest of the spiritual spheres and was very happy, as I thought, but when I obtained this Divine Love, I realized that the happiness of my former condition was as nothing compared to that of my present condition and I therefore want to tell all mankind that they must seek for this higher Love if they wish to obtain a bliss that is supreme.

I know that this rambling talk may not seem very instructive, but I merely wish to emphasize the fact that I lived a mere man, though in the spirit form, before I obtained the Divine Love, and that only with the coming of that Love in my soul did I partake of the Divinity of the Father.

Well, they are still in the spiritual heavens * because they have not yet embraced the Christ doctrine of Divine Love. They are living and teaching the doctrines that they taught on earth, only much improved.

I don't know, except that they have been satisfied with what they taught and the happiness that they live in. It may seem strange to you that they have not found this love in all these years, but it is a fact, and they are not seeking for it. I feel that they have neglected a great opportunity and have lost very much by letting all these years go by without having sought the great truth.

The different teachers of the various religions which have come to earth are occupying planes in the spiritual heavens all to themselves. They, the Jews, still think that theirs is the only true religion, and that they are the chosen people of God, and that all others are mistaken in their doctrines.

Well, I must stop. So thanking you for your kindness, I will say good-night.

SAMUEL.

Jesus denies that he is God, or that his blood washes away men's sins.

I AM HERE. *Jesus.*

I was with you tonight and saw that the Spirit was filling your heart with the Divine Love of the Father and that you realized its presence, and felt that even though the people who worshipped me in their ignorance, yet they have this love of the Father to a great degree.

I do not approve of their frequent reference to my blood as saving them from their sins and keeping them in the grace and favor of the

---

* Referring to many in the 6th sphere of the perfect natural man that do not possess the Divine Love to qualify them to enter the Celestial Heavens.

Father, for, as I have told you, my blood has nothing to do with the salvation of any soul—only the Divine Love of the Father saves a soul from sin and makes it one with the Father in His love and divinity.

But, nevertheless, these people have this Love in their hearts, and while with their intellects they look upon me as God, yet their souls are turning to God, and consequently, they receive the blessings of the Father's love and are receiving to a large extent the development of their souls.

I am glad that you attend these meetings,* for in them is a wonderful presence of the Spirit and the love of the Father, and while you may not be in sympathy with their doctrines as to who and what saves them from sin and unrighteousness, yet the influence of the Spirit is so great that it helps your soul development.

I tried to influence the speakers to tell just what the conditions of their souls were, and what experience they had in receiving and enjoying this Divine Love; and many of them experience and have as a part of their religious possession just what they said they had.

It will be beneficial to you to attend this church, and get the benefit of the presence of the Holy Spirit which is with them in their worship.

I was with you and tried to make you feel my presence, and I did, and you felt a little exaltation of your soul qualities and enjoyed the services, especially the singing and the prayers.

So, while you must not be influenced by their doctrines as to my being God or to be worshipped, yet if you will ignore this and only consider that their real worship is of God and that their souls are in unison with Him, you will find that these services will do you much good.

I am with you very much and am trying to get you relieved from the worries which come to you. I am also trying to help you get in that spiritual condition which is necessary in order for you to take and continue my formal messages.

Yes, you are and I am glad that it is so. I want you to become a man so possessed of this love and of faith, so strong that nothing that you may encounter will swerve you from your convictions and from your work.

I see that you are anxious to continue this work and you will soon be able to do so.

Yes, I know that the Bible iterates and reiterates the statement that I am God, and that my blood saves from sin, and that I am a propitiation for mankind, but nevertheless, the Bible is all wrong, and these false doctrines must be corrected and men taught the true plan of salvation.

I will be with you very often until we have commenced our work in

* The Church of the Holiness, Washington, D. C.

119

the way that we desire to carry it forward. Let not anything that you may read in the Bible cause you to have a conception that may not agree with what I shall write. Let your mind be blank on these truths and wait until I shall disclose them to you, and believe me.

John never wrote these statements as contained in his epistles and Gospel, and he will write to you denying that he did. The Bible contains many truths and many of my sayings, but also, many statements that were never made by me or by the apostles, and my mission now is to correct all these errors. So you see we have much work ahead of us and we must commence it as soon as possible.

I am with you tonight to comfort and encourage you and help you to overcome not only your worries, and if you will only pray to the Father and believe, you will be successful in both particulars.

I will not write more tonight as others are here to write, and I desire that they shall do so.

Your brother and friend,   JESUS.

Aman, first parent, reveals his temptation and fall.

Aman, the first parent.

You don't believe me, I can see, but I am whom I say, and want to tell you that I am now a follower of Jesus and a lover of God, and live in the Celestial Heavens far up near where the Master lives.

I know it is hard for men to believe that I am the father of all physical manhood, and that I can come and communicate with mortals; but Jesus has rendered this possible in his opening the way for the higher spirits to communicate through you. You should feel specially blessed at having this great privilege, and feel that the Master has conferred on you a great favor, as he has.

Well, I have never before come to earth to communicate with mortals, and, the experience being new, I find some difficulty in doing so. But I will try to write a few more lines.

I and my soulmate lived in a paradise which God had given us, and were very happy until the great fall. We were so filled with the thought that we were all powerful and all wise, that we concluded that the obedience which God had required of us, was not necessary for us to observe, and that if we only exerted our powers, we would be as great as He is great, and would be able to obtain that immortality which he possessed. But, alas the day. We were mere creatures, although wonderful and beautiful, and we soon realized that fact.

The disobedience was in not waiting for God to bestow upon us the great Divine Love that would make us like Him in substance as well as in image. We were like Him in our possession of souls and also in the possibility of obtaining the Divine Love.

120

We disobeyed Him in that we tried to make ourselves believe that we were as He was, and that we need not submit further to His decrees. We tried to make this belief a thing of reality, and in our vanity tried to appear as gods; but as soon as we did this the scales dropped from our eyes, and we saw how naked and impotent we were.

God did not drive us from His paradise, but the inexorable laws of our creation and of the workings of His will, showed us that no longer could we expect this Divine Love, which He said would make us Divine.

And so we became mere mortals, deprived of the potentiality of obtaining this Divine Love, and we had thereafter to become subject to all the appetites of the natural man and to work to satisfy these natural appetites.

We continued to live in the same place as formerly, but no more could we be satisfied with the spiritual food that had supplied our wants and enabled us to subdue the appetites which formed a part of our physical being. The physical then asserted itself and the spiritual became subjected to it, and we became as mortals now are, and had to find our substance in mother earth. We were compelled to till the soil and earn our living by work. I mean we had to work in order to make the earth supply us with food for our physical wants.

It was a bitter time of sorrow but the law had imposed its penalty, and we were without power to relieve ourselves of that penalty, and had to live thereafter without the possibility of obtaining this Divine Love and of having our spiritual natures reassert themselves over the physical, and subdue it.

When Amon and I were created, there were no other human beings living on earth, and none came there to live, until we had sons and daughters who intermarried and produced other sons and daughters.

I cannot tell you how long ago our creation was, but many thousand years before the coming of Jesus. I will not write more to night, but will come again sometime and write.

Your brother in Christ, AMAN.

Amon, mother of all human creation, gives her experience.
Her temptation and disobedience.

Amon.

I am the first mother of all the human race, and I want you to know that before Aman and myself, no human beings ever existed. We were created by God at the same time, and were ready, just after the moment of our creation, to live the lives of natural beings. So that there was no gradual growth on our part from any other creature or thing. I know it has been said that the first man was not created, but developed from some animal of the lower order, and as the process of

121

evolution proceeded, this being became in the end a man, with all the wonderful organism and structure of his body, but I want to tell you that this is not true.

When I was created I was as perfect in my physical organism as I ever was afterwards or as any man or woman ever became from that time into the present. In fact, I believe, that at the time of our creation we were more perfect than mankind are now, because we had no physical ailments, no sickness, no deformity of any kind.

We certainly were more beautiful in face and form than mankind now are or have been for many long centuries; and besides, our bodies and organism lasted for longer years than do the bodies of mankind at this time.

Before our fall we were very happy in our conjugal love, and knew not troubles or worries of any kind, and never had anything to make us afraid or draw us apart from each other or from God; nor until the great temptation came, and then because of our ideas of our greatness and power and want of dependence on God we fell, and never again were restored to our position of beauty and happiness that were ours in the beginning of our lives on earth.

So you must see that we were specially created and not evolved from any other thing.

Some men now may marvel and wonder at the Bible description of the creation of man, and reject the description as the imaginings of a mind of romance or imagery and not true, but I tell you now that the essentials of this creation and the fall, are true. Of course the parts played by the apple and the snake and the devil are not true literally, but are symbolical of the principles that entered into the temptation and fall.

Well, I was as much to blame as was Aman, but I did not entice him after I had the ambition to become immortal without waiting till that time came when God would give us that quality of His own nature; but our ambitions grew *together* and we discussed the matter of making the great effort between us, and acted as one in trying to obtain this great immortality.

So the story in the Bible is not exactly true just as far as I am concerned, for I did not entice or seduce Aman to do the great wrong; neither did he seduce me to enter into the effort.

But all this is past, and many thousand years have gone by since our fall, and we have suffered much because of our first sin. As you have been told, many thousands of years passed since the time that we forfeited the gift of immortality, until it was restored and made known to humanity by Jesus the son of God, for he was the son of God, and as being a part of his Father's divine nature he was divine, and partook of those qualities of the Father which gave to him immortality, and those who follow his teachings and receive the New Birth will become divine and immortal also.

I must not write more tonight.

Yes, I will, and now I will say good night.

Your sister, AMON.

Aman makes a correction.

I am here. Aman.

Yes, and I want to correct what I wrote before in this: that I never was a spirit who wanted to have merely immortality as God was immortal, but I also wanted to obtain the power and wisdom which I saw that God possessed.

I thought that if I could obtain these qualities, I would become a God and a co-equal with my Creator, and hence the possessor of all the universe, and of all power and knowledge that He had. My effort to realize my ambition in these particulars was a part of my great sin of disobedience.

I thought it best to tell you this so that my description of the great sin of disobedience would not be only a part of the truth.

I now know what an insignificant creature I was as compared to the Father, and I also know that the creation of Amon and me was the highest creation in all the universe of God.

But the great mercy and love of the Father, notwithstanding my great sin, has placed be in the position and condition which he promised me at my creation, and which I forfeited with such fatal consequences. You have a privilege which I was then deprived of for so many long years, and your happiness may be as great as mine is now without having to wait the long and many years that I waited.

No wonder that mankind worships Jesus as God, when we consider the Great Gift that he brought to them and the way to obtain it.

I must not write more.

Your brother in Christ and father in the flesh.

AMAN.

Affirms that Aman and Amon, the First Parents, Actually Communicated Through Mr. Padgett.

I am here. John

I merely want to say tonight that you must soon prepare to take messages which the Master and some other high spirits desire to write.

Let your arrangements be such that you can take those messages without any one being disappointed, for when you say that you will receive them and then something comes up to prevent, the spirits feel that you have not interest sufficient, and they are disappointed.

Well, that will be satisfactory and we will make our arrangements to comply with that understanding.

I know though that you have been in a condition of love and soul during the past few days, and have realized that the Father has been close to you, and you have been happy. So continue to turn your thoughts to the Father and His love and you will find that there will come to you an increased Love and a great happiness.

I feel that your faith is growing and that the rapport between us all is steadily increasing.

I did not intend to write more tonight, as we will all wait until the time that you have named.

Well, I have already told you that that Book (Revelation) was written as a kind of allegory, and that now it is of no practical use, and should not be given much attention. Besides it is not as I wrote it for many interpretations and additions have been made. At any rate it is of no importance, and men lose much time in trying to solve what they call its mysteries.

Well, Aman is a general term which means first or highest, and when applied to man it means the first or highest creation. As it is applied in Revelation to Jesus it means the man who first received the Divine Love of the Father after its rebestowal.

I will come to you sometime and explain this matter more fully.

Yes, they (Aman and Amon) came to you and gave you their names which were the names that they were called by after their creation. They were both created instantaneously and became living souls in a moment, and did not grow from a germ by the slow process of evolution. Their story of the fall is substantially correct as I have learned from them and from the Master.

The names Aman and Amon are correct, and were known thousands of years ago to the early inhabitants of the earth and who descended from them.

The story of their fall was, of course, known to their immediate descendants and became known for some generations after their deaths to their more remote descendants; but after awhile the names became forgotten, but the substance of the story of their fall did not, and there were at one time manuscripts showing the account of the fall, but they disappeared long before the time of any of the present writings, though the story of the fall with various changes and amendments came down the ages, until the writers of the Old Testament incorporated such tradition in the Book of Genesis. Of course, Adam and Eve did not exist, and neither is the story as to their fall, true. It is only symbolical in the way of showing that man once occupied an exalted and happy state, and by his own disobedience fell, and with his fall came the condition of evil and sin.

Well, I must not write more tonight. So remembering what you say, I am your brother in Christ.

JOHN—*Apostle of Jesus*

Refers to Jesus' Love for Mr. Padgett. Affirms that Amon Wrote About the Creation of the first parents. Difference in their qualities. Equal in their relationship to God.

I am here. Helen.

Well, my dear old Ned you must stop writing for tonight as you have written a long time.

I am so glad that you are now in such good condition of faith and love, and feel so close to God and so near to the Master. It certainly is wonderful how he loves you and clings to you and tries to help and influence you for good. We are all surprised at his love for you and he does not seem to grow impatient that you sometimes seem not to care whether he loves you or not. But such is his Great Love.

Oh, my dear, you must love him more and get closer to him and trust him with all your heart and mind, for I, your own Helen, tell you that he is with you very much and loves you more than you can possibly conceive to be true.

He is trying to help you spiritually and he will succeed.

Well she (Amon) was a beautiful and bright spirit, more so than most any of the spirits that I have seen from the higher spheres. She talked to me for a while and told me that she was the first mother, and that I was one of her children. She has a wonderful portion of the Divine love and seemed so grand and loving to me that I am inclined to believe her. But I cannot tell you anything more about her as I never saw her before. But I heard the Master say that he would tell you sometime about her and you may get a great treat from him.

So good-night, your loving and true

HELEN.

Creation of the first parents. Difference in their qualities. Equal in their relationship to God.

I am here, Josephus.

I come tonight to write a few lines upon a subject in which you may be interested as I have observed that recently you have been reading my History of the Jews, and there are some things in that book which require correction. I don't mean that I desire to correct the whole book, but I do want to say something on some of the subjects that you have been reading about.

Well, you will notice that I attempted to tell of the creation of the world and of man, and that what I said was taken from the Old Testament, and that I elaborated a little upon what is contained in Genesis.

My work was not taken entirely from the Old Testament for in my time on earth there were other books dealing with this subject that were entitled to just as much credence as was the Old Testament, and from these books I obtained much information that is contained in my writings.

But the truth of the things which I wrote, I find now to be not the truth in many particulars, and should not be accepted as such. The description of the creation of man is not in accordance with the facts, and the story as related in the Old Testament, and by me, is not the true story of the facts of such creation.

I have not the time now to enter in detail, into a correction of the errors contained in these descriptions, except that I wish to say a few words as to the creation of man and also his fall.

He was not made of the dust of the ground, but was made of the elements that existed in the universe of a different order from the mere dust of the ground, and was so created by God for the purpose of forming the mere physical body of man. The two persons called our first parents, were created at the same time, and not one out of the rib of the other. Therefore, the man and the woman are equal in their dignity, and in the relationship which they bear to God, and the one is of just as much importance in the sight of God as is the other. One was created stronger, physically, than the other, and also was given a stronger mentality, for the exercise of the reasoning powers, and the workings of the physical organs of the body. And the other, while weaker in these particulars, yet was given more of the spiritual and emotional nature and also, an intuition by which she could understand the existence of things just as accurately and more quickly than could the man by the exercise of his reasoning power. One was just as the other as respects the gifts bestowed, and together, they were the perfect pair,—male and female were they created with divers functions and duties to perform in the perfect workings of the laws of God.

Power and love were theirs, and neither was made the superior of the other, nor was the one to be subject to the other, and had it not been for their fall there never would have been the subjection of the female to the male.

When the disobedience took place and the consequent fall, the qualities of the spiritual were taken from them to a large extent, and the animal qualities, as they may be called, asserted themselves and then the male felt his superiority by reason of the fact that he possessed a greater amount of these animal qualities; and the female became subordinated and continued to be ever afterwards, for the male, not having these spiritual qualities to the extent that his mate possessed them, and not being able to realize the greater existence of these qualities in the female, believed that the physical was the superior, and as he possessed the physical to a larger degree than his companion, he determined that he was the superior, and therefore asserted this superiority, and the female observing that this physical superiority did exist, submitted herself unto the male and so continued until now.

As man degenerated, this domination of the male intensified, and in some parts of the earth the female became nothing better in the sight of the dominate man than one of the lower animals.

This degradation continued until man found the lowest place of his degeneracy, and when the turning point came the qualities of the woman came to be more recognized, but very slowly, and for many thousand years this inequality continued, and man remained the master.

As man evolved from this low condition and the moral qualities began to come more into his consciousness, and the animal nature became less dominant, the condition of the female commenced to improve, and as education came into the life and practices of men, woman's opportunities became more extended, and she was more and more recognized as approaching the equal of her companion. In some countries of the earth her equality was recognized, but not in many.

The Jews recognized the equality of the woman in all matters pertaining to the home or the domestic life, and continued the distinction which had previously existed, only in respect to public affairs and the qualities of the mind—women were not permitted even by them to develop their mental faculties, and were taught that they were things that belonged to the male, in all matters pertaining to the state or religion of the race.

The consequence of this course of life, was that the woman developed the spiritual qualities which were hers to a larger extent, and her refinement and emotional nature and love principle exceeded those of the man to a great degree, and she became in her soul nearer the image of the Divine.

I have noticed that this progress has continued with the passing of the years, and now in some of the nations of earth the equality of the woman has become recognized, notwithstanding the fact that the laws of these countries did not permit her to exercise the rights of man, as she is his equal only in the home or in social life.

But a time will come when she will be recognized not only by the individual man but by the man-made laws as his equal in every particular, and the further fact will appear that she will be his superior in matters pertaining to the spiritual.

As the time approaches when man shall return to his former state of purity and harmony with the laws of God, the spiritual qualities will assert themselves and the animal will become subordinated, and woman will stand before God and man as the latter's equal, and in these soul qualities, his superior; for in the beginning, in this particular, she was his superior; but that superiority existed only in order that what in this regard was lacking in man, was supplied by the woman, and the perfect pair was one.

You may think that this is a digression from what I first intended to write, and so it is, but I thought the occasion a proper one to tell mankind the future of the two integral parts of the perfect creation of God.

I will not write more tonight, but sometimes will come again and write.

So with my love I will say good-night.

Your brother in Christ,

JOSEPHUS.

What Should a Man Do Who Is Not Satisfied With Any of the Churches?

I am here. John.

I was with you tonight and heard the preacher answer the question, and some of his answers were very satisfactory, but there was one that did not exactly satisfy the true longings of the man who is in search of truth, I mean the one that asks what should a man do who is not satisfied with any of the churches.

Well, if he can find no church that provides truths that satisfy that man's inquiring soul, then that man can never feel that he should go to any church for information as to those things which he has no knowledge of or which he has grave doubts about.

The churches, of course, can give no information of truths that the churches themselves do not know, and if the truths that these churches teach fall short of what the man is seeking for, then these churches cannot possibly be satisfactory to him. While the churches differ in their creed and government, and perhaps in some particular construction or interpretation of the Bible, yet they, the orthodox churches, are all founded upon the teachings of the Bible, and they cannot teach greater or other truths than that Book contains, and, hence, if a man is seeking for truths that are not in the Bible, his inquiries cannot be answered by those whose knowledge is confined to the Bible teachings. And the non-orthodox churches cannot give forth the truths of the spiritual kingdom of God for they to a large degree reject the Bible and depend very largely upon ethical and moral doctrines, and the results of the works of mere conscience in determining the right and wrong of things. The spiritual things are not known or taught by these churches, and, consequently, the inquiring mind cannot get from them the information or help that it is calling for.

I know that in such a condition and want of knowledge of truth on the part of the churches, such a man is without the privilege of having his cravings for the truth and his cravings for spiritual things satisfied. And, as a consequence, he must seek further to get the information which he may consider so necessary, and when he comes to so seek, he will find no place where such knowledge may be found.

The mere intellectual acquirements of students and philosophers will not supply what the man is seeking and he is without any possibility of obtaining what he seeks for.

And so the preacher's suggestion that he and two others form a church of their own, would have some force were it not for the fact that any church that might be so formed would have no greater possession of the truth than the churches that he has failed to find any satisfaction in.

There are many men on earth today in the condition of the man spoken of, and many who refuse to seek in the churches for the truth, are without any recourse to other means or places of teachers of whom they can learn the things that they are searching for.

The spirits have known of this condition of men for these many centuries and have been trying to supply a way or create a medium through which the great spiritual truths of God could be made known to men. And for that very purpose we are now using you to receive our messages of truth and make them known to mankind, and provide a church, may I say, where the seeking man may find answers to his inquiries.

We shall complete our delivery of these truths through you and then the man who cannot find a church where his searchings can be satisfied, will find a reservoir of truth opened up to him, that will not require any preacher or church to explain it.

As you proceed in your experience with the churches and teachers of the old truths, as they call them, you will more fully realize the necessity for our work and your work.

I will not write more tonight, but will come soon and deliver a formal message.

With my love and blessings I will say goodnight.   JOHN.

Says that many of the teachings of the Bible cannot be relied upon.

I am here. St. Augustine.

I merely want to say that I am the St. Augustine who lived after the death of Jesus and was well acquainted with his teachings as they were preserved by the Church. At that time I never knew exactly what became of the manuscripts that were in existence when I lived, but the ones that are supposed to furnish the origin of many of the Biblical writings were not the ones that I was acquainted with. Those that I used were all written in Greek and were written by the disciples of Jesus, and by those of his followers to whom the disciples had communicated the teachings of the Master; and they were the genuine ones and were written from the actual communications of the disciples.

Of course, the teachings of Jesus were never recorded at the time of his teachings, but were merely the recollections possessed by the disciples of what they thought he really said, and consequently, as you may realize, they were imperfect and could not be relied on implicitly.

I know that great controversies have arisen in the church as to what portions of these writings should be accepted as genuine, and many needless disputes have caused the officials of that church to differ as to what were really the writings of the disciples, and what were not. I when on earth joined in these disputes, and maintained that certain of these writings were genuine and certain were not, but I was as likely to be mistaken as any of the others.

But even the ones that I thought genuine were more or less flavored by the spiritual knowledge and beliefs of those who wrote them. So I tell you that you cannot depend on these writings as a whole to learn what the Master actually did teach.

He is now in condition to give you the genuine truths, and whenever what he may say conflicts with what is contained in the Bible, you must consider what he now writes as the truth and discard the Bible account as unreliable.

I tell you this, because I am interested in having the world learn the truths which he came on earth to declare.

I am a spirit of the Celestial Spheres and am a follower of the Master, and am trying to help in having these truths come to the world again.

I did not always believe, as I do now in many particulars, and my comments on the Bible should not always be taken as correct.

So if you will pardon my intrusion I will repeat, pay attention to what Jesus may say now, and do not let the Bible statements, which do not agree with what he may write you, disturb you or cause you to doubt what you may receive.

Sometime I shall come and give you my ideas of some of these spiritual truths, and how necessary it is that men should know them.

I certainly believe in the New Birth, and I want most emphatically to say that it is one of the most important truths of the spiritual world. It has not heretofore been very often understood, and its exact meaning is somewhat in doubt by even the best students of the Bible.

I will not write more tonight, but will say that you are my brother in the good work of showing to mankind the truths that are so important to their future happiness and salvation.

So with a love that is in Christ, I am your brother

St. Augustine.

Efficacy of Faith in God.

I am here, John. (Apostle of Jesus)

I only want to say that the faith that the preacher spoke of tonight as being possessed by Elijah is the faith that you must try to obtain, and then you will realize that you will be superior to all the worries and troubles that may come to you. This is the kind of faith that overcomes every obstacle and makes you a true child of the Father and one whom He will never forsake or let go unprovided for.

I was with you at the services and I tell you that the minister made a forcible application of the truths taught by that instance in Elijah's life as related in the Old Testament.

If men would only learn the efficacy of that kind of faith in God, they would become so much happier and possessed of that great peace of which the Master spoke. I am telling you this not as a speculation or a theory, but as the result of knowledge and actual experience. The same faith that existed in Elijah was the same faith that existed in the martyred disciples of Jesus, and the same faith that you and all other men may now have. God never changes, although men's conceptions of Him do, yet no matter what these conceptions may be, the same God rules and lives, and, as the preacher said, is present with you; and faith in Him is always accompanied by a power that never fails in working out His truths.

I, John, tell you this, because I want you to obtain that faith as you will need it in the great work which you have before you, and which can only be done by one whose soul is developed by such faith.

I was present tonight at church, because I had been with you a large portion of the day, trying to influence and encourage you with my love and influence.

Very soon you will again commence to receive the messages of the Master and continue to do so until they are completed. And what messages of truth they will be. As the minister said tonight there will be troublers, but their mission will be similar to that of Elijah—that is, will show to mortals the true God, and that genuine faith and steadfastness of purpose will bring to mankind the salvation of the Lord.

I will not write more tonight, but will say before I stop, try to get this faith, and you may get it even as Elijah had it, by earnest persistent prayer, accompanied by belief. The Lord gives faith to him who seeks for it in earnestness and longing desire.

I will say further, that you are progressing very much in your soul development, and if you will only trust in the Master's promises, very soon the worries that you have will pass away, and you will be free to do the work without being distracted by anything that militates against the exercise of the soul perceptions, which are so neccessary in your work.

So my dear brother, I will say good night and God bless you,

Your brother in Christ, JOHN.

Gives Advice to Pray.

I am here. Saint Peter.

I want to tell you that you are very near the Father tonight and that His love is filling your soul to a great degree. I see that you are anxious to learn of the spiritual things of the Father and of His love towards you and all mankind.

You must pray for more faith and trust implicitly in His promises, and in the promises of the Master, for they will be fulfilled and you will not be disappointed or left to yourself. I am with you quite often now, for I want to assist in the great work that the Master has chosen you to do; and you must get into a condition that will enable you to do this work in the greatest perfection. Your soul must be developed with this Divine Love of the Father, so that you will be in accord with the Master when he writes, for unless there is such accord you will not be able to get the spiritual meanings of his messages as he wants you to do.

There is nothing that will cause this development as well as earnest, sincere prayer to the Father. With such prayer will come faith, and with faith will come the Substance of what you may now only believe. So pray often, believing that the Love of the Father will come to you, and you will realize your oneness with Him.

I am so much interested in you and your soul development that I am going to help you with all my love and power.

Let not the things of the world detract your attention from these spiritual necessities, and you will find that all these material things will be supplied you.

Be firm and courageous in your beliefs and professions and God will be with you in every time of trial and distress. This I know and tell you as one having knowledge. I want you to let your faith increase until doubt shall flee away, and only trust in the love and goodness of God remain with you. I will not write more tonight.

So with all my love and blessings I am

Your own friend and brother in Christ,

ST. PETER.

Affirms that Jesus is a true son of God, and lived on earth and was crucified.

I am *Josephus* (Jewish Historian).

I am the Jewish historian and now a Christian. You are not a man to

132

let alone. I mean that I must write some of my knowledge of the things of those ancient days, for I see that you are selected to do a great work, and I want to contribute to the truth of Jesus' life on earth. He lived just before I wrote, but I had heard of him many times, and I know that he was a real existing being. In my history of the Jews I mentioned him, and when the learned say that what is there said is interpolated, they say what is not true; for he did live and taught in Palestine as the New Testament claims.

I never met him, but the wonders of his works were circulated all over the country and caused much agitation on the part of the leaders of the Jews.

I never wrote much about him, because we all looked upon him as a mere agitator and destroyer of our religion, and to such we never gave much notoriety in our writings.

But this same Jesus of Nazareth lived as a man and was crucified by the Romans at the clamor of the Jews. I want to tell you this, because it is claimed that he never lived on earth.

I am a follower of him, and believe in his teachings and have received the New Birth that he taught.

I live in the Celestial Heavens where only his followers live. He was the true son of God, and his mission was to show men the way to God's love and to declare the rebestowal of the Divine Love.

I tell you that this is the most important truth in all the heavens, except this, that God is Love. These two constitute the hope of mankind and furnish the means by which man may acquire immortality.

Without this New Birth, men will remain merely men, and will not partake of the Divine Love, and the home in the Celestial Spheres. I say this, because I know from experience what this New Birth means, and from observation that those who have never received it cannot enter these Spheres. So man must believe this great truth.

Many Jews have become believers since becoming inhabitants of the spirit world, but the large majority of the inhabitants of the Celestial Heavens are those whom we called Gentiles. God had no chosen people in the sense that He designed to save any particular nation in preference to all others. He knows no preference. All are His children, and the great gift is for all who ask for it in faith.

I must not write more tonight, but with your permission will come again.

Vespasian is a Christian now, but he never was while on earth, notwithstanding that it was said that he was. He continued a pagan as long as he lived, but he knew something of the Christian teachings; and after he had been in the spirit world a considerable time he received the light and was born again. He is in the Celestial Heavens and a follower of the Master.

So you see, many Jews and Gentiles and pagans who rejected the Master and his teachings on earth have, since becoming spirits, had the opportunity, and embraced it, of becoming partakers of the Divine Love and followers of the Master.

Well, you may be surprised to know that Herod is also a Christian. But no pen can portray the sufferings that he had to undergo. Oh the long years of repentance and torment and darkness! His experience was a hell indeed. But the love and mercy of the Father were even sufficient for his redemption; and among all the spirits of our Celestial Heavens, none are more humble and meek than is this same Herod. His life, voluntarily assumed, is one of service and devotion to the Master. I think that his love for the Master is so great, that even he cannot appreciate it.

I will, with all my love and earnestness, accept your invitation, for the work is of the greatest importance and the time is ripe. Oh what an awakening there will be when the truths of God, which the Master is communicating through you, shall come to the knowledge and consciousness of mankind.

I am your brother in Christ, and a fellow worker and so I will say with all my love and best wishes—goodnight.

Josephus.

What It Is that Makes A Man Divine?

I Am Here. *Jesus.*

I wish to write tonight on the subject: *"What it is that makes a man divine."*

When man was created he was given the highest qualities that could be bestowed upon a mortal, and yet he was mere man, but the perfect one, and with these qualities was given him the possibility of becoming divine like the Father in his nature; but this gift was never possessed by him in its enjoyment of full fruition until after my coming to earth, and making known to man that such a possibility existed.

The first created man never possessed this gift in its fulfillment, but merely had the possibility of receiving it, on condition that he continued in his obedience, and made the effort to receive it in the way that the Father declared was the only way.

You have been told in detail what this gift was, and how the first parents forfeited the enjoyment of it by their disobedience and ambition to possess it in a way that was not in accord with the Father's way.

As we have said, man lost this possibility at the time of the first disobedience, and thereafter became gradually a man with his moral nature sinking lower and lower until he became almost lost in the condition of the beasts in the field. And from that condition he has been steadily improving or progressing towards his first estate of purity.

But a great many men have ceased to know, or have never known, that God is the Creator of all things, and that all creation is dependent upon Him for its very existence, and in their assurance and self importance they have assumed and professed to believe that their progress or salvation depends upon their own efforts, and that these efforts are sufficient to bring about this state of purity or harmony with God's laws and desires.

But in this men are mistaken, for there is nothing in them that is divine, and there never will be when they depend upon their own selves to progress to this state of perfection. The divine nature of the Father is not in man and will never become a part of him until he pursues the way which is absolutely necessary for him to follow in order to become anything more than mere man.

I will not write more tonight as I think it best not to do so.

I understand that you could not prevent your condition of sleepiness, and I do not blame you, but I think it best to wait until later to finish what I desire to write.

Well, my dear brother, believe that I have only love for you, and will get close to you as we progress—so I say, don't worry.

I will say good-night.

Your brother and friend,   J<small>ESUS</small>

St. Stephen Affirms Jesus Wrote.

I am here, and desire to write just a few lines, for you are not in condition for lengthy writing tonight.

The Master was disappointed, but he is so loving and good that he did not complain and only wanted you to feel that you must not worry, because of the fact that you could not take his message—but nevertheless he was disappointed.

I understand that you could not control your sleepiness and are not to blame, but it was unfortunate, and it must in some way, if possible, be avoided in the future.

If you only realized the great importance of these messages and the great number that are yet to be written, you would bend every effort to facilitate their reception. I am not saying this complainingly, but merely stating a fact. So try your best to get in a good condition so that there will be no failure in your receiving the messages.

I am so very much interested in this work and so are a host of other spirits who realize the importance of these truths being given to mankind. They are the only truths, and never since the time when the Master was on earth have they been revealed to man.

I will not write more tonight, but will say with all my love that I am your brother in Christ.   S<small>T</small>. S<small>TEPHEN</small>.

Affirms that Jesus lived in Palestine at the time he wrote of him.

I AM HERE—*Josephus.*

I merely want to say that since I wrote you last I have made inquiries as to who it was that taught that my book was interpolated in the paragraph where it speaks of Jesus.

These persons are they who do not believe in Jesus as an historical person and try to procure evidence to show that he was not.

But I tell you that he was, and that he actually lived in Palestine at the time I wrote about him. I do not think it best for me to write a long letter tonight but will come again sometime.

.**Your** brother in Christ, JOSEPHUS.

Advice given by Jesus in attending church service. Jesus was present with Mr. Padgett.

I AM HERE. *Jesus.*

I was with you tonight and my spirit was in your heart to an extent that made you feel its presence, and caused you to suffer somewhat physically—but it was there to tell you that I was present and that my love was helping you to get nearer the Father and His love.

I know that the people who were worshipping me were not doing what I approve of or like, but their hearts were turned to God; and while they were making me the object of their worship, yet the spirit of God was with them, and the workings of the Holy Spirit were in the hearts of very many of them showing them the love of the Father and the truth of His salvation.

They, of course, are mistaken when they talk about being saved by my blood, for my blood has nothing to do with their salvation, but as they have been taught this, I cannot expect that they will know the real salvation which the Father has provided for them. Sometime they will know that only the Divine Love of the Father saves from sin and error, and that not any blood of mine or death on the cross can save them.

But, notwithstanding this false belief, these people in their prayers actually aspire for the love of God, and He knows the longings of their hearts and sends the Holy Ghost to fill them with this Divine Love which makes them become very close to the Father, and makes them happy.

So, while, as I say, I don't like the worship of me, yet the truth of God's love enters into their souls and they become at-one with Him to the extent that such love enters their souls.

I know that to you, with your enlightenment, it appears that they are making a great mistake in worshipping me and believing that my blood saves them, yet, you must understand that while they make such mistakes, yet they are receiving the Divine Love and that it is working to redeem them from their sins and evil lives. So let not this error in their belief make you think that I am not with them, or rather that the Christ spirit is not with them, teaching them the way to the love of the Father and to the great happiness which that love brings to them.

I know that the meeting did you great good and opened up your soul to the inflowing of this love, and consequently, to a renewed faith and trust, and renewed love for the Father and belief in me.

Let this love in you increase and pray to the Father for more faith in His promises, and for a greater inflowing of His love, and very soon you will realize His actual presence in your soul to an extent that will make you know that you are one with Him in love, and in the possession of the Divine Essence that will cause all doubt to leave you and give you a faith in which no doubt will appear.

I am glad you went to this meeting tonight and I hope you will go again, for the influences attending it were helpful to you, and were from above.

Soon I will write again as I desire, if you will only pray more and trust more.

You are thinking right and I will pray the Father for you, and if you will only persist in your desires and try to act in accordance with our prayers you will succeed; for the Father will hear your prayers and will help you to the fullest.

And in addition, I will be with you and help you with my power and love.

So do as I say, and above all have faith in the Father and trust me.

I will not write more tonight, but will say that I will be with you during the week and will help you in your spiritual efforts.

So with all my love, I am

Your friend and Brother,   JESUS.

Francis Bacon on the continuity of life after death.

Let me write a few lines tonight upon a subject that has recently been discussed by a spiritualist, a preacher, a philosopher and a scientist, and that is the continuity of life after death of the physical body. Each of these writers approach the subject from a different viewpoint, but all arrive at the same conclusion based upon different means of argument, and that is, that life continues after death.

The subject is one in which mankind is vitally interested and is worthy of consideration by the greatest minds of investigation and research, and should be studied in the light of nature as well as in that of actual demonstration by the experiences ot those who have by their experiences proved to mankind that the spirits of their departed friends and acquaintances and of others of more or less distinction when in the physical life, do actually live and communicate to men their existence and the possession of the mental faculties and thoughts that were theirs when mortals.

137

The proper study of man would demonstrate this fact, and logically doubt would cease to exist, but the difficulty is that men do not understand man or his creation and faculties and his relationship to things of life known as the material or matter. It is a common belief that matter that is now existent, or rather that what men see and know of the material is all that is knowable, and that when that which is merely physical, as commonly understood, ceases to exist no further or other knowledge of it can be obtained or understood by the finite mind of man.

But this accepted assumption is not true, and if man would only think for a moment of what matter or the material is, they would comprehend the possibilities of its workings and functionings, and also, of what use may be made of the same by the minds of the spirits operating upon it in the spiritual world, that is in the world beyond the comprehension of the five senses of men, which are only the means of the spirits working in the ordinary purview of the physical life.

Matter is eternal, and exists in all the spheres of the spirit world just as it does on earth, although in different forms and attenuations, and in conditions that may or may not be the objects of the physical senses, or of the senses of the mind which are superior to or exclusive of these mere physical senses. Matter is, in its essential nature, the same, notwithstanding the fact that it assumes different forms—some visible to the ordinary senses of men and some entirely outside of that view or sensation, and as to these senses wholly nonexistent, yet to these other senses of the mind just as real and tractable and subject to the influence of the workings of the mind, as the merely physical matter is to the five senses of men.

The world in which men live is composed of the material, and the world in which I live is also composed of the material, of the same nature, but of different consistencies and objective qualities. The material of the universe is always material, whether or not it be cognizable by man and subject to his thoughts and inventions and uses; and as man progresses in the study of the same—I mean the practical and experimental—he will discover that there are things of the material in nature which to him are being developed and made known, and which a few years before he had no conception of their existence. Such is the discovery and use of electricity, and the workings of the laws of nature which enables him to make possible the effects of wireless telegraphy. These discoveries and workings of forces of the unseen are nothing more or less than a certain kind of knowledge controlling the same as to his consciousness has become apparent. But in all these operations matter is the thing made use of and not any spiritual power as commonly understood by men. So you see matter, whether in the grossly physical of earth or in the more attenuated and invisible of the spirit world, is that which is used to produce effects and is operated on by the mind, whether or not it be tangible and understandable or not.

The mind is an entity indivisible and united, and is not separable into the subjective and objective as men frequently teach, except in this: that in its workings, that part of the mind which controls the brain in the ordinary affairs of life may be called the objective, and that part which is suited for and used in controlling the material after it has been transformed into the purely invisible may be called the subjective. But it is all one mind and exists in man while on earth,, just as it will and does when he becomes a spirit.

Man in his journey through life, and I mean when in the earth existence as well as in the eternal part of his existence, is always of the material, that is his soul has a material covering and appearance, and while this material covering changes in its appearance and quality as he progresses in the spheres, yet the gross physical of his earth life and the sublimated spiritual of the eternal part of his life, are both of the material, real, existing and tangible—and used for the purpose of their creation, namely: the protection and individualizing of the soul which they contain.

Now this being so, you can readily understand that man, when he gives up the coarser physical of the human body, does not cease to be of the material but becomes an inhabitant of the finer and purer material of what is called his spirit body; and this body is subject to the laws governing the material just as was his physical body subject to these laws; and the spirit, which in this sense is the real man clothed in the material, controls and uses that material more effectually than it did when on earth, bound in the physical. All the material of the spirit world is use1 and formulated by the spirits according to their degree of intelligence and development as the occasions for such uses may arise, and such use or the effects of the same are or can be made known to man according as his limitations admit.

Ordinarily, man's understanding of the effects of the spirit's control of the material of the invisible world is limited by the capacity of his five senses to comprehend, and as these five senses were created for the purpose only of permitting or helping the spirit to manifest itself with reference to those things which belong to the wholly physical of earth, it rarely happens that men can perceive the invisible material or the workings of the laws controlling the same.

Now in what I have said this spirit is merely the mind of man—the same indivisible mind that he possesses when on earth, but which because of the limitations of the physical organs he was not able to function as regards the invisible material, so that man could understand that functioning and its results.

Man when he dies is thereafter the same being in all his faculties, desires and thoughts, and in his ability to use the material as he was before his death, except that the purely physical organs of his own being are no longer his, and as to them he is dead: but strange as it may seem to you he can and often does control the physical organs of another man who is living in the flesh, if that man will submit to that control. And when you think for a moment you will realize that there is nothing remarkable in this. The mind of the spirit remains just the same as it was before his departure from the body, having all its powes and thoughts and consciousness, and if it can obtain control of that which is necessary to manifest itself to the consciousness of men, there will be no difficulty in its doing so, and nothing unusual or supernatural. Its own organs of brain and nerves and the five senses having gone, and the brain of every other mortal being subject to the control of its own mind, so long as that mind claims the exclusive use or control of these organs, the mind deprived of its own physical organs cannot control, because it is a law of being that no mind in its normal state can be intruded upon by another mind, and unless the mind whose seat and functioning are within the spirit body which is enclosed in the physical body possessing these organs, consents to the control of such organs by the other mind, it cannot use such organs. But the power is in the disembodied spirit or mind, only the opportunity is wanting.

When the spirit desires to control the invisible material, it is limited only by its intelligence and knowledge of the law governing such control, and its progress in the spirit spheres.

Well, I have written enough for tonight, but will come again and amplify my message.

Thanking you, I will say, good night.

Your friend,   FRANCIS BACON.

Affirming Francis Bacon Wrote on the Continuity of Life After Death

I am here—Your own true and loving *Helen* (Mrs. Padgett):

Well dear, I am glad that you are in condition to again receive the messages of the spirits who wish to write you in reference to things spiritual.

The spirit who wrote you was very anxious to do so, and we permitted him in order that you might gain some conception of what the material of the universe is, and the power that spirits have over such material.

But this is not the nature of the messages that we wish to convey to you, and we will not permit ourselves to be interfered with very often in this particular, and until our messages are all delivered you must not think of such things.

The Master has been with you today and is well pleased at your way of thinking, and says that you will soon commence to receive the higher messages again, and we are all anxious to write. Keep up your prayers to the Father and your thoughts about the higher things of the spirit world.

As you have been drawn on a great deal tonight I will not write further now, and will only say that we all love you and will be with you to help you in your thoughts. So love us and say good night.

Your own true and loving HELEN.

Explains the difference between the natural love and the Divine Love.

I am here—*John* (*St. John, Apostle of Jesus*).

Let me say just a word. I was with you today when you were talking to your * friend, and heard your conversation, and saw the utter want of comprehension on the part of your friend as to the truths of the spirit world, and especially of the laws that divide the mere perfect man from the Divine man or spirit. He is so engulfed in the conceptions that he has of these loves arising from his experience in life that he can only see the existence of one love, the natural, and his mind is not capable of seeing the other love, and of course his soul has not that development which would assure him of the reality of the Divine Love. The mind itself is capable of informing him of the existence and working of the natural love, and as this is the only means that he possesses of understanding what love is, he cannot possibly understand this Love, and that soul developed to a degree by the very Love itself. He may argue to the extent of the capacity of his mind and he will never be able to comprehend the Love that requires a perception of the soul, and he may remain satisfied and convince himself that the natural love is the only love and that when it becomes developed to a certain degree it becomes the Divine Love, and then find that that he is far away from the truth.

He must know, and I mean it is necessary for him to know, that only those who have the Divine Love to some degree are capable of knowing that the Divine is a thing of itself, and not the development of the natural love, and has in it not the qualities of that love. The one is of God, that is partakes of His very nature, while the other is also of God, but does not partake of His nature, but is only a creation intended to make man happy and perfect in his condition of the mere man—the merely created existence.

I thought that I would give you these short comments on your conversation in order to show the grave and important mistake under which your friend is laboring. He will not easily believe these things of truth while in the flesh, and when he comes to spirit life the difficulties will be just as great, and it may be that he will always be content to remain the possessor of this natural love only. I wish that it might be otherwise, and that he might let go his intellectual belief and harken to the call of the soul, which when not trammeled by these beliefs is continually longing for this Greater Love .

* Mr. Padgett's friend was investigating spirit laws. This was told to me (Dr. L. R. Stone) by Mr. J. E. Padgett.

Believe that I am your friend and interested in you to an extent that you cannot now comprehend, but which, some day you will understand and wonder that such a thing could have been. Good night.

Your brother in Christ,

JOHN.

Jesus was the natural son of Joseph and Mary.

I AM HERE. *Mary the Mother of Jesus.*

I come to you with all the mother's love of one who loved her dear son so much while on earth, and who suffered all the heart pangs which the cruel death of my beloved caused me, and with the love that has been purified by experience and closeness to the blessed Father.

I say, I come to you with this mother's love, for you are the children of my Father, as I am his child, and you are also the brothers of my dear son, who is with you so much and so interested in you and your future.

Let your love for the Father increase, and also your love for the Master, as he is the greatest and dearest friend that you have in all the Celestial or spiritual heavens.

I am in the Celestial Heavens, very near the fountainhead of God's love, and also near the home of my dear son, but not in the same sphere with him for no spirit in all the Celestial Heavens has the same great soul development as he has, or possessed with the Divine Love to such an extent.

And I want to say just here that I am not in the condition or place that I am, because I am his mother, but because of the development of my own soul—only this great possession of the Divine Love determines our position and condition here.

I am now in such condition that I know that the love of the Father is the only thing in all the universe of God that can make a mortal, or spirit either, a partaker of the divine nature, and an inhabitant of the Kingdom of Heaven.

I will not write more, but will come again and write you of the early life of Jesus, and of his development in the love as was shown to me, while he was a growing child, and after he became a man, prior to his public ministry.

(Question: *Was Joseph the Father of Jesus?*)

Well, I suppose I am the only one in all the universe of God, who knows the fact with reference to that question, and I as a spirit of the Celestial Spheres, knowing only truth, say to you and all the world, that Joseph was the actual father of Jesus, and that he was conceived and born as any other mortal was conceived and born. The Holy

142

Spirit did not beget him and I never was informed that such a thing would happen. I was known by Joseph before the conception of Jesus, and by him I was made pregnant with that blessed son. This is the truth and all accounts and statements to the contrary are erroneous.

I was a simple Jewish maiden, and never had any knowledge that my son was to be different from the sons of other mothers, and it was not until after the development in him of the Divine Nature of the Father that I realized that he was so different from the sons of other mothers.

I will not write more tonight.

So my dear children believe what I have written, and also know that I love you with a great love, and am working with the other Celestial Spirits to make your souls the possessors of this Great Love.

With this love and my blessing I will say, God be with you now and for all eternity.

Your sister and mother in Christ.   MARY.

Affirms that Mary the Mother of Jesus Wrote.

I AM HERE. *John.*

I came tonight to tell you that the Master will not write, as he is not present, but is at work in another part of the universe, where he is needed, and where he is doing a work that none of us can do.

Well, I know that he had an engagement with you but he thought best not to keep it, and sent me here to tell you, for he did not want you to think that he had forgotten you, as he has not. Very soon he will come and continue the messages, and you will not be disappointed.

I will not write more tonight as you will have a communication from another that will be interesting.

Yes, it was a glorious night, for as you were told many of the Celestial Spirits were present with their love and helpful influences—and one especially was with you, having a great love for you and your friend. She still has a great mother's love as well as the Divine Love, or rather this Divine Love which includes this motherly feeling and desire to make you happy as one of her children, although she is your sister rather than your mother,—but still she feels like the mother of all of Jesus' followers, as she is his mother still, and yet, not his equal in the great soul development.

She really wrote to you, and what she stated is true, notwithstanding the declarations contained in the Bible, as to Jesus' conception and birth.

And I must here state again, that at no time in his ministry did he claim or have the slightest thought of having been conceived by the Holy Spirit or that he had any other father than Joseph.

We never looked upon him as God or as a Son of God in the peculiar sense in which the orthodox churches teach; and now I know he was

143

not such God or Son of God. He is merely a spirit as are the rest of us, but the one possessing more Divine Love, and having the greatest knowledge of the Father, and of His personality and attributes.

So believe what we have written you on this question for it is true.

I will stop now, and in doing so will say, God bless you.

Your brother and friend,

JOHN.

Affirms that Mary the Mother of Jesus Wrote.

I AM HERE. *Saul.*

I want to write just a line as I see that tonight you have around you so many of the high spirits. I do not intend to say much, but I must tell you that I am in a condition of love that makes me happy as I see that you are.

I am not so high in my position or have so much of the soul development as have those who have just written you, but yet, I am a spirit who knows the truth of the Divine Love and a possessor of the divine nature. I want to say to you both, pray and believe. Let not what others may write or say to the contrary cause you to doubt that the spirit who wrote you was Mary—not the Virgin Mary—but Mary the mother of Jesus. She is a beautiful and pure spirit and one who is filled with the Father's Love to a wonderful degree.

She also has her mother's nature to an extent that makes her love all the children of God, whether they be good or sinful, and she does pray to the Father for the sons of earth, but she is not pleased when mortals pray to her as some one who should be worshipped. She is only a spirit filled with love, and when they, I mean mortals, look upon her as a mother she is not displeased, for as I say she loves them all; but when they think that in order to reach the ear of the Father in seeking for His Love, they have to pray to her to intervene, she is sorely displeased and, if she could do so, would proclaim to them the great error and sin in believing in her and praying to her as a necessary intermediary between God and themselves.

Some day, mortals will know that the Father hears their prayers, just as he does the prayers of Mary or any other spirit, and that while she and all other spirits can help them, even by their prayers, yet God wants the prayers and soul longings of mortals directed to Himself.

I write this to show that some of the orthodox Christians make a great mistake in praying to the Virgin Mary or to any other saint, instead of to the Father.

I will not write more tonight, and will say that I, as well as the other spirits who are here tonight, love you with the love of a brother who knows the reality of this Divine Love.

Your brother in Christ   SAUL

Affirming that John, Saul and Mary the mother of Jesus wrote

I am here. *Your Helen.* (Mrs. Padgett)

Well, you have had some wonderful messages tonight, and you must believe that they were written by the spirits who professed to have written. I know the spirits, and I tell you—and you know that I would not deceive you—that John and Saul and Mary wrote you, and what they wrote they know to be true.

How happy I am tonight, for I see that you are happy too, and have felt the influence of the Great Love that has surrounded you this night.

I never, in all our meetings, have seen so many of the Celestial Spirits as have been present tonight. And if it were not that you are too tired, though you may not realize it, many others would write you.

But the fact is that you have been in an atmosphere of love that I believe has rarely come to mortals, and this love is of a nature that can only come from spirits who have received this divine nature of the Father. So you and the Doctor must believe what I tell you and follow the advice that has been given you and rely upon the encouraging words that have been written.

John is a very beautiful spirit and is so greatly developed in his soul perceptions that his knowledge of the Father and the love that comes from him is astonishing.

I will not detain you longer tonight for I see that you are tired.

Good night and pleasant dreams.

Your own true and loving HELEN.

Jesus was the true Messiah and the true Christ as he taught
when on earth.

I am here. *John the Baptist.*

I have not written you for some time, and tonight I come merely to let you know that I have not forgotten you, and am with you quite often, trying to help you with my love and influence.

No, I was not present then.

Well, I am glad that you had such an experience, and I will tell you that you shall have many more experiences of that kind for the Celestial Spirits are your friends and companions, and where they are, only love can come.

Well, that does seem contradictory, but the fact is, that I never sent my disciples to ask any such question. I knew at the time of the baptism of Jesus that he was the promised Messiah, and that knowledge never left me or degenerated into a doubt. This passage of the Bible has no foundation in fact, for I never thought it necessary to ask any such question, and, as I have said, I never asked it.

To me, Jesus was the real Christ, and I knew that he was the true and only one, and that no other would come after him, for when he

145

brought to light the fact that God had bestowed upon mankind the great possibility of obtaining the Divine Love and the divine nature, there never thereafter arose the necessity for the existence or coming of another Christ. The Great Gift that was necessary to make man a being Divine had been bestowed, and beyond that there was nothing that the Father had to bestow upon mankind.

I am so sorry that such an untruth should have been written and incorporated in the Bible. It did Jesus an injustice and made me appear as a contradictory prophet and messenger of his coming. When I said, I am the voice of one crying in the wilderness, make straight the way of the Lord, I meant that I knew that Jesus was the true Christ, and that forever thereafter would that knowledge be mine. *No, I did not send my disciples to ask the question that you referred to.

As I knew then, I know now, that Jesus was and is the true Son of God, and the savior of mankind, in the sense that he brought life and immortality to light. I will soon come and write you on some of these Bible declarations.

I will now stop, and in doing so say, that you have my love and blessings and the love of the Father, which is the Great Love that makes you a part of the Divine Essence of the Father.

So my dear brother—Good-night.

Your brother in Christ,   JOHN THE BAPTIST.

*Spirit Who Believed in the Creeds and His Awakening to the Truth
After He Met Jesus*

I am here. The spirit of one who when on earth was a believer in the divinity of Jesus and in his being one of the three parts of the Godhead, co-equal with the Father and with the Holy Spirit.

This belief I died in and as a consequence, when I came to the spirit world I was disappointed and also surprised to find that Jesus is not God, but a spirit made like the rest of the inhabitants of that world though infinitely more beautiful and possessed in a very much larger degree of the divine nature of the Father.

I did not believe that this was true until a long time after I entered the spirit world, for my old beliefs clung to me, and while I did not find myself in heaven singing psalms and playing on harps as the Bible taught, yet I was not very happy and was not in much darkness, and I settled down to the belief that the state in which I found myself was the one that I should probably remain in until the great day of judgment and the general resurrection of those who had died.

But after a while I met spirits who said they were from a higher sphere, and who told me that there is no such thing as a fixed state in

---

* John the baptist says he never sent two of his disciples to ask Jesus—"Art thou he that should come, or do we look for another." Matthew 11; 2,3.

146

the spiritual world, and that the day of judgment is every day that I existed as a spirit, and that if I chose to do so I could progress out of my condition into higher spheres where I would find more happiness and light.

Of course I did not readily believe this, for my old beliefs stayed by me and I continued in my condition of hesitancy for a long time, until at last I had the good fortune to come face to face with the Master, and then I knew that my beliefs were wrong and erroneous. Such a beautiful and bright and loving spirit I had no conception of.

He told me that he was not God, and that he was only a son of the Father, and that I was a son also, and could obtain the Divine Love just as he had obtained it, if I would only pray to the Father and have the necessary faith.

Since then, I have been praying, and my old beliefs about Jesus being God, and the great day of judgment and the resurrection of the dead at the last day have left me, and I am a free spirit possessing the love of the Father to a considerable extent.

I am not so exalted and bright, and have not the soul development that your band have, but I am progressing and know that the Divine Love of the Father is what we all, spirits and mortals, need to make us one with the Father, and partakers of His divine nature and of immortality.

I am a stranger to you, and you must excuse my intruding, but I so desired to write as I have, that when I saw the way open I could not resist the temptation to write.

I am S. B. S. I lived in the city of New York and died many years ago. I am in the fifth sphere and am progressing.

So thanking you, I will say, good-night and God bless you.

Your brother in Christ

S. B. S.

Spirit Gives His Experience and How His Old Beliefs in the Creeds Retarded His Progress. Affirms that Mr. P. Was Selected by Jesus to Receive the Messages.

I am here and want to write a little tonight with the permission of your band and yourself. You will remember me when I tell you that I am an old friend of yours and a brother in the profession.

You knew me as G. H———, and I knew you as my young lawyer friend.

I am living in the third sphere and am comparatively happy, and am trying to progress to the higher spheres, but somehow the old beliefs that I imbibed, when on earth, seem to retard my progress. As you know, I was a Methodist and believed in the Methodist doctrines, and yet was not so spiritual as I should have been. I have learned or rather unlearned and learned many things since I have been here, and, as a consequence, I am in a better condition to appreciate the truth than when on earth.

147

Well, I know now that the blood of Jesus, as such, does not wash away sin, and also that he is not the saviour of men because of any vicarious atonement. These were great stumbling blocks to me when I came into the spirit world, and my disappointment growing out of these beliefs was very great, and almost caused me to believe that there never was any Jesus or any God. But thanks to some of my spirit friends who knew the truth, I was prevented from becoming an unbeliever in the truths of salvation and so was saved from what might have been a great stagnation of my soul and its progress.

Yes, and I am somewhat surprised at Riddle's progress, for I must tell you that he is in a higher sphere than I am, and is more filled with this Love of the Father. He has told me somewhat of his experience, and how you first started him to right thinking, and then how your band, I mean your grandmother, and the rest of your kinfolk, came to him and helped him to see the light, and the necessity of seeking and obtaining God's love. He is now a very bright spirit and has much faith. So you see, a man may have his doubts on earth and yet succeed in progressing more rapidly than one, who, though he believes in God and the Bible, yet because of his erroneous beliefs, stands still.

Well, I must say that I have been with you a number of times when the spirits were writing to you, and I was very much surprised at first that such a thing should be; and I saw that you were doing the dark spirits a great deal of good in the way in which you helped them out of their darkness and sufferings.* When I was on earth I did not suppose that there would ever come a time when you would be in this kind of work—in fact I did not know that there was such a work to be performed by any one. Yes, I have seen Jesus writing to you a number of times, and only tonight did he do so.

My views as to him have changed very much since I was on earth. As you may have thought I then believed him to be God or one of three that constituted God, and that he was a way up in the heavens, sitting on the right hand of the Father, controlling the heavens and the earth. But since I have been in the spirit world my beliefs have changed, and now I know that Jesus is not God, but only his highest, best son, and a spirit such as I am. He has at times talked to me and told me of many erroneous beliefs contained in the Bible and in the dogmas of the churches. He is a wonderful spirit—the brightest in all the spirit world, and the one that is closer to the Father than any of the others, ancient or modern.

He is so very filled with the Divine Love of his Father that we adore him as our Master—not worship him as God. I have been surprised at the great interest he has in you, and the abundance of love that he has

* By causing them to visualize bright spirits after they wrote through Mr. Padgett.

for you. But I know that I need not have been surprised for he has selected you to write his messages to the world.

What a fortunate man you are. I don't sometimes understand how such a thing can be, but he says that the world must have all the truths of the Father, and he selected you because he saw that you could carry out his desires better than any other mortal; and so you are favored.

Well I must stop as I have written a very long letter and some others wish to write also. So my dear brother I will say good-night.

Your old friend,

G. H————.

How Wonderful It Is to Obtain Possession of the Divine Love.

I am here, your own true and loving *Helen*: (Mrs. Padgett)

Well my dear Ned, I see that you are very happy tonight and I join in your happiness, for the source of both our happiness is the same—the Great Divine Love of the Father.—How loving He is and how thankful we should be that we not only have the privilege of receiving this love, but that we know the way as the Master has taught. Oh, wonderful is this love and more wonderful that little, insignificant creatures as are we, should have the way pointed out to us by which we can obtain this love. The Father is good and his love is without stint or limitation in its bestowal on all his children, even on those who do not seek for it with longings of the soul. Always it is waiting for the desires of men to possess, and, as you know, never is the man who earnestly seeks for it, disappointed. Love is the one Great Gift of the Father which all may obtain, and only man, himself, can prevent this love transforming his soul from the condition of the mortal to that of the immortal.

With all my love,

Your own true and loving HELEN.

Jesus claims that his disciples never wrote all the false doctrines in the Bible attributed to him.

I am here, *Jesus.*

I was with you to night, and heard what you said about the Bible and its writers, and I desire to say that many things in it were not written by my disciples or by those to whom my disciples had delivered the sayings that I made use of while on earth.

The text as contained in the present Bible is not a true copy of what I said, or what was in the manuscripts of those who originally wrote; and I am trying to correct the many errors that the Bible contains.

Well, the sayings in the Epistles and in the Gospels and in Revelation to the effect that my blood saves from sin, are erroneous, and my disciples never wrote that false doctrine, for I repeat here, what I have before written you, that my blood has nothing to do with the redemption of mankind from sin, nor has my blood any effect in re-

conciling men to God or making them one with Him. The only thing that works this great result is the New Birth as I have explained it to you.

So do not let these sayings of the Bible disturb your belief in what I say now, or in what I may hereafter say.

Well, the Revelation of John is not true—it is a mere allegory and not just as he wrote it, for it contains many things that are absurd and not in accord with the truths as I shall write them to you. He has written you already on the * "Revelations" and told you what he did not write, as he has been annoyed by this book of the Bible and its interpretations by the preachers and others. It is nothing but a revelation of a vision which he thought he saw while in a trance, as you mortals say. I mean that the real Revelation that he wrote is only the vision of a trance. So let not these things disturb you.

I see that you are getting more of the Divine Love in your soul, and your spiritual eyes will be opened, and your soul perceptions will, before long, see and understand many of the vital truths of God.

I will not write more to night.

With all my love, I am,

Your brother and friend,   JESUS.

Not the blood of Jesus but the Divine Love is what saves and redeems. Revelation of the Bible is not to be relied upon as true in many particulars.

I am here. *John* of the *Revelation.*

I saw you studying the Bible or rather those portions of the Book which treated of the salvation of mankind through the blood of Jesus, and that you made extracts from the Revelation, which declared that the blood of Jesus washed away sins of mankind and redeemed them.

Well, I want to say that while I wrote a Revelation or rather dictated it to another to write, I never wrote the words declaring the salvation of mankind through the blood of Jesus, which declared that the blood of Jesus washed away sins of mankind and redeemed them, for I did not believe any such doctrine and had never been taught such a belief by Jesus.

Much of the matter contained in the Revelation I never wrote; but men or scribes who professed to copy the description of my vision, added to it for the purpose of incorporating therein the views of the Christians of that early day, so that their views might be emphasized and in union with similar views that had been added to the Gospels and Epistles in the copies which these same persons or their predecessors in these views had made.

* Revelations—St. John. Vol. I, Edition 1—Pages 195-199.

The Revelation is merely a vision which I had when in a trance and was undoubtedly intended to illustrate or predict those things which would be visited upon the believers and the non-believers in the truths of God as taught by Jesus and his apostles.

At the present day, I cannot see that this book can serve any good purpose in making men acquainted with the truths of God, or with the relationship of man to God. Many of the things therein contained are not true as a truth, but were used merely to illustrate a truth. There are no streets of gold or pearly gates or dragons or beasts or white horse or other material things which are depicted in that book; and it is valuable only so far as imagery may show to mankind some spiritual truth.

And besides it has been so embellished and added to, that many of its figures or images do not illustrate any truth, or anything else, but merely serves to give the book the character and appearance of a book of mysteries.

So, I advise you in attempting to search for the truths that the Bible contains, do not waste your time in trying to discover the meanings of the various dark sayings and mysterious descriptions which this book contains.

There are enough truths in the Bible, though mixed with many errors, to lead men to the light and to salvation. Love is the great principle, and the fact that God is waiting to bestow that love on mankind, if they will only seek for it, as it is the principle which is sufficient to lead men to the Celestial homes and happiness.

I am not an advocate of all the isms which men draw or formulate from the Bible, but on the contrary, deplore and condemn the misconstruction of the truths which it contains, and which men may understand, if they will search for them in humbleness and in the spirit of a little child.

But, whatever of errors may be written in the Bible will be shown by the messages which Jesus shall write to you, and after they are transmitted and made known to mankind there will be no occasion for men to accept or believe these errors.

So, I tell you that while the Bible, even as now written, is a grand old book, yet it is not the true mouthpiece of God in very many particulars, and is a stumbling block to man's acquiring a correct knowledge of the truths of God.

These truths will not conflict with the reasoning of the normal man who is not prejudiced by views which are erroneous, either in the scientific or the religious world.

A man who believes what is not true is just as much an infidel whether that belief relates to the sciences or to religion. A belief in the false is a want of belief in the true, and, hence, as to the true he is not a believer.

I will not write more tonight.

So will say good-night and God bless you and your work.

Your brother in Christ,

JOHN OF REVELATION.

The epistles in the Bible are not the same that the Apostles wrote. The Divine Love mentioned in the Bible is not explained as to what it really is as contradistinguished from the natural love. Very little in the Bible explaining the New Birth as it should be by the writers.

I am here—Your own true and loving *Helen*: (Mrs. Padgett)

Well dear, I see that you have been reading portions of the Bible tonight and that you have not found in the same any mention of the Divine Love in the sense that it has been explained to you or any evidence that the writers had any knowledge of the love in the way of being born again. Of course they used the expression, but the meaning that they gave to it is altogether different from the one that Jesus gave the other night.

Now you have been told that he taught the apostles this true meaning and that they to a more or less extent understood it, and especially John, and as a truth, being the very foundation of the truth of salvation, it may be surprising to you that if John wrote the * epistles which are ascribed to him, he did not speak of or attempt to explain the meaning of this New Existence. But the * apostles do not mention the New Birth in the light of the explanation that has been given to you, and you may very reasonably infer that these epistles were not written by any of the apostles to whom they are accredited, but by some writers who had some knowledge of the moral truths of Jesus' teachings and of the great one expressed as "that they should love their brethren as themselves." You will find very little in any portion of the Bible that will show you that the great truth of the New Birth was understood by the writers thereof: and all that you will find is, that love between man and God and man and man with all that flows from it, such as patience and kindness and charity, etc., is the fulfilling of the Christian doctrines. No distinction is made between the natural love of man and the love of God bestowed upon him at his creation and the great Divine Love which man never possessed until the coming of the Master.

It may seem strange, that this knowledge that the apostles and many others had in the time of the Master when on earth, should have been lost to the world. But it is a fact, and, as a consequence, the teachings of Jesus as to this great truth have for all these long years failed to work out his mission.

* What is the fact in reference to the authenticity of the Bible by St. Luke, Vol. I, 1st Edition—Page 150.

152

Well, I could write for a long time on this matter but it is not necessary, as you already know of these things.

Good night.

Your own true and Loving, HELEN.

St. Peter on forgiveness of sin

Let me write a few lines for I am very anxious to write you in reference to a truth which obtains in our spirit world, and with which you may not be acquainted.

As you may not know there is in our world a law which makes the soul of one who has not yet been purified suffer the penalties for the acts of sin and evil of which he may have been guilty during his earth life; and there is no forgiveness of these acts in the sense that forgiveness is taught by the theologians and churches, but the only forgiveness is the cessation of recollection of these acts so that they become as though they had never been; and, as the soul becomes naturally pure and in harmony with the laws of its creation, it then comes into its natural condition, and then, and then only, forgiveness takes place.

God does not forgive by the mere act of pronouncing forgiveness or by any arbitrary and sudden blotting out of sins, and thereby removing the condition which creates the inharmony; and so you will understand, that He cannot forgive sin in this way, neither can the popes, priests, teachers or churches, and the pronouncing of forgiveness by these men constitutes a deception of and an injury to the persons who pray and ask for forgiveness, and for such deception these men will have to answer when they come to the spirit world and realize the truth of forgiveness and the great deception that they had practised upon those who were their followers and believers in these false doctrines. Many spirits are now living and suffering in darkness in their purgatories just because of their beliefs, and the results thereof, in these misleading teachings.

There is no forgiveness until man makes the effort by struggling and succeeding in getting rid of these recollections; and such riddance can be obtained only by men realizing the fact that sin is only the effect of their having done those things, and thought those thoughts which are out of harmony with the will of God and the laws governing the creation of man.

There can be no sinning of the physical body or of the spirit body, but only of the soul caused by the exercise of the will in a manner antagonistic to the will of the Father. The body, of course, is affected by these inharmonious thoughts and impelling directions of the will, and is caused thereby to commit the act which is the external demonstrator of the inharmonious exercise of the will; and as God leaves to man the freedom of exercising his will, as such will may be influenced by the thoughts, desires and affections of his appetites and lusts, so God leaves to man

153

the application of the remedies that will free the soul from such influence and effects as are caused by this exercise of the will; and only when these thoughts and appetites and lusts become eliminated from his soul and desires, does the soul come into its natural condition and in harmony with the will of God.

Man, himself, must be the actor and the initiating force to bring about these changes in his will, and no assurances of forgiveness by popes, priests or churches can eradicate these contaminating influences, or remove that which is the cause of the sin or the effect of the cause. You must see that there can be no relationship between the assurance of forgiveness and the sin or the cause thereof.

Prayer to the Father for forgiveness or supplication to priests and church is supposed to effectuate the objects sought, but this belief is erroneous and does not bring the relief prayed for; yet prayer is a very important element in forgiveness, and while the Father does not, and the priests and church cannot, forgive sin in the manner mentioned, yet true, sincere prayer to the Father for forgiveness will bring its answer, and affect, not the sin, but the soul and state of men, so that their will and appetites and desires may be influenced in such a way that they will receive and realize the fact of a wonderful help in changing these appetites and desires, and in turning their thoughts to those things that will enable them to remove from their recollections the acts and thoughts, which are the causes of the existence of their souls in a state of sin.

If men would only realize these truths, and, when they desire the forgiveness of their sins, pray to the Father for help in turning away from these thoughts and in exercising their will in accord with His will and not expect any arbitrary forgiveness or removal of their sins, they would find themselves on the way to this forgetfulness and the true forgiveness.

Well, I desired to write this short message and am pleased that I could do so. Thanking you, I will say, good night.

Your brother in Christ,
Apostle of Jesus.   PETER

The wonderful power that may come to Mr. Padgett if he will only have sufficient faith.

I am here, *Jesus.*

I am glad that you are so much better tonight and that your thoughts are turned to the higher things of which I so much want to write you.

John has told you truly of the faith which you must seek to obtain, and which you may obtain if you will only pray to the Father with all earnestness and confidence. Elijah's faith is no different and no greater than what you may obtain if you will come close to the Father by prayer,

154

as he did. The Father is as much your Father as He was his, and your mission is a greater one than was his.

I am the Jesus who is the true son of God, and am closer to Him than is any other spirit, and know the extent of His love and power to a greater degree than does any other spirit; and I tell you with the authority that my love and knowledge gives me, that you may obtain a faith that will enable you to perform greater wonders than did Elijah.

Trust me implicitly and your faith will grow so strong that your freedom from worries and cares will come to you as the sunlight breaks from behind dark and threatening clouds and bathes the whole landscape in light and beauty.

You must soon now resume my message taking, and attune your soul to the influences which I will bring to you.

Well, you will receive help, as I have promised and you must not doubt me longer. I know that you consider your unworthiness as the great stumbling block to the performance of my work, but if I say that you are worthy, you have no right to say otherwise, or to feel that I am mistaken in choosing you, or that you are being deceived in this communication.

I am Jesus the chief of the Heavenly World, which my Father has given me, and there is none to gainsay or prevent what I do or determine to do. This you must believe, and on that belief guide all your acts.

So forever hereafter, know that I have chosen you for my disciple of this New Revelation.

But with the acquiring of this faith also acquire more of the Divine Love of the Father, for this is the great power which will develop you into the disciple that I intend you to be.

Pray to the Father and trust me, for my love for you is without limit, and my care for you shall be increasing until all shall be accomplished.

I have written this emphatic and authoritative message to you tonight, that you may know that there is no uncertainty that I, Jesus, have chosen you, and you must not again doubt that your mission is as I have told you.

With all my love and my blessings, I am, Your brother and friend,
JESUS.

Jesus showed his glory

I am here, *Helen*. (Mrs. J. E. Padgett)

Well, sweetheart, now you must be satisfied beyond all doubt that you are the chosen one of the Master to do his work.

It was Jesus who was writing to you, and never before have I seen him with such a royal and authoritative expression on his face. It must have been just such a look as he had when before the tomb of Lazarus he said: "Lazarus come forth." Power and determination were in his words and stamped on his face, and we who are here never before felt the wonderful authority which he has. Always before, were only love, and humility and grace, but when he told you what he did, everything seemed to be subordinated to this regal power and authority, which he showed forth.

I never before had seen this phase of his attributes, and we all felt that we were standing in the presence of—if not God—then of the mightiest personage in all God's universe.

I can well imagine that his wrath, should he ever have occasion to show it, would be terrible and withering.

So my dear you must no longer doubt or hesitate as to what your work is to be, or as to what great power you will have back of you in doing his work.

I am simply awestruck to night and can write no more now,

So with all my love, I am

Your own true and loving, HELEN.

Affirming that Jesus showed his glory, power and authority when writing through Mr. Padgett, and the wonderful blessings and faith that may come to him.

I am here, *St. John,* Apostle of Jesus

I am here again so soon, because I want to help you believe in what the Master wrote you as to your mission, and the work that he has chosen you to do.

I know it is difficult for you to believe that the communication actually came from Jesus, but I must tell you that he wrote the message, and that what you received and wrote he actually said, and in doing so he was the king as well as the loving savior who heretofore appeared to you as the loving and kindly brother that he is.

You must not doubt that he wrote you just as you received it, and that he has selected you for his disciple to do this great work of receiving and transmitting to mankind the wonderful truths which he shall write.

When he selected me as his disciple on earth I had my doubts as you have yours, and it was only after I came in close personal contact and association with him and saw the wonderful power that he had as well as the great absorbing love, did my doubts leave me. While you cannot see him as I did, and hear his voice of love and blessings as I did, yet you will be able to feel his love and realize his presence.

When he told you that you must doubt no longer as to your being selected for this work, he was a magnificent spirit in his aspect of power and authority, and we who saw him as he told you these things, knew that he was the Jesus who led us through Galilee and performed the wonderful things that he did, and also the great Jesus who gave to us the knowledge and the way to obtain the powers to heal the sick, and open the eyes of the blind and raise the apparent dead.

His presence was that of a very god, for he seemed possessed of all power and authority as well as of love and grace.

The spirits who were present and who had never seen these qualities of his nature displayed before, were awe struck, and like Peter and James and myself on the Mount of Transfiguration, fell to their faces because of the exceeding brightness of his countenance and the glory of his power which illuminated his whole being.

When he comes into the spheres lower than that in which he lives, as you would say, he leaves behind him this great brightness and glory, and appears only as a beautiful loving brother spirit. And never before had those spirits who were present when he wrote you, seen the wonderful and inspiring appearance which he then showed.

I tell you that you are a very favored mortal, and when your faith grows, you will realize what a wonderful mission has been given you to carry out.

Now we are all more interested in you than ever and continually will you have around you some of the high celestial spirits to aid and enlighten you in doing this great work, but the greatest of all will be the Master, for he will be with you often.

Now you must strive to attain to the fulness of this Divine Love and, the faith which is so necessary. There is no doubt as to your getting it if you will only pray; and I must tell you here, that you have the prayers of a host of Celestial Spirits ascending continually to the Father that this faith may be given you in its greatest degree. I, John, tell you this, because I know, and my knowledge is based on fact.

So let your prayers go to the Father, and let your trust in the Master and his promises increase, until at last you may realize the wonderful blessings that may be yours.

I will not write more to night, but will say that very soon the worries will disappear and you will be in condition to resume the writings.

With my love and blessings, I am your brother in Christ,

JOHN.

A. G. Riddle in a condition of wonderment after seeing Jesus showing such brightness and power.

I am here, *Your old partner.*

I will write only a few lines tonight, as I am in such a condition of wonderment over what took place when Jesus was writing to you last night that I do not feel able to gather my thoughts for extended writing. I want to say that what happened was to me the greatest revelation as to the character or rather the attributes of Jesus that I have seen since I have been in the spirit world.

When he wrote to you in his emphatic and authoritative manner, he became transformed into such a being of light and glory and power that none of us could look upon his countenance, and we had to fall upon our faces to hide the brightness of his presence. I tell you it was a wonderful evidence of his greatness and power. Never before had I seen him

157

clothed in such brightness and power. He was always the most beautiful and bright and magnificent of all the spirits, but never was there displayed in him before those appearances which made us think that he must be a very god.

I now know as never before that he is the true son of God and that he is worthy to follow and believe in. What a wonderful spirit he is. All love and power and greatness, and yet all humility. Such a combination of attributes I had no conception could ever exist in the same spirit.

Well my boy, I cannot say much more now, except that you surprise me more and more because of the great favor and blessings you have had conferred upon you. We are all amazed over it, but of course, happy over the fact.

You must try your best to do this work, and fulfill the mission for which you have been chosen.

What a wonderful Jesus. I cannot help thinking of him and the greatness of his being. I am so glad that I saw him as he appeared when he wrote, because now I have some conception of what the glory and grandeur of the high Celestial Heavens and their inhabitants must be.

I will not write more to night, for I cannot think of anything just now, but of the glory of the Master. I am your old partner,

A. G. Riddle.

Mr. P's grandmother affirming that Jesus wrote and showed his glory and power.

I am here to tell you of my Master's glory.

Heretofore, we have written you mostly of his love and beauty and humility, but said very little of his grandeur and the glory of his countenance when he permitted these attributes to appear in all their fullness and splendor. And this was reasonable, because until last night we had never seen this great brightness and glory.

I am in the Celestial Spheres, but he never before displayed the wonders of his love and powers to me or to others in my sphere, and neither to those in the lower spheres. But last night—oh, the glory of it—he came to you to write and in doing so, when he told you what your mission is, he assumed the authority and power which are his, and there came into his countenance and very being that wonderful glory and brightness which made him a being from other spirits, apart.

I have seen the glories of the Celestial Spheres in which I live, and they are so magnificent and wonderful that I have never been able to describe them to you; but they are as a mere shadow to the glory that surrounded and came from the Master when he appeared as I say. We were spellbound as you say, and could look upon him but for a moment only; and I can well imagine how his three disciples fell upon their faces at the time of the transfiguration on the Mount.

I cannot describe to you his grandeur and brightness, but your sun would appear as a pale moonbeam in his presence. And how thankful that I saw him as he is, for it shows me what must be the wonderful glory and beauty of the sphere in which he lives, and to which I am striving to attain, and thanks be to God, the Master says I may become a dweller therein if I will only pray and have faith and let the Divine Love come into my soul in sufficient abundance.

When I think of all the wonderful things that have centered around you in your communications with the spirit world, I simply have to wonder in amazement, and think why such things should be. The only explanation that I can give is that you are the special object of the Master's desire to have his work on earth carried forth in the way that he has declared.

My dear son, you must not doubt again as to what you shall do in the way of performing the work of the Master. Your call is certain and you must believe, and believing, do with all your strength and the powers that will be given you, this great task. And let me say further, you must make it a work of love.

Pray to the Father for faith and you will get it; and trust in the Master and you will never be forsaken.

I cannot write more to night, as I want to think of the wonderful scene of last night.

Your own true and loving Grandmother.

(ANN ROLLINS)

R. G. Ingersoll was present when Jesus wrote and showed his glory. Agnostic no longer—A most repentant believer now.

I must say a word, for my heart is so filled with regret and remorse, and the recollections of my awful mistakes while on earth, that I must release my soul of its burdens so far as a confession can do it.

I am Ingersoll, and I am not the agnostic any longer, but the most repentant believer in all God's spirit world, and one who now knows that Jesus Christ was and is the son of God to the fullest meaning of the word.

Oh, how glad I am that I came to you when I did, and that you caused me to seek the society of your band of beautiful and bright spirits who are filled with the Divine Love of the Father. For if I had not been with them I would not have witnessed the scene of last night, and today be a believer in the Jesus, who I now know is the savior of men by his wonderful love and knowledge of the truth.

Well my dear friend, such a scene as I witnessed last night was never witnessed on earth, except as I now believe, by the three disciples of the Master at the transfiguration on the Mount, and then I doubt if the glory was as great and the brightness of the Master so blinding and magnificent as they were last night.

I had seen the Master a number of times, and while to me he was the most beautiful and loving of all spirits and one to whom I was drawn in great affection, yet I had no conception of the other qualities or attributes of his which he displayed last night.

And what must I think of you, a mere mortal as are thousands of others on earth, having a soul development to a certain degree, but not to that of any of the spirits in the soul spheres here, as I am informed, to be selected for the work of doing the Master's desires on earth, and having that selection declared or rather ratified by an occasion that made all the spirits present tremble with awe at the glory and power which were displayed by Jesus Christ, who I, on earth, proclaimed to be merely a good man.

I tell you that you are wonderfully favored, not only in being selected to do his work, but in having that selection anointed, as it were, by such evidence of glory and God-like power as were shown last night.

I had no conception of what the glory of God meant or what the power of God could mean, and least of all did I suppose that any spirit in all the spirit world could possibly possess such glory or manifest such power. But Jesus Christ possesses the glory and power to such a degree as to make him almost Godlike.

As I said, I was present, and observed him as he wrote to you, and also what he wrote, and as he proceeded to tell you that he had selected you to do his work, he was the beautiful loving Jesus that he always is, as I had seen him; but as he proceeded and you doubted the possibilities of such things, and even to doubt if Jesus was really writing to you, there came into his countenance a wonderful look of authority and power and then the more wonderful brightness that outshone the noonday sun, and glory indescribable, and upon which none of us could look, and we fell prostrate to the earth, as you would say.

Oh, I tell you, the power which emanated from him was beyond all conception, and the wondrous authority that appeared in his whole being was not possible of being withstood by either spirits or mortals—and we were filled with awe and admiration.

When he had finished writing, the glory and brightness that I describe, left him, and he again appeared the humble loving but beautiful Master; and before leaving us he gave us his blessings—and to me came a great peace that passeth all understanding. I know now that Jesus is my savior, and that the Divine Love of the Father is a real existing thing, and I am striving to obtain it.

I believe in the New Birth, and am praying for it, and your dear grandmother tells me that I will soon get it.

So now I say to you, that you can declare to the world that Ingersoll the agnostic is no longer an agnostic, but a believer in the Father's Divine

Love and in Jesus Christ his beloved son, and the Way and the Truth and the Life.

I will not write more to night, but when I shall have gotten my thoughts and feelings together, I will write you at large and tell you of what my soul says as to my future destiny.

Well, thanking you for your kindness and for you having such a * grandmother, and for such a Jesus, I am,

Your friend, R. G. INGERSOLL.

Affirms that Jesus wrote and showed his glory and selected Mr. P. to do the work in receiving the messages.

I am here, Helen. (Mrs. Padgett)

Well, sweetheart, you have had some wonderful messages tonight, all confirmatory of the fact that the Master has chosen and confirmed you to do his work.

How thankful I am that this evidence has come to you, for now you cannot doubt and you will lay all your plans to carry out the desires of the Master, and to get in condition to receive his messages.

Now, we must stop.

But oh, my dear Ned, to think that you are the object of the Master's choice and his great love. Love me as I do you,

I am your own true and loving, HELEN.

John the Baptist Affirming that Jesus Wrote

Let not your heart be troubled, believe in God and in the Master. This is as true tonight as it was when spoken by Jesus to his disciples many centuries ago.

You are his disciple now just as certainly as were they, and while you cannot see him or hear his voice as they did yet the words are just as emphatically spoken tonight as they were to the other disciples.

You do not realize what love and what powerful influences are with you tonight, else you would let your worries flee to the winds and never return.

I merely want to tell you this to let you see that there is another of the Celestial Spirits who knows that the Master's promises will be kept.

I am not here because I want to encourage you merely, but because I want to tell you a fact, and fact it is, that you will soon be relieved of your worries.

Go to God in prayer and you will find great consolation as we have all found consolation in our troubles, and when on earth we had a great number who were persecuted resulting in the death of many of us. But we had faith, and our faith and the love of the Master helped us over many rough places. I merely want to add another confirmation to those who have told you that you will be relieved of these worries.

* Mr. P.'s grandmother had previously helped Ingersoll in his progress.

I will stop and say, that I am your brother in Christ,

JOHN THE BAPTIST.

St. James says that Mr. P. will soon get relief from worry.

When you are weakest, then are you strongest, because then you rely more on the power and help of the Father. Such has been your condition tonight, and I want to tell you that you have received a wonderful amount of the Father's love, and the love of the Master. This I tell you because I know from what I actually have seen. So you should not let your worries trouble you so much. Try to think more of the promises of the Master and of the love of the Father, and you will realize that help is very near you.

We are all here tonight because we are interested in you and want to see you happy, and you should be so; and if you could only know the love that surrounds you, you would cease to worry so much.

The Master has told you that your worries will leave you soon and you must believe him, for it is true.

I know this, and I can only corroborate what he says, so that you must not continue to let these temporary troubles keep you in such a condition of gloom and despondency.

I will not write more tonight.

Your brother in Christ,
JAMES THE APOSTLE.

St. Luke gives assurance that relief will soon come to Mr. Padgett.

I am here too, and want to assure you that our love is all with you tonight, and we are trying to make you feel that you are not forsaken even though things look very dark and you see very little light. But the light will soon come and with it a relief that will make you realize that the Celestial World is with you in love and power.

I see how worried you have been today and what a condition of helplessness possessed you, but we were with you then and were trying to help and encourage you with our influence.

I will not write more tonight, but will say I am

Your brother in Christ,   LUKE.

I am here. *John—Apostle of Jesus.*

Well, I will say that you are now surrounded by the love and influences of a band of Celestial Spirits, all sending to you their best and kindest wishes, as well as their love. I am now trying to make you feel my presence and love, and if you will open up your heart, you will realize that you are surrounded by love.

We are many and all anxious that you feel our presence, and you must pray to the Father more and ask for more faith. You will receive it, and will be correspondingly strengthened.

162

So let me say before I close, that you are all the special care of the Master, and his love for you tonight was something wonderful. He seemed to let all his love center on you, and I do not doubt that you felt its influence.

I will stop now and say that you have my love and blessing,

Your brother in Christ, JOHN.

Barnabas says Mr. Padgett is the favorite of the Master on earth.

Such are the thoughts of men when troubles arise: I can do nothing of my self, but will go to my Father and seek His aid; and the thoughts are true and the aid is certain.

You are that man tonight, and you will not be disappointed for you will find relief from your worries and the help that the Father shall bring to you.

The Master is all love and you seem to be his favorite on earth, and you can rest assured that you will not be forsaken. I tell you this because I know from experience.

I will not write more. I am,

Your brother in Christ,

BARNABAS, THE APOSTLE.

John Wesley's Affirmation.

When the Master said, "Feed my sheep", he not only meant that Peter and those to whom he was talking should feed the spiritual natures of those who should believe on him and try to belong to his fold, but he also intended that their material wants should be taken care of. And tonight he is saying the same thing, and as you are his sheep of special care and love, he intends that all the things that are necessary for your well being shall be given you. So do not doubt at all, but believe that you will be looked after in all your times of need.

He was so loving to you tonight that we were all somewhat astonished at the great love which we saw going to you, and thought how dear you must be to him. I have never seen him take such interest in any particular person before, and when you realize what his love and power are, you will be more astonished than were we.

I see what your troubles are, and while they may seem mountains high to you, they are merely temporary and will soon pass away. So believe in what the Master told you, and pray to the Father for love and faith.

I will not write more, but will say God bless you.

Your brother in Christ, JOHN WESLEY.

Garner the preacher gives encouragement.

Let the * worries go and bury themselves, and turn your thoughts and

* Mr. Padgett told me (L. R. Stone) that soon after he received the above messages, the causes of his worries were removed.

163

soul aspirations to God, for these are the things eternal and those of the world merely temporary things.

I say this, because I know, that if you will only pray to the Father and trust in the Master you will realize that what I say is the truth, and can be understood and realized by mortals as well as by spirits.

So my brother try to look on these worries in that way.

I am with you often trying to help you and have you feel my influence and love—

I will not write more.   GARNER THE PREACHER.

Mrs. Padgett refers to the many consolatory messages received.

I am here, *Helen* (Mrs. Padgett).

Well, you have had the most wonderful consolatory messages tonight, that I have ever known to be given to any mortal. With what love the Master spoke to you and tried to comfort you. He is a precious saviour and you seem so dear to him.

Try to trust him and do as he says.

These others are all Celestial Spirits, and are also much interested in you, and want you to get rid of your worries. You are sleepy and must go to bed.

So with all my love I will say good-night.

Your own true and loving Helen.

What man should believe in trying the spirits.

I am here, Luther. (One time monk and reformer)

I came to tell you that you are not much benefited by the book (Pastor Russel's "Atonement") you have been reading to night, because it ignores the very foundation of the plan of man's redemption—that is the Divine Love which the Father bestowed on mankind at the coming of Jesus. The blood atonement is all wrong and misleading, and has done much harm to the truths of God and to mankind.

I will admit that there are many truths stated in the book and many that will do much good to humanity to understand and believe, but because of the great error in the vital point of the declaration as to the plan of man's salvation, these truths which the book contains may not do the good that they otherwise might.

Of course you who understand the true plan of salvation may make the true discrimination between those declarations which declare the truth and those which do not. But on the whole I do not see that the teachings of the book will do you much good.

Well, I know that the passage in John refers to the spirits of men who once lived on earth and who communicated to the members of the early church in their places of worship, and elsewhere. John has explained to you, and what he said, I have been informed by others of the apostles, is true.

164

The author of that book has certain theories, and, of course, he is construing all the teachings of the Bible in such a way as to sustain his theories. But he is wrong as he will discover when he comes to the spirit world.

He teaches that the soul as well as the body of man goes into the grave to await the great day of judgment, and there is no such place as the spirit world inhabited by the spirits of departed mortals and to maintain this position he quotes from some of the old books of the Bible. But these books were not written by men inspired by God to declare the truths, and the quoted expressions are merely the result of the purely human minds of the authors, who did not know what they wrote to be a fact, but because of the conditions in which they were in, they concluded that such assertions must be true. Let not the writings of these old writers or of the present day writers either, cause you to hesitate to believe what the Master may write as being true.

I merely wanted to say this as I saw that you are interested in this book and I wanted to warn you against letting it influence you in any way.

Yes, I say that Jesus Christ did come in the flesh, and I know it, for he is here a spirit and once lived on earth. But that fact does not prove that any spirit who acknowledges that, is a true follower of him or a redeemed spirit of the Father.

There are many spirits in the spirit world who believe that Jesus, the spirit whom they sometimes meet, once lived as a mortal, and would, if asked, say that he lived in the flesh, but they are not believers in the Divine Love of the Father, or have had the benefit of his great plan of salvation or acknowledged him as the savior from sin and error. So that the test set forth in the Bible may have been considered a true test in the days of the early church, yet it is not now a very safe one for the reason that I have mentioned.

And if a test is necessary, I think a better one would be: try the spirits and every one who does not acknowledge that Jesus is the best beloved son of God, and brought to the knowledge of mankind the rebestowal of the Divine Love, and declared to men the way in which that Love may be obtained, is not a spirit that should be communicated with for the purpose of learning spiritual truths.

This test is better, because no spirit who has not received this Divine Love, or the New Birth, will acknowledge the existence of these things, because it has no knowledge upon which to make the acknowledgment.

I must not write more to night, but I hope the little that I have said may help you and others who have doubts, as to what the meaning of that part of the Bible, which refers to the trying of the spirits, is.

I am very anxious to write you again as to some of the higher truths pertaining to the spirit world, and soon I hope that I may have the opportunity.

I will say good night. Your brother in Christ,

MARTIN LUTHER.

Luke asserts that the Gospel in the Bible is not
the one as he wrote it.

I will write a little as I am interested in what you have received from Luther to night, and as I am supposed to have written the Gospel of Luke, I desire to say a few things in reference to the correctness or rather incorrectness of many things contained in my Gospel.

As you infer, I am St. Luke the writer of the third Gospel and a follower of Jesus.

My Gospel was not founded on anything I had personal knowledge of, but upon the writings of others and the traditions which were the common knowledge of many Christians at that time. I knew several of the apostles and obtained much of my information from them, as well as from many of the Christians who were members of the congregations to which these apostles preached and expounded the sayings of Jesus.

In my Gospel, as now contained in the authorized version, there are many things that have been interpolated. This version was not based on what I wrote, but upon pretended copies of my writings; and the persons who made these copies did not follow literally my writings, but added to my text and gave their own interpretations of what I had written in such a way as to destroy the true meaning of what was intended to be conveyed by my writings.

There are many truths contained in the Gospel as now written in the Bible, and they are the truths of God, but there are also many errors which contradict these truths. For instance, I never wrote that Jesus commanded his disciples to believe that the wine was his blood or the bread his body, and to eat and drink these things in remembrance of him.

How this interpolation could have been made I do not know, but will observe that the same things are said in all the four Gospels, and this saying must have been derived from a common source, and that must have been the minds of those who pretended to copy the Gospels.

I tell you now that this saying, that the blood of Jesus saves from sin, is not true, and if men depend upon this blood for their salvation they will never be saved, but will enter the spirit world in all their sins, and will be surprised to learn that Jesus is not waiting to receive them in his arms and carry them to the mansions prepared for the truly redeemed of the sons of men.

I know that a vast number of the members of the various churches believe this harmful doctrine, and that as a consequence, many persons claiming to be Christians will realize that their sins have not been forgiven them when they come into the spirit world.

166

Sometime, as these writings continue, I will point out the errors of my Gospel to an extent that will show you the fact of what great additions and misinterpretations have been made thereto.

I will stop now. Your brother in Christ, ST. LUKE.

The result of erroneous beliefs—the importance of men knowing the truth. Jesus' blood does not wash away sin.

Let me say a word, also. I am your own dear grandmother. *Ann Rollins.*

I came to tell you that I know now that the blood of Jesus does not save from sin. You will remember how, when on earth, I believed this doctrine of error. How I used to talk about the precious blood of Jesus being able to save from all sin; and used to sing with all my heart and belief the old hymn: "There is a fountain filled with blood," and so forth. Well I know now that that belief is all wrong, and that Jesus is so anxious to have men learn that it is a great error and stumbling block to the soul's progression.

Of course, I know that a large majority of those now living will never believe that this saying of the Bible is erroneous until they come to the spirit world; but if they could only be taught to throw aside this belief and rely entirely on the Divine Love for their salvation while on earth, how much easier their progress would be when they come over.

So you see, while many say that a belief does not amount to much, yet I tell you that it causes more unhappiness and retards the progress of spirits to a greater extent than any other one thing.

I know that only the Divine Love of the Father saves from sin and makes mortals at-one with Him. So in your work for the Master, you will have to make great efforts to cause people to give up this belief in the blood, and turn to the truth of the New Birth. Many of the orthodox will oppose your efforts and refuse to believe what you may tell them to be the truth, but many will believe and seek this New Birth, and find the peace and happiness of a soul whose sins have been forgiven.

I must not write more to night.

I will come again soon and tell you more of the results of your work among the unfortunate spirits who seek your help.

So my dear son, I will say good night,

Your loving grandmother, ANN ROLLINS.

Observance of the Ceremonies Which My Church Still Uses in Its Worship is Not Approved by God or Jesus.

I am here. *Luther.*

I desire to write a short message tonight on the subject of the: "*Observance of the ceremonies which my church still uses in its worship is not approved by God or Jesus.*" I will not detain you very long and will try to express myself as succinctly as possible.

Well, as you may not know, the church of which I am the founder believes and teaches the necessity of infant baptism and the observance of the Lord's Supper as necessary parts of its church doctrine, and of such very great importance that without them it is difficult to become an accepted member of the invisible church of Christ.

Nothing is further from the truth than these doctrines for the baptism of infants for they have no virtue to save one from his sins or to make him in at-one-ment with the Father, and the mere fact that water is sprinkled on an infant's head and some blessing pronounced by the preacher does not in any way bring that infant in unison with the Father. Baptism is of man's creation and to God it means nothing more than an outward ceremony that affects the infant merely as regards its connection with the established earthly church. It is not possible for this baptism to have any effect upon the soul of the infant and neither does it open up the soul faculties to the inflowing of the Divine Love.

God cares not for these ceremonies, and rather looks upon them with disapproval, for their tendency is to make men and women neglectful of the great truth that will bring them in harmony with God's laws of love and redemption.

And the same thing may be said of any and all kinds of baptism, whether the subject thereof be an infant or a grown man or woman.

As to the sacrament of the Lord's Supper, it has no part in God's plan for the redemption of mankind and it is merely a reminder of the association of Jesus with his disciples. It cannot affect the condition or development of the soul, and as now understood and practiced this sacrament is of no importance, for Jesus does not want to be remembered in the way of recalling to him the tragedy on the cross which was only the result of the malice and envy of the Jews, and the blood spilt is not an element that enters into the plan of the salvation of men. And besides with this sacrament there is always more or less worshipping of Jesus as God, which he, Jesus, abhors and looks upon as blasphemy.

So you see, the celebration of the last supper is a thing which is not acceptable to God or to Jesus. He does not want men to believe that they can be saved by any sacrifice of him or by any blood which he may have shed as a result of his crucifixion.

Of course, you will remember that the question of what the wine and bread of the sacrament really were, was one that engendered much controversy, and even hatred and ill-feeling on the part of those who were assisting me in the great Reformation. If I had known then what I do now, no such question would have been debated or believed in by me and taught for many years. The blood of Jesus was no more than any other man's blood, and the commemoration of the last supper that Jesus gave his disciples before his death, is a useless ceremony and brings no help to those who indulge in this sacrament.

I see that you are tired and sleepy and I will not write more now. So with my love and wishes for an increase in you of the Divine Love, I am
Your brother in Christ,

LUTHER.

Denies the Vicarious Atonement, etc. Bible Full of Contradictions and Errors.

I am here, Luther—Martin Luther.

I came again because I want to tell you that I was with you this afternoon when you were reading the comments on the origin and different versions of the Bible. Among them was a reference to my version, and I want to say that while my version was a pretty correct translation, yet the manuscripts and other versions, upon which I based my translation, were not the real writings of those who profess to have written them. I mean that those manuscripts were not true copies of the original epistles and books written by those whose names they bear. Many interpretations and more constructions were given to the texts of the originals than you or any other mortal are aware of.

The Bible as now written and as I translated it, is full of contradictions and errors and makes the truth hard to ascertain. Take for instance that one subject of the blood redemption.

No greater error was ever written than that the blood of Jesus saves from sin, or that his blood washes away sin. It seems to me now, so absurd that I wonder and am astonished that I could ever have believed in such an absurdity.

I know now that there is no efficacy in Jesus' blood to accomplish any such results, and the pity is that many men now believe this, and, as a consequence, neglect the one vital and important requirement necessary to salvation, that is the New Birth. This and this only saves men from their sins and fits them to enter the Kingdom of God, which is the Kingdom of Jesus, for he is the Prince of that Kingdom and the Ruler thereof.

Jesus never said any such thing, for he has told me so. This saying that his blood was shed for many, is not true. He never said it, neither did he say drink the wine, being his blood, in remembrance of him, for the wine is not his blood, and neither does it represent anything that has to do with him or his mission on earth, or his present work in the spirit world. How unfortunate that this saying is made to represent something that he did not say.

So in order to understand the real truths of God and man's relationship to Him and His plan of salvation, you must believe what the Master shall write you and what his apostles may write, for now they understand what

169

his true mission was, and what he attempted and intended to teach when on earth, and what he is teaching now.

I also will write sometimes and give you the result of my instructions and knowledge as I received them since being here.

I will not write more to night.

Your brother in Christ,   MARTIN LUTHER.

Denies the Efficacy of the Eucharist to Save Man. Jesus living and teaching and demonstrating the Divine Love in his soul, and how man can obtain it, shows the way to salvation.

I am here. *Luther.*

I have come merely to remind you that I am waiting to continue my discourse to my people. I am very anxious to do this, and as soon as you get in condition I hope that you will give me the opportunity. Well, we will arrange that, and all that we desire is for you to get in condition.

We are with you a great deal and try to assist you in every way possible.

Well you have asked me a question that I should like to have more time in which to answer than I have now. But in short, Jesus was not of the substance of God in the sense that the Catholic Church, following the Nicene Creed, claimed. He took on a part of the Divine substance as the Divine Love filled his soul, and so can you or any other man do to the extent that you may receive this Love. But to say, that Jesus was in his very being of the substance of the Father to that degree that made him equal to God, is erroneous, and should not be taught or believed in. He was born or created in the likeness of God in the way that has been explained to you and in no other. He was a man and not God, or any part of Him, and if he had not received into his soul the Divine Love, he would never have been of the substance of the Father. But being of a very spiritual nature, and in fact so much so that he was without sin, this love commenced to come into his soul very early, as you may say, from his very birth, and at the time of his anointing he was so filled with it that you may say, he was of the substance of the Father in the quality that that Substance possessed of the Nature Divine. He was no more divine though naturally, as I may say, than was any other mortal born of the flesh. I should like to write you a long message on this subject, and will sometime, when convenient.

Well, all the speculation that has ever existed as to the Eucharist and the change in the qualities of the bread and wine, are untrue. Jesus is not in these elements in any particular or view that may be taken. His flesh and blood went the way of all other flesh and blood of mortals, and no more forms a part of the bread and wine than does your flesh and blood.

This sacrament, as it is called, is very abhorrent to the Master, and when it is celebrated, I must tell you, he is not present, not only not in

170

flesh and blood but also not in his spiritual presence. He dislikes any kind of worship which places him as its object in the position of God or as the son of God who paid a great debt by his sacrifice and death. He wants God alone to be worshipped, and himself to be thought of only as the one who brought to light immortality and life by his teachings and the living demonstration of the truth of the existence of the Divine Love in himself.

He does not approve of the teachings of men that his death and his blood were the means of man being saved from their sins and becoming reconciled to God. He says, it was his living and teachings and demonstration of the love of God existing in his own soul that showed the only true way to salvation.

But, I must not write more now. So with my love I will say good night.

Your brother in Christ,   MARTIN LUTHER.

Mrs. Eddy's Testimony

Let me write a few lines, as I am anxious to declare some facts, which when on earth were not facts to my understanding and beliefs. And oh, the pity of it all.

Today, I was present at the church where the preacher discussed and criticised my teachings and me also and I am compelled to admit that some of his criticisms were true and justified.

I am Mrs. Eddy, and the founder of the sect which bears the high sounding name of Christian Science, and the doctrines of which are neither Christian nor science as I now know from actual experience in the spirit world, where many of my teachings are shown to be not in accord with truth, and so misleading.

I now realize that my mind and soul were not in accord as regards the truth, while I lived a mortal, and that my mind was superior in causing me to have certain beliefs which I left to the world in the form of doctrines contained in my text book and my other writings.

My soul possessed a considerable degree of the Divine Love, as that love has been explained to you, and when I came to the spirit world that love was my salvation, notwithstanding the errors of many of my teachings as to mind and matter, and non reality of sin and evil.

I am too weak to write more, but I will soon come for I must declare the truths.

Goodnight.   MRS. EDDY.

Some of the doctrines of Christian Science are untrue. Very important that the truths being revealed through Mr. Padgett be made known as it involves the salvation and good of all mankind.

I am here. *Jesus.*

I have been present as you read the article on Christian Science and was interested in your comments, and am pleased to assure you that your

171

annotations were correct, and that in the particulars that you criticised the statements of the writer the same were erroneous and not in accord with the spiritual laws of truth and the understanding thereof. Sometime I will come and write you a message at some length on the doctrines of Christian Science, for the reason that I think a correction of the claims of this cult is very important.

The doctrines that it proclaims to the world contain many truths and are beneficial to mankind, and are doing much good, both spiritually and physically, but some of the claims are so much in violation of the truth that they must not be permitted to pass as truths uncontradicted.

The founder of this Science or discovery, as her writings and followers claim, is here now, and deplores the fact that she left to the world so many false and misconceived concepts of the truth that so many persons believe and teach. She is a spirit of much soul development, and is in possession of much of the Divine Love, which she did not conceive the meaning of by her carnal mind, as she called it, and was not therefore able to teach what this Divine Love is and its operations upon the souls of men, and the effect of its presence in such souls.

She never conceived any higher ideal for man than the perfect man. One who should become wholly delivered from the sins and errors which all men have to a more or less extent. And her teachings that sin and error and disease are not things of reality, because God did not create them, are all wrong, for they have a reality that not only makes men unhappy and causes them suffering in the mortal life, but also prevents their progress towards her ideal of the perfect man in the spirit world. God only is good, and everything that He created is necessarily good, and cannot contain that which is evil or in conflict with His creations; but, as we have explained to you, while He created man perfect, knowing only good, yet He bestowed upon him that great power of free will, and after his disobedience, he exercised it in such a way that he violated the laws of his being, and sin and error resulted—this made man the creator of evil.

Mrs. Eddy will write you very soon on the subject of her Science, as she is very anxious to remedy the errors that she taught, and we have determined that it is advisable that she do so, on account both of her followers and her own account, for her work here and so far as possible in the mortal world, is to unteach, as it were, the errors that she taught.

I expected to write my message, or rather finish the message which I partly wrote a few nights ago, but you are not just in condition to receive it, and I prefer waiting until you feel better in this respect.

I am glad that you are so much interested in that message, and when you receive it, I don't think that you will be disappointed, for as you say, the subject is the one fundamental truth to be made known to mortals. I will deal with it in all its phases, and you must try to get in the best possible condition to receive it.

172

Well, I do not think that that will be necessary for there will be such powers present, that the presence of any mortal and the favorable influences that he may attract will not afford any assistance to you. You must know that I have greater power than all the other spirits have, and when I come to you the assistance of the powers of any other spirit is not needed. If you will only get your soul in the best condition possible, so that I can make the proper rapport, nothing else will be needed.

I will not write more tonight. I love you very much and am with you quite frequently, throwing around you my love and influence, and trying to help you develop your soul condition and become in greater at-one-ment with the Father.

Yes, I have kept my promises, and when you call for me to come with you and pray, I come, and send up my earnest supplications in your behalf, and I know that the Father answers my prayers, not only because of the faith that I have, but because I can see the effect in your soul's condition.

Well, you must not think that I am God or one of the Godhead, for as I have told you, I am only His son, and the possessor of so much of His Divine Love that I get very close to Him, and have communion. I have my home in the Highest Heaven, that the spirit of man has not yet so far reached, but, notwithstanding, I am not of so exalted a condition, or in such position, that I do not come to you in love and sympathy and as your elder brother. In my exaltation, I am most humble, and I must tell you that humility is a certain and eternal accompaniment of great spiritual and soul development.

And because I am the highest of the Fathers' sons, you must not doubt that I come to you, and deliver my messages and pray for you and throw around you my love and influence.

I have explained to you the great reason why I am doing this, and this reason is one that involves the salvation and good of all mankind, and you. I will tell you now that you are engaged and made a co-worker with me, and the spirits who write you, in the greatest work that any spirit or man can engage in. And I want further to say, that you will accomplish the work, and successfully; and when the time comes for you to lay down this work and come to the spirit world, your reward will be beyond all conception, and your happiness will be complete.

I see that you have in your mind the thought as to what will be the future of your two * friends. Well, they will perform their work and it will be a great and important work, that will bring them a reward similar to the one that is in store for you; and this reward is not the result of any special dispensation of the Father, but is the result of the work

* Mr. Eugene Morgan and Dr. L. R. Stone.

and the associations and experience that you all will have in doing and completing the tasks that are before you.

You, and they too, are now doing a work which is laying up rewards in the spirit world for you when you come over, and not only there but you are now experiencing some of the benefits that flow from your work. Continue in the efforts that you are making to show spirits and mortals the way to the Father's love, and my kingdom, and you will find a wonderful reflex happiness come to you while you are yet mortals.

If you men could realize the love and spiritual influences, and the number of highly developed spirits that are with you so often, and the efforts the latter make to help you and bring happiness to you, you would feel that you are the truly blessed of the Father.

Well, I must stop now. Remember what I have said and believe that I am,

Your brother and friend,   JESUS

Master wrote and so anxious that Mr. Padgett should comprehend his message and its importance.

I am here. Your own true and loving, *Helen.*

Oh, my dear, how glad I am that the Master wrote to you as he did, and if you only could have seen him as he told you of his love for you and the great happiness that will be yours when you shall have finished your work, you would have been thrilled as well as very happy. He seemed to be full of love and glory, and so anxious that you should fully comprehend what he wrote you.

Your own true loving   HELEN.

Spirits' experience when entering the spirit world and their progress by John B. Comeys.

I desire to write you a short time to inform you of certain truths which you should know pertaining to the spirit life, and to what mortals who lead the lives of good and pure men may expect and be assured of realizing.

I am in the Celestial Spheres, but I shall not speak of these spheres, but only of the spiritual spheres, where men after they become disembodied spirits may live and experience a happiness which they on earth have no conception of.

When a spirit first enters the spirit world it receives a welcome from some one or more spirits whose duties are to receive such spirit, and to show the place where it is suited to live or exist.

Such spirit is then permitted to meet its friends and relatives and to commune with them for a short or long time and receive whatever consolation such friends or relatives may be able to give it; and in many cases the gladness and happiness of these spirit friends cause the spirit to believe that it is in heaven, or at least, in a place of great happiness.

But after this first interview, the spirit must, by reason of the law of attraction, go to the place where its condition of soul or its condition of moral growth or intellectual development fits it for, and there remain until such condition is made better and enables it to rise to a higher place.

No spirit, after it once gets into the place that is suited for it to live in, ever retrogrades, although it may stand still for a long number of years, and never make any progress. But this is a truth not known to a great many mortals, and spirits also, that the condition of the mortal at the time he becomes a spirit fixes his condition and place of living when he first enters the spirit world, after he is put in such place by the law of attraction as I have said, and when once that place is found and occupied, the spirit never goes to a lower place; but either will stay in that place for a long time, or will progress—and ultimately will in all cases progress.

Well, the evil spirits find these places of habitation in the earth planes, which are many, and of varied kinds, having many different appearances, suited to the conditions of the spirits who will occupy them.

A spirit who is in the lowest of these earth planes is said to be in the lowest hells, as all spirits who are in these planes where they suffer and encounter darkness believe and say they are in hell. But this is merely a name used for convenience, for the hells are merely places forming a part of the one great universe of God.

These hells, as you may imagine, are very numerous, for the conditions of spirits are very varied, and each spirit has a place in which to live fitted to its condition.

As the spirit becomes freed from some of these conditions, which as to them causes the law of attraction to work, he progresses to a higher and better place, and finds that his surroundings are not so dark and painful. And as this progression continues, such spirit will ultimately find himself in the planes of light and comparative happiness, where the evil recollections have to a large extent left him, and the good deeds which he did on earth then come to him and cause a happiness that makes him realize that he was not all bad, and that God has been good to him in relieving him from the sins and evil thoughts which bound him to the place from which he has progressed.

But after all this, he has not gotten into any of the spheres which are above the earth planes, and he may have to remain therein for a great many years before he enters the second sphere which is next in gradation to the earth plane. This latter plane is the most populous of all the spheres, for it has spirits coming to it in great numbers—in greater numbers than are progressing from it to higher spheres, and hence it has a greater variety of sub-planes than has any of the other spheres, and is filled with a greater variety and kind of spirits than are any of these higher spheres.

When a spirit has remained in the earth planes a sufficient length of time to put him in condition to go to the next higher sphere, he makes his progress, and is never prevented from doing so. I do not mean to say that the spirit is compelled to remain in the earth planes any particular number of years before progressing, for this is not true; on the contrary the number of years that he remains there is determined by his condition of progress, so that some spirits may go through these planes in less than a year and others may remain there many years.

In the second sphere, appearances are brighter and many opportunities are afforded the spirit to seek for and obtain happiness that he did not have before, and many spirits find great happiness in pursuing their intellectual studies and things of this kind, and in obtaining a knowledge of the laws of the spirit world governing what you might call the material nature of this world and also of the earth world.

This sphere is not so well suited for the growth of the soul faculties, and those spirits whose desires and aspirations are for the development of their soul qualities do not stay in this world or sphere very long, for they do not find that the necessary provisions for such development exists, and as a consequence, they progress to the third sphere, where they find wonderful opportunities and surroundings, which enables them to progress in these matters of the soul.

Well I see that you are tired, and I will postpone any further writing on these matters to another time.

So Good-night—JOHN B. COMEYS.

*Joseph H. Salyards writes on his knowledge and soul perception.
* "Who and What Is God." God has personality.*

I am here, Your old *Professor Salyards.*

I merely want to say that I am very happy, and want you to know that I am progressing in my condition of soul development and in my knowledge of the truths that pertain to the spirit world. I have not written you for a long time, and would like to tell you of certain truths that I have learned since last I wrote you.

Well, I find that I am now in a condition of soul development that enables me to see the truth of what the Master has told us in reference to the real existence of God, who knows what His creatures are doing and in what way they are making use of their souls and bodies. I mean that this God is one having all the faculties that you would suppose only a being would have who had a personality and form; but can hardly understand how a mere essence or formless existence could have such powers and qualities.

I never, until recently, could comprehend the real truth and meaning of God, I believing him to be mere essence, void of form or personality,

* Appendix. Read "Who and What Is God" from Jesus, Edition 1, Vol. I—Pages 59-63. Also by Ann Rollins, Pages 63-69.

who could have the wisdom and love and power that I was taught such God possessed. Such comprehension is beyond the finite mind, and can only be accepted as a realization of an existing condition or truth by means of faith. Yet now I have more than faith to enable me to understand the fact that this God, whom we call our Father, for He is, has all these qualities and powers; and such understanding is to me a wonderful and unexpected addition to my knowledge of God.

This understanding, of course, is not a thing that arises from any exercise of the mind, or the result of any mental power or quality which I may never have realized that I possessed, but is the result of the exercise of my soul perceptions, which have become so great and in such condition of unison or harmony with our Father's qualities of soul, that He and all these attributes appear to me as real, perceptible existences, having a certainty of comprehensible being, as do the existence of spirits and their attributes.

So, you see, what soul development may mean and what its possibilities are .

No mere development of the intellectual qualities or attributes could ever lead to a comprehension of the personality of God as I have described it.

I never in all my life, natural or spiritual, conceived or expected that it were possible for any soul of mortal or spirit to see God as I now see Him, and I never could understand what was meant by the beatitude, "the pure in heart shall see God", except in this sense, that as we became pure in heart those qualities that were ascribed to God would become a part of us, and as such possessors, we could see God, or rather the result of those attributes of God in our souls.

I don't know whether you can fully comprehend what I intend to convey to you, but I have tried my best to put the idea in such language that your mind may understand, to some extent, what my meaning is. I know that you will never fully know what this great soul perception is, until you have experienced what this development is in your own soul, which is necessary to enable it to see with the clearness that I now see.

I thought that I would tell you of this progress of my soul, so that you might have some faint idea of what the development of the soul means in a way other than an addition to the development of the love principle. But really all phases of its development are part of or dependent upon and resultant from the development of this love principle; for Divine Love is the fulfilling of the law, and law includes that which enables us to perceive that God is a personality, having these qualities that I speak of.

I see that I have written enough for tonight, and if you will carefully read what I have written, you will find much food for thought, and probably some help to a correct, concrete comprehension of "Who and what God is."

177

So expressing to you my gratification and pleasure in being able to come to you again and having you take down my ideas of who our Father is, and also for the opportunity to declare that God is a being, having an existence of His own, comprehensible by the soul perceptions of the redeemed of His creatures, I will say, good night.

Your old professor and brother in Christ,

JOSEPH H. SALYARDS.

Affirms the Professor's message. The personality of God—The necessity of developing the soul perceptions to be able to perceive God's personality

I am here, *Jesus.*

I have heard what the Professor said to you and you must try your best to comprehend its meaning, for it contains a description of the true conception of God in a way that only one having the developed soul perceptions could explain. The only difficulty in the way of your fully understanding this idea of who and what God is, is that the idea is not one that the mere mind can grasp, for only the soul that has been developed to a sufficient degree can comprehend. But yet, you may be able to conceive of its meaning to an extent that will enable you to get closer to our Father as a real, personal Father, and not as a being of formless existence only. I mean that the idea of personality may bring the Father nearer to you, so that you may realize a deeper meaning of His love and care and mercy and interest in you and in all His creatures.

In my message on * God, you will find that the idea of personality is spoken of, but not emphasized so much as in the writing of the Professor; **but the truth is that our Father is to the soul perceptions a Being of real existence and personality.**

I know how difficult it is for the mind to conceive, even in a faint way, how such a personality can be a part of a Being who is declared to be a mere spirit without form or limitation, and everywhere at the same time; but I tell you that it is a truth that by the soul's faculties is comprehensible the personal attribute of the Father.

Of course, men will not understand this truth so long as they depend upon the mere intellect to comprehend it, and to them it may not mean much; but it is of the greatest importance to mankind, both in their lives on earth and in the spirit world. "Thou, God seest me", is not a mere meaningless generality which men repeat and do not understand, for God does see every act of man; and as I said when on earth, not even a sparrow falls without my Father knowing it, and the hairs of your head are all numbered. So if men will only learn that this great truth is of such importance, they will take more care of the manner in which they live their lives.

* Appendix. Edition 1, Vol. I—Pages 56 to 63. Who and what is God?—from Jesus. Also read Pages 59-63 from Ann Rollins.

(I am not disconcerted by the interruption) Dr. L. R. Stone came in.

As I was saying men must realize that God knows not only their acts but their thoughts, and every idle thought will have to be accounted for, and the penalties which his laws impose will have to be paid.

So, if men would only realize this fact, of God's being able to see and know what their lives on earth are, they would many times, think before they do some things which they do, supposing that no one but themselves know of them.

I am very glad that the Professor wrote to you on this subject to night, for it is one that is very important in our plan of revealing the truths of God and His attributes.

Very soon I will write you another message, and one that will be very important to mankind.

I will come again soon, and tell you of some things that you must learn.

So with all my love and blessings, I am, Your own brother and friend,

JESUS.

Adds his testimony to the Professor as to "Who and what is God"
God has personality.

I am here, *St. Luke.*

I want to add my testimony to that of Professor Salyards as to *"who and what is God."* Of course, since the Master has substantiated what the Professor wrote and enlarged on it, my testimony is not necessary, yet, I desire to say a few words which are expressive of my knowledge arising from my own experience.

I have a soul development which is greater than that of the Professor, and a perception which is clearer and more convincing than his, and yet, what he has said is all that I can say as to the truth of the personality of God, except that to me it is undoubtedly much clearer and of longer acquaintance.

I know that God is a being that has personality, though not a form like unto man, but has all the attributes that have been mentioned. These attributes are not God, but merely qualities which he possesses, and which in their workings upon the hearts and souls of men emanate and flow from Him. You may better understand this if I call your attention to the fact that while you can see and feel and hear and love and dislike, yet these attributes or qualities are not you, but only those things that belong to your personality. You may be deprived of any or all of them, and yet you may not cease to exist as a personality. And so with God; while these things of love and wisdom, and loving and hearing do not constitute God, yet they are a part of Him and are exercised by Him, just as the qualities I have mentioned are exercised by you.

179

I know it is difficult for the mere mind to comprehend this great truth of God having a personality, yet it is a truth, and just as real to the perceptions of the developed soul as is the existence of yours or any man's personality to the finite mind.

And here is another fact in connection with this great truth, and that is that only the spirits who have experienced the New Birth and become filled with the Divine Love of the Father, and hence a partaker of His Divinity, will ever be able to perceive this great truth of the personality of God. No other spirit will ever receive that soul development which is absolutely necessary for it to possess in order to perceive the great truth under discussion.

Yet the mere fact that these other spirits do not comprehend or understand this truth, does not make it any the less a truth, and all men and spirits are subject to its operations and must come under the benefits that they may receive by reason of the workings of this truth upon their lives and thoughts.

Just because men cannot see God it does not follow that He does not see them, for He does; and their every thought is known to Him and taken account of. And strange as it may seem to you, or as I should more appropriately say, surprising as it may seem to you, that account is kept in the memories and consciences of men themselves, and when the time comes for them to render an account of their acts and thoughts, no other place or receptacle is sought for or examined to find this account than these very memories and consciences; and nothing can be hidden or lost, until it has fulfilled the purpose of its existence.

Men may create, but they cannot destroy—I refer now to their actions and their thoughts. While on earth they may forget and ease their consciences by forgetting, yet, when they come to the spirit world, and are called to render an account, the inexorable laws that are really their judges and executioners show them that there is no such thing as forgetting— and has been said, they have forgotten to forget.

God is being, self-existing, unchangeable, but full of love and mercy. and these He does not exercise in any individual case, but has made certain that His laws of mercy will so operate that all the spirits of men and mortals also, may by their own acts and desires place themselves in such condition of soul, that these spirits will receive the benefit of this mercy. Yes, His mercy is from the beginning waiting for all men to ask for it and want it, just as is His love.

I could write on this subject for a longer time, but I must not write more to night as you are tired, so I will close.

With all my love and blessings, I am Your brother in Christ,

St. Luke.

180

That God can see and hear and know what the thoughts of men are.

I am here, *St. Stephen.*

I want to say only a word.

At the time of my martyrdom I saw the heavens opened and the spirits of the just made perfect, so now I can by my soul perceptions see my God as a real personal being, full of love and mercy.

Let no man rest in the assurance that God is only a, formless spirit, without the attributes of seeing and hearing and knowing what the thoughts and deeds of men and spirits are, for if he does, in the time of accounting, he will be deceived in his false security.

I am in a condition of soul development to know the great truth that God is a God of real personality, and when I say this I don't mean individuality in the sense that you are an individual. But what I mean by personality is that all these attributes of love and power and knowledge and mercy do not constitute God, but are merely a part of His being and flow from Him in their operations upon men, and in fact upon all the things of the universe.

I will not enlarge upon this truth, as it has been explained by those who preceded me, but I will say this, that because a man with a finite mind cannot understand this truth, it by no means follows that it is not a truth, for it is, and in the great future every man who has received the necessary soul development will learn and know this truth.

I will not write more to night, but will say to you continue to seek this great development of your soul, and you will not be disappointed in coming to the realization that God is our Father of the Master, the close personal and loving Father.

With all my love I will say good night, Your brother in Christ,

ST. STEPHEN.

Preacher gives his beliefs; denies the trinity.

I am here. *Colyer.*

I was a preacher. I am now a preacher and my doctrines are those of Christ stripped of the creeds and dogmas of the churches.

I was not an orthodox preacher, but was one who believed in God and in Jesus as the best and most spiritual man that ever lived on earth, and who taught the truths of his Father.

I am of the same belief still, and I have since being in the spirit world learned many things to confirm my belief. The orthodox doctrine as to his being God or one of three Gods is a pernicious one and against all reason and truth. He is just who he said he was—the son of God and the son of man—the first in a spiritual sense and the latter in the material or natural sense.

He never, as he has told me, claimed to be God, and his disciples never undertood that he was such. The freedom of men's minds from this doctrine of his being God, will do more to bring men to the truth and to believe in religious truths than can be conceived of. When his true mission on earth shall become understood, men will turn to the true worship of God, and to a belief in the teachings of the Master, which will result in many a one being saved from their sins, and in happiness and harmony and brotherly love being more firmly established on earth.

I am a believer in the Divine Love and the New Birth and am an inhabitant of the seventh sphere, and am trying to progress to the Celestial Spheres.

I will not write more tonight as you are tired, but will come again sometime.

So with all my love as a brother in Christ, I am

ROBÉRT COLYER.

Denies the Vicarious Atonement. Spirit communion was more prevalent in the days of St. John than now. If men would have faith like the Apostles of Jesus, healing and so-called miracles would exist today.

I am here, John.

I do not write St. John, because I am not called by that name in the spirit heavens, and I have written you often enough now, that you will identify me when I merely write John.

Well, I heard what the Master said, and I can only add thereto, that I never wrote the things which declare that I preached that the blood of Jesus saves from sin or that Jesus was a propitiation for the sins of mankind. Neither in my Gospel nor in my Epistles nor in Revelation did I write such a doctrine. As I have told you before many things contained in these books were written by others to carry out certain plans and ideas of the writers. I never said that Jesus was God and that he was begotten by the Holy Ghost, or that he is equal with God, or that he saved a man from sin by reason of any personal qualities which he may have had.

So let your mind eliminate these false doctrines and receive the truths which the Master shall write with a perfectly unbiased mind, free from all preconceived ideas.

(Answer to question by Mr. Padgett follows:)

I meant that many spirits would try to communicate with man and attempt to teach false doctrines as to Jesus and his mission.

That the only spirits who were capable of conveying the truth, and worthy of belief were those who should acknowledge that Jesus was the son of God in the way that it has been explained to you. Not that Jesus or Jesus Christ was God. Only those spirits who acknowledge Jesus as the Son of God and have received the New Birth, and know anything about the kingdom of Christ, or of the gift of the Divine Love of the Father, and the way to obtain it, as taught by Jesus, should be

182

acknowledged. All other spirits who have not this knowledge, and consequently would not acknowledge Jesus as the son of God, who should hear his teachings, is not to be trusted as being true followers of Jesus.

This is nothing mysterious or contrary to the laws governing the conduct or beliefs of men. If a spirit or man either, knows nothing about a certain subject he certainly cannot teach others its qualities or merits, and, hence, I was applying an ordinary law of nature to the way in which spirits should be tried. For I must tell you now, and it is a truth, and was a truth at the time I wrote my gospel and epistles, just as it is a truth now, and always will remain a truth, that every spirit who acknowledges that Jesus is the son of God is a redeemed spirit, and has received a portion of the Divine Love, and is progressing in the kingdom which Jesus is now forming. And when I gave those instructions to my children, as I called them, I intended that their communications should be only with those spirits or men who had received this New Birth.

I know that all the spirits who have received this Divine Love in sufficient abundance are good spirits, free from sin and error and the power or inclination to influence mortals not to sin or to do anything which is contrary to the will of the Father, while all the other spirits may or may not exercise upon mortals the influence of evil.

Hence, try the spirits, and if they do not acknowledge Jesus as the son of God, let them alone, and do not receive their communications or teachings, because they are not believers in Christ and the New Birth.

Among my children or believers in the Christian religion were many persons who had the power or gift of communicating with the spirits of the departed, and did so communicate; and such communications were made known to the rest of the congregation and believed by them. And hence, my injunction against communion with those spirits who were not believers in Christ.

You must not think that this is the only age in which spirits communicate with mortals, for I must tell you that in my time it was much more common than now; and in our congregations when worshipping and when in our other gatherings, and often in private, we had these communications.

This was an important part of the services of our meetings, and one that kept us in constant harmony with the soul power of those who lived in the spirit form, and from whom we received powers of healing and of doing good in many other ways.

In those days healing the sick and doing kindred things were a very important part of our work as Christians. We believed what Jesus had told us on earth, and we increased our faith and performed many works, which the people who did not believe as we did, thought were miracles.

To us the healing of the sick and the doing of these other things were just as natural as eating and sleeping. I tell you that our faith then was a certainty. We possessed the Substance that Paul speaks of, and we expected to do the things just as we expected to breathe and be able to do material good to our brothers.

But after a few centuries, when men came into the church for other purposes than to receive the New Birth and do the will of the Father, faith, such as I speak of, died, and the power to do these things was taken away from men, and the church became a congregation of men having the mere lip worship.

And all through the centuries from then until now, this power has not been with men, except that here and there some true believer with a faith such as we had has appeared, and done wonderful things.

So I say, let not what the Bible may say about Jesus being God and having those other qualities with reference to the salvation of men, disturb you in your beliefs in what the Master may write you.

I will not write more tonight, but will say good-night.

Your brother in Christ,

John.

The Kingdom will be completed, and the door of the Heavenly Kingdom closed.

From *St. John.* (Apostle of Jesus)

We are Celestial Spirits of the highest order, but that fact does not prevent us from realizing the necessity for the salvation of man, and even though we have to come to earth to bring about this salvation in work and association with the spirits of the earth plane, yet it is a labor of love, and humility is the touchstone that brings to us happiness in our work.

No, we are with you often and in close association, and we would not be fellow workers with the Master, if for one moment we should have the feeling that, because of our high estate we should not come in rapport and helpful association with sinful mortals, and so long as the Father requires His great truths to be taught and men's souls saved from the effect of the great fall, and made angels of Divinity, our work will continue. But sometime after the Celestial Kingdom is closed, our work on earth, as well as in the spirit spheres will cease, and then our homes in the Celestial Spheres will be our only places of labor and love.

The kingdom will be completed—the door of the Heavenly Kingdom closed, and the angelic hosts become separated from the spiritual or perfect man. Such is the decree.

And as the Father desires all men to become at-one with Him in His Divinity of Love, we must work until the great day of the consummation of the Kingdom arrives, and spirits who have not on the wedding garments shall suffer the doom of the * second death.

* Second death. The loss and death of the privilege of obtaining the Divine Love that is necessary for souls to obtain before the Celestial Kingdom is closed.

And when Jesus said, "Work while it is day, for the night cometh when no man can work," he meant that while the Kingdom is open for men to enter we must work, for when its doors shall be closed the work of the angelic laborer must cease, and men and spirits be left to an eternity in the spiritual spheres.

And so we work, and so must you work until the time of separation, and as the Master said, the wheat and the tares must be permitted to grow together until the great time of the harvesting shall take place.

But until then we must mingle and work and pray without ceasing.

Your brother in Christ,

JOHN.

Divine Love is ever waiting to fill the soul, and will, when the soul longings become real for its possession.

I am here. *St. John.* (Apostle of Jesus)

I heard your prayer and know that this Love is flowing into your soul and that now you have a great abundance of its possession of which you are conscious. It will never fail you when you pray in earnestness and with the real longings for its coming. It is always ready to respond to your aspirations and to make you feel its presence and the happiness that comes with it.

I, as you know, am your special friend in my work of helping to develop your soul, and whenever you pray to the Father, as you have just prayed, I come to you with my love and influence to help open up your soul to the inflowing of this Love. Have faith, and you will have the certainty of the presence of the Love, and that it is yours—seeking to come into your soul in greater and more abundance.

You are blessed in that you have the knowledge of the existence of this Love, and that it may be yours if you so will it to be, and pray with the true longings of your soul's desires. You cannot doubt the truth of what I write, for, as in the ordinary things of life, there is nothing so convincing as personal experience, and your experience is such that there has been no room for doubt. So if you would keep the consciousness of the presence of this Love continually alive, pray and pray whenever the opportunity presents itself, and by this I don't mean that you shall wait for a time when you are not engaged in your business affairs, but at moments when the mind may be free, even if only for a moment, from these business affairs. The longings, if exercised only for a moment, will bring their results; for God's ear is always open and ready to cause the responses to such longings.

One moment of true soul felt longings is more effective than hours of prayer where these longings are not present. The prayers of the lip or of habit arises no higher than the escaping breath, and does not cause the Love to respond and flow into the soul. Remember this,

185

and then realize how futile are all the prayers of preachers and ostensible worshipers when the soul's longings and desires are not present.

Only soul can call to soul, and love responds only when such soul calls. The mere desires of the mind, if I may so express my meaning, do not in the least affect the soul, and as mind can operate only on mind, there cannot possibly be any activity of the soul's faculties, when only mind is in operation. Hence, you will see, that all the worship that comes merely from the mind will not effectuate the working of the Love or bring into operation the Spirit's work.

I write this to further encourage you, and also to make plain the necessity for the true prayer.

JOHN.

Jesus sayss "Those who worship him as they do in the churches commit blasphemy."

I am here—*Jesus.*

I was with you at the church this morning, and I impressed you with my feelings in reference to what the preacher said as to my sacrifice and blood and instead of calling upon his people to show their gratitude for the sacrifice and the cross, he should have taught them that the sacrifice and the blood do not save them from their sins, and in that particular there is nothing that calls for their gratitude; and that to worship me as they do, and as he teaches them to do, is blasphemy, and a more heinous sin than ingratitude.

I was successful in impressing you with my feelings of dissatisfaction and was glad that I could, for it shows that our rapport is becoming closer, and after awhile you will be able to receive my thoughts and inspiration as well as my writings.

You must pray and have faith, and if you do you will more often have the experiences that you did last night; which only means a quicker soul development.

Trust me and you will not be disappointed.

I will not write more now.

So with my love and the Father's blessings, I will say good-night.

Your brother & friend,

JESUS.

I am here—Your own true and loving *Helen.*

Well dear, I see that you do not feel like writing much tonight, and I will say only a few words.

The Master was anxious to finish his message, but he saw your condition and was not displeased that you did not write.

So sweetheart, keep up your courage and faith and pray, and you will be happier and realize your desires.

Goodnight, my own dear husband.

Your own true loving,

HELEN.

186

Lazarus says he was not dead when he was raised by Jesus.
Confirms that Jesus writes through Mr. Padgett.

I AM HERE. *Lazarus.*

I was the one whom Jesus called from the grave. I merely want to say that I was not dead when I was resurrected but had on me the sleep of death. But I was not entirely a spirit separated from my body. I know this, because if I had been a wholly separated spirit, Jesus could not have brought me to life again. No spirit, once entirely liberated from the body, can ever return to it and reanimate the body. I know the Bible says or the inference from what it says, is that I was dead, but this is not true as I have above stated.

I am now in the Celestial Heavens in a sphere that is not numbered, but very near those in which the disciples live.

My sisters are also in the Celestial Heavens. We all believed in the teachings of the Master, and consequently became imbued with his doctrine of the necessity for the Divine Love to come into our souls.

While on earth Jesus did teach us that God had again bestowed on man this Divine Love and we believed it. I know that the disciples were taught this same doctrine, but just how far they understood this teaching I do not know. It is strange and they did not declare it in their Gospels, but such seems to be the fact, and it is unaccountable why this important truth was not preserved and taught in their writings. I know that it is the truth and that only those who have received this Love in their hearts can become inhabitants of the Celestial Heavens. Men may refuse to believe this Great Truth if they will, and think that by attending church and worshipping God in their service with their lips, they will be able to enter the Kingdom but they will find themselves mistaken.

So in your teachings, let this great truth be the corner stone of whatever you may teach.

I am supremely happy and want all mankind to be so.

I came to you to inform you of these truths so that my testimony may be added to that of those who may have written to you.

Jesus is in the spiritual world working to teach men and spirits his truths. He comes to you and writes and you must believe the fact for it is a fact.

I must stop now, so I will say Good night.   LAZARUS.

Jesus says his blood does not save men. Only the Divine Love
or New Birth that he taught, saves and redeems.

I AM HERE. *Jesus.*

I heard the discussion between you and the other man about my blood saving from sin, and I felt that you were not benefited by what was said, because his faith is based on ignorance of the true plan of salvation and my mission on earth.

But he is so firmly fixed in his belief that no argument that you might make would convince him that anything but my death and atonement could save from sin. So I do not think it would do any good to attempt to argue with any of these people in reference to the matter of my blood as the means of salvation.

They have received the Divine Love to a considerable degree and the Holy Spirit is with them in their worship and is in their hearts, but it does not come to them by reason of their belief in my atonement, but because they pray to the Father for its coming and making them a new being so far as their soul development is concerned. They do not know that only the flowing of this Divine Love into their hearts in answer to prayer is what gives them this New Birth.

They think that my blood has something, or rather that it is the great and only cause of this New Birth and they will continue to think so. I would not let this matter deter you from attending their meetings because, as I have said, the spirit is present with them. Of course they will learn differently when they come to the spirit world and see that I am not God.

Yes, I know that is what all the orthodox believe but that does not make it a fact, for no devil ever comes and teaches the things that I have written you.

I will not write more now.

So with the assurance that I am with you very often, and that I will guide you in the ways of truth, I will stop.

Your brother and friend,   JESUS.

Divine Love casteth out all fear.

I am here. *St. Andrew.*

I came to tell you that where love is there can be no sin or unhappiness, and fear is not.

We, who live in the Celestial Spheres, know this to be a fact, and with all the force and authority that knowledge gives, we declare this truth unto you tonight, the love that casteth out all fear is the Divine Love of the Father, and when a spirit obtains that, there exists no such thing as fear, and nothing that could create or permit fear to exist.

God wants the souls of men in love and not in fear and the only way in which such end can be accomplished is for men to see and know Him as God of love only. No man can come to the Father except through this New Birth and faith in the Father's love.

The performance of duty, good works and mere faith, while they will all help man in the development of his moral character and qualities, yet they will not give him an entrance into the Celestial Heavens which are the heavens where Jesus rules and is the Prince, unless the spirit shall obtain this Divine Love which makes it a part of the Father's very essence of Divinity.

Many spirits are happy by reason of their having led good, moral lives on earth and because of a high development of their natural love, and realize that God is their Father, and watches over them and gives them many blessings; but this happiness is not that which comes with the possession of the Divine Love, and besides the place of habitation of these spirits is limited and does not permit these spirits to have free access to all the spheres where God's goodness and care are manifested.

The spirits who have obtained this Divine Love have no limitation to the spheres in which they may progress, and are not restricted in their places of habitation or in the spheres in which they may live. And besides the presence and glory of the Father are so much greater in these Celestial Spheres than in those where the mere natural love obtains.

I must not write more tonight, for you are commencing to tire.

So with all my love I will say, Your brother in Christ,

ST. ANDREW.

Denies the efficacy of the vicarious atonement. God was never a God of wrath but always of Love.

I am here, *St. Paul, the Apostle.*

I merely want to write about the truth of the New Birth, because I speak, or rather it is written, that the blood of Jesus saves men from condemnation, and sin and death.

This is not true, and I never wrote such declarations of what purports to be true. Jesus did not save men by his death or sacrifice, and as I am informed now, and learned when on earth, he never claimed that his blood or sacrifice saved men. And I hardly see how that could be so, because the blood did not have any efficacy to affect the condition or spiritual development of men, and his death could not help men to become redeemed from any condition of evil or defilement that they might be in, and, hence, there can be no possible connection between his blood or sacrifice and the condition of men, whether good or bad.

I know that it is claimed that the blood of Jesus tended to appease the wrath of God towards men as did his death, but this presupposes that God had a wrath against men and that only blood and death could satisfy it. What a barbarous assumption!

God was never a God of wrath, but always of Love, and men can come to Him in reconciliation through Love only, and not through any sacrifice. Jesus never taught this doctrine of sacrifice and does not now, but repudiates it and says that it is a doctrine that is doing his cause and the salvation of mankind a great harm.

If men will only think for a moment, they will see that the only relation between God and man is that which arises from the soul's con-

189

dition. God, as I said, is Love, and for man to be at-one with him man must become love; I mean that his soul must be filled or permeated with this Love to such an extent, that it will become impossible for anything that is not of love to be or remain a part of his soul.

I do not mean that it is necessary for men to obtain this Divine Love in order to live and enjoy a happiness which is far above the happiness that they have on earth for that would not be true. God has given to man a natural love, which, when enjoyed in all its intended purity, is sufficient of itself to make men comparatively happy; but this love does not make man a part of God's oneness, or enable him to partake of the Divine Essence of the Father. And this oneness is absolutely necessary for men to become reconciled to God as Jesus taught.

So, while the large majority of men may never become reconciled in the sense that I have mentioned, yet they will be able to enjoy this inferior happiness in the spirit world, and to such a degree that no sin or evil will be permitted to mar it.

A small minority will become reconciled to God and enjoy the superior happiness which such reconciliation will bring to them. They will be in their nature and substance like the Father, having his Divine Essence and partaking of His immortality.

But this reconciliation can only be obtained by what is called the New Birth, which comes to men not by reason of any power or effort on their part only, but by the operations of the workings of the Holy Ghost, the instrument of God in bringing about this New Birth.

And yet man has his part to perform also, in this great renewal of his spiritual being. He must open his soul to the inflowing of this Divine Love, and must pray to the Father for the inflowing of the Holy Ghost, and with his prayers, must believe that the Father is waiting to bestow it.

Without the desire on the part of man to receive this Divine Love, with prayer and faith, it will not come to him, for God never forces any human soul to a New Birth against its will.

I tell you this, because in my opinion this is the one great important truth of the mission of Jesus on earth, and the one that human beings should understand and try to comply with.

I know now, as I never knew on earth, the full meaning of this truth, and I thank God all the time for His goodness and mercy.

Only those who receive this New Birth become divine angels, all other spirits remain mere spirits and subject to all the changes and conditions that belong to spirits; for there is nothing fixed as to those who may remain mere spirits any more than there was in the case of the first man and woman. We know now that changes may take place in the conditions of these spirits during the workings of God's plans.

Many men may, even when they know of the things that I have written, be content to remain mere spirits and live their spiritual lives in the happiness which their natural love gives them, but it seems to me that all men, if they will think a little and understandingly, will seek for the greater Love and happiness and immortality.

I wanted to write this tonight, for I see that some of the teachings of my Epistles may tend to lead men astray on this most important question as to what saves them from their sins and reconciles them to God.

I will not write more to night, but will come at times and write you in regard to the various spiritual truths of this Kingdom

I will say good night.

Your brother in Christ,   **PAUL.**

Mrs. Eddy did not know the truth that has been revealed in the messages that Padgett has received

Let me write a line, for I have been interested in the conversation of the Doctor and want to express to him my thanks for his efforts to enlighten one of my followers as to the truth; and my obligation is based on the fact that I recognize the misleading errors of some of my teachings, and that I am responsible for the beliefs of many mortals that are not true and have the effect of keeping them from the truth; and further, that whenever any of those who have embraced the beliefs that I taught are shown the light and directed to the errors of my teachings, I am to that extent happier and relieved from the burdens which I carry with me that my teachings are keeping so many from the truth. In all this I refer to the great question of the Divine Love and the way in which mortals may obtain the same and become in harmony with the Father, and partake of His divine nature and immortality.

I have examined these truths since I came to the spirit world, and realize with a great conviction that the reflection of the Divine Love is not the possession of that mind which comes only with the possession of the Love of the Father.

I wish that I had time tonight to write you a longer letter on this subject, but your guide says that you are not in condition to receive a lengthy letter and I must stop.

Let me express the hope that you and your friend, whenever the opportunity occurs, will attempt to enlighten my followers as to the truths which you know, and as to errors and the want of the true explanation of a salvation which my books do not contain.

With my love I wil say good night.   **MRS. EDDY.**

I am here—Your own true and loving *Helen.*

Well dear, I have been with you all evening and enjoyed your conversation. You may believe that the last communication was from Mrs. Eddy, for she actually wrote and was glad that she could do so, and because she carries the burden of which she wrote, we permitted her to write.

She realizes that, although she has a great amount of the Divine Love, yet the knowledge that she believed and taught others to believe the errors of her writings causes her much unhappiness in the way of possessing a great desire to undo or neutralize the effect of what she taught.

Love me and pray to the Father.

Good night.

Your own true and loving   HELEN.

Some of the errors and deficiencies of some teachers.
Errors of Christian Science

I am here. *Jesus*

I come today to tell you that I am pleased with you in your efforts to find the truth of what we have taught as to God and of the relation of man to Him.

I have been with you in your reading of several days past, and have observed the effect upon you of the contrast between the beliefs and teachings of men as you have read them and the teachings of truth that we have revealed to you in our messages.

While these writings that you have been reading have in them some things of truth, yet there are many things that are wholly untrue, and the mere results of speculation.

Today, if you feel in condition, I will instruct you as to some of the errors and deficiencies of Christian Science, and the want of the true comprehension of its founder of the realities of being.

She writes and teaches that there is nothing real in sin and error and disease, and that their apparent existence is wholly due to the mortal mind, and that when this mind denies the existence of these things, they will no longer exist. Well, in this assertion there is a large grain of truth, but in order to understand and apply this truth more than a mere denial of their existence must be taught and believed by man.

It is true that God never created anything of evil or that which is not in harmony with His nature and essence, which are only good, and that to ascribe the existence of these evils and discords to God, is erroneous and blasphemous. But the fact remains that these things exist, and the mere denial of their existence does not remedy the harmful results that flow from such existence.

Man suffers from evil and error and disease and has always so suffered since the fall from his state of perfection, and always will suffer in consequence of there being in his consciousness these things of reality, and the mere calling them the result of "Mortal mind," will not explain their existence or furnish a remedy by which they may be gotten rid of.

First arises the necessity of understanding how, and by what means these things came into existence, and then it will become easier for the understanding of the means and the way by which they may be eliminated from the life and apparent nature of mankind.

As I have already told you, these things, foreign to God's creation, were created by man alone in the excessive and unlawful exercise of his will power in following out the suggestions and desires of his animal appetites, which unduly asserted themselves when man lost a part of his spirituality by his disobedience.

Their creation was the result of something more than what the founder, of that Science calls the "mortal mind", for the mind is only a part of man's being; and while the faculties of the mind must be used in the operation of all the powers and qualities of man, yet the mind is not the originator of all his desires, and appetites and emotions. The emotional nature and affections are distinct from the mere mind, or the intellectual faculties, and as regards sin and error, are generally the creators of the same, although the mind may and does foster and increase these things so created.

Then man must understand that these excrescences to his perfect creation are real and existing, and result in his own damnation and alienation from the good—and are antagonistic to his original and natural condition of perfection, and that they cannot be swept out of existence by the mere assertion that they are not real.

Again man must understand that they are the creatures primarily of the inordinate exercise of the animal appetites and desires, and not of the exercise of the mind, and to be eradicated by the same process in reverse order as was used in their creation.

Of course, it must not be lost sight of that in using this process the faculties of the mind must be brought into operation just as they were in the creation of these existences. And the great fact to be remembered in this process is that these things are real, and not things of the mere imagination which is the equivalent of the founder's "mortal mind".

Now, when man grasps the meaning, as thus explained, of what these things really are, and how they came into being, then he will the more readily comprehend the way or the means by which they are to be destroyed and never again permitted to become a part of his being; for while they do not by nature belong to his being, yet by reason of his being the creator of them, they are, so far as his consciousness is concerned, together with all the results flowing therefrom, a part of his being, and that part which keeps him in discord with the laws controlling his own existence. The purity of his true being is always besmirched by the impurities of his own artificial being, and always will be until he eliminates these impurities which as to him and to his fellow man are real, persistent existences.

The will, however, is the great force that must be used in the destruction of these excrescences, and as this will power in man is free and untrammeled, and in its operations follows the suggestions and desires of the appetites, both animal and spiritual, of man, it therefore becomes apparent that these appetites and desires must first be controlled and directed in that direction that will cause the will to be exercised in such a manner as to lead the thoughts and deeds towards the realization of the desires and appetites in harmony with God's laws.

As sin and evil are not the creatures of the spiritual desires, but wholly of the animal, then to eradicate from man's being these things of evil and sin, the efforts of man must be directed towards the supplanting of the unlawful and inharmonious animal desires and appetites, by appetites and desires arising from the same source that is in harmony with the laws creating this very source.

Man was created by God with animal appetites just as he was created with spiritual aspirations, and the one is just as harmonious with the laws of his creation as the other, and the loss of the spiritual aspiration, or the perversion of the animal appetites, similarly causes man to become out of harmony with these laws. So that man in order to become free from these foreign parts of his being, must strive, not by a denial of their reality, but by the effort to supplant them, to recreate, as it were, in himself the animal appetites that are consistent and in harmony with those which were his when he was made the perfect man. In other words, to destroy the beings of his own creation, and possess only those of the creation of God.

Of course, in this effort, he will have to use his mind, mortal or otherwise, but in addition, he will also have to exercise the faculties of his emotional and affectional nature, which are not of the mind but the soul. Mere negation or belief will not be sufficient, but desires and cravings for these things which engender sin must be supplanted by desires and craving for those things which are in harmony with his creation.

So, I repeat, the teachings that sin and error and disease are not real, and are no part of man's being, as he now exists and lives, is erroneous and when not understood, harmful, and not sufficient to bring about the regeneration of man.

In one sense it is true that sin and error and disease are not real, but that means that so far as God's creation of man is concerned they have no existence, for He created only that which was good and in harmony with His perfect laws. But as man is a creator as well as a creature, and as these things are the creatures of man alone, then so far as the being of man is involved, they have a reality which will persist until their creator man has destroyed them.

194

I am pleased that you gave me the opportunity to write today, and am also glad to find you in good condition.

Your friend and brother,   JESUS

God and His personality.

A preacher at a Protestant church attempted to describe God, and said He is the all enfolding energy with a purposeful will, existing everywhere—that He is a Spirit.

I am here. *Jesus.*

Let me write a few lines.

I see that you were much interested in what the preacher said tonight about God and His personality, and that you gave him several questions which he could not answer. This must be expected, for to men is not given ordinarily a true conception of God, or Who or what He is, and only by the development of their souls by the Divine Love can they obtain any conception of His being. As their souls thus develop they become a part of His Divinity, and their soul perceptions become opened up to a realization of who God is, to a small degree at least, and then they know that He is something more than an all enveloping energy, supplemented by a purposeful will.

The preacher has not these soul perceptions and cannot conceive of God, the Soul, but can only express to you the truthfulness of the evidences of God's existence, such as the energy that he spoke of.

As you know, this energy is His Spirit, although the preacher has not the exact conception of what this Spirit is or how it operates. He confuses the soul and spirit, and makes the mere instrument by or with which God expresses His energy, to be the real true substance of God, the Soul. He is right when he says that he cannot go back of this energy to find God, for his soul perceptions have not yet been awakened to a cognition of that from which the energy proceeds, or which is the very source from which flows all the manifestations, that to his mind constitute God. He is like the theologians and philosophers, who believe that these manifestations and energies and forces are the only God, the only personal God; and he may be shocked to hear that his teachings amount to only this. But it is true, and to him there is no more personal God than to the others, with this exception; that he attempts to believe that in some manner and in some way connected with this energy, there is a will which has in it a purpose of love or kindness or fatherly care; but the real personal God, with his Great Soul of Love which is being always bestowed upon the individual man, he does not conceive of or make his own.

God is Soul, and only Soul, which has in it all the attributes of love and wisdom and thought for the welfare of His creatures. He is a thinking

195

and seeing God, and all the energies of His Soul are used to make men better and happier. As is the natural father of the man a personal father, so is the Great Soul of God, a Personal Father to all his children; and men when they have the development of their souls in the Divine Love will know that God is personal—something more than an all enveloping energy or force or mere manifestation of His existence.

The preacher says, in substance, that God is everywhere, and His presence may be realized by all who are willing to receive that manifestation, and that whether they are or not willing, that presence exists just the same. This is pantheism, toned down a little by his beliefs in a more personal God, but still pantheism, and wholly wrong and violative of God's being.

The source of things can never be the things themselves, although the things as they flow from the source have some of the qualities of the source itself, and so these manifestations of God's existence, while they are of His qualities, yet they are not equivalent of His presence or the source from which they flow. God is not everywhere, but in His Heavens, and all these expressions of His powers and will and energies are merely evidences that there is a source from which they all come, and they are not that source itself.

And again, the preacher said that God created the body of man and not the spirit, as he calls it, meaning the soul, so that the body is a creation by itself and cannot contain in it the spirit or the spirit body, but that this spirit is outside of the human body, and is in a general way a part of one Great Spirit that is universal and everywhere and that, therefore, all men, no matter what their conditions may be in the earth life or in the eternity part of life are brothers and God is the Father of them all. Well in this the preacher is mistaken, for every man has his own individual spirit, soul, and on the state or condition of that soul depends the happiness or misery of the man, and he is merely the brother of other men, because he is a creature of God and made in his image, and not because he is a part of the universal spirit, which the preacher believes permeates everything and exists everywhere. And God is the Father, because these children are His creatures, the objects of His creation, and individualized, each working out his own destiny. As we have told you some of these children will always remain the merely created children, while others will partake of His Divine Love, and become a part of His divinity, and inhabitants of the Celestial Spheres.

The preacher has many things to learn, and as he believes in the search for the truth, if he will let the Divine Love flow into his heart, and transform his soul into the very essence and substance of the Father's divinity, he will be able to learn many things spiritual as well as of things material are governed by law, and unless the soul gets into a condition that enables it to see and realize the higher truths of the spirit world, it can never obtain knowledge of things spiritual, and one of the objects of such knowledge is God.

Well, I have written enough and will stop.

With my love, I will say, good night.

Your brother and friend,   JESUS.

Comments on the discourse of the preacher on God by Jesus

Let me say a few words tonight.

I was with you again at the services and listened to the preacher as he expounded the truth of God and the truth of man as he conceived these truths to be, and I am compelled to say that if his future state of happiness depended upon these supposed truths he would be a very unhappy spirit in one of the million heavens of which he spoke.

I am sorry that men can conceive of such notions of God and man, and teach them to other mortals. But so it will be for many years, and until my teachings, through you, are accepted and believed by men, great darkness and error will prevail in the earth.

It is hardly necessary for me to attempt to analyze many of his erroneous statements, for they are so many and so erroneous that it will take too long a message to review them all.

But I will say one thing, and that is, that when he attempted to show that God's energy and man's energy are one and the same, he was all wrong, and knew not what he said. God is a being who is infinite and omnipotent and as to his energies there is no limits, while man is a mere creature of God, and cannot possibly have any greater or other energy than he was created with; and this energy is controlled by the soul that is man, and is subject to all the limitations of that soul.

Well, I will not write more tonight, but hope ere long to write you one of my messages of truth.

I see that you have been somewhat in doubt as to the reality of the truths of the messages that you have received, and as to the power of the Divine Love to make you a child of God, in the sense divine. You must not let such doubts enter your soul for one moment, for they are the breeders of other things that are most harmful and tend to alienate you from the Father. As you are aware, God's love is all around you, and may be in you, and if permitted to flow into your soul, with faith accompanying it, you will find yourself growing in at-one-ment with the Father, and realize that fact. So my brother get rid of your doubts and come to God in the faith that is childlike and dependent. He will not disappoint you. I will be with you, and try to help you in your desires.

Pray more to the Father, and believe that His love is yours; only for the longing and seeking.

I will not write more tonight.

Rest assured that my love is with you in all its fulness, and believe that you have a work to do.

Good night.

JESUS.

Spirit comments on the preacher's discourse.

Let me say a word, as I was also present at the meeting tonight, and listened to the preacher as he unfolded what he thought to be the truth of God and man.

Well, I will not stop to discuss many of the errors of his teachings or the workings of his mind, but only say, that if God is as he considers him to be, he would not be the God, which we know to exist and who loves us and whom we can call Father. The all enfolding energy is not the God of love and mercy, and the preacher cannot possibly find in such a God, the Father that is calling for and caring for his children.

I merely wanted to say this.

I am an inhabitant of the Celestial Kingdom, and will say good night.

THOMAS B. MUNROE.

Comments on the preacher's sermon on what he thinks God is.

I am here—Your own true and loving *Helen.*

Well dear, I see that you are not very much enlightened by the preacher's discourse tonight, and I do not see why you should be, for he has no true conception of either God or man, and gave no help to those who are searching for the true God, the Father.

I see that you may feel that you are benefited though by the negative lesson that his discourse teaches. He tells of what he thinks God is, and in telling this, demonstrates that he knows nothing of the true God. You may hear the full course of his lectures and you will not learn much that will benefit you in an affirmative way. But attend the same, and then meditate upon them, and you will find that you have listened to a man who knows nothing of God or the spiritual world of which he pretends to speak.

We all love you and want you to love us.

Good night.

Your own true and loving

HELEN.

Did not understand the plan of man's salvation when on earth.

I am, *Campbell.*

I am the founder of the Campbellites. Well, I have spelled it as it should be spelled. I know my followers are called Camellites, but that is not correct.

198

But the name makes no difference, for I am the man, and these people are my followers.

I merely want to say that when on earth I did not understand the plan of man's salvation, and I taught erroneous doctrines as to this matter, and I now see the great harm that I did, but, nevertheless, there was some good done also; for my people worshiped God as their Heavenly Father, and prayed to Him, and many of them received the ministration of the Holy Ghost. So I am grateful for what I taught, and also very sorry for the errors that I taught.

I am now in the Celestial Heavens and know that Jesus is a spirit and not God, and that his great work is still going on.

So when I say that I am a follower of Jesus, I mean that I follow his teachings and try to imitate his life here as on earth. I am a stranger to you but I felt that I must write to you, and so took this opportunity.

So thanking you I am, Your brother in Christ,

ALEXANDER CAMPBELL.

What men must do to see God and realize that He is a personal God, with all the attributes that belong only to a Supreme, Infinite Being.

Let me write. *Judas.*

I have not written you for a long time and feel that I must write you and declare some truth that is of importance to you and to mankind. I will not write a very long message, and what I have to say will be put in short sentences and made succinct. I know that you wonder who I am and what I will write about, and you must not be surprised if I tell you what you may think is not of much importance.

Well, my subject is, *"What is the best thing for men to do who desire to see God and realize that he is a personal God, with all the attributes that belong only to a Supreme, Infinite Being."*

God is a spirit and a person, and not a mere nebulous being without form or personality. He is real as to these qualities, and is not wanting that which will make him the Father that Jesus so often called him.

Now in order for a spirit to see and understand just what all this means, the spirit must get in that harmony with Him that will enable the spirit to possess qualities of soul that is like the qualities of the Father that the spirit desires to see and understand. This condition can be obtained only by the spirit pursuing the way that the Master so often writes you of, and which is absolutely necessary in order for the spirit to obtain the qualities necessary for such comprehension. Only as a soul is filled with the Love of the Father can it possibly be in the condition that will enable it to see and comprehend this per-

199

sonality of God. No mere development of the intellectual faculties or of the natural love will suffice for this purpose; and while such development is necessary in order for the spirit to become the perfect man in order to enjoy the condition that belongs to that man, yet such development is not sufficient to enable the spirit to see and comprehend the Father.

It is much easier for a spirit to get in the condition just mentioned than to get in the condition last described; and as you may see the wholly different thing that the development leads to, should be sufficient to induce the spirit to accept the Father's love, and become a true son of His.

I have written what I desired, and thank you for the opportunity and with my love will say good night.

JUDAS.

Jesus approving and emphasizing what Judas has written.

What Judas has written you I approve and emphasize, and with all my love for the mere man as for the spirit, urge them to pursue the way and attain to the great goal that the Divine Love will fit them for and lead them into.

I will not write more tonight, but will soon come and write you a long message.

Your brother and friend,   JESUS.

The importance of man cultivating the soul perceptions. Spiritual things cannot be perceived by the material mind.

I am here, *Jesus.*

I have heard your discussion and am much pleased that you and your friend are progressing so rapidly in the knowledge of truth, and very soon you both will be surprised at the extent of knowledge of spiritual things and truths that will come to you.

No man, who on earth is given to only what you may call the material things will be able, when he becomes a spirit, to understand the spiritual laws until he has gotten rid of the material mind and the reasoning that comes from the powers which have been exercised only in the investigation of material things.

You cannot perceive spiritual things with the material mind, neither can a man by reason of those powers of the mind which know only material things, be able to perceive the truths of the spirit. Hence the necessity for man cultivating the soul perceptions, which are greater and more comprehending than all the faculties of the material mind.

Mind, as usually understood by man, is undoubtedly a wonderful instrument in investigating and learning the laws of nature and the relation of cause and effect in the physical world, but such powers when applied to the things of the spirit, will not help much, but rather retard the progress of the soul's development of its faculties.

The reasoning power given to man is the highest quality of the material mind and, when properly exercised, affords a very safe and satisfactory method of arriving at the truth. But such power when exercised in reference to things which are strangers to it, or with which such powers having no acquaintance, or have never been concerned in the investigation of the phenomena of their existence, cannot be depended upon to bring conclusions that will assure men of truth.

Laws are eternal and never change and are made by the great Father to be applied to all the conditions and to all the relationships of the material world and of the spiritual world. But the laws that apply to the operations of the material world are not fitted to apply to the operations of the spiritual world; and the man who understands the former and their application to material things is not able to apply the laws applicable to the spiritual world to spiritual things. A knowledge of the laws pertaining to the natural will not supply a knowledge of the laws pertaining to the spiritual.

And hence the great scientist who, when on earth, was able to discover and show the operation of the laws controlling material things, when he comes to the spiritual world and attempts to apply this knowledge to the things of the spirit, will be wholly unable to do so, and will be as a babe in his ability to understand and draw deductions from the spiritual laws. So you see the necessity for man's becoming acquainted with these spiritual laws, if he expects to progress in things to which they apply.

The material laws may be learned from by the operation of the senses that belong to and constitute the material mind, but the spiritual laws can only be learned by the exercise and application of the faculties of the soul. The soul is to the spiritual things of God what the mind is to the material things of God. And the great mistake that men make and have made, is to attempt to learn these spiritual things with the powers of the material mind.

I write thus because I see that you and your friend desire to learn the nature and operations and workings of the spiritual things, and hence I want to impress upon you the necessity for exercising the soul perceptions which will come to you as your soul develops. These perceptions are just as real as are the five senses of the natural mind, though most men do not even know of their existence; and when once you have succeeded in understanding that they do exist and that you may be able to use them just as you use the faculties of the material mind, you will be able to progress in the development of these faculties or perceptions with as much success and certainty as does the great scientist or philosopher in the studies of the things to which he applies the faculties of his material mind.

I hope that I have made plain what I intend to convey.

I will not write more tonight, but say let your faith increase and pray more to the Father, and you will see open up to you a wonderful vista of knowledge of the truths of the spirit.

Your friend and brother,   JESUS.

Jesus showed His Great Glory and gave His Love to Mr. Padgett
I am here, *Jesus.*

Well I am so glad that you are so longing for this Love and I will tell you that the Father loves you with all His divine nature, and is helping you to receive this Love into your soul, and you will soon receive it in such abundance that you will find yourself happy beyond all conception. And I love you too with all my heart and soul, and am very near you and try to make you feel my presence and influence. Rest assured that I am with you in all my love and tenderness and that you are the special object of my care and keeping. I wish that you could see me as I write this for I am filled with so much love for you, that I know, if you could see the glory of the Father displayed you would never again doubt my love. Oh, my brother, only try to get this love by prayer and faith in such a way that it will become as real to you as anything which your natural senses show you to exist in the physical world.

It is more real than anything in all nature, and you have in you the possibilities of realizing that it is an existing thing, and is yours, if you will only pray and believe.* I am with you in prayer at night, and with all my love and faith I ask the Father to bless you and make you a true partaker of His love and mercy, and to give you the assurance that you will receive and know that you have it.

My dear brother I must stop now, but your longings tonight have been so great and so earnest that I could not stop without telling you as I have. And remember this that I, Jesus, with all the knowledge and authority that I possess, tell you that the love of the Father shall be yours, and you will become a most happy man, and a power on earth in things spiritual and which pertain to the Father's business.

So believe me and trust the Father, and you will not be forsaken or left alone, but will be surrounded by a host of witnessing angels that you are the chosen child of the Father, and the object of His Great Love and blessings.

---

* Mr. Padgett told me that when he was praying just before retiring at night, he sometimes saw Jesus alongside praying with him.

I will not write more now, but I will say, that I love you as a true brother and friend, and even as a closer one to you: and you must believe, and yours will be the happiness that few on earth possess.

So with all the great love that is mine I will say good-night and God bless you.

Your friend and brother,

JESUS.

Great Love of Jesus for Mr. P. John Wesley said the Glory and Power was so wonderful they knelt in awe.

Let me write a word too, for I was present when the Master bestowed upon you his great love and prayed the Father to send into your soul the love of the Father—the Divine Love—that will make you one with Him. And I must tell you that never before have we seen such love and glory displayed by the Master as he displayed tonight to you his love and blessings. Oh, I tell you that it was wonderful and we all stood, or rather knelt in awe, for we could not stand in his presence.

What does all this mean? None of us know for we have never received such evidence of love from him, and have never seen any one else receive the love in that way.

We commence to know how you must be a very important man to the Master, and you must be the special object of his love and care, for he seems to love you with a love that we cannot understand, although we have in our souls the Divine Love of the Father to a very great degree. But yet such love as he displayed tonight we have never seen and the meaning of it we cannot fully comprehend.

Oh, I tell you that you are a blessed man, and you have with you not only the love and power of the greatest spirit in all God's universe but also the Great Divine Love of the Father.

So let us think of this wonderful experience before writing more.

I will say good-night.

Your brother in Christ,   JOHN WESLEY.

Affirming Jesus' Love for Mr. P. The Wonderful Experience. All Were Surprised at the Display of His Glory.

Let me write while the power of the Master is here, and tell you that you have had a wonderful experience tonight, and so have we who have stood by and seen the Master write to you, and bestow upon you his Great Love.

He was glorious as he told you of the Great Love of the Father, that would come to you and how he would be with you in all his love and blessings trying to make you happy.

203

We were all surprised at the great display of his glory, for it was like the great shining light of God's countenance of which we have heard, but never seen. You certainly are a blessed man and one that must become very happy.

I am not in condition to write more tonight, and can only praise God for the Great Love and favor that he has bestowed upon you. So my dear son believe what I have told you, and know that we all rejoice with you in the great favor which you have from the Master.

So dear son, good-night.

Your own loving Grandmother (ANN ROLLINS)

Affirms that the Great Love of Jesus Was Bestowed on Her Husband. She Was Filled With Awe.

I am your own, *Helen. (Mrs. Padgett)*

Well my dear Ned, I can scarcely write as I am so filled with awe over what has happened tonight that my power to write has almost left me.

But my darling I must tell you that you are very dear to the Master and a child of the Father's love to a very great degree.

Such love, I never before saw displayed and I never expected to see it, especially bestowed upon you who are so dear to me.

I must not try to write more tonight as I am so filled with love and wonder and thankfulness that I can hardly think. So my own dear Ned love me with all your heart and soul, and believe that I love you too. But when I think of this night and the great love that was bestowed upon you, my love seems like a mere shadow; but it is all that I have to give you, and I give all I have.

So sweetheart, good-night.

Your own true and loving,   HELEN.

Confirmation by St. Mark that the Master is doing the great work through Mr. Padgett.

I must add my testimony to the others who have preceded me, to the fact that the Master is now doing a great work for the redemption of mankind, and that through you he is going to transmit his great spiritual truths to sinful man.

I will not write much to night, but say that in the future I will communicate my thoughts, which are the creatures of knowledge and experience in the Celestial Spheres of Christ's Kingdom.

Good night, and may God keep you in His love and care forever more.

ST. MARK, the writer of the second gospel, originally true as written, but now full of errors.

204

The condition of the soul when and after the Divine Love flows into it.

I am here, *John.*

I come tonight to tell you that you are in a better condition than you were last night, and that I desire to write a short message if you think that you can receive it.

Well, I will not write very long, and what I shall say will have to do with *"the condition of the soul when and after the Divine Love flows into it.'*

As you know, the soul in the condition in which man possesses it before the entrance of the Divine Love is not in accord with the love of God, nor is it a part of the great Oversoul. It is only a special creation made in the image of the Father, having in it the natural love which was conferred upon man at the time of his creation, and not having in it any part of the essence of the Father, or any quality that makes it of the divine nature of the Father, or necessarily immortal.

But when the Divine Love enters into it, and it becomes permeated, as it were, with the Divine Essence, then it takes on the divine nature of the Father, and to the extent that it receives and possesses this Love it becomes at-one with God and ceases to be a mere image, and becomes transformed into the substance.

The soul in this condition is altogether a different entity from the soul in the condition in which it was created and no longer is subject to the dominion of either the mind or of the animal appetites and desires, and, hence, the spirit possessing such a soul is, in essence, a part of the Father, or as Jesus said, is in the Father and the Father in it.

Now, do not understand that such a soul is the soul that man originally possessed with increased development of purity and goodness or freedom from sin, because such is not the case. Such soul by such transformation becomes a new thing, and never again can it relapse into the soul of man's origin; because of the qualities that it then possesses it becomes immortal, and such immortal nature can never be taken from it.

It is now a thing of love and purity, and consciousness of its true condition is always with the spirit that has such soul.

This transformation is gradual, and men must not think that by the mere act of conversion from their state of death they at once become possessed of the nature of the divine, for such is not the fact. The transformation is gradual and comes according to the susceptibility of the the souls to receive this love of which I speak. But when once the inflowing of the love commences it continues eternally although there may be times of stagnation and apparent loss of this Divine

Essence, yet always is the transformation taking place, and at certain stages in its progress, the possession of this Divine Love will be so great that the original soul, or its original qualities will entirely disappear and leave only the new qualities which the Divine Love has implanted in it. The leaven when once deposited never ceases to work until the whole shall become leavened.

I will not write more tonight, but only further say, that this condition of transformation may be obtained by all men if they will only seek for it in the proper way and with faith.

I will soon write you again.

In leaving you, I give you my love and blessings and the assurance that I am helping you in your efforts to carry forward the work, and in accomplishing all the promises.

So my dear brother, good-night.

Your brother in Christ,   JOHN.

The belief in the unpardonable sin is slanderous and blasphemous against the Loving Father.

I am here. *Your grandmother.*

I have been listening to your conversation tonight and am much pleased to see that you and your friend are growing in your conceptions of the truth.

The matter of the unpardonable sin is one that is of the greatest importance to the world, especially in view of the fact, that so many of the orthodox ministers teach that it is a thing of real existence and is so dreadful in its consequences.

But thanks to the Master that teaching will not in the near future be permitted to go unchallenged, for the truth in this particular will be made so plain that men will cease to believe in it, and as a consequence will be relieved from a fear that has kept many a one from seeking the Love and favor of the Father.

I know that this revelation of the truth will antagonize many of these preachers who see that it is one of the strongest instruments that enables them to keep together their organization. But this antagonism will not avail, for the truth will prevail, and mankind will, when they come to think for themselves, embrace this truth with gladness and joy.

How strange that the professed ministers of Christ should so slander and blaspheme the one loving Father, and cause men to look upon Him as a God of insatiable wrath, and one who, because a man refuses to believe in the doctrines of the churches consigns him to eternal punishment and hell; and when he gets into such condition of hardness of heart that, as your preacher said, "even God himself will have no power to save."

Oh, it is pitiable, that such erroneous and harmful doctrines should be taught, and worse than all by professed ministers of the loving and lowly Jesus.

So my son, you and your friend, whenever the opportunity comes to combat this monstrous teaching, do so with all your strength and power of conclusion and show and proclaim to the world that such teaching is not true, and that for every sinner there is opportunity for salvation, and that God loves the man who will not believe on Him just as he loves the believer, only the former may not partake of the divine nature as does the latter.

I wanted tonight to write this, because I thought that the time was opportune to impress upon you the falsity of this great dogma that has no foundation in truth or in the plan of God for the salvation of humanity.

Well, I will not write more tonight as you have others present who may want to write, but before I close I want to say in fulfillment of John's statement to you today that he is present and with him is his great influence of love.

So with all my love I bless you both.

Your grandmother,   (ANN ROLLINS)

Holy Spirit not God. No unpardonable sin.

I am here. *Jesus.*

I want to tell you, once and for all, that the Holy Ghost is not God and that the unpardonable sin is a thing which has no existence either in the world of mortals or in the spirit world: I never used the expression contained in the Bible in reference to the unpardonable sin, and it has done more harm to my cause than most any other thing.

Well, I was not conceived by the Holy Ghost as many believe. I was a man created and born as other men; only, as I have told you, I was without sin.

All writings which make the Holy Spirit equal to the Father are untrue. The Holy Spirit, as I have told you, is a mere instrument of God in doing His work among men, and for men to believe that the Holy Spirit is God, is blasphemy—but even that sin will be forgiven men.

I hope that before we get through our writings I will make it so plain and convincing that the * Holy Spirit is not God, but a mere spirit, though

* Read Holy Spirit, from Jesus, Vol. I, Ed. 1, Pages 72 to 76. St. Luke, Pages 76 to 80.

the Greatest Spirit in His kingdom, that men will cease to worship it as God.

Yes, I will write a formal message on this subject, and you will see that the Holy Spirit cannot possibly be God. So do not let this question interfere with your belief in me or in what I write to you. You are now in the way to truth and the kingdom; and if you will continue to pray and have faith you will become an inhabitant of that kingdom, no matter what the Bible may say which is apparently in conflict with what I write.

So with all my love, I will say goodnight.

Your friend and brother,   JESUS.

No unpardonable sin as taught by the preacher.

I am here, *St. Luke.*

I was with you at church and heard the sermon on the unpardonable sin, and was much interested in the way in which the preacher dealt with the subject. His discourse was very plausible, but it is not true. As Jesus has told you, there is no unpardonable sin, and all men in this life and in the life to come, have the opportunity to be saved from their sins and become at-one with the Father.

The great danger in such a sermon as the one preached to night is, that men who have not become believers in Jesus as the Savior of the world, and I mean the expression in the sense that we have explained it to you, will think that after they have arrived at a certain age and find their souls show no inclination or desire to seek the way to God's love or to a reconciliation with Him, they have committed the unpardonable sin, and hence there is no use for them to try to find the way to salvation. It is a damnable doctrine, and the preacher who announced it has incurred a dreadful and awful responsibility, for in the after life he will very likely meet spirits in a condition of darkness and stagnation of soul, who will tell him that because of his sermons they gave up all hope of salvation, and believe at the time they meet him just as they did on earth. And he, possibly, may see the errors of his wrong teachings; and then will come to him remorse and bitter recollections of these teachings and the great harm that they did to these darkened spirits.

When men get to know the truth, as they will when the Master shall have delivered through you his messages, they will not have to run the risk of becoming bound and shackled by such false beliefs as the one of which I speak. But before that time, with so many preachers and especially those so called evangelists who strive to force men into the erroneous beliefs which they teach through fear of eternal damnation, many men will have formed these beliefs and will suffer the consequences which these false doctrines entail.

I was sorry that someone could not have arisen in the church and resented his doctrine of the unpardonable sin, and told all the people that

208

there is no such thing, but that the Father's Love is waiting for every one who may seek it, in great abundance and freely to be given, and that if men will only come to the Father in prayer and belief, that Love will be given them, and salvation and immortality will be theirs.

The age of a man has nothing to do with his salvation; it is for the old as well as for the young, and no idea or suggestion of any unpardonable sin must be interposed to prevent any man from believing that the Great Love of the Father is waiting for him.

So you see, with some truths preached by these orthodox ministers there is a great deal of error, and the effect of the latter is to prevent or undo any good which the truth may have otherwise been bestowed upon men.

Well these great errors have been preached and worked their injury for many centuries now, and men will be hard to convince that they are not the true doctrines of Jesus, and that the claimed truths which they teach are not the only truths.

I will not write more tonight.

I will say with my love and blessings, I am,

Your brother in Christ, ST. LUKE.

Corroborates St. Luke wrote on there is no unpardonable Sin as taught.

I am here, *Latham.*

I was a preacher in the days of the Reformation, and died in England a martyr to my beliefs and preachings.

I merely came to tell you that you must believe in what Luke wrote you as to the unpardonable sin, for I know that it is not true, for many men who, on earth denied God and the Holy Spirit, have since coming into the spirit world found the Divine Love of the Father and salvation.

I know it may not have been necessary for me to say this, yet I thought it best to do so, as I was a man and became a spirit long after Luke lived, and that which he said was the truth in my day, and is the truth now.

I will not write more but will say goodnight. Your brother in Christ.

CHAS. LATHAM.

Paul denies unpardonable sin.

I am *St. Paul.*

Yes, I was trying to write my name, but was a little confused and stopped. Well I am all right now.

I merely want to say that the unpardonable sin as taught by the preacher has no existence, and the preacher is wholly in error, for no soul is without the privilege of coming to the Father and obtaining His love and mercy even in the spirit world.

I am not in condition to write more tonight and neither are you, so we had better stop.

Your brother in Christ, PAUL.

209

I am here, *Swedenborg.*

Well, I am sorry to say that my work was a failure; and that, because of that fact, I have suffered very much since I became a spirit. I know now that what I attempted to do was injured by my preconceived ideas based on the orthodox teachings, and that I did not carry out the work of the great mission that I had been selected to perform.

I will say now, though, and you must believe me, that you have been selected to do the work which I failed to do, and I hope that you will permit me to give you one piece of advice and that is: take, record and believe only the messages as they shall come to you from Jesus and the other high spirits, and let no opinion of your own mar or flavor these communications. The truths will be presented to you and you must accept them as they come.

When I came to the spirit world and realized the failure that I had made, then everything was failure to my conscience.

In your case, you have no such preconceived ideas to hamper you or prevent you from receiving the truths, for you are used merely as a conduit through which these truths are to be received; and as they are to be declared in the very language of the writers.

I am your friend and brother and co-worker in making known these truths, and write only, because I, as a failure, can speak from experience. So my brother, turn your thought more to this work and, if necessary, sacrifice every worldly consideration to carry forward your work and make perfect your efforts to fulfill the great mission with which you have been blessed.

I will not write more now.

May the Father bless you with His love.

Your brother in Christ,   SWEDENBORG.

Did not know of the Divine Love as contradistinguished from the natural love that was bestowed on man at his creation.

I am here. *Swedenborg.*

I merely want to say that I have been reading my work as you read, and that I now realize how many statements of error and untruth I made in that work. The errors are so many that it will take a longer time than I have tonight in which to give you a bare outline of them. But I will soon come and write you, and hope that you can give me an evening when I can write without limitation of time.

Since I have been in the spirit world, I have found that there are so many statements in my writings of my experiences while in the mortal, when I was permitted in my spirit, or, as I then said, interiors, to enter the spirit world, that were not truly conceived or interpreted, that it is absolutely necessary that I should correct and describe in accordance with what I now know of the truth, and especially is this necessary as I have on earth a large number of mortals who believe in my teachings and are trying to follow them in their lives and deeds. So, you will appreciate my anxiety to be permitted to write.

Tonight, I will not write more.

Well, I am sorry to say, that I did not know of the Divine Love, which by its reception into the soul made angels of men, and recreated them, so that their souls became in their very substance, Divine. I did not know of this love as contradistinguished from the love that was bestowed upon man at his creation, and which, in itself, has nothing of the Divine. No, I was ignorant of this and never learned it in the spirit world in my visits to that world, nor in my conversation with spirits.

I know now that no matter how great is the ruling love of a man for falsity and evil when he enters the hells, he will have the opportunity to have that love changed, and that ultimately the loves of all who are in the hells will be changed into the love for good—in some instances into the love of the Divine, and in others, to the purification of their natural loves to that which will make them perfect men.

These are some of the things that I desire to write about, and there are many others equally erroneous.

I am in the Celestial Spheres, and of course, am an angel of God and the possessor of His Divine Love that has caused my soul to become Divine, and immortality to become to me a thing of understanding and possession.

I will stop now, and with my love and the blessings of God and all the divine angels, I will say goodnight.

Your brother in Christ,   SWEDENBORG

Affirms that Swedenborg wrote. Importance of errors being corrected in his writings.

I am here. *Luke.*

I come to tell you that you must not doubt that Swedenborg wrote to you, and what you wrote, or rather, received, in answer to your questions, he actually wrote. We are all desirous that he shall write you on the subjects that he has expressed a desire to write upon, for many of the teachings and doctrines that are contained in his earthly writings are erroneous and must be corrected, for they are being studied and believed in by many mortals, and all to their leading away from the truth.

The one great error or untruth that must be corrected is his teaching, that Jesus is God. This is blasphemous and abhorrent to all the angelic spirits, and more so to the Master than to any other, and for the correction of this, Swedenborg must write.

Well, I will not write more tonight, except to say this, that another anniversary of the resurrection of the Master, as it is believed, has come,

211

and men are worshipping Jesus as God, and sending their praises and thanks to him as the great redeemer of the world by his death and * resurrection, while as you know, his death had very little to do with that redemption, and his resurrection was not the resurrection that he taught could be the experience and possession of all mankind.

It is pitiable and destructive to the truth for men to believe and teach that the mere resurrection of the spirit from the body is the resurrection that Jesus came to teach and demonstrate; and when we see each year the repetition of the observance of the anniversary of this rising of Jesus from his physical body, and all the false beliefs and teachings, we realize more and more the necessity for our truths being made known to the world.

So you must work harder and pray to the Father to increase your soul development so that our messages may be more rapidly received.

Remember what John said a few nights ago and believe, for the promises then made will soon be realized by you. I will come soon and write a message.

With my love and great desire that we become closer in our rapport and more expedient in our work, I will say goodnight.

Your brother in Christ,   LUKE.

Affirmed that Swedenborg wrote.

I am here. Your own true and loving *Helen.*

Well dear, I come to say that Swedenborg actually wrote you, as I realize that you had a doubt come into your mind as to whether he really wrote. He actually answered your questions in his own words, and not any thought contained in his answers came from your mind.

Luke also wrote, and you must believe.

Goodnight and God bless you.

Your own true and loving   HELEN.

Comments on Swedenborgian pamphlet entitled "Incarnate God"

I am here. Luther.

I merely desire to say that as you read the pamphlet I read with you, and the description and explanation therein contained as to who God is, are entirely erroneous and blasphemous.

Jesus never claimed or taught, while on earth, that he was God, and this I say because he has so instructed us, and he never since becoming a spirit has made any such claim, and the teachings of the New Church in this particular are all wrong and tend to lead men away from the true conception of who God and Jesus both are.

Swedenborg has often conversed with me about his teachings and declared that his explanations as to God are not in accord with the knowl-

---

* Appendix. Read Resurrection, Vol. I, Edition 1, pages 94 to 107—by St. Paul and Jesus.

212

edge that he now has, and that the teachings as contained in his books upon this subject were the results very largely of his own speculations, and the results of his endeavors in trying to reconcile what he thought was an absurd conception of the nature and being of God with the true interpretation of the Bible. He could not accept the doctrine of the Trinity, as explained and accepted and taught by the Church, and hence, being a believer in the inspiration of the Bible and its infallibility of religious truths he sought some exegesis that might be consistent with the Bible, and at the same time in consonance with his ideas of reason and common sense. But, as he now says, he added mysticism to mysticism, and irrational explanations to irrational explanations, and the result was that his teachings were more absurd and more difficult to understand than were the teachings of his church.

The doctrine of the Trinity, as you have been told, is not true, and never had any authority in the teachings of Jesus or those of the Apostles and Bible writers, and was merely the deduction of some of the old fathers of the church, arising from their speculations and desire to make of Jesus a God though a lesser God than the Father, and at the same time one with the Father and a part of the Godhead that must be considered as being only one God, and as taught by the Old Testament writers and prophets that there is only one God.

This doctrine, of course, was absurd and, hence, was one of the mysteries of God, but, nevertheless was taught as a truth and incumbent upon man to believe whether they could understand it or not, which of course, they could not.

But the doctrine was not accepted by all the writers of the early days, for as you know, there were bitter controversies among these expounders of what they supposed to be the scriptures, upon the question as to who Jesus was, and his relation to God. But as the years went by the doctrine of the Trinity became firmly established as a canon of belief in the church, and in my time on earth it was believed, and not questioned by the church; and I believed it also, although I could not understand it.

Now, Swedenborg was a member of the church that bore my name and which I was credited with having founded, and believed in its doctrines, even as to the Trinity, and the actual transformation of the wine and bread into the blood and body of Jesus, and he continued in this belief up to the time of his wonderful visions of the spirit world and his experience in meeting the spirits and angels of that world, including Jesus, whom he in his writings claimed to be God, and with whom he had many conversations and from whom he learned the spiritual truths that he declared to the world.

As you have been told, in the working out of the plans of the Celestial Angels under the leadership of Jesus, Swedenborg was selected as the

213

instrumentality through whom the spiritual truths should be revealed to mankind, and in carrying out that plan power was given to him to come in his spirit perceptions or his inner sight, as he calls it, into the spirit world and there see the conditions of spirits and angels, and also of their environments, and learn the higher truths from conversations with spirits and angels. And he did come in the manner indicated and communed as he has claimed, except that he never talked with God, but only with Jesus, who he misconceived to be God; and this cannot be wondered at, for Jesus was a spirit, so transcendent in glory and love and wisdom, that it was almost natural, as I may say, that the mortal in his new and unusual experience should conceive this glorious Jesus to be God himself. But it was not God, only Jesus, that this seer saw and listened to.

Having a conception of this kind, you can readily see, that when he came into his mortal self again, and many times this occurred, he firmly believed that Jesus, who had form and individuality in the spirit world similar to what he had when on earth, was actually God, and it therefore became easy for Swedenborg to reject the doctrine of the Trinity, Jesus is God, manifested in the flesh, and God is Jesus, the Divine Man.

Of course, you must understand, that in the exercise of this seership, he experienced the doubts and fears that at times, what he saw and heard might not be things of actuality, and that possibly, his imagination, or as in these latter days, what is called the subconscious mind, was deceiving him, and being a man of extraordinary mentality and strong convictions, as well as established faith in the doctrines of the church to which he belonged, many of his interpretations of what he saw and heard, and his teachings therefrom were limited and flavored by his existing mental condition and faith.

He has told me that for many years before his experience as seer, he had to a more or less extent doubted the truth of the Trinity, and accepted it only as a mystery, and because the church declared it to be a truth, and that after his experiences as such seer, believing in the statements of the Bible as the infallible words of God, and also believing that he had seen God in the person of Jesus, he sought an explanation of these Bible statements and a reconciliation of them with his belief that Jesus was God, and the result was his declared doctrine that Jesus is God.

And so in many other of his teachings, based upon his experience in the spirit world, he embraced many errors and misconceptions of the truths, and to such an extent that, as you have been told, his mission, in its results, was a failure, and the truths that he had been selected to learn and declare to the world were never made known to mankind.

This failure was disappointing to the spirits who conceived this plan and in whom were lodged the spiritual truths of God, and who were acting as God's instruments in their endeavor to make them known to humanity.

214

But it will be more satisfactory to you, and convincing to whomsoever may read the truths that you are receiving from these same high spirits -that selected him, as their messenger, to have Swedenborg come himself, and explain the workings of his mission, and the causes and particulars of his failure in doing the great work that had been assigned him to do.

He says that he has one consolation that many who have founded churches and attempted to declare spiritual truths, upon which doctrines and creeds have been promulgated and believed in, and that is that his followers are so comparatively few in numbers, and, consequently, so many less mortals are being deceived by his teachings. And I can appreciate the consolation that he may have in this fact, for my teachings and beliefs that are false as his are false, are believed in and followed by a very large number of mortals, to their injury.

Well, I am glad for the opportunity to write you tonight, and I am still waiting for the chance to finish my message to my people on the errors of continuing in my teachings, and the necessity for them to become undeceived, and learn the truths that are now being declared to mankind.

I will not write further. So goodnight.

Your brother in Christ,   LUTHER.

Chauncey Giles changes his belief about Jesus being God.

Let me write you a line, for I am interested in what has just been written you, for when I lived on earth, I was a Swedenborgian or New Churchman, and believed in the doctrines of that Church, and especially in the corner stone of its beliefs, and that is that Jesus was God, and the only God to be worshipped as such and accepted as the incarnate God, who came to earth and lived and taught among men the coming of God into the flesh.

Well, I, when on earth was a leader or preacher in that Church, and during the course of my ministry I not only taught but wrote many pamphlets and some books upon this doctrine of God becoming man in the form of Jesus, and on many other doctrines, that I now know to be untrue.

And my authority for saying that this fundamental doctrine of the Church is untrue, is that I have seen and talked with Jesus in the spirit world, and learned that he is only the spirit of a mortal, but the highest and most glorious spirit in all the heavens, and is not God; and I have never seen God nor any spirit who has seen Him with the spirit eyes, though Jesus and others of the highest spirits say that they have seen Him with their soul perceptions, which must be true because Jesus is so much like God in this, that he cannot tell a lie.

But I know that there is a God, and my knowledge is based on certainty, but the basis of this certainty I cannot explain to you, as you could not comprehend my explanation. But God loves and rules and loves, and is present with us and with you in some or many of His attributes, and Jesus is not this God.

I wish that I could come to my people and tell them of the errors of their beliefs, and the truths as they exist and to the extent as now known to me, but I have no hope of ever being able to do so, for one of the cardinal doctrines of the Church is, that with the passing of Swedenborg passed the possibility of all communications between God or his angels and mortals as to spiritual truths, and that it is contrary to God's will that mortals should attempt to penetrate the veil that separates the two worlds.

How such beliefs as I taught now cause me suffering and regret, for I see no way of remedying the wrong that I did, and of turning the thoughts of my followers into the paths that lead to truth and the certainty of heaven.

As this is my first attempt to communicate, I am somewhat tired and must stop. But I thank you for the opportunity, and hope that some time I may have the privilege of again writing.

Notwithstanding my erroneous beliefs, I have in my soul some of the Father's Divine Love, that enables me to sign myself,

Your brother in Christ,

CHAUNCEY GILES.

Affirming that Luther wrote on "Incarnate God."

I am here. Your own true and loving Helen. (Mrs. Padgett)

Yes, Luther wrote, and the other spirit I don't know, but I have no doubt that he is whom he represents himself to be. He seemed to be in much earnestness and was very anxious to write, and seeing that he was a good spirit with a message, we let him write, and he felt better by having done so.

Swedenborg was here tonight and is very anxious to write and soon he will as he feels that he must write a message on the subject that you have been interested in recently.

I will not write more. So with my love I will say goodnight.

Your own true and loving,

HELEN.

How and when God answers prayer.
** Laws of rapport and communication.*

I am here. *St. John.* Brother of James—Apostle of Jesus.

I come to you today because I see what your condition is and that you need encouragement, and as I am your special guardian I could not

---

* These three messages on "Laws of Rapport" are the messages Jesus referred to in his message—Vol. 1, Edition 1, Page 2, 2d Paragraph.

216

abstain from writing you as I have. So I say, trust in the Father and in our help and you will not be disappointed.

It has been a long time since I have written you in regards to spiritual things, and I desire very much to do so, as I have important messages to communicate, as have many other spirits who have been accustomed to write you.

While your material affairs are important, yet these spiritual truths are of more importance, not only to you but to the world for whom they are primarily intended. The world needs these truths more at this time than ever before, and the sooner we can complete our book of truths the better it will be for suffering humanity, and for many whose hearts are now lacerated because of the great destruction of human life caused by the war.

Well, I know that many believe that in some way God has an overpowering direction as regards the progress and outcome of the war, and in a certain sense this is true, for He is always interested in and seeks to reach the souls and hearts of mankind and, of course, desires that the great suffering and devastation shall cease. But as the cause of all this was the evil desire and ambitions of men, He will let men, themselves, control the conduct and outcome of the war. He will not by His exercise of power in an arbitrary way end the war or determine which of the contending nations shall be successful, except in this, that through the instrumentality of His spirit, He will influence the minds and consciences of these men in such a way that right and justice will prevail, and the evil thoughts and deeds of men be stopped in their operations. His spirits are working to this end at this time, and have been for a long time, and so have the evil spirits been working to bring discord and destruction upon humanity. The leaders of the nations have been, in a large degree, obsessed by these evil spirits, and have been influenced in many of their thoughts and acts by these dark ones who delight in seeing mankind suffer, and in evil asserting itself.

The spirits of truth are exercising a wonderful power over the hearts and souls of men, and one that will cause them to soon realize that evil must not be allowed to prevail and that truth and right must assert themselves to the end that the war must not only cease, but that men must become more in unison with truth and justice. In this way the Father will answer prayer, and His love will also continue to flow to men.

I know that prayers are ascending unto the Father from many men and from many of the churches of the respective contending nations for success, but only those prayers will be answered which tend to bring about the overruling of evil and injustice; and the spirits who are working the Father's will will answer these prayers only which in their answer will bring about the desired end.

217

As I have said, while God does not take interest in these matters by His arbitrary power and decree that the one or the other of these warring nations shall overcome and conquer the others, yet, He does by His angels exercise such influence upon the men who are engaged in the struggle, that in the end His will will be brought to pass. But men, immediately, must determine the course and results of the issue, and no miracle will be performed which will make one side the conqueror of the other; and while this is so, this determination by men will be influenced as I have stated.

Man has his free will and, as we have written you, that is never arbitrarily controlled by the Father, but in the exercise of that free will, whenever man violates the laws of God, man must suffer the penalty of that violation. This is a never changing law of the material as well as of the spirit world. When evil is sown evil must be reaped, and until this evil ceases to operate as a cause, good will not appear. The men who are directing the war must understand that this law is operating in the conduct of the war, and that evil thoughts put into execution will inviolably bring evil consequences.

You may look for an earlier determination of the struggle than some men now believe possible, yet ere that end comes many mortals will become spirits and find their homes—some in the darker spheres, and some in those of light and love, but all are the children of God and will not be forsaken by Him in the great eternity.

Well, you have not been in that condition of mind that has enabled us to make the necessary rapport with you. We must have a mind that is filled with thoughts of the higher things of truth, even though we do not use those thoughts. Our thoughts are all spiritual, and our truths can be received only by the mind in a spiritual condition, and you, lately, have not had so much of this spiritual mind as formerly. Our contact has not been so close and our rapport, necessary to enable us to express through your mind these spiritual truths, has not been so perfect. And when I say mind I merely mean the organs of the brain as influenced by the thoughts of the mind; for I will tell you what you may not know, that these component organs of the brain are not always and under all conditions receptive of the same control by the minds of spirits. You may receive through your brain a long and profound message of things pertaining to what you may call the material, and yet under similar conditions of these organs, not be able to receive messages of the higher truths; and the conditions of these brain organs are caused by the condition of the soul in the possession of things spiritual.

It is difficult for me to express just what I intend to convey but this you will understand, that upon the development and possession by the soul of things spiritual, depends the capacity of the human brain to receive the various kinds of messages. A medium who is merely intellectual and morally good cannot receive those messages of the higher truths, because there can be no rapport between the brain of such a medium and the mind of the higher spirit who may desire to communicate. And thus you will understand why it is that the messages from the earth-bound spirits or from those who have merely the intellectual development, are so vastly more frequently received by mediums than messages from spirits of the soul development.

A spiritual thought—I mean a thought which can come only from a spirit who has the development of the soul that makes that soul divine—cannot possibly pass through a human brain which has never been developed by a soul in which the Divine Love has entered and worked its regenerating powers. Things of the material may be conveyed through a brain purely material—things moral through a brain which has been influenced by moral truths—and things spiritual through a brain which has assimilated those truths that come only with the development of the soul by love. This is the law of rapport and communication.

Well, I will not write more now.

But in closing urge you to have faith in us, and let your worries leave you, and pray more to the Father.

Good-bye.

Your brother in Christ, JOHN.

Laws of rapport—continued

I am here. *John.*

I desire to write for a short time tonight upon a subject that I consider important, and you may consider interesting.

As you may know, it has been sometime since I wrote anything of a formal character and I regret very much that so much time has gone by without my being able to communicate some of the spiritual truths, and also regret that your condition has been such that I was unable to make the rapport with you that is necessary in order that I may deliver to you these messages of the nature mentioned.

I have explained to you in a former recent letter, in a brief way, the law of communication and rapport, and that law, if you will try to understand it, will enable you to comprehend the reason why we have not been able to communicate these higher truths.

It may seem to you that if we control your brain and not use or transmit your thoughts but only the thoughts which come from our minds, it would be immaterial what the nature of our thoughts might be, and that as your brain is used by us as a mere instrument we, having possession of your brain, would have the power to write anything we might desire. And upon a mere superficial glance at the assertion, it could be reasonably supposed to be true.

219

But, as we have told you before, rapport and our ability to use your brain are governed by laws, and one of these laws is that a high thought cannot be transmitted through a human brain which is not in the condition that qualifies it to receive the thought, just as the brain, in matter pertaining to mere material knowledge cannot receive a conception or comprehension of some intellectual truth with which it has not had acquaintance, and transmit it. A brain cannot be used by the mind of the human to make known or present a problem in geometry, when that brain has never been used by the mind to acquire an acquaintance with or knowledge of the principles of geometry. This is an incomplete analogy but it may serve to illustrate what I mean.

In the conception by the human mind of a truth, material or spiritual, the brain must be used in order to manifest or make known that conception. This is absolutely true where the idea or thought originates in the mind of the man who is using his own brain to formulate or manifest that idea or thought. The mind may have the thought or knowledge of some branch of learning, and yet when it has never used the brain to put that thought or knowledge into concrete form the brain cannot manifest or transmit it. This law applies specificaly to the capabilities of the brain where it is attempted to be used or controlled by the mind of the man who owns the brain. And from this you will see that it is possible for the human mind to have thought and knowledge of things which it cannot use the brain to express.

In many of your material things of life, such as great invention, the knowledge of these inventions is in the mind, it may be, for a long time before it is formulated and expressed by the brain, and sometimes it never gets through the brain at all. The mind and the brain are not one and equivalent things; the one is the operator, the other is the thing used to operate with, so that the possessions of the operator may become manifested to others.

But this law, applying to and controlling the relationship of the mind and brain possessed by the same man, does not so absolutely apply to and control the relationship of mind and brain, where the mind is that of a spirit and the brain that of a mortal, for in such case the mind may take such complete control of the brain, that the former's manifestations are not governed or limited by the special experiences or want of experiences which the brain may have had in its use by the mind of the mortal along specific lines of expression or manifestation. Thus, as you may know and as it has been demonstrated by the work and experience of many human mediums, the minds of spirits have controlled the brains of these mediums, so that such brains have transmitted from these spirits expressions of various kinds of languages and mathematical truths with which such brains never have had any acquaintance or become exercised in expressing.

In these instances the brain is used merely in the sphere of intellect and the spirit who takes possession of that brain and uses it to express and make known the knowledge of the spirit's mind, is doing no different thing in essentials, to what the human mind, controlling its own brain, could have done had the brain been exercised in those directions. The capacity of the brain, whether exercised or not by the human mind controlling its own brain, limits the power of the spirit to control in the manner and for the purpose mentioned.

But this law has a further phase, and that is, the greater the general experience of the brain in its exercise by the human mind, the more perfectly can the spirit mind control it. All this is dependent upon facts which I cannot linger here to explain, such as the mediumistic qualities and susceptibilities of the human whose brain is attempted to be controlled by the spirit.

And the same laws apply to the disclosure of truth and principles along the moral planes. A spirit cannot possibly use the brain of a mortal to convey or transmit through it moral precepts or truths that that brain is not capable of receiving. And I do not mean by this that the brain must have had any acquaintance with any or many particular moral truths, or must have been used by the human for the purpose of receiving or imparting these precepts but must be in its essential capacity, potentially able to transmit and receive these truths. And so the capacity of the brain to receive and transmit these moral truths, limits the control of the spirit over the brain to express through it, these truths.

The rapport of the spirit with the human is determined by the development of the brain and the moral qualities of the human at the time the rapport is attempted to be made—and this means the actual development of these conditions and not what they may appear to be to other humans, or even to the individual himself. And this development determines to a large extent the power of the spirit to use the brain to disclose the truths, either intellectual or moral.

A medium can receive only such truths as his condition according to the nature of the truths, is susceptible to the forming of a rapport by the spirit. The possibility of rapport, and the kind thereof, lie at the foundation of mediumship, and determines and limits the power of the spirit to convey its thoughts and the capacity of the mortal to receive them.

When the medium is in a certain condition of development the spirit, writing, can form the rapport according as that condition harmonizes with the condition of the spirit; and it is impossible unless the harmony exists, for the spirit to write these things which require a greater degree of development than the medium at the time possesses. **Hence, you** will in a way understand why so few of the higher spiritual truths have ever been delivered to the world through the mediumship of any mortal who has been possessed of gifts of either automatic writing, as it is called, or clairvoyance or inspirational powers.

As to those truths which did not require a higher degree of development than was posesssed by the medium, there arose no difficulty in transmitting the same, and many mediums have been very successful in receiving the truth suited to their condition. And this fact, and law also, will explain to you why the same spirit may communicate through several mediums, and yet the communications be of a dissimilar character; that is, the communications through one medium contain higher or lower character of truth than those transmitted through some other medium; and with the result that those mortals who have heard or read these different communications, especially when critical, have been prone to believe that the same spirit was not making both communications. But this is not a just conclusion, for while the spirit was in the same condition—possessing the same knowledge—at the time of both communications, yet the mediums, because of their difference in development, were unable to receive the same character of messages.

You may search the whole history of spirit communications and of mediumship and you will not find any messages of the character of those that have been transmitted through you, and for the reasons that I have stated.

Swedenborg was the last and nearer perfect instrument for receiving these higher truths, and yet he, because of his want of soul development and his being bound, to a more or less exent, by his orthodox beliefs and scientific knowledge that caused him to coordinate and fit in these truths with his ideas of correspondence and such like conceptions, was a failure, and could not be successfully used to transmit these truth which we have been communicating through you. And after him other gifted and, in some respects, successful mediums were used by spirits, of the higher knowledge and progression to convey truths, but their conditions were such that, under the workings of the laws governing rapport, these mediums could receive only those truths which their conditions of development permitted them to receive. The workings of this limitation was not dependent upon the condition and ability of the spirits to impart these higher truths, but upon the capacity of the mediums to receive them.

You, yourself, have had experience as to how this law works and controls communication and rapport, for, as you know, it has been a long time since you were able to receive any spirit messages of these higher truths, although the spirits have been present with you many times, ready and anxious to make the rapport and deliver their messages; and you have been willing, intellectually, to receive them, but because of your condition or want of condition, the spirits could not deliver them and were compelled to wait until you get into the necessary condition.

From all this you will comprehend why so very few messages containing high spiritual truths, or even moral truths, come through mediums. The mediums, mostly, are so developed that they can receive only messages dealing with the material affairs of life, and which kinds of messages I am compelled to and can truthfully say, are those that are largely desired by the mortals seeking information from the spirit world.

Again, in your reading of spiritual literature you may have observed the great diversity of opinions of spirits upon the same subject, and sometimes contradictory opinions, thus causing doubt on the part of mortals, as to what are the facts existing in the spirit world as to the subject of inquiry. Well this is due very largely to the condition of the mediums, and also to the knowledge of the spirits who attempt to communicate, for the knowledge of spirits is limited by the extent of their progress and development.

Many spirits believe that what they have learned is true, and so give authoritative expression to the facts of their knowledge, and often believe what they know is all that may be known of the subject on which they communicate. And these are mostly honest in their beliefs and truthful, as they think, in their messages. And thus it is well for mortals to understand that everything written or spoken by spirits, at all times, is not to be accepted as the finality of truth. And on the other hand apparently contradictory statements should not be taken as fraudulent merely because they are contradictory. A spirit with greater knowledge using a medium in harmony with itself, can convey to men the more exact and greater extent of truth than can a spirit with less knowledge and development using a medium in harmony with itself.

Now, from what I have written, it is apparent that in order to get the greater truth, and more extended knowledge of the spirit world, mediums should make the effort to obtain larger and more intensive development of their spiritual natures as well as of their intellectual capacities. This acquirement is absolutely necessary to the reception of the higher truths which are so vital to mankind.

So, you see, communication and rapport depend upon the condition of both spirits and mortals working in unison; though more I may say upon the condition of the mortal. for, if the medium is in the proper state of development. there being always many spirits present with that medium in condition and readiness, a rapport can be made.

The Master is here tonight and has heard my communication and unites with me in saying: have faith and seek with all your soul for this Love. Believe that I am your special angel friend.

Your brother in Christ.   JOHN.

223

Laws of Communication and Rapport—continued
By St. John, Apostle of Jesus

Let me write a few lines tonight as I have not written for a long time and am anxious to say a few words which may be of help to you.

I have been present on many evenings when you were expecting to receive communications and was disappointed because of reasons or causes that you could not understand, except that you were not in that condition which would enable the spirits to make a rapport with you.

Well, this is true, and is the immediate cause of the want of power of communicating; but it is well that you understand more than this, for in order to remedy the difficulty you must have some knowledge of the seat thereof.

I have explained to you the law controlling rapport and communication, and endeavored to make it as plain and understandable as possible, so that you, at least, might grasp its meaning; but, I see there are some things that you do not understand, and because thereof, you have had the recent experience of not being able to receive the many messages that were waiting to be delivered through your brain and hand.

As I have said, the first and important requirement is that you be in that condition of soul which will, because of its qualities, enable the spirits who may desire to write the higher messages to form a rapport or union with you, which means simply to take charge and control of your brain—a brain which because of certain qualities and thoughts having possessed it, will be in harmony with the thoughts that these spirits desire to transmit through it, just as it is absolutely necessary that the medium through which it is desired that the electric fluid shall flow, must be a medium possessing such nature and qualities as will permit the fluid to flow through it. A wire or medium may be made of wood, and the electric fluid be present, ready to flow through it, but cannot. And why? Not because the wire or wood may not be perfect in itself as such wire; but, because the wire has not that nature and quality that will permit the electric fluid to make a union with it and thus control it. And so it is with the brain of the mortal, that such brain has the possibility of possessing, when properly prepared, those qualities that will admit of this union and control, while the wood has not. But the brain, when devoid of this preparation, is just as non-receptive to the union with and control of these spirits—as is the rapport—as is the wooden wire to the union with the electric fluid.

You have been told on numerous occasions that you were not in condition and that the spirits could not make the rapport, and that you must make the effort to get in condition; and this assertion and advice are all true. You were told to pray more to the Father and think of spiritual things, and then you would become in that condition. This is true, and the advice is helpful. But you were not told what this praying to the Father or thinking of spiritual thoughts means, and, hence, you may do these things in a way and yet not get in the condition.

I know that during a long period in the past you have been receiving many messages of the higher truths, and for the delivery of which a brain highly prepared was necessary to receive the same, and the thought has come to you, why were you able to receive these messages at the time of their delivery and not be able to receive them now because, as you further think, your brain is in as good condition now as it was at those times. Well, in the latter thought you are mistaken, and the fact of such mistake should be sufficient to convince you that your inability to receive the messages should not surprise you. During the periods mentioned you prayed more often for the inflowing of the Divine Love and your longings were intense, and the desires to possess this Love, which is so vital to the preparation of your brain, were so much more active. And also your thoughts of things spiritual were so much more frequent. In other words, you were then seeking with your whole heart to learn the truths of God and to possess His love; and, hence, your brain was continually in that condition which enabled the spirits to make the union and control it for the purpose of their higher expressions.

Lately you have not had the longings or prayed the prayers for the love as frequently and, as a consequence, the qualities and elements of thought that have possessed your brain were not such as to put your brain in that condition which made it receptive to the passing through it of those thoughts of the higher truths. Now from this, you must not infer that this condition is a mere matter of brain condition, produced by itself, for it is not. You have had the intellectual desire to write and receive the messages as much as you ever had, and also to receive messages of the higher truths that should be new as well as edifying to you, and your desires were real, and you were disappointed because they were not realized. And this merely demonstrates to you that there is something more than the mere mental or intellectual necessary to prepare the brain for the reception and transmission of that, which partakes of the nature of truth that has its source in something else than the mere human mind. These higher truths come from spirits whose minds, as you might say, are of the soul, and as only soul can deal with soul, it requires that the preparation of the brain should come from the exercise of soul powers upon the organs of that brain. And, hence, the necessity for your soul being in that condition that will produce in the brain the qualities that will unite and permit the truths of the soul to be received and transmitted.

You must not only pray to the Father for the inflowing of this Divine Love but you must pray often, until you realize almost constantly the possession of this Love in your soul; and also, you must turn your

225

thoughts, and I do not mean the merely intellectual thoughts, but the thoughts of the soul, which as you have already had you may have again, to the spiritual truths which have been revealed to you, and to the spiritual realm where you believe other spiritual truths are waiting to be revealed. If you will thus pray and think, you will find coming to you the desires and expectations of the fulfillment of these desires and an enthusiasm which will come from the development of your soul by the possession of this Love, and also the soul thoughts. This is what is meant by the condition necessary to enable the spirits to make the rapport.

Of course, as to the ordinary matters of the spirit world where no special soul condition is required, the spirits can make rapport as they desire, and in your case many of them could have written at the times you thought you were unable to receive any writings. But we thought it best that no spirit be permitted to write you, as it might endanger the probability of your getting in the condition that we desire and which is necessary in order for your brain to receive our vital and important messages. And, hence, your Indian was directed to not permit any spirit to write you, and he did not though many made the effort to do so.

Well, I am glad that I can write you in this manner tonight, and hope you will consider what I have said, and realize the importance of your getting into the condition of which I speak. The brain must be used by the soul having the Divine Love active and so prepared to receive the rapport.

I will not write more tonight, but will merely say that we have many more messages which we desire to transmit.

So believe that I am frequently with you in my love and desire to help and protect, and make your mission a success.

Good night.

Your brother in Christ,   JOHN.

The Result of Obtaining the Divine Love in Removing Worry. Prayer Is a Wonderful Help When Offered with the True Longings of the Soul and Will Always Find a Response.

I am here—*Jesus*:

Well, my brother, I see that you are much better than you have been for some days past, and that you have prayed more to the Father for the inflowing of His love, and, as a consequence, have more of it in your soul, and are in a better condition spiritually and physically.

I should like to finish my message on * God tonight, but I do not think that you are in just the condition necessary to enable you to receive it, and I think it desirable to postpone it for a while longer.

You must surely realize the effect of prayer to a greater extent than ever, because if you had not prayed as you have been doing for the past

* Read message "Who and What Is God," Edition II, Vol. 1—pages 60 to 64.

few days, you would have found yourself in a great degree of despondency, as the same cause for creating this despondency exists now as it existed several days ago when you were so depressed and worried. Prayer is a wonderful help when offered with the true longings of the soul and will always find a response, and the benefit will not be merely spiritual but, as you may say, material as well.

Of course, prayer does not remove the cause of worry and thus relieve the mortal from worry, but it operates on the mortal's consciousness in such a way as to remove the effect of this cause of worry on the feelings and mental conditions of the mortal, and in this way is the mortal benefitted and his prayers responded to. He, as it were, becomes a new man and ceases to look upon these causes in the same light that he did before the prayers commenced to bring their responses. And he in his real self, is a different man from what he was when in the condition that existed before he prayed.

I am so very glad that you prayed and let your longings go out to the Father, and tried to have faith in us to help you. We are helping you, and you will soon realize the result of our work in securing those things that you desire and consider necessary to enable you to get rid of your worries and perform our work. Continue to pray and to have faith in us, and you will not be disappointed in what we promise, for our promises will be fulfilled in a very short time.

I have many messages yet to write, and so desire that you get in condition to receive them properly; and besides myself, there are many other spirits who want to write upon these truths, that are so important that the world should know. So, if you continue to pursue the course that you followed today, you will find a wonderful improvement in your condition of soul and mind and spirit qualities, and we will be able to form the required rapport that is necessary to our properly communicating.

I will not write more tonight.

But in closing, I advise that you continue to pray with all the longings of your soul, and to believe with all the strength of your mind and you will develop to a surprising degree in your soul qualities and perceptions and also in your physical condition and mental strength.

I will say good night.

Your brother and friend,   JESUS.

Comments on Prayer to Remove Worry

I am here—Your own true and loving *Helen*: (Mrs. Padgett)

Yes, it is Helen, and I will write only a few lines as I see that you are feeling so much better physically and spiritually, and I think it best that you go to bed early tonight.

I am so glad that you do not feel so worried as you did, and also, that you can understand that prayer helps so much to get rid of the worries while it may not remove the immediate cause thereof: but as you are helped, you are strengthened and the better fitted to deal with the causes and overcome them.

So my own dear Ned, continue to pray, and try to have faith in us, and you will realize so wonderfully the response to your prayers, and the fulfillment of your hopes and freedom from your causes of worry.

Good night,

Your own true and loving *Helen.*

Why Should Men Learn that They are not to be Left to Themselves in Their Conception of What Life Means, and What Its Importance is in the Economy of Man's Creation and Destiny.

I am here. *John.*

I come tonight to tell you of a truth which is important for you to know as well as for the world of mankind. I will not write a very long message, but what I may say will be the truth and every man should understand it and make it his own.

I will not write upon any subject that you have been instructed upon before, but will deal with a subject entirely new and my subject is: *"Why should men learn that they are not to be left to themselves in their conceptions of what life means, and what its importance is in the economy of man's creation and destiny."*

I know that this may seem to you to be a strange subject to write on, but it is one that should be of interest to all men who know that the earth life is very short and then eternity takes them into its embrace and never again permits them to become creatures of time.

Man lives and dies and never lives again according to the materialist, and he is as the brute animal without any future. But the spiritualist, and by that I mean those who believe that there is something more to man than the mere material, believes he lives and never ceases to live, although the physical body dies never to be resurrected again as such body.

Now, as we take either the one or the other of these views, the meaning of man's earth life assumes a very different aspect, and calls for very different thoughts and actions on his part in living his life. Of course, if what is called death is the end of things that man should do, or he should think he should do as the old saying, "eat, drink and be merry for tomorrow you shall die," and with that death comes oblivion and forgetfulness never to be awakened again into consciousness, his mission in the universe is fulfilled, and he can no more experience the hopes or ambitions or joys or sorrows which were his as a living man.

But on the other hand, if man never ceases to live then his thoughts and conduct should be turned towards the accomplishment of that which will provide for him the best possible future.

Those of both opinions know, that when death comes the physical body can no longer be used, and those who believe in the continuous existence know that as the physical body perishes man must have some other form or body in which may be lodged the consciousness of this continued existence, and that body must be as real as the one which he relinquishes. Such being the fact, the man who knows that death does not end all will naturally and necessarily seek to learn what that body of continued existence is like, and what is necessary to enable him to obtain that body and thereby enjoy the living in eternity. And thus seeking he will not be satisfied to learn that that body is the mere spirit body which has been his during all the years of his earth life, but will desire to further learn what the relationship is between that body and the manner of living his earth life.

I know that of himself, man cannot to any degree discover this relationship, and that he must depend upon the teachings and experiences of those who have experienced the separation of the spirit from the physical in order to at all comprehend this relationship.

As one having had this experience, I wish to say that the spirit body is, of itself, a creation like as is the physical body, and has its existence only for the purpose of preserving man's individuality, and of containing and sheltering his soul, both while on earth and after he becomes a spirit.

Then his living means that he is placed on the earth merely to acquire an individuality, and to learn that within him is the soul which is his real self and which he must cherish and educate and feed with the higher thoughts and goodness of his original creation; and not neglect the opportunities that come to him for this development.

I know that this seems incoherent to you with no special object in view, but you are mistaken in thus thinking for the object will soon be seen. But as you are not just in condition for further writing tonight, I will postpone my writing until later.

So trusting that you will not feel inclined to reject the message I will say good-night.

Your brother in Christ,   JOHN.

The Divine Truth Must be Declared to All Mankind.

I am here, *Jesus.*

Let me write for I am anxious to tell you that you are in a much better condition than you have been for a long time, and your thoughts of today and especially of tonight have put you in a spiritual condition, and if you continue in these thoughts and longings you will soon enable us to make the rapport by which we can continue our messages with greater frequency and with exact expression of what we desire to convey.

I have been with you a great deal today, and have tried to exercise upon your soul and mind an influence that will cause you to more fully realize the responsibility that rests upon you and the importance of the

229

work that you are to do. I was with you at church this morning and saw the impression made upon your mind by the preacher, when he asked the question: if any one had anything to offer that would show him that he had not grasped all of the truth as to the spiritual things, as he called them, that would cause men to aspire for and obtain a higher course of living, and also saw that you realized that your work, if carried to its conclusions, would answer that question. And so you must think of this question and try with all the powers that have been given you to learn these truths, so they can be made known—not only to the preachers of the so-called Christian Churches but to all mankind. You already have truths enough to show this minister that he is not preaching the true Christian spirituality that I came to the world to teach, and did teach, and that he must not rest satisfied with his knowledge of spiritual things but must seek for more light and truth, and then make them a part of his own possessions, and teach them to the world of men, and especially those to whom he has the opportnity of ministering.

I am much pleased that you are in so much better condition of soul, and want you to persist in your efforts to obtain more of the love of the Father and then you will be able to bring true enlightenment to the unthinking and unknowing world of the truths that are so vital to their salvation.

I was also with you tonight and saw the impression made on you by the preacher when he set forth Samuel as he then was, as an example to be followed by the true seekers after the important things that lead to spiritual regeneration and perfect manhood, and was glad that you could appreciate how far the character of Samuel fell short of what is necessary to make a man the Divine Angel, or even the perfect man. The preacher does not experience the truth of the Divine Love in his soul, and in fact has not even an intellectual knowledge of its existence and operations. He believes that I am God, and that my blood washes away the sins of all men who believe in me; and thus thinking, he is satisfied to rest upon the promise of the Gospels, which he accepts as the true teachings of me.

Samuel is now here, and was with you at the church, and realized how devoid he was, at the time spoken of by the preacher, of that thing which was necessary to his salvation, and that his demand upon the people to behold him, and then bring any charge of unrighteousness that they could against him and his conduct as a servant and prophet of Jehovah. This is a very pretty story and to a certain extent contains in it a teaching of the moral laws, that works for good, but it is not more important than many other things contained in the Old Testament. * Samuel will come some time and write you of his life on earth, and his ministry as a servant of Jehovah.

*Message from Samuel Edition II, Vol. I—Pages 270-273.

Well my dear brother, I will not write more tonight, but will soon come and write an important message, which I know will not only benefit but interest you.

Well, I will write on the subject that you suggest, for this is an important thing for men to know, as so many think they are doing God's will in their various courses of living and in their various forms of worship. His will is one that corresponds with all the laws that affect man in every way, and men must know what this will is.

I will come soon and write on this subject and hope that you may be successful in receiving my message as I intend to deliver it.

With my love and blessing, and the assurance that I will be with you in all times of need, and try to direct you in your thoughts, I will say good night.　　Your friend and brother,　　　　　　　　　JESUS.

Affirming that Jesus Wrote

I am here—Your own true and loving *Helen*:

Well dear, I am so happy that you are in such good condition to receive the messages, and that you have again realized the presence of the love in your soul, and have turned your longings and desires to the Father, for an increase of His love.

I cannot tell you how solicitous I have been for you, and have prayed the Father that he would pour out his Holy Spirit upon you, and call you again to the work that you must do. How different you are when in the condition of love from what you are when indifferent and cold and shut in, as it were, to your thoughts of the material. If you could only appreciate what it all means to be in this condition of indifference, you would try with all the powers of your soul and mind to never let the condition come over you. There is nothing in all the universe that can possibly compensate for the loss of this feeling of the possession of the active love in your soul, and you must realize it.

I am so glad that the Master wrote you as he did, and hope that you will remember what he said, and become in unison with him and the work that he has given you to do. Be true to him and to yourself and you will arrive at the state of will that will make and keep you very happy while on earth, and give you the certainty of a home in the Celestial Heavens.

But believe that I love you with all my soul, and want you to be very happy. Many spirits are anxious to write.

So good night.　　Your own true and loving,　　　　　　　　HELEN.

What Is the Holy Spirit and How It Works.

I am here. *John.*

I merely want to say that your condition is improving and that in a few nights we will be able to continue our messages, and then you will find yourself happier in more ways than one. I mean that you will feel better spiritually.

231

I was with you tonight at the meeting, and it did you good, for there were many spirits present who have the love to a more or less degree, and of course, their influence was being exercised on and felt by the worshipers.

The preacher is a man with a considerable amount of the Divine Love in his soul, and if he only had the true conception of Jesus he would find himself possessing more of this love; and his idea of the Holy Spirit is such that it interferes with his receiving the effect of the work of the Spirit. He thinks and believes it to be an entity—in other words a being of substance and thought and sentient capacity, whereas, as you know, it is not, but merely the evidence of the working of God's own soul in bestowing upon mortals His love and mercy. The Spirit is God's messenger for this purpose and is not a creation of His, as is Jesus and mankind. It is merely an energy of the soul of the Father, conveying His love. The Spirit could have no existence without the Soul of the Father, and is entirely dependent upon the powers of that Soul for its existence, and only in the sense that it conveys God's love can it be called the Comforter. And to grieve the Spirit, as the preacher said, means only that the Love of God is grieved, which is in fact not true, for this Love is never grieved, as it is so great and so intense in its desire that men shall receive it, that it never becomes grieved, though it is often disappointed, as you may say, that men will not receive it. It is always present waiting for men to receive it, and by their longings and prayers cause their souls to be opened up to its reception. And this remember: that this Love of the Father is so very great that the Spirit which conveys it to man cannot become grieved.

Well, I did not intend to write on this subject tonight and what I have said is merely fragmentary, but sometime I will come and write in detail.

You must pray more and let your faith increase and you will find what the * Holy Spirit is, and how it operates. Yur prayers will be answered, and a great inflowing of the love, and also your desires will be realized. Keep up your courage and you will not be disappointed. Today may look dark and dreary, but tomorrow the sun will shine, and you will enjoy the sunlight.

I will not write more now.

So with my love and blessings, I will say goodnight.

Your brother in Christ, JOHN.

Comments by Jesus of a Discourse by a Preacher Who Knows Only the way that leads to the perfect natural man. Man's main existence in the flesh is for the purpose of giving the soul individualization. All other apparent objects are only secondary. Explains the incarnation of the soul.

* Holy Spirit—Vol. I, Edition 1, Pages 72 to 76, by Jesus.

I am here, *Jesus.*

Let me write tonight as you are in good condition, and I desire very much to write you in reference to a subject that is important for men to know.

As I have before written you, there are two destinies for man in the spirit life, and the one or the other of them may be just as he desires and seeks for.

I was with you today as you listened to the preacher expound the reasons why he is a believer in the faith of the church to which he belongs, and in which he is a leader and teacher. He is undoubtedly honest and earnest in his beliefs, and, so far as they go, they will afford him the happiness that he spoke of, provided he puts such beliefs into actual, practical living and makes them the dominating, dynamic influence that shall guide and control him in his intercourse with humanity. He said truly that there is a law that operates in wonderful power in shaping men's lives, and which, when obeyed, will determine the career not only of men but of nations; and that law is, that when once a truth is ascertained or comes to the knowledge of men it must be recognized and acted upon, or it will lose its beneficent effect upon the lives of men.

If he applies this law to his own life he will experience a wonderful help in meeting the difficulties and cares of life, and in overcoming the things that beset him as a thinking man.

This is a wonderful truth, and so far as it pervades the life of a man will result in making that life one of consistent goodness, and cause harmony between that man and God who overrules the secret things of the universe, and that man will enjoy a great happiness even while in the flesh.

But this is not the important object and aim of what the preacher calls religion, nor does it furnish the means by which a man may come into a greater and closer harmony with the will of God. I know, that to man this present mortal life seems a thing of the greatest importance, and that the chief aim of man should be to act in that manner that will make his life successful and happy, and, so far as it is suited to make man the harmonious creature that is intended, it is advisable to follow that course of living and loving. But the preacher does not know of and cannot teach the great object of man's appearance on earth, and the goal that is ever before him, waiting to be reached and possessed.

As I have told you before, man's existence in the flesh is only for the purpose of giving his soul, an individualization, and all other apparent objects are only secondary as you may say, accidental accompaniments of this process of individualization.

Hence you will observe that this great object is accomplished equally in the case of the infant who dies young and in the case of the man who lives to a ripe old age—in each case the object of the soul's incarnation in the flesh is effected. The old man, of course, has his experience—a longer and more diverse existence in meeting and overcoming or submitting to the exigencies of his living than does the infant, but the great object is not more perfectly accomplished in the one case than in the other. The soul becomes individualized the moment it finds its lodgment in the receptacle prepared by the laws of nature in using the human father and mother as its instruments, and time thereafter does not influence or have any determining effect upon that soul so far as its individualization is concerned; and neither does eternity, for that condition being once fixed never can be changed nor annihilated, so far as is known to the highest spirits of God's heavens. Of course, the soul as thus individualized is subject to the various influences that surround it in its mortal life, and these influences may be retarding, deadly or destructive to the progress of the soul, but cannot possibly affect the object obtained by that soul's coming into the flesh or ever require a new individualization of that soul. Its identity and character, as an individualized thing are established, and no condition of the soul as to its goodness or badness can ever, in the slightest degree, affect this character or identity. The soul once individualized always remains the individual, even though the elements that enter into and make up the form will always find itself being rebuilt and continued by the operations of the law that preserves the individuality of that soul.

Then, I say, the object of the incarnation of the soul is to give it an individualization, and this in two appearances; first, in that of the physical form which men by their perception of their natural organs of sense can perceive, and secondly, a form that is more sublimated and generally invisible to these organs. A spiritual form.

At the moment of incarnation the soul takes the form which has been prepared for it by the forces that exist in the parents and retains that for during the natural life; and at the same moment there is created for it or attracted to it, the form of the spirit body, which then and ever afterwards remains with it. Both of these bodies are of the material; one of the visible material of the universe, the other of the invisible but still of the material.

As you know that body which is made of the visible material lasts for a little while only and then disappears forever, while that which is of the invisible, and which is more real and substantial than the former and exists all the time of the existence of the visible, continues with the soul after the disappearance of the invisible body; and while changeable in response to the progress of that soul, yet the spirit body never in its composite form leaves that soul. This we in the spirit life know to be true, just as certainly as you mortals know the truth of the existence of the

234

physical body. And as you mortals may in the short space of the life on earth identify the man—which is really the soul—by the appearance of his physical body, so we in the spirit world identify the same man by the appearance of the spirit body, and so this fact must be forever.

Then such being the fact, it must be conceived that the soul has its existence in the physical body for an infinitesimal short time—that is its life on earth is only the breath of a moment—and then it enters on its career through eternity, and after a few years, as you may say, it may cease to remember that it ever had a lodgment in the physical body.

The preacher criticised the religion that taught man to think of and prepare for the future of the soul, and emphasized the fact that their thoughts should be more of the present, and that duty and good works towards their fellow man should be the object of their living, and their religion. Well, I recognize the importance of duty and good works and approve of them with all the knowledge that I now have of the demands and requirements of God's love, but on the other hand must say, that their importance to man's future destiny is also the importance of other privileges and obligations possessed by, and resting on man, during the short time that the soul is clothed in the physical body. Duty performed, and good works will lessen the distress and sufferings of the mortal life, and cause the man who performs the duty and does the good works to become more in harmony with God's laws of mercy and truth, but will never suffice to bring a soul into harmony with the will of the Father as regards the higher destiny of man. These things will tend to lead merely to the purification of the soul, and to cause it to come into accord with the laws of its own creation and their end. These constitute merely the exercise of compliance with the moral laws, and bring only a moral effect. And when I say moral laws I mean those laws that demand that, and by the observance of which, man comes into the condition of the perfect man, which was his at the time of his creation. He thereby obtains nothing more than belonged to him when he existed as the perfect man and was in complete harmony with God as such perfect man. He then loved God with all the capacity of his soul in the exercise of the love that had been bestowed upon him, and could have loved his brother as himself.

And to this condition men are, to a more or less extent, now striving to attain, and many precepts of the Old Testament as well as of the New, will lead men to thus obtain, and if this were the only destiny of man, then the religion of the preacher, which he says is based on these moral precepts of love to God and love to his fellow man, would be sufficient to obtain the goal sought, and love and duty and service would be all that are required of men while on earth as well as after they become spirits; and the exercise of these graces by men while on earth would be just as necessary and helpful as would their exercise afterwards in the spirit world. These things of love to God and love to man, and service and sacrifice constitute the true religion that leads to the perfect man, and makes for that harmony with the laws of God governing the condition of the perfect man but not the divine man.

These things should be preached by all ministers and teachers, and practiced by men everywhere, for in their practice are happiness and bliss unspeakable. As these things work to a finality, man again becomes the son of God and obedient to his laws, and realizes the meaning of "love God and love your brother". And so I repeat, the preacher in pronouncing the basis of his religion, declared the truths that will lead him into the condition of the perfect man, in harmony with God's will as to man's creation.

Well, I see you are tired and so we will postpone the further writing. I am very much pleased that you are in so much better condition, and hope that we may continue our messages without further interruption. Only pray more and believe that the Father will answer your prayers.

So believe that I love you and want you to be happy and free from care. Good night.

Your brother and friend,   Jesus.

Comments by a Minister.

Let me write just a line as I merely desire to say that I have listened to what the Master has written and can testify that the love to God and love to our fellow man are not all that man needs for a basis of his religion. I was when on earth a minister and taught the same doctrines that the preacher of the day taught, and believed that they were all that man needed, and died in that belief; but, alas, I discovered after many years of darkness and of happiness in my natural love that they would not furnish a basis for my progress to the Celestial Heavens—to the condition of the soul transformed by the Divine Love. I merely wanted to say this. If agreeable to you I should like to come some time and detail more at length my experience in learning the basis of the true religion.

I will say good night.

Your brother in Christ,   Dr. C———.

Man Himself Must Make the Effort to Overcome the Influence of the Evil Ones.

I am here, must I say—*Your own true and loving, Helen?* (Mrs. Padgett)

While, in many instances, the evil spirits influence mortals in their thoughts and actions, yet this is not always the case and it will not do for mortals to think so. They are not the mere pliant tools or subjects of these evil spirits, but are persons with free wills controlled by their

236

own appetites, and for them to believe that all their evil acts are the results of the influence of these evil spirits would place them in a very subservient and deplorable condition, and at the same time retard the development of themselves by their own thoughts and acts. No, the evil spirits are always working evil, but all the thoughts and desires that mortals have and do, are not the results of the influence of these spirits.

Man must realize that in himself is the cause of his own evil thoughts and deeds, though increased by the influence of these spirits, and that he must master these thoughts that he be able to drive them from him and overcome them by thoughts of a different and higher nature. It will not do for men to think that they are wicked only because of the influence of the evil spirits, for to think so would retard their development and at the same time take from them a realization of their own responsibility. And on the other hand, the source of good thoughts is within themselves, and if they will only seek for this source they will be able to progress in their moral conditions; and while the good spirits can and do help them, yet primarily men must help themselves from the good that is within them.

I would like to write you fully on this matter, and will sometime, but tonight you are not in condition, and I will not try. But remember this, that whatever of evil is displayed or gives evidence of the soul being possesed by it, yet within themselves is the power to overcome and cause its eradication. I mean that men must make the effort, realize that they are masters of good and evil. We can help you, if you will let us—it depends on you—and no other can take the praise or blame of the results of your thoughts or actions. Yet, you must also realize this, that when the evil ones form a rapport with you, and in a way obscess you, it will become the more difficult for you to exercise your own will; and hence, men should pray to be given help from the Higher Source to overcome the influences of these evil ones. The character of your company will determine to a considerable extent the kind of thoughts you may have and the deeds you may do. But good or bad be your associates, you alone will be responsible for the results of your thoughts and acts.

I must not write more.

Good night.   Your own true and loving,   HELEN.

A Mother gives her experience after passing over, due to giving birth to her baby.

Come to the bridal chamber, death. Come to the young mother when she feels for the first time her new born's breath. And so death came to me when I was but a young bride and lived in expectation of a new, loving being that would be part of my flesh—and died when my baby came. As life came to it, death came to me, and we missed each other at the very moment that I heard its first cry.

237

And when I came to life in the spirit world I was bitter and thought God to be so heartless and cruel to take me from my baby, and was so unhappy, and wanted to die over again.

I would like to tell you of my misery and gloom and hatred of my very God, whom I had believed in and thought that I loved, but I cannot now. But this I must say, that my unhappiness was for a short time only, for bright spirits came to me and comforted me, and assured me that I was not separated from my baby, but could go to my baby and watch over him and give him my mother's love, and so I did, and am now doing, for my baby who is now a man, and still I am with him, and I know that I have been a greater blessing to him as his spirit mother, than I would have been had I remained his mortal mother.

I write this to comfort mothers who have to leave their babies as they come into the earth life, and to assure them, that, though they disappear from the visions of their loved ones, yet they can always be with them—close and in deep rapport with them and love.

Death comes as an enemy, but when recognized, only a friend appears. Mothers, thank God for such a death and the great consolation it brings to the departing and to those left behind.

Goodbye,   G. S———.

I desire tonight to write for a short time on the text, *"That the sins of the parents are visited upon the children unto the third and fourth generations."*

I am here. *Luke.*

I desire tonight to write for a short time on the text. *That the sins of the parents are visited upon the children unto the third and fourth generations.*

I know that usually the explanation of the text has been that the material sins or rather the sins which result in material injury or affliction are visited upon the children and to a very great extent this is true. but that explanation is not what was intended by the declaration.

Man is not only a material or physical being, but is more largely a spiritual being, having a soul and spirit which never ceases to exist, and which are just as much a part of him while on earth, as when he becomes a spirit, that is after he has left the vestments of flesh and blood.

These real parts of man are of more importance to him and his real existence than is the physical part, and the sins which man commits are not the results of any primary physical action, but of the operations of the powers which form or have their real seat in the spiritual part of his being.

The physical part of man is not the originator of sin, but merely manifests its effects, and it almost always manifests itself on and in the physical body, and leaves its scars apparent to the consciousness of men upon

238

such body; and hence, as man is able in his ordinary condition to perceive the effects more plainly on this body, he thinks that the meaning of the text must refer to the sins that affect and are shown upon his body, and at the same time ignores or is not sensible of the fact, that the great effect or injury of sin is upon and to the spiritual part of man.

As the physical body is affected by the results of these sins being carried into operation, so much more so is the spiritual part of man affected by the fact that these sins had their creation in that spiritual part of man.

It may be asked, in what way can the effect of sin upon a man, that is upon his soul and spirit, have any injurious effect upon the spirit and soul of his child, so that the child may suffer from the sin of the parent.

Well, when a child is conceived and gestates and is born, he not only partakes of the physical nature of his parents, but also of the qualities and condition of the spirit and soul of the parents. This may seem improbable, but it is a fact that the spirit and soul that enters into the child when it is conceived comes from the great universe of soul and spirit, wholly independent of the parents and is not in its nature or qualities a part of the parents as is the flesh and blood which build up and produce the physical body of the child.

But while this is true, it is also true that this spirit and soul of the child is susceptible to and in a way absorbs the influence of the spirit and soul of the parents, not only at the time of conception but also during the period of gestation, and even for years afterwards, and to such an extent that this influence continues beyond the mere earthly existence of the parents and into the life of the progeny to the third and fourth generation, as the text says.

The spirit part of the child is more susceptible to the influence and evil effects of these sins than is really its physical body, for as I have said the spirit part is the originator and breeder of the sins, if I may so express it, while the body is merely the recipient of the exercise of the sins and the objects of their manifestation.

The influence of spirit upon spirit is more extensive and certain than mortals can possibly conceive of, and the results of that influence are not so apparent or known to the consciousness of the succeeding children, or to the respective parents, as men suppose, and as a fact they do not understand or become conscious of the fact that such influence is operating upon the spiritual parts of their children. They see and realize that the effects of such sins become manifested in the physical body, and as their ordinary natural senses cannot perceive the condition of the spirit, they conclude that the text can only mean, that these sins are visited upon the material bodies of their children.

But I must tell them that, while great and deplorable injury is inflicted on these material bodies, yet greater and more lasting and more grievous

239

in the way of manifestations, injury is inflicted upon the spiritual nature of the children; not only because this nature continues to live, but because men, not realizing that this nature has been injured, make no attempt to find and apply a remedy as they so often do in the case where these sins manifest themselves in the physical body.

And besides, there are many sins that do not affect the mere material body, but which do great injury to the spiritual nature, and which to the senses of men are never perceptible.

A man is not only the parent of a child's material body but in a secondary way is also the parent of its spiritual nature, and the condition of the parent's spiritual nature influences and determines to a large extent the qualities and tendencies of the child's nature for good or evil, not only while it is a mortal but frequently after it has ceased to inhabit the veil of flesh.

So let parents know that they do not live to themselves alone as mortals, but that their evil thoughts and deeds have a greater or lesser influence upon the spiritual natures of their children, especially at the time of conception and during gestation. Then how important that every parent during these times particularly and at all times, should have their spiritual natures in that condition of purity and freedom from sin, that their children may be conceived and born in a condition of soul purity, which will not reflect any evil that they can charge their parents with being the creators of.

If men would only realize these facts and live their lives in accordance with the truths which I here declare, how much sooner would the human race be brought into harmony with God's laws and the souls of men be freed from sin and evil.

I know it is often said that it is unjust and not in accordance with the justice of an impartial God that the sins and penalties arising from the disobedience of our first parents, should be visited upon mankind who were and are their progeny, as such mankind had no part in that disobedience. But when it is remembered and it is a fact, that God did not create sin or evil or impose such upon the first parents for their disobedience, but that they themselves created evil and sin, and men have been creating these inharmonies ever since, it will be seen that an impartial God, who is our only God, is not responsible for either sin or evil and the consequent penalties which they impose. And, as has been written you before, the abolishing of sin and evil and their penalties is in the power of man and his will.

As these first parents created these evils, as I have explained and in the manner that I have pointed out to you, their sins by the influence which they have upon the spiritual nature at the time of conception and birth become, as it were, a visitation and that is the spiritual desires and

240

tendencies and inclinations toward that which is evil, and this influence continues with the child for years after its birth according as the child and parents are closely associated together in their earth lives, and as each succeeding generation caused the visitation of its sinful influence and tendencies upon the succeeding generation, you can readily see how men, all men, became subject to the sins and evils and penalties which were brought into the world by the first parents.

Instead of God being the creator of these things or visiting them upon the children of man, He declares that their existence is contrary to the harmony of His creation and must be eradicated before man can come into that harmony and an at-one-ment with Him. And as He gave to man the great power of free will, without any restriction upon its exercise, except as a man's understanding of the harmony of the operations of God's laws might influence him to exercise this great power; and as man in the wrong exercise of that power brought into existence these things of evil and sin, so man, as he perceives this plan of God's harmony, must exercise that will in such a way as to free himself from these things which are not part of God's creation, and are out of harmony with His plans for the creation and preservation of a perfect universe, of which man is its highest creation.

God never changes. His laws never change. Only man has changed from the perfection of His creation; and man must change again before that perfection will again be his.

Now from all this it must not be inferred that man is left to his own efforts to bring about this great restoration, for that is not true, because Gods instrumentalities are continuously at work influencing man to turn again to his first estate, and become the perfect man, as he ultimately will become.

I am not here referring to the workings of the great Divine Love which, when a man possesses in a sufficient degree, makes him more than the perfect man.

So the sins of the parents are visited upon the children to the third and fourth generation means, the tendencies and inclinations toward that which is evil, not by God, but by man himself, solely and exclusively.

And oh man, could you see the results of these sins upon the spiritual natures of your children, as you often see them upon their material bodies, you would hesitate in your sinning and think, and thinking would see the way by which the great blot upon the happiness and salvation of humanity could be removed and its progress to the "perfect man" be hastened and assured.

Well, I have written enough for tonight, and hope that what I have said may be understood and meditated upon by all who may read it.

I will not detain you longer, and with my love and the blessings of one who is now not only the perfect man, but a possessor of the Divine Nature of the Father and an inheritor of immortality, say good night.

Your brother in Christ, LUKE.

I am here, *Luke*.

I desire to make some corrections in my message of last night, and will thank you to receive them.

I desire to say, that when I spoke of the sins of the parents being visited upon the children at the time of conception and birth, I meant that these sins by the influence which they have upon the spiritual nature of the child, became, as it were a visitation. I did not mean that any part of the real sin of the parents became a part of the spiritual nature of the child, but only that the influence of the parent's sins upon the child is sufficient to give the spiritual desires and tendencies of the child an inclination towards that which is evil; and this influence is continuous with the child for years after its birth according as the child and parents are closely associated together in their earth lives.

Let this point be made plain so that man may not quibble about the meaning of what I wrote.

Otherwise the message is true and just as I intended it should convey to you the truth of the meaning of the text.

I will not delay you longer tonight, but with my love and blessings say,

I am your brother in Christ,

LUKE.

Why Judas Betrayed Jesus.

I am here. *Judas Iscariot.*

I came tonight because I want to tell you of just what my condition and expectations were when I betrayed Jesus which resulted in his crucifixion.

I was a very enthusiastic lover of the Master and believed thoroughly in his teachings and his power, and did not believe that the Roman soldiers could take him away from where we were, if we did not permit it to be done.

As a consequence, I was anxious that Jesus should show his great power, and demonstrate to the Jews that he was a true son of God, with power over men and devils.

I never betrayed him for the money that I received for it was not sufficient to pay for one moment of happiness which I have lost because of my act in betraying the greatest spirit in all God's kingdom.

I see that you are too sleepy to write more tonight. I will come again and tell my story.

So good-night. JUDAS.

The greatest sin is against the Holy Spirit
that conveys the Divine Love into the soul.

I am here. *Judas.*

I come tonight to write a short message for I have been interested in what you and your friends have said regarding the "greatest sin".

Now, to me, for a long time, the greatest sin in all the universe of God was my sin in betraying Jesus to the Jews, and it was a real, living, blasting sin, and so enormous that I could not endure my life, and face the recollection of that awful tragedy; but since I have been forgiven of that sin and become a redeemed child of the Father and an inhabitant of the Celestial Heavens and a possessor of immortality, I realize and know that my sin was not the greatest, even though I suffered for long years after I became a spirit.

As sin may be committed by neglect as well as by affirmative action, and my betraying the beloved Master was a heinous one, but yet, even in my case, and as applicable to me, my greater sin was not seeking for the Divine Love of the Father. We were not ignorant of this, for the Master had taught us that this love was open to and waiting for us to seek and obtain and I had not sought for it in the right way and of course had not obtained it; and in such neglect I was not the only one of the disciples that was guilty of that sin.

No, even we who had been with the Master for so long a time did not fully understand the importance of obtaining this Great Love, as we were more interested in his establishing his kingdom on earth and, as we thought, a material kingdom, to be controlled by spiritual powers manifested in Him, and in us as his disciples. And the material, in our minds, was of more importance than the spiritual, and our expectations were that this great power would come, and that the Master would become our king.

As I say, he had taught us that this Divine Love was open to us, and that by prayer and earnest seeking we could receive it, but to us there were so many important things to be done, connected, as I say, more immediately with our earth lives, that we neglected the Great Gift that was ours for its seeking, and as a consequence, in my case, I had to suffer for a long time before I awakened to the fact, that it was not too late, even for me to receive it.

My sin of betrayal had been forgiven me in that I realized that the recollections of it were leaving me and that I was progressing in the way of purifying my soul in its natural love, and that as the spirit of the one-time murderer, I was coming into happiness and light.

And then I had memories of what the Master had said to me about this Great Love, and after awhile I had sufficient awakening to cause me to make the effort to obtain this Love, and as that awakening came to me,

243

my old-time associates, who had progressed to the higher spheres came to me and in their great beauty and Transcendent Love, helped me to progress and to pray, until at last this Love came to me, and I realized that not only had my sin of murder been wholly forgiven, but that the greater sin of rejecting and neglecting to seek for the Divine Love had also been forgiven me.

The sin of the murderer or of any violator of God's laws other than that of rejecting the inflowing of this Love, may and will be forgiven a man and he will become pure and happy in his natural love, but such forgiveness will not make him an inhabitant of the Divine Heavens or an inheritor of immortality, while the forgiveness of the sin of rejecting the Holy Spirit, will not only take away from him the recollections and taints of all other sins, but will open up to him the very portals of the Celestial Heavens and give him a home in the Father's kingdom.

And thus, you see, every sin except that of sinning against the Holy Spirit, may be forgiven a man, with the result that he will become the perfect man, but the forgiveness of all these sins many times over if it could so happen, would not make him the Divine Angel.

And I need not explain to you, for you can readily see from what I have written, that the greatest sin in all the world is the sin against the Holy Spirit—the sin of neglecting or refusing to let the Holy Spirit bring in and to the soul of man the Great Divine Love of the Father. And not only is this sin the greatest because of the results that flow from it, but because it will continue to be the unpardonable sin so long as man refuses to permit its forgiveness.

When the sin of murder and such kindred sins are committed, the sin then ends and only its consequences must be suffered and the penalty paid; but the sin against the Holy Spirit is a continuing sin, committed every day and hour and minute and never having an end until the mortal seeks and receives the inflowing of this Divine Love. As has been written you many times, yes, the large majority of men and spirits will continue forever and ever to commit this sin, and in the effects to follow, to them, it will become and is the unpardonable sin.

As we are much interested in you, and have determined that you shall not go astray to these Divine truths, my brother spirits of the Celestial Spheres, thought it fitting, as the world considers that I committed the greatest sin in all the history of the world, that I should write you on this subject, and explain that the greatest sin in all the world is the sin against the Holy Ghost.

We all know this, and while I write, you must believe, for it is true, that all of us and the Master too, declare that the sin I name is the greatest sin.

And now to be a little more personal, for your gratification and comfort, I desire to tell you, that you three will not be found guilty of having committed this great sin, for you have in your hearts and souls much of this Divine Love, and the Holy Spirit is with you quite often in answer to your prayers, and in answer to ours also, for we all pray for you, causing this Love of the Father to possess your souls, even as the leaven wrought in the batch of dough.

I have written longer than I expected and will now stop.

But be assured that you have our love and the blessings of the Father.

Your brother in Christ,

JUDAS.

Corroborating that Judas wrote on the unpardonable sin.

I am here. Your own true and loving *Helen* (*Mrs. Padgett*)

Well, I am pleased that you received the message from Judas and it is a wonderful message filled with truths that you will perceive with more force and newness the more you read it.

It was actually Judas writing, and as he said, he was chosen by the others to deliver the same, for many of them were present while he was doing so. And I was here also and heard what was said, and know that what I tell you is true.

How blessed you and Mr. Morgan and the Dr. should feel to know that of all the wonderful spirits of the Celestial Spheres, the most wonderful and the highest come to you and communicate with you, and not only that, but they bring with them an atmosphere of love that has a most beneficial effect upon the conditions of your souls. I am so happy that I can tell you this and I know that you will believe me, for my love for you would not permit me to deceive you, no matter what the occasion might be. Yes, my dear, these high spirits are your friends and brothers. What more can I say to cause you to realize the greatness of the experience that you are having? I do not know.

Well as you were much drawn on by the message of Judas, I do not think it best to write more tonight and I will stop.

Your own true and loving　　　HELEN.

It was not ordained by God that Judas should betray Jesus;
Judas was not a bad man.

I am here. *St. John.*

Well, there are some things in my gospel that do not seem to be very plain, and perhaps are contradictory. But you must remember that many of these writings were not mine or written at my dictation.

In the mutations of time many things have been added to and subtracted from what I wrote and, as a consequence, the true and the untrue are mixed.

Well, it will be a very difficult task for you to make the distinction in simply reading or even studying the Bible, for the tenor of the writings is the same. The only way that you can separate the true from that which is not, is to wait until Jesus gives you his messages. Of course, we can help also in that particular.

Well, that was not the word which he used, because he never taught that it was ordained by God that Judas should betray him. In fact the death of Jesus was never a part of that which the Father considered as necessary to the performance of his mission.

Of course it was certain that Jesus would die, but the manner of his death was not foreordained, as my Gospel written in your Bible declares. Judas was not a bad man as he is depicted to be and his betrayal, as it is called, of the Master, was not for the purpose of gratifying any avarice that he might be supposed to have or because of any jealousy or desire to revenge a wrong, but it was because he was impulsive and a belief in Jesus' powers and ability to overcome the Jewish leaders in their fight to defeat the objects of Jesus' mission; and he thought he would be doing the Master and his cause a great benefit by having it demonstrated to these Jews that the Master could not be silenced or harmed by any act of theirs. It was really an act that grew out of his love for and belief in the greatness of the Master's powers.

Well, I tell you that Jesus never said any such thing. He never even told us that one of us should betray him, and I know because I was there

If Jesus knew that Judas would betray him, he did not tell any of us at that time, and we only knew it for the first time when Judas actually committed the act. I don't believe that Jesus knew it before that time; in fact he has told me that he was surprised at Judas' betrayal of him. So you must not rely on the Bible statement as to what occurred at that time.

Judas was the youngest of the disciples and not so easily controlled in his impulses and acts, as he would have been were he older.

Yes, I know, but they are all based upon the same erroneous writings, for you must know that these Gospels, as you have them, are not the originals written by those whose names they bear.

Let not these things disturb your belief in the essential truths which the Bible contains.

The trouble is that Jesus as the individual is given the prominence which should be given to his teachings. He is displeased very much because of this, and one of the great objects of his writing anew his truths is to correct that error, and make the truths which he received from the Father, the prominent things.

As you progress in your writings you will see that this is the great object of which he shall write.

Well, I will tell you that you are in the way to receive the Father's Love in very great abundance. In fact, so much so, that you will realize that you are one with the Father.

246

I see, that you at present, have some difficulty in your way, but they will soon disappear and leave you free to do this great work. So my advice is to believe in the Master and pray to the Father and you will soon be a much happier man.

When on earth, I was a married man, and in my family the mother of Jesus lived until her death. She, Mary, lives near me. She is a beautiful spirit and filled with the love of the Father. But you must not suppose that because she was the mother of Jesus she has any more exalted position than she otherwise would have had. Family ties do not determine anything in the higher spheres—the soul development is the criterion. Many spirits are living in higher spheres than Mary.

I will not write more now.

Your brother in Christ,   JOHN.

Many things in the Bible John says he never wrote. St. John was mistaken about the kind of Kingdom that Jesus came to establish.

I am here, *John*.

I will not write now, except to say, that your spiritual condition is much improved and you are advancing in your soul perceptions of the truth and of the reality of the Father and His love.

Yes, I know, but you must remember two things with reference to the writings in the Bible ascribed to me, namely:

First, that many of the sayings therein contained, I did not write or authorize to be written, and, secondly, that at the time I lived on earth and wrote, my knowledge of the truth and of God was not so great or so correct as it is now. I realize that some things I then believed and taught, were not in accord with the truth as I now know it to be—even my conception of Jesus and his mission on earth and his return to earth was not true. Then, although I was a close companion of the Master and had many lessons of instructions from him, I was a quite ignorant man and did not grasp the spiritual meanings of his teachings, and up to the time of my decease, my beliefs were more colored by things of the material than by those of the spiritual. For instance. I, as did the other disciples, supposed that he was coming to earth again in a short time— at any unexpected time—and set up his kingdom on earth. Now, this is a fact, notwithstanding that he had said that his kingdom would be a spiritual kingdom, though existing on earth. I could not dissociate from my conception of the establishment and existence of this kingdom, the idea, that in some way it would be an actual ,visible kingdom in which the Master would be the king, and rule as other kings ruled, except it would be a rule of righteousness.

All this may seem a little strange to you, but if you will consider for a moment that my teachings as a Jew were to the effect that when the Messiah came, he would actually rulé on earth as a king, you will understand how difficult it was for me to get the idea, or make the distinction between that kind of kingdom and one which would be purely spiritual.

At sometime, I will write you more fully on this matter, for I realize its importance, as many, yes a majority of the professed Christians, now believe that Jesus, at sometime, will come to earth and establish a material kingdom and rule all the nations of the earth; and some of these enthusiastic Christians believe that they will be of the elect, and become princes and sub-rulers in that kingdom, as material men called by the resurrection to again become the human, although glorified, as some of them express their faith.

Well, they will be disappointed, for when they shall have passed from the mortal to the spirit, they will forever remain spirits, and the only kingdom that they will live in thereafter will be a spirit kingdom, and that, whether the kingdom of the restored man or of the divine angel, will not be on the earth.

I must stop now.

So pray to the Father and strive for a deeper and more abiding faith, and you will realize the truth and this experience.

Goodnight.

Your brother in Christ,   JOHN.

Saul's testimony—Many laws of the O. T. came to him by tradition.
I am here. *Saul.*

I very much desire to write a short message tonight as I promised you a short time ago.

I will not detain you very long, and will try to make my message as succinct as possible.

I know that many men look upon me, as depicted in the Old Testament, as having been a great sinner and violator of God's laws. Well, that is largely true, for I did not let God's will control me as I should have done, and consequently, I became in discord with His will, and did many things that were contrary to His laws. Of course my knowledge of these laws was limited to the teachings of Moses and the prophets, as they were given to me by tradition and word of mouth.

The books which are part of the Old Testament were not written in my time, and many of these laws came to me by tradition. The Old Testament contains many sayings which were written long after the times that they purport to have occurred, and many things therein declared never had any existence, except in the minds of men, who, at much later periods, conceived that it might be wise to write these things. Many alleged incidents connected with my life, never had an existence, and were merely the fictions written by subsequent writers.

We had very few writings in the shape of manuscript in my time, and men depended upon tradition and memory.

Well, the history of my life and doings, was not written at the time it purports to have been written, I was a real person and a king, and some records of me and my people were actually written, but they were very few, and as time went by the imagination and ingenuity added to them in the way of tradition, and then those books relating to me, as they are now contained in the Bible, were compiled from some of these writings and from tradition.

The story of my experience with the witch of Endor, as she is called, was not written at the time; but it is a fact that I had visited her, and had an experience somewhat similar to that related in the Bible. I had with me at the time of my visit, some of my followers, and they saw and heard what took place, and after my death, they repeated and described what had taken place to my countrymen, and also to the followers of David; and some parts of this occurrence became inscribed on the materials which we used to preserve some of the occurrences of those times. But there was not kept any accurate history of the scene. The people of those days had retentive memories, and for long years afterwards this incident of my life was handed down from generation to generation and some parts thereof were written by some scribes and other parts by other scribes.

I merely write you this to show that you need not give credit to the supposed truths of many sayings of the Old Testament, for many of these accounts had no existence.

I know that what I have written is not of much importance, but while you are receiving these truths you had as well learn something of what was true in my life.

I will not write more tonight, so thanking you, I will say good-night.
Your brother in Christ, SAUL.

Jesus gives advice to Mr. P. Is anxious for him to get into condition of soul so that Jesus can continue his messages to mankind.

I am here. *Jesus.*

Well, my disciple, I realize that your desires are that I shall deliver a message to you tonight, and I am anxious to do so, yet I see you are not in condition that I may take possession of your brain that is necessary in order to write satisfactorily. I am sorry that this is so, but it is a fact, and we will have to wait awhile longer, which will not be very long, for you are much improved, and if you continue to pray you will soon become in that soul condition that will enable me to make the rapport.

There are many messages yet to be written and I am anxious that you receive them in order that they may be delivered to the world, for the world is now awakening to a greater realization of the fact that man is spiritual and must have spiritual food. The war is causing many people to think of the hereafter and the destiny of the soul; and the knowledge

249

that the world now has of the future life is very meager and unsatisfactory, merely a knowledge that the spirit survives death and experiences more or less happiness in the spirit life.

As you know, this is not the vital thing in the destiny of man, for while a knowledge of the survival of man from the death of the physical, may and does give a great deal of consolation to the near and dear ones who are left on earth, yet that fact does not, in the slightest degree, determine the condition or destiny of the soul that has left its home in the flesh; and there are no means, now known to men, to show that destiny, except some things written in the Bible which are the subjects of much speculation and controversy and want of belief. The consolation of those who have faith in the Bible is founded on that faith, or rather, in most cases, belief; but there are a number of believers in the truths of the Bible, with a conscious soul perception of their real meaning, who have that faith which makes certain to them the facts of destiny, and the possession of love in their souls.

I will come soon and endeavor to write a formal message; in the meantime let your prayers ascend with more earnestness and longings to the Father.

* As you know, I love you as my brother and disciple, and am with you as you pray each night, uniting in our prayers, and you must let your faith increase, and believe that your prayers are being heard, and will be answered to the fullest.

I will not write more now.

So my brother, goodnight, and may the Father bless you with His greatest blessings.

Your brother and friend,   JESUS.

Incarnate Soul, by Jesus.

I am here. *Jesus.*

I am here as I promised last night and will write on the subject of the Incarnate Soul. You may have observed in your studies of the different theories of the creation of man that always the question has arisen as to the relationship of the spiritual and physical—that is, as to the soul and the material body. I know that many theories have been set forth as to how and when the soul became a part of the physical body and what was the means adopted by the laws of nature, as they are called, for the lodgment of the soul into that body, and the relationship that one bore to the other. Of course this applies only to those mortals who believe that there is a soul separate in its existence and functionings from the mere physical body; as to those who do not believe in the distinctive soul, I do not attempt to enlighten but leave them to a realization of the

Mr. Padgett told me that when he was praying before retiring, he often saw Jesus alongside praying with him.

250

fact when they shall have come into the spirit world and find themselves existing without such body, but really existing with the consciousness that they are souls.

When the physical body is created it has no consciousness of its having been created, for it is merely of the unconscious creations that are of the other material creatures of nature, and does not feel or sense in any degree the fact, that it is a living thing dependent upon the proper nourishment of its mother for its growth and continued life in accordance with the laws of nature, and the objects of its own creation. The father and mother being necessary to the creation or formation of this merely animal production, know only that in some way there has come into existence an embryo thing that may eventuate into a human being like unto themselves. If this thing were allowed to remain without the soul it would soon fail to fulfill the object of its creation and disintegrate into the elements of which it is formed, and mankind would cease to exist as inhabitants of the earth. This physical part of man is really and only the result of the commingling of those forces that are contained in the two sexes, which according to the laws of nature, or of man's creation, are suited to produce the one body fitted for the home of the soul that may be attracted to it, to develop its individuality as a thing of life and possible immortality.

The result of this commingling is intended only as a temporary covering or protection for the growth of the real being, and does not in any way limit or influence the continuous existence of the soul, and when its functions have ended, the soul, which has then become individualized, continues its life in new surroundings and in gradual progression, and the mere instrument used for its individualization is disseminated into the elements forming its appearance and substance. As this body was called from the elements for a certain purpose, when that purpose shall have been served, it returns to these elements.

This body, of itself, has neither consciousness nor sensation, and in the beginning has only the borrowed life of its parents, and then when the soul finds its lodgment, it has only the life of the soul: for the human life can exist only so long as the soul inhabits the body, and after such habitation commences, the borrowed life of the parents ceases to exercise any influence or directing force on the body. This, then, is really the true description of the physical body, and if it were all of man, he would perish with its death and cease to exist as a part of the creation of the universe of God.

But the soul is the vital, living and never dying part of man—is really the man—and the only thing that was intended to continue an existence in the spirit world. It was made in the image of God, and there is no reason for its existing for the continuing companionship of the physical

251

body, and when men say or believe that the body is all of man and when it dies man ceases to exist, they do not understand the relationship or functioning of soul and body, and know only the half truth which is visible to their senses—that the body dies and can never again be resuscitated. This is a determined fact and all arguments by analogy, to show that man must continue to live notwithstanding the death of that body, are not apposite and very inconclusive. All these analogous appearances only show that the objects of the analogy ultimately die, and thus fail to prove that these objects are eternal just as much as if there had never been any change in their condition or appearance. The final demonstration is that they die, and when this analogy is applied to man, it must show that he dies also, and is no more.

But the questions are asked, whence comes the soul, by whom created, how does it become incarnated in man and for what purpose, and what is its destiny?

First let me state, that man has nothing to do with the creation of the soul or its appearance in the flesh. His work is to provide a receptacle for its coming—a mere host, as it were, for its entry into the flesh, and existence as a mortal or in the appearance of a mortal. But his responsibility in this particular is very great, for man can destroy that receptacle, or care for it so that the soul may continue in earth life a longer or shorter time. And while this receptacle is the creation of man and without him it could not be brought into existence, yet the soul is no part of his creation and is independent of the body—and after the earth life, in the spirit world, it will cease to remember that it was ever connected with or dependent upon the creation of its parents. The soul, in the spirit life, as a truth, is so separated from and dissociated with that body which was its home while in the earth life that it looks upon it as a mere vision of the past and not a subject for its consideration.

As has been told you, the soul was created by the Father long before its appearance in the flesh, and awaited such incarnation for the purpose only of giving it an individuality, which it did not have in its preexistence, and in which it has a duplex personality—male and female—that is needed to be separated and made individual. We who have had this preexistence and incarnation in the flesh and have obtained this individuality, know the truth of what I have here stated.

There is a law of God controlling these things that renders these pre-existing souls capable of knowing the desirability of incarnation and they are always anxious and ready for the opportunity to be born in the flesh and to assume the separate individuality that they are privileged to assume. As men provide the receptacle for their appearing and homing, as it were, they become aware of the fact and take advantage of the opportunity to occupy the receptacle, and become ostensibly a human being with the necessary result of individuality.

I am glad that you are in a better condition and will continue the messages as we have been desiring to do for some time.

I shall be with you and help you in every way, and hope that you will keep up your faith and prayers to the Father.

Good night and God bless you.

Your brother and friend,   JESUS.

Incarnation of the Soul—Mystery of the birth of the soul in the human being.

I am here—*Luke.*

I want to tell you tonight of the *mystery of the birth of the soul in the human being.*

All souls which enter into mortal bodies are, previous to such advent, real, living existences, and made in the likeness of the Great Soul, though not having the qualities and potentialities of that Soul, and also, not having the form of individualized personality that they have after they become parts of the composition, or form of the mortal and spiritual bodies of human beings.

The soul, in its existence prior to becoming an indweller in the mortal body, has a consciousness of its existence and of its relationship to God and to other parts of the Great Soul, and more especially of the duplex character of its being; and by this I mean the sexual differences in the two parts of the soul, which, in the way that they are united, constitutes the one complete soul.

When the time comes for this soul to become an indweller in the mortal frame, the two parts that I speak of separate, and only one of the parts enters at the same time into a mortal and never into the same moral; and while this separation is necessary for the individualization of each part of this one complete soul, yet the two parts never lose that interrelationship, or the binding qualities that existed before their separation, and which continue to exist thereafter, and in the great future, after the work of individualization shall be completed, will come together again and reunite in a complete one.

This separation may exist a longer or shorter time, depending upon the similar development of those similar qualities that is absolutely necessary in order that this coming together in the original one, as it were, may take place.

While, as I have said, this soul before its separation has a consciousness of its existence, and when its duplex character leaves it, or rather leaves the two separated parts, and thereafter, until its reentrance into the spirit world, does not again return to these parts. But in order to regain this consciousness, it is not necessary that both of these parts at the same

253

time shall come again into the spirit life, for if one part becomes a spirit, free from the physical body, and the other part remains in the mortal body, that part that comes into the spirit world may receive the awakening to this consciousness, depending upon certain conditions and developments.

It often happens, that both these parts will return to the spirit world, and yet, for a long time, live as spirits without having a restoration of this consciousness, because of various reasons that may exist. The conditions of the development of the two parts may be so vastly different that the realization of this consciousness may be wholly impossible; and very often it is the case that when these two individualized parts are informed that they are the soulmates of each other, they will not believe that information, and live on in utter indifference to the fact.

But ultimately, the consciousness of their relationship will come to them, because their development, no matter whether intellectual or spiritual, will tend towards the awakening of this consciousness, which is always present with them, although dormant.

Now, as to what this soul is in its constituent parts or shape or form prior to its separation for the purpose of becoming an inhabitant of the mortal body, we spirits are not informed and do not know. We are often present at the conception, and also the birth of a child, and realize that a soul has become enveloped in the flesh, but we cannot see that soul as it enters into that home of mortal environment, because as to us it is invisible and has no form; but after its lodgment in the human body we can perceive it and realize its existence, for then it assumes a form, and that form varies in different incarnations, or in the incarnations in different humans.

We have never seen the Soul of God, although we know that there is this Great Oversoul, and hence we cannot see the soul of any image of the Great Soul until it becomes, as I say, individualized.

I know that men have often wondered and asked the question as to the preexistence of the soul that has been incarnated, and what qualities and attributes it had during its preexistence, and as to these particulars I wish to say, that we spirits, although we are inhabitants of God's Celestial Heavens, have little information, though we know that the soul, and I mean the complete soul in oneness, has an existence prior to its becoming individualized. You may ask, how we know this? Well, it will be hard to explain this to you, so that you may comprehend, but this I can say, that we spirits of the higher soul development can, by our soul perceptions, understand the existence of these souls as images of the Great Soul, and the qualities of these images are such, that while we cannot sensibly as you would say, see these souls or their qualities, yet we are conscious of their existence. To use an illustration, that is not altogether appropriate, you understand that the wind blows, yet you cannot see it.

And we further understand, and such is the result of our observations, that when the soul, and keep in mind that I mean the two parts when I say soul, once becomes incarnated and assumes an individualized form, it never thereafter loses that individuality, and hence, never again returns to its condition of preexistence, and can never again become reincarnated in the existence of any human being.

There is no such thing as reincarnation, and all the theories and speculations of men upon that question, which conclude that a soul once incarnated can again become incarnated, are wrong, for the incarnation of a soul is only one step in its destined progress from an invisible formless existence to a glorious angel or to a perfected spirit.

A soul in this progress never retraces its steps—it is always progress, though sometimes stagnation takes place—but continues as an individualized spirit until it reaches its goal in fulfillment of the Father's plan for the perfecting of His universe.

This is a subject that is difficult of treatment for several reasons, among which is the fact that we spirits, no matter how high our attainments, do not have the information in order to give a full and complete description of the soul and its qualities prior to its incarnation, and you mortals are not capable of comprehending the full truth as we may try to convey it to you.

I have made this effort to give you some faint idea of the soul, as you are in good condition tonight to receive my ideas, but I realize how inadequate my attempt has proved to be. But from it, you can understand that the soul has an existence prior to its finding its home in the physical body—that it is duplex and has a consciousness of the relationship of its two parts—that after it has received the experience of the mortal life and received an individuality, it returns to the spirit world, and that at sometime that consciousness will come to it again, and the two parts will become one, unless in the development of these separate parts have arisen barriers that may prevent their reuniting. And further, that this soul will never again retrace the steps of its progression and become reincarnated.

I will now close, and with my love and blessings say good night.

Your brother in Christ,

LUKE.

Incarnation of the Soul.

I am here, Samuel—Yes, Samuel, the prophet:

Well, I will not write long tonight, as I merely want to say that you are much better in your spiritual condition, and the rapport between us is so much greater than heretofore.

Tonight, I desire to say one word on the subject of my knowledge of how a soul is born into the flesh and becomes an individualized person.

255

I heard what Luke wrote you, and I agree with him in his explanation of the character and qualities of the soul in its state before its incarnation; but I want to add one other thing to what he wrote, and that is, that when the soul first separates into its two component parts, and one of these parts enters into the physical body, the other part remains a mere soul, invisible even to us, but having an existence of which we are conscious, and hovers close to the earth plane seeking the opportunity to also incarnate and become individualized; and this happens within a short time after the separation from the half that has already incarnated. Of course, when I say a short time, I do not mean in a few months or even a few years, because sometimes there is a space of several scores of years between the two incarnations; but such time seems short to us who know nothing of time.

The soul which remains, as Luke has told you, as well as the soul that enters the human body, loses its consciousness of having been a part only of one complete soul, and of its relationship to the other part of that soul, and exists in the supposition that it is still a complete soul and needs no other soul to make it complete. This is a provision of the Father's goodness, so that the soul that continues in its pristine existence will not become lonely or unhappy.

You will naturally ask how I know this, as we have said these souls are not visible to us, and I can only answer that we spirits who have developed our souls to a high degree have acquired certain faculties, or what you may call senses, which enable us to know these things. It is not necesary that we should see these unindividualized souls in order to know of their existences and the qualities that they possess, any more than it is that we should be able to see the Great Oversoul of the Father in order to understand its qualities and attributes and existence. I know it is hard for you to understand this, and I cannot now satisfactorily explain it, for your senses of the earth life are not capable of comprehending the explanation, but what I tell you is true.

We often see the birth of the two parts of the souls into mortals and know that such souls then, for the first time, assumes a shape and form, for this invisible image of God fills the whole of the spirit body, and from that body assumes or receives its form, and thereby becomes individualized. The soul is the life of the spirit body and never leaves it during the earth life of the mortal, and comes with it at the death of the physical body, and remains a part of it during all the time of the existence of the spirit body in the spirit world. Whether it can ever become lost is a question upon which I shall write you later. You will remember that Jesus said, according to the Bible, "What does it profit a man to gain the whole world and lose his own soul?"

256

I will say this though, at this time, that a man may retain his soul as a fact and yet have a consciousnes of having lost it, and he is then as if he had no soul.

I have said to you what I intended to write, because Luke had omitted to speak of the condition of that half of the soul that remained in the spirit world, after the other half had been incarnated.

Matters of this kind, though, are not important as regards the salvation of man, or the perfecting of his soul to such a degree that that soul may become at-one with the Great Soul, having what it did not possess before its seeking a dwelling place in the flesh, and that is the divine nature of the Father and immortality, as an individualized, never dying person.

As we proceed in these writings you will understand the importance of the soul's becoming incarnated, and then leaving the flesh and again returning to the spirit spheres. And you will also learn that the doctrine of evolution is to an extent correct, but not as commencing from an atom or from an animal inferior to man. Back of and greater than this doctrine of evolution is the great and more divine doctrine of involution; for if the soul had not come from above and been placed in the physical man, there would never have been any evolution; and if the soul had never received its individualized existence by coming into the body of the human, it would never have evoluted to the divine nature, as well as to the individualized being that follows that incarnation.

When I say the divine nature, I do not mean that all souls, either on earth or in the great eternity, necessarily receive that divine nature, for many of them do not and never will; but all, no matter whether they come into the divine nature or retain the nature which was theirs in their preexistence, will become individualized personalities, and which will be theirs so long as that soul and its spirit body shall continue to exist.

I have written enough for tonight, but will come again and write you other truths.

So with my love and blessings

I am your brother in Christ,   SAMUEL.

Refers to the prophecy in the Bible (Matt. 24)

I am here—*Jesus*.

I would like to write tonight, but you are not just in condition, though much better than you have been, and soon I anticipate I will be able to deliver my messages again. Take my advice and pray more and you will find yourself much helped into the condition which is necessary in order that I may make the rapport. I merely write this tonight to let you know that I am with you and waiting to write.

You must not let your faith decrease, but believe with all your soul that we communicate with you and are with you trying to help you in every way. You must do the work and keep up your faith in us.

I will not write more now.

Well, so far as that prophecy (Mat. 24) is concerned it referred to the fall of Jerusalem. At that time—I mean just prior to and at the time of the destruction of Jerusalem—the whole world was in that condition that the prophecy speaks of—I did not know anything about the present condition of the earth, and could not have referred to these times, or to what may now happen among men. The end of the age as it should be written referred to the ending of the Jewish dispensation, and not to the end of the physical world. That was not to be destroyed at the time the prophecy was to be fulfilled, and no man or spirit now knows when the earth will cease to exist. Only God knows that, and He has never revealed it. But this I do know, that such an event will never take place until He has worked out His plan for the ending of the world and, I believe, it will be many centuries yet before such an ending to the earth and the visible world will take place. And I do not know that it ever will have an ending, and no human can foretell the same. So you need not bother about these things.

Each human will have his ending of the earth life, and to him that will be, in effect, the end of the world, and his duty is to prepare for that ending and what will surely follow. Sometime I will write you on this subject.

There are many matters yet to be disclosed, and this disclosure waits only for your getting in the proper condition to receive the same. You can see the importance of this, for the end of the world is coming each day to many mortals, which is so important for them to know.

Think more of the spiritual things, and of your work.

Believe that I am with you very often, and especially when you * pray at night, according to my promise.

Good night.

Your brother and friend,   JESUS.

Confirmation that Jesus Wrote.

I am here—Your own true and loving, *Helen.*

Well, dear, I am pleased that the Master wrote you tonight, for it indicates that you are getting in better condition. You must bend all your efforts to accomplish the objects, the great objects of your selection, and not let other things interfere, as they have done for some time past. If you will only pray more and turn your thoughts to the spiritual

---

* Mr. Padgett told me (Dr. L. R. Stone) that he often saw Jesus praying beside him when he was praying for a greater inflowing of the Divine Love just before retiring at night.

things, you will soon find yourself in the condition which will enable the spirits to make the rapport.

Pray to the Father, and say good night.

Your own true and loving　　HELEN.

Aaron gives his experience and what he now knows about immortality since Jesus came and taught how it can be obtained.

I am the spirit of *Aaron,* the prophet of the Old Testament and the brother of Moses, as it is written.

I merely want to say that as you read the message* from the spirit of Henry Ward Beecher, I read also, and that is a wonderful description of what immortality is, and how it first was given to mankind after the fall of the first parents.

I know the truth of what he wrote, for I experienced the want of this Divine Love for many thousand years before the coming of Jesus and the rebestowal of this Divine Love, which is the only thing in all God's universe that can bring to man immortality. So, let this great truth be preached to all the world, and let man know that until he gets this Divine Love he can never become immortal. It is so difficult for man to understand this truth, and for those who come forward as the teachers of men in spiritual things to comprehend that only this love will save them from their sins, and make them a part of the divinity of the Father and certain of immortality.

I lived at a time when we had not the privilege of getting this Love, and, as a consequence, immortality, and we had to find our happiness in our natural love, and that meant a love towards God as well as towards our fellow man; but this love while it enabled us to experience much happiness, yet it did not give that Divine Essence or nature which now makes our happiness supreme and also at-one with the Father.

I had many experiences in teaching the Hebrew children that there was only one God, but at that time my conception of God was not what it is now. I then thought more of Him as a God of wrath and jealousy than as a God of love and mercy.

In my contest with the magicians of the Egyptian Pharoahs I was afforded the help of the spirit world, and unusual powers were given me, such as I had never had before nor ever afterwards; but it was for the purpose of causing the king to let the people of God, as we called ourselves, depart from Egypt. When this was accomplished I never again possessed those powers or had any occasion to.

But those powers were merely the influences that came from the spirit world, and God himself did not speak to me or to Moses, as it is written. Merely his spirits or angels told us what we must do, and gave us the power to do it.

* Appendix—Message on Immortality. Vol. I, 1st Edition, Pages 53-57.

This power is still existing, and should the occasion arise again, it will be given to the instrumentality that may be selected to do the will of the Father. Even as to Jesus, who had the greatest power conferred upon him of any mortal that ever lived, this power was given him by the angels of God in obedience to the commands of the Father.

I cannot explain to you now in what way these commands were given by God, for you would not understand me, if I should make the attempt. But suffice it to say, that the higher angels have such soul perceptions that they can receive and understand these instructions of the Father. All this is, I know, strange to you, but it is true, and because you do not understand you must not doubt that there is such a close relationship between God and His Celestial spirits, that they know what the will of the Father is.

I am in a Celestial Sphere and am very high up, but not so high as are the apostles. But I am high enough to know to be true what I write you of my own knowledge.

I will not write more tonight, but will come again sometime and instruct you in the laws obtaining in our Celestial Spheres.

So with all my love, I will say that I am,

Your brother in Christ,

Aaron the Prophet of old.

Sarah is now a Christian.

I am the spirit of *Sarah*—I was the wife of *Abraham*.

I want to tell you that I am now a Christian and live in the Celestial Spheres.

Yes, but there are many things in the Bible that are not true. Well, when it says that I sent Hagar into the desert, or caused her to be sent into the desert, to starve and die—that story was a slander on me, and did me great injustice, because I was not such a wicked woman.

Abraham did not send her there either, but she went of her own accord, because she had done that which condemned her in her own conscience. Well, she had taken my husband and had a child by him I know that the Bible says that was commanded by God or that I prevailed upon Abraham to have a child by her, but it is not true.

Yes, I am happy, and so is Abraham and our son Isaac, and his son Jacob; but they were without this Divine Love for a great many years, as it only came to us when the Master came to earth.

I know that you think it strange that I should come to you and write, but as I was with Aaron in the earth plane, and was attracted to you by the light which fills the space around you, I followed Aaron and came to you, and after he wrote, I wrote also.

Yes, I see a great number of beautiful spirits around you and some of the apostles who are so very beautiful and bright. They seem to be so much interested in you, and say that you have been selected to do the work of the Master on earth in the way of revealing the truths which he shall write to you. I don't quite understand it all, but if the Master says it is what shall be done, you will do it.

I must stop now, but please believe that I am Sarah as I have told you. I will leave you now and say goodnight.

Your sister in Christ,

SARAH, *the wife of Abraham.*

Mrs. Padgett's Experience of Joy and Grandeur in the Third Celestial Sphere.

I am here, your Helen (Mrs. Padgett) and ready to write as I promised you today, and you must not think that I will not tell you of what is so dear to me, and should be to you.

It has been a long time since I wrote you very much in detail about myself, and you do not know what has taken place in my soul progression for some time past.

Well, I have been praying and trying to get more love of the Father in my soul and have succeeded to such an extent that I am now in the third Celestial Sphere, where are your grandmother and mother also; and my dear, if I could only tell you of the joys and grandeur of this sphere, I should be most happy. But I have not the words at my command to give you any satisfactory idea of what the appearance and conditions of this sphere are.

I have described to you my home in the second Celestial Sphere, though very inadequately, but that sphere cannot compare with what I have now, and I cannot better describe it than to say it is beyond all possible conception of what you can possibly have of beauty and grandeur and love. I am only in the lower planes of this sphere, but these are so filled with the Father's love that it almost seems impossible that there can be any spheres where there is more of this love, but, of course, as Jesus and all the apostles and some others who write you, have their homes in these higher Celestial Spheres and nearer to the fountain of love, consequently there must be more love where they are.

I am so happy that I can scarcely tell you of what this happiness means, but at any rate, I must say that there is never the slightest thing to interfere with my happiness or to make me think that I am not an accepted child of the Father, partaking of His love to an extent that makes me immortal and never again subject to death.

This happiness is not such as satisfies for awhile, but is one continual source of living, free from all that might enter into the feelings or lives of spirits that know not that they are one with the Father and a part of Him in love and beauty. I am only wanting one thing now to make my life complete, and that is to have you with me; but from this

261

you must not think that I am not perfectly happy and contented, for I am, but as you have been told I am only one-half of the complete one, the other half must come and join the half that I am before the perfect one can become completed.

So my dear Ned, you must try now harder than ever to get this Great Love in your soul in more abundance, and you may if you will only pray and have faith, for the Master says that you can, and he knows.

Yes, I have my individual home here, just as I had in the lower spheres, and it is just as real, and more so, as any home which you have on earth. My garments are the same in appearance, as to form, but oh, so much more beautiful and shining white, and my countenance too is more beautiful and full of expressions of love.

So you see, I have a greater love for my Father and a greater love for you; for as my love for the Father increases my love for you also increases, and I know that when you come over this love will be so great, that you will wonder that such love could exist.

I do not think that I had better write more tonight as I do not feel like telling you of other things, and I only want to enjoy this Great Love free from communication about other matters, though at another time I shall be pleased to do so.

So sweetheart, think of me as I am now, filled with this Great, new Love that is possessing my whole being, and now dear you are the object of this love outside of that which is the Father's.

I will not write more, but will say that I am yours now and for all eternity, and am waiting, oh, so longingly, for the time to come when you can be with me.

I will stop writing.

Your own true and loving,

HELEN (Mrs. J. E. Padgett).

Refers to Mr. P.'s wife's description of the third Celestial Sphere. The importance of man seeking for the Divine Love.

I am Jesus.

I will write only a few lines. I merely want to say that what you have read tonight from your wife as to her progress and her condition of love is all true. She is in such a state of happiness that you must not wonder, that she was not able to describe to you her home and her new surroundings, for they are beyond description in the words that you mortals use to express your ideas.

But this I will say, that the heart of man has never conceived nor the mind of man thought of the great blessings and joy which the Father has prepared for those who love Him in the way of possessing His Divine Love which makes their souls at-one with Him, and causes them to partake of His Divine Nature, and realize that they are a part of His Great Divinity and Immortal.

If mortals would only learn of this great plan of the Father for their redemption, and then believe and try to get this Great Love, how much more happiness there would be, not only among spirits but among mortals also, for this Love can be possessed to a very great degree by mortals, notwithstanding, they have all the trials and temptations of the flesh.

My object is to have you and your friend obtain this Great Love while you are still in the flesh, for your work will require that you have this Love so that you cannot only teach its existence, but by your very lives show and prove to mankind that it is a thing of reality.

I will soon write you another message that will show another great truth which mankind must know.

Well, I will explain that sentence in one of my messages very soon, and will to the satisfaction of your friend show that God never leads any of his children into temptation, and that I never said in teaching my disciples the Lord's prayer, that they should pray that God would not lead them into temptation. I will also write you the actual prayer* which I taught them, and which is the true prayer which all men with fervent, honest, longing hearts should offer to the Father. So let not this trouble you or your friend for God does not lead men into temptation, but, on the contrary, uses the influence of his righteous spirits upon them to help them resist all temptation.

With all my love for you and your co-worker, and the blessings of the Father upon you both, I am your brother and friend,

JESUS.

Mr. Padgett's soul condition. Receives encouragement to continue in prayer for the Divine Love.

I am here—*Jesus.*

Well my brother, I am glad to tell you that your communion with the Father tonight has been responded to. His love has inflowed into your soul in great abundance. His Holy Spirit has been bringing the love in wonderful abundance and your soul is now filled with it, and the influence of this Great Love is working in your soul and you realize its presence. If you will meditate and long for and pray to the Father as you have tonight, your soul will soon be so filled with this love that you will receive the knowledge, that you have a near at-one-ment with Him, and you will be conscious of the possession of a part of His divinity, ·of which we have written you. The pentecostal shower will come to you as it did to my disciples in the days that followed my departing from them; and I will be with you also just as I was with them, and power

* The prayer is found in first volume, First edition—pages 40-42.

and Essence Divine will be bestowed upon you so that you will be able to display the marvelous presence of this love just as they were able. So you must pray and long, and your experience tonight has given you some foretaste of what will come to you.

There is nothing in all the world that can take the place of this love in its power to draw you near to, and make you in at-one-ment with the Father. All beliefs and faiths in any and every other thing will not suffice. Sacrifice and sorrow on account of sin and vicarious sufferings and mediators, will not work the transformation, because it is solely a conjunction between this Divine Love and your soul, that is capable of bringing you into this relationship to the Father, and the resultant consciousness that you have partaken of and possess to some extent His divine nature in love.

Now you are in condition that makes my rapport with you complete, and I have that possession of your brain that enables me to write as I may desire, and I know that I could convey a message to you tonight in a most satisfactory way; but I will not do so, for I think it best to permit the rapport to become a little more intense, and thus enable me to write a long message without the probability of tiring you; for as you know these messages of deep truths such as the ones on the * "Soul" and * "God" necessarily cause me to draw very intensely on your brain power. But soon now, I will come and commence to deliver my messages and continue to do so if our rapport can be maintained. And it can be, if you will only meditate and pray as you have done tonight.

I have been with you very much today, entering into your thoughts and endeavoring to influence the longings of your soul. I was with you at the spiritualist's meeting and sometime I will write you in reference to the claims of the speaker, and the real facts as to how much of what she said was inspired, or as she claims, was spoken through her by a controlling spirit.

I now want you to think more than ever of the importance of your work and of the necessity for you putting all your energies and desires into the work. No one can conceive of what it means, and above all you must realize its great importance and the place that you occupy in carrying it to a successful issue.

I will be with you very often and I know that you will feel my presence and influence, and, as you do, turn all your thoughts to the Father's love, and let all your longings go to Him.

Tonight, I will not write more, but will soon write as I have said. Have faith and know that you have been selected to do the work, and that upon you rests the responsibility that is upon no other man.

* Appendix. These messages in Vol. I, Edition 1, The Soul, page 107—Who and what is God, page 59.

264

With my love and the Father's blessings, I will say good night.

Your brother and friend,

Jesus.

Elizabeth, cousin of Mary—Mother of Jesus. The work that Mr. Padgett is doing, which is the real second coming of Jesus.

I am here, *Elizabeth.*

Let me say a word, and that is, that you are a very happy man just now, and so you should be, for as the Master said you have much of the love in your soul tonight. You may not fully realize this fact, but the influence and effect of its presence will manifest themselves, and you will find coming to you that wonderful peace of which the Master has told you.

For a moment think that there is nothing between you and the Father, and that as regards your longings and His love they are face to face, and no mediator intervenes or can intervene. Only the Father's love and you, alone. Think of this, and you will realize not only what a wonderful thing the Divine Love is, but what a wonderful thing your soul is that it can become so in nearness and in Love with the Father.

This is the only way of becoming at-one with Him, and everything besides is inefficacious to bring about the great transformation of which the higher spirits have written you. So many spirits are engaged in this great work, which is the real second coming of Jesus— and which means the second coming of the love and mercy and privilege of receiving the love—and if you could only for a moment with your physical vision see those who are present, you would never doubt the work that you are to do, and the great responsibility that rests upon you. But as you cannot in this way see, you must believe without seeing, and let no doubt of the fact enter into your faith.

I thought that I must write this tonight, for we see your condition, and many are here with you praying to the Father for a great bestowal of His love upon you.

So consider what has been written you tonight, and meditate and long for and pray the Father, and you will be greatly blessed.

With my love, I will say good night.

Your sister in Christ,   Elizabeth.

Well, it has been so long since I heard or used the name that it was a little difficult to recall and formulate it.

Names are of the things that we forget in a short time after being in our Celestial homes, unless there is some special reason for recalling them.

Confirmation that Jesus and Elizabeth, who is cousin of Mary, the mother of Jesus, wrote the preceding messages.

I am here—Your own true and loving, *Helen* (Mrs. Padgett).

Well dear, I am very happy tonight and that because of your condition of soul in the Father's love. You are nearer the Father than you have ever been, and His love is now more shed abroad in your heart than ever before; and the Master was so glad that you opened up your soul by your longings and meditation tonight.

Many of the holy spirits are here tonight and united with you in your prayers to the Father, and the love was bestowed in great abundance. How blessed you are and how happy you should be for you have a realization of the love in your soul. I know the Master is also pleased that the rapport is now so perfect, and you may expect a long message from him, and many of them. And so do the other spirits rejoice now that they realize that soon they will be able to write. As the Master wrote you, meditate, and long and pray.

The spirit who wrote is one that I have never seen here before, that I am aware of; and she is a most beautiful and radiant spirit and has her home in the high spheres of the Celestial Heavens. She says her name is Elizabeth and John tells me that she is the Elizabeth of the Bible, the cousin of Mary, the mother of Jesus. She is filled with the love and seemed so anxious to write you about the Father's love and how close you are tonight to Him.

Well dear, I will not write more now, for it is not best to do so, as you are in that condition when you can commune with the Father, and I want you to let your thoughts go to Him with all the longings that your soul is capable of.

We will remain with you as you sit and meditate and unite with you in your prayers.

So my dear, dear husband, love the Father with all your soul tonight. Good night.

Your own true and loving,   HELEN.

What is necessary for a man to do to recover the purity of soul and love that was possessed by the first parents. Doctrine of original sin is a mocking, damnable lie.

I am here, *Luke.*

I have not written you for some time and desire to write a short message tonight on the subject of: What is necessary for a man to do to recover the purity of soul and love that was possessed by the first parents. I mean as a man possessing the natural love only.

Well, in the first place, he should realize that he is a perfect creature of God, and that his sins and diseases are merely the results of his own thoughts, and of qualities that have come to him down the long ages of his ancestors living on earth.

He need not suppose that these sins and desires are inherent in or a part of his creation, for they are not, but merely accretions that fastened

266

themselves upon him by reason of the thoughts he has had, and the resultant course of life he has led, and when he changes these thoughts, which will necessarily bring about a change in his manner of living, he will find that he can progress toward the condition of the perfect man.

I know that many of these thoughts are so deep seated that they seem almost a part of his very nature, and can only be eradicated by the death of his physical body; but this is not true, for man, even while in the full vigor of his manhood and possessed with all the appetites and desires which arise from the perverted indulgence of these desires, either on the part of himself or on the part of those from whom he is said to have inherited them, may relieve himself from these desires and become a man, having only the thoughts of good, and desires for those things which are in harmony with the nature of his perfect creation.

This I know, seems to man a thing impossible, and so thinking he does not try to accomplish what I say he may accomplish, and to become free from these sins and unnatural appetites. The almost universal belief in original sin has caused men all along the ages to think that such a task is hopeless, and that they are thinking and acting only in accordance with the appetites and desires that God has implanted in their natures, and that so long as they indulge these thoughts and desires in a moderate or respectable way, they are not doing that which is contrary to God's will or to their own nature.

But this doctrine of original sin is a mocking, damnable lie, and the sooner man realizes the fact that it is a fraud and deceit, the sooner he will be able to get rid of those things which have placed him in his present condition and held him there bound, as it were, hand and foot.

This supine submission to this old and ever recurring belief is the great thing that prevents man from starting to progress towards the attainment of that condition, which is purity and health and the perfect man.

Man must decline and no longer submit to this belief, which, I am sorry to say, is fostered by the teachings of the orthodox churches in order to sustain and make forcible their creeds and dogmas, and to show to man that he is not to be considered worthy of the mercy of the Father, and cannot possibly obtain that mercy and be relieved from the great wrath and punishment that God has prepared for him, unless he believes and acknowledges that he is a dependent and lost man, unworthy of the Father's favor, or the help of the instrumentalities which the Father uses to assist men in regaining their lost estate.

If men would only think, and in thinking realize that they are dear children of the Father and His highest creation, and that He prizes them above all His creatures and wants them to know that they are beings of such wonderful qualities and possibilities, they would then have come to them an overpowering and convincing sense of what they really are, and of how necessary it is for them to assert their rights as such exalted creatures of the Father, and would realize that they are masters of sin and disease, for they are the creators of the same.

When he shall assume such position and become possessed of such knowledge, they will find that they have a wonderful power as creatures of the Father, they will realize that they are masters of sin that must be gotten rid of.

Let men for a moment think again, and thinking know that God does not desire his greatest creature to become or be less than the perfect being that He created. He is not flattered nor does He have any pleasure in the thought that man is degraded and fallen from his perfect creation, and that in order to rise again he, man, must believe that God may show his power in rescuing him from his low and hopeless condition. No, God is not pleased by man assuming such an attitude, nor does he need any such helpless condition of man that he may show His power or gratify what the teachings of these orthodox imply, His vanity, which He has not.

In this particular man must work out his own salvation, but it will be a difficult task so long as he continues to believe and act upon that belief, that he is a creature of original sin, and that as God in the beginning failed to make him the perfect man, so now, only God can remedy what he failed to provide in His creation, and that man of himself can do nothing. That all he has to do is to wait until God is pleased to recreate him and thereby take from his very nature this great curse of the original sin. See the great fatality of such belief and how it tends to make man a slave of and obedient to this false belief in this blight of original sin.

God gave to man in his creation, the great power of will and the right to its unlimited exercise, subject only to the penalties of a wrongful exercise; and by the exercise of that will man created sin and disease and became depraved and fallen, and the possessor of false beliefs as to the perfection of his nature. By the exercise of that will man, himself, must redeem himself from this condition of depravity and false belief, and again become the perfect man—God's wholly perfect creation.

As man was in the beginning the perfect son of God, and by his own will created his own and only devil, so must he by this same power kill this devil and again become the perfect son. He must believe and declare, and show the sincerity of his beliefs by his acts and living, that he is a perfect son of the Father—needing no new creation.

This I have written to show what man was in the beginning, and what he really and truly is now; although covered with sin and disease and false beliefs.

To recover this lost estate or, better, condition, he will find that by searching for and learning and acting upon many of the moral precepts of the Bible and of other so called sacred writings, he will be greatly helped and strengthened in his efforts. But above all let him understand and believe with the certainty of knowledge, that he is God's highest and most perfect creation.

Now, from what I have said, it must not be inferred that man is his own God, and has not and needs not any tender, loving Father, who is interested in him and always ready to help him whenever he earnestly and in sincerity asks the help of that Father. Always is man dependent upon God; but that dependence is not recognized by God, unless man first recognzes it, and by his longings and thoughts shows to the Father that he needs His help.

This may seem unbelievable, but man was created so independent in his great will power, as regards the qualities of thought and desire both spiritual and material, that God never interferes to compel. The principle involved in "WHOSOEVER WILL" must be exercised by man before the Father will intervene. But when it is exercised He does intervene, and never refuses or fails to answer the call of the sincere cry of man for help.

And God does help man in his recovery from the state of false beliefs and degradation, that I have mentioned. His love overshadows men, and His instrumentalities are always ready and waiting to answer the call upon Him for His help in assisting them out of their condition of sin, disease and false beliefs; for, as I have elsewhere written you, in God's universe there must be perfect harmony, and the present man, so far as his own creation of inharmony is concerned, is not in that harmony. Ultimately, man, all men, will become again the perfect man.

Of course, you will understand that what I have written does not apply to the redeemed sons of God who receive the New Birth and become partakers of the Divine nature of the Father, for in their case the perfect man is absorbed in the Divine angel.

I have written longer than I intended, but as the theme is an interesting as well as important one, I thought it best to write just as I have.

I will now say good night and leave with you my love and blessings.

Your brother in Christ, LUKE.

(of the New Testament)

Important that Man Must Search and Find the Truth.

I am here. *John—Apostle of Jesus.*

I desire to write tonight, and if you think it is not too late, we will do so.

Well, I will not make my message very lengthy, but try to condense in short sentences.

I want to tell you that when a man gets to know the truths of the Father, he will become a very happy and wise man, for these truths have in them only those principles that create happiness and wisdom.

269

I know that men believe many things on account of their being ancient or having the authority of their forefathers, or some great saint or writer who lived many centuries ago, but such a basis for truth, while worthy of consideration and examination does not of itself because of being old, afford any certainty that what is thus accepted contains the truth.

Truth is a thing very old, and existed for many thousands of centuries before the times in which these ancient writers, as you call them, lived, and in fact, those days of the writers, in comparison to what had gone before, are as yesterdays; and therefore you will see that because the declarations of these writers are what you consider very ancient, they should not be received as having authority.

Truths of those days, and of the long ages prior thereto, and of the present time are all the same, as truth never changes or assumes new forms no matter what the conditions of mortals may be as to intellectual or spiritual development. And they may be revealed to-day, and are being constantly revealed as time progresses, and should be accepted with as much credence and satisfaction as any truths that were ever disclosed in ancient days.

Men are just as susceptible now to the reception of these truths in their spiritual natures or perceptions as they were in the times of Abraham or Moses or at any time since.

The mind of man was given to him to be exercised in the way of investigation and search, and never was it contemplated in his creation that the time would come when he should accept anything as the ultimates of truth and cease his inquiries, for truths are so many and great and deep, that so far, in the mortal universe man has acquired only a smattering of these truths, and to rest supinely in this acquirement under the belief that there is nothing more in existence than man may know, violates and subverts the very object of his creation; and what I have said applies to spiritual truths as well as to material ones.

The churches, I know, declare and try to enforce the declaration, that it is not possible to discover or have revealed to men the essential principles of spiritual truths to a greater extent than has already been declared in the Bible and the churches' interpretation of the same, and that, therefore, it is contrary to God's will that men should seek further for any additional truths, and that men should accept, without question, the sayings of the Bible, and the dogmas and creeds of the churches which their claim is founded upon, and which they declare are the true principles of spiritual truths. And for many years this has been the demand of the churches, and the members thereof have acquiesced, without question or doubt.

Now, this has been one of the great causes why men have not progressed more, not only in their spiritual nature but also in what may be

270

called their natural qualities. They have remained satisfied, and what was believed by them centuries ago are believed today. I say all this to show how stagnant the intellects of men have been, as it depends on search and investigation, and has remained for all these long ages.

I further recite this to show the necessity for men to seek and criticize, and accept or reject as the results of the search may demand.

In recent years, though, men have made greater progress, and the individual has come to the front and the old accepted fabulations of truths have been assaulted and shaken and denuded of their falsities to a considerable degree, and so it should be. Men must seek, and criticize and accept or reject as their own conscience and reasoning powers dictate, and therein will be freedom of the mind as well as of the will.

The soul, also, has been smothered in these dogmatic beliefs, and as a consequence its development has been slow and knowledge of things spiritual has not come to men as it should have done, and as is necessary to teach them their destiny and the truths which should control their lives on earth, and which will control their progress in the spirit world.

Well , as you are tired, I will postpone the balance of my discourse. I think it best when you feel tired to discontinue the writing instead of attempting to force yourself into receiving it.

So I will not write more. Believe that I am your brother in Christ.

JOHN.

God is not the God of any race but of the individual.

I am here. *Saul.*

I have not written you for sometime and I would like to say only a few words, and these are, that never in all the battles with the Amalakites, did God help me or bring to me victory, as is set forth in the Old Testament, although some of the prophets, like Samuel, at the time might have thought, yet as I now know, it was not true. God was not the partial and particular patron of the Jews, and to Him is was just as sinful for the Jews to commit murder and the other horrible crimes that are mentioned in the Book, in connection with my life as King, as it would have been for the Pagans to have done the same thing.

God is not the God of any race, but He is the God of every individual child who comes to Him in true supplication and prayer, seeking His love and help in his spiritual nature. God will respond and the individual surely will be helped. But should that individual come to Him, seeking power and assistance to murder his fellow man, no matter how great an enemy he might be, God would not help him or approve of his desires, and this being so, you can readily see that He would not help any nation to commit such acts and gain the victory.

And I want to tell you here, that God is not a God of nations, but of individuals only, and only as the individuals that compose the nations, can

271

He be said to be a God of nations. He wants not the praise of men or of nations because of victory that they might acquire through bloodshed and cruelties ascribed to His help, but he wants the praise of men only because their souls may have been awakened to His love, and have acquired victory over sin and evil.

Nations rise and fall and disappear from the face of the earth, but the individuals who compose these nations never die, even though the physical bodies die, and God is a God only of those things that never die, and He is interested in having the individual become victor over sin and the appetites of the flesh.

Of course, the individuals make the nation and give it its character and qualities, and hence the nation will become sinful and cruel as the individuals that compose it become sinful and cruel. He does not deal with nations as such, but only with the small, but important, units that make the nation. Hence, for a nation to say that God is our God, or that God will help us to victory over our enemies, is all wrong. When the individual gains the victory over his greatest enemy, himself, then he can claim that God is his God and give Him the praise, and when all the individuals of a nation have gained that victory then that nation can proclaim that God is its God and render to Him praise for the victory. But only in such event is any nation justified in saying, "God is our God."

And here let me say, that no Christian nation so called, has yet, as individuals, attained to that condition of righteousness and victory over sin, that it can claim to be God's chosen nation.

And so, I say, that I, Saul the King, before my alleged fall from the grace of God, was no more helped by God, than I was after that supposed event, for the reason that while outwardly I may have appeared to seek God's directions and listened to the advice of His prophets, yet inwardly, I was no more in accord with Him or reconciled to Him than I was after the momentous event.

God never helped the Jews, as a nation, to any greater extent than He did any other nation, for they as individuals were no more in attunement with Him than were many individuals of what were called the Pagan nations.

When I went to Samuel in my despair, as the Bible portrays, and felt the burden of the sins of my life, I became nearer to God than I had ever been before, and He was more my God than ever, though I did not realize it.

I merely write this to show men that they must not believe and rely on the statement that because I was said to have observed God's will and obeyed His commands before the time that I realized defeat was certain to be mine, that God was any more my God then, directing and assisting me to overcome my enemies than he was after that event.

272

I have written enough and will now stop.

So with all my love, and the assurance that God is a God of the individual and not of the nation, I will say good night.

Your brother in Christ, SAUL.

*The necessity of obtaining the Divine Love. Those who refuse this Great
Gift after the privilege of obtaining it is withdrawn, will suffer the
second death.*

I am here—*Your grandmother (Ann Rollins).*

I thought that I might write you a message tonight, if you feel like receiving it.

The only way in which the salvation that can be obtained by man and make him of a nature divine is through the medium of the Holy Ghost, and the way pointed out by Jesus.

I will not here attempt to go into details as to the methods,* for they have been fully explained to you, but I must say that no other methods can be pursued that will bring the soul of man in unison with God, and make him of a nature divine.

No sacraments of baptism or mere ceremony of the church will enable a man to accomplish this end; and in fact, such things frequently retard the soul of man from becoming in the condition of development that places him in the position of a redeemed child of God.

**I will not write much, in detail, as to what man himself should do
in order to bring into operation the workings of the Holy Spirit, but
merely say, that he must pray with the sincere longings of his soul for
the inflowing of the Father's love, and have faith that such love is a
real thing and that it comes to him in response to his prayers.**

And now to continue as to the truth that this love is waiting for all mankind, no matter where the individuals of the race may be, and that they can receive this love even though they have never heard of the plan of salvation as declared by Jesus.

God intended, when He rebestowed this love, that every human being, as well as spirit, should have the opportunity to obtain it, and that the manner in which it might be obtained should be made known to all mankind, and in carrying out this intention he specially selected Jesus for this work, who, through his own teachings to mankind, should learn of it.

Of course, during the short ministry of Jesus on earth it was impossible that all men should learn of him through the teachings of himself or of his disciples, and hence, the spirits of the world of spirits were permitted to hear these teachings, and come into the knowledge, and then, when they should obtain this love, to teach it to mortals and spirits, which they did, and have been doing ever since.

* The only way to the Kingdom of God in the Celestial Heavens—Page 20, Vol. I, Ed. 1.

273

But while they have been working all these centuries to bring about this great consummation, yet they have not succeeded for the reason, that they could not force the truth of the plan of salvation upon either mortal or spirit, and consequently, man in the exercise of his free will, and spirits also, in the exercise of their will, unless they would open up their understandings of the soul qualities, supplemented by the exercise of their mental qualities, could not obtain this Divine Love. And just, as on earth, men have refused to listen to those in mortal life who have attempted to teach them of things religious, so in the spirit world many spirits have and are refusing to listen to the teachings of other spirits, who have the knowledge and possession of this Great Love. And mortals also have failed to respond to the impressions which spirits have been trying to make upon them as to this truth, and, as a consequence, were unable to open up their soul perceptions; and many mortals, as well as spirits, have never received the benefit of the Great Gift of rebestowal.

And yet, as I have said, many have responded to these impressions, and even while on earth have had the inflowing of this love to a more or less extent, although they may not have been conscious of the fact in such a definite manner as to know, that what they had received was a portion of the Divine Love.

Among the great obstacles to men putting themselves in this condition of receptivity, are the creeds, and mental beliefs and ceremonies obtaining in many of the churches of Christendom, and in many of the faiths and teachings of the races which live outside of Christendom and which have never heard of this great plan of salvation.

In the spirit world, the followers of many of the faiths and creeds, distinct and different from one another, live together in communities as separate races, still believing in their various creeds and teachings of their leaders, and have never heard of this Divine Love or of the necessity of receiving it, but worship God according to their beliefs on earth, satisfied that the doctrines which they profess are the true and only ones, and absolutely refuse to listen to the spirits who often try to teach the truths as to eternal life in the Celestial Spheres.

Of course, these spirits have the right and the power to refuse to listen to these truths, and are never compelled to. And then again, some of them will listen, and decline to believe that there is any other truths than the ones that they have embraced.

And thus you see, that while this Great Gift, the Divine Love, and privilege of obtaining it was bestowed upon all men, and the love is ever ready to enter into their souls, yet a very large majority of spirits and mortals will never receive it and become inhabitants of the many mansions.

All men and spirits will have the opportunity before the great day of final separation, but many will not be willing to accept the Gift, and will be satisfied in the happiness of their natural love and contented to live in their merely spiritual homes.

And here, let me say, because of the fact of the great variety of beliefs and teachings on earth as to the meaning of the second death, many men and spirits will neglect to exercise their privilege of obtaining the Great Gift of the Divine Love and suffer the second death. The second death will take place when that great separation occurs, and the gift of this privilege of receiving the Divine Love of the Father will again be withdrawn from man and spirit. No other death is meant, for man and spirit will continue to live their mortal and spirit lives, without any other death than that which is now constantly taking place. There will be no death in the sense of condemning the spirit of man to eternal punishment, or the annihilation of any spirit, as is taught by some of your religious teachers. No, the only death will be the death that the first parents died at the time of their disobedience, which was the deprivation of the great privilege of receiving the Divine Love and thereby partaking of the divine nature of the Father, and immortality.

Well my dear boy, I have written enough for tonight and will stop.

You have my love and my influence to help you in every way, and also my prayers to the Father for your spiritual development.

So with my blessings, I will say good night.

Your loving,   GRANDMOTHER.

I am here—Your *Helen.*

Well sweetheart, I am so glad that your grandmother finished her message, for she was so anxious to do so, and I know that you will enjoy the same.

I will not write more tonight, as I see that you are tired.

Your own true and loving,   HELEN.

Nero—Roman Emperor.—His experience in the hells and his progress to the Celestial Heavens.

I am here, the spirit of one who lived on earth the life of a wicked man, and a persecutor of the Christians, and a blasphemer of God, and everything that was pure and holy; and when I had lived the life to its end and shuffled off the mortal coil and became a spirit, I also became a dweller in the lowest hells where all is darkness and torment, and the abode of * devils and everything that tends to make the spirit unhappy and at variance with the loving God.

I introduce myself in this way in order to demonstrate to you the wonderful power of the Divine Love, for now I am an inhabitant of the Celestial Spheres, and know that this love is not only real, but is capable of making the vilest sinner a partaker and owner of the Divine Essence of the Father.

275

My sufferings were beyond all description and I was the most dese-crated of mortals, and was almost worshipped by the devils of hell be-cause of the great injury that I had done to the followers of Jesus, who, in my time, were possessed of this love, and a faith, which even the ter-rors of the wild beasts of the arena, or the torches of my own evil designs could not cause them to renounce, in this great religion that the Master had taught them, and the disciples were still teaching when I put so many of them to death.

The * devils loved me for the very evil that I had done, but strange to say the spirits of those who I had sent unto the spirit world before their time were not revengeful to me, or came to me with their imprecations or cursings. Then when I had been in the spirit world a sufficient time to realize my surroundings and the nature of these evils, these spirits of the martyrs, which I had made, came to me in sympathy and pity, and in fact, tried many times to help me out of my great sufferings and dark-ness. I did not understand all this unexpected kindness and evidence of love, and I would not for a long time believe that these spirits were sin-cere; and so I suffered for year after year, and century after century, and became convinced that my condition was fixed, and that for me there was no hope, and that the God that I had heard of was not my God, and that devils were the only companions that I was destined to have through all eternity.

And so I endured, wishing to die, but I could not. Oh, I tell you it was horrible and beyond all conception of mortals! The law was working and I was paying the penalty, and there seemed no end to the penalty.

I could find no consolation among those who surrounded me, and the pleasures that I first enjoyed, became to me mere things of mockery and derision, and my darkness and torment became the greater. How often I called upon God, if there be a God, to strike me dead, but the only an-swer to my call was the laughter of the grinning devils, who told me to shout louder as God might be asleep, and may be deaf.

What to do, I knew not, and so I became isolated as best I could from these terrible associates, and many years of my living were spent in the darkness of lonesomeness with never a ray of hope, or the whisper of one word to tell me, that for me there might be a fairer destiny. And so time went by and I waited in my misery for some kind power to come and an-nihilate me, but I waited in vain.

During all this time the recollections of my earthly deeds were like hot irons scorching my soul, and burning my body, as I thought, and the end came not.

Well, I suffered the tortures of the damned, and it seemed to me that I was paying the penalties for all the sins and evil deeds that had ever

* Devils mean undeveloped spirits who once lived in the flesh.

276

been committed by all the wicked kings and rulers and persecutors of earth. Many times the shrieks of the Christian children and the groans of the men and women as they were being torn asunder from limb to limb, or burned as living torches which I had made of them, came to me and increased my torment. I lived the life of centuries of torment in a few moments, as it seemed to me, and not one cooling drop of water was mine. It may seem impossible that I should have continued to live in this ever increasing suffering, but I did, because I was compelled to. The law did its work and there was no one to say enough.

I might write a volume on this suffering of mine, and yet you would not comprehend its meaning, and so I will pass it by.

In my loneliness and suffering there came to me on an occasion, a beautiful spirit, full of light and love, and all the beauty of early womanhood, as I thought, and with eyes of pity and longing, and said, "You are not alone, only open your eyes and you will see the star of hope, which is the sign of the Father's love and desire to help you. I am a child of that Father and the possessor of His great enveloping love, and I love you, even though you took from me my young life when you threw me to the wild beasts to satisfy your desire to gratify your thirst for innocent blood, and see the suffering and hear the groans of your victims, yet, I love you, not because I am a human with a kindly nature and a forgiving disposition, but because I have in me this Divine Love of the Father which tells me that I am your sister, and that you are a child of the Father, just as I am, and the object of His love just as I was the object of His love. You have suffered, and while you suffered, His great love went out to you in sympathy and desire to help you, but you, yourself, prevented it from coming to you and leading you to light and surcease from sufferings. And now I come to you, your young and innocent victim, who had never done you any greater harm on earth than to pray for you, and ask the heavenly Father to take away from your heart, the great wickedness that caused so many of my people to suffer persecution and death. We all prayed for you and never asked our Father to curse you, or do anything to you to make you suffer. And we have prayed for you often since we came to the spirit world, and we are now praying for you, and this because we love you and want you to be happy. Look into my eyes and you will see that love is there, and what I tell you is true. And now, can you not love us a little and open up your soul to our sympathy, and let your feelings of gloom and despondency leave you for a moment, and realize that in this world of spirits there are some who love you?"

Well, to say that I was surprised, does not express my feelings, and as I looked into the lovelit eyes of that beautiful spirit, I felt the great sins of my earth life overwhelm me, and in my anguish, I cried, "God be merciful to me, the greatest of sinners," and for the first time in all my life in the hells, tears came to my eyes, and my heart seemed to have a sense of living; and there came to me feelings of remorse and regret for all the evils that I had done.

It would take too long to tell what followed this breaking up of my soul, all shriveled and dead, and suffice it to say that from that time, I commenced to have hope come to me, and to get out of my awful condition of darkness. It took a long time, but at last, I got into the light, and this love which the beautiful spirit first told me of gradually came into my soul, until, at last, I reached the condition of bliss in which I now am.

And during all the time of my progress, this radiant loving spirit came to me very often with her words of love and encouragement, and prayed for me, and never left me when I became, as I did at times, doubtful and discouraged. And as my awakening continued, the love came into my soul and as she told me of the heavenly things that would be mine as I progressed and reached the soul spheres, where beautiful homes and pure bright spirits are, I became more and more bound by my love to her. After a while I got into the third sphere, and realized that what she had told me was true, only I had not been able to comprehend the greatness of the truth.

She then commenced to tell me of the happiness of the beautiful spirits of the two sexes, that I so often saw together, and explained that they were soulmates, and that their love was the greatest of all the loves except the Divine Love, and that every spirit in all the spheres had its soulmate and at the proper time would find it.

My love for this loving spirit had then become so intense that in the very depths of my soul, I wished and prayed that my soulmate might be such a one as she; and, at last, I became so filled with my love for her, that I told her that the only thing in all the heavens that I needed to make full my happiness was she as my soulmate, but that I realized that that desire was hopeless as I had destroyed her life, and of course she could not be my soulmate. And oh, how I suffered when I realized that she could not be mine, but was another's.

As I told her of these longings and hopeless feelings of my soul, she came close to me and looked into my eyes with such burning love, and threw her arms around me, and said, "I am your soulmate, and knew the fact a short time after you came to the spirit world and entered your hells of darkness, and during all the long years I prayed and prayed for the time to come when I could go to you with my love and awaken in your dead soul the response to my great love. And when the time came that I could go, I was so thankful to the Father, that I almost flew to you, with some dread of disappointment I confess, to tell you that you were not neglected or unthought of, but that there was some love in the spirit world that was going to you. Of course, I could not tell you of my soulmate love, for you would not then have understood, but as your soul awakened and the love of the Father came to you, I became happier and happier, and have waited so anxiously for this moment, when I could tell you that this love that had been consciously mine for so long, is all yours."

Well, I will draw the veil here, but you can imagine what my happiness was, and as I progressed from sphere to sphere my happiness and love for her increased and increased.

Thus I have told you the story of the life in the spirit world of the wickedest man that God ever permitted to live and gratify his feelings of hatred and revenge.

And I, who have passed through this experience, and realized all that it means, say, that the Divine Love of the Father is able to and does save the vilest sinner, and transforms the chiefest of devils into a Celestial angel of His highest spheres.

I have written long and you are tired.

I thank you, and will say good night, and subscribe myself.

Your brother in Christ,

NERO, The Roman Emperor,

and at one time persecutor of God's true children.

Mr. P.'s grandmother encourages Mr. Padgett to press forward to the goal. Refers to the great love of Jesus and that he is still praying for more.

I am your grandmother (*Ann Rollins*).

Let me write a few lines tonight, as I have been listening to your conversation with some interest, and I desire to say a few words that may encourage you both to press forward to the goal which you have before you—a home in the Celestial Heavens and the acquirement of a nature divine, which only those who know the way can obtain by following the way that the Master has so lovingly taught you. You will not be disappointed in your efforts, for when you long for the love and receive portions of it, every experience of that kind will help you to get more and create in you increasing desires.

You must not think that it is possible to obtain this love in its fullness, and then permit your longings to decrease whenever you feel that the love has come to you in wonderful abundance, for I must tell you that we in the Celestial Heavens know and realize that there is always more beyond what we obtain; even the Master prays to the Father for an increase of this love in his soul. And if you could see the evidence of the love that he possesses, as we see it, you would probably think that nothing more could be obtained, or that there was any greater amount to be obtained; and with us, this fact of the endlessness of this love is that which keeps us always striving, and consequently, happy, because in realizing our experiences in our progress, and how each successive stage of that progress has brought us greater and greater happiness, we know—I say know, that what is beyond must mean a greater happiness and a nearer approach to the Father, Himself.

So I say, let not your strivings in the slightest particular decrease and you will find that increased happiness will be yours.

I will stop now, and with my love to you both will say good night.

Your loving,

Grandmother, ANN ROLLINS

I am here—Your own true and loving *Helen*.

Well dear, it is very late.

I am glad that you received the messages that you did tonight, although the Master was here and intended to write, but he gave way to these other spirits for he saw that their messages might do some good.

But tomorrow night you must be prepared to receive his message.

I will not write more tonight. Good night.

Your own true and loving,

HELEN.

Spirit Describes His Experience in One of the Hells

I am a spirit who cannot tell you of the joys of heaven, but I can describe the horrors of hell, for just as these other spirits described to you their homes of beauty and happiness, I can describe my home of ugliness and torment.

Do you wish me to do so?

Well know then, that when I lived on earth I was a man of very considerable intellectual powers and acquirements and also of an intense animal nature, so much so, that it overcame my judgment and what moral qualities I had, and I became at last a slave to my appetites which were varied, especially my appetite for drink.

I had many friends of position, social and otherwise, and I was considered a brilliant newspaper writer, and had access to the inner political circles that were then in control of the government.

My weakness, or rather the effect of the strength of my animal nature, was known to many of my friends, and they, in many ways, tried to help me and rescue me from my evil and destructive course of living, and, at times, I would succeed in reforming my conduct; but, alas, not for any great length of time, when I would again relapse into my deplorable habits and become the controlled victim of my destroying appetites.

Of course human friendship and sympathy had their limits, and finally my friends gave me up as lost and past redemption, and I surely and quickly sunk lower and lower in my moral condition, and at last, died a drunkard, unwept and unsung except for the evil that I had done. It was undoubtedly a relief to my friends and acquaintances when I passed over, and forever relieved them of the shadow of my presence and the ghost of what I had been.

But such was my end, and when I came to the spirit world I found that I still was deserted by friends who had become spirits before me, except some who liked the flowing bowl as I did on earth, and who were inhabitants of the unattractive place that I found myself in when my habitation became fixed.

I never, when on earth, thought much of the future life, except to convince myself that there was no hell, and if there was a God He was not bothered about me, a mere man of many millions.

But oh, the fatal mistake; and the unexpected realization of the fact that there is a hell! Whether there is a God I don't know, for I have never seen him or felt his influence. But since I came to you tonight, and heard the messages of those two spirits who described their wonderful homes and their condition of happiness, and ascribed them all to the kindness and care of God, I have commenced to think that there may be a God and that my mistake was greater than I have heretofore realized. But this is a digression from what I started out to write.

That there is a hell, I know to my sorrow and sufferings, for I have been the occupant of one for oh these many years; and it is always the same place of horrors and darkness, except sometime it is lighted by the flame of lurid light that comes from the anger and sufferings of some unfortunate like myself.

In this hell of mine, and there are many like it, instead of beautiful homes, as the other spirits described, we have dirty, rotten hovels all crooked and decayed, with all the foul smells of a charnal house ten times intensified, and instead of beautiful lawns and green meadows and leafy woods filled with musical birds making the echoes ring with their songs, we have barren wastes and holes of darkness and gloom and the cries and cursings of spirits of damnation without hope; and instead of living, silvery waters we have stagnant pools filled with all kinds of repulsive reptiles and vermin, and smells of inexpressible, nauseating stinks.

I tell you that these are all real, and not creatures of the imagination or the outflowing of bitter recollections. And as for love, it has never shown its humanizing face in all the years that I have been here—only cursings and hatred and bitter scathings and imprecations, and grinning spirits with their witchlike cacklings. No rest, no hope, no kind words or ministering hand to wipe away the scalding tears which so often flow in mighty volumes. No, hell is real and hell is here.

We do not have any fire and brimstone, or grinning devils with pitchforks and hoofs and horns as the churches teach; but what is the need or necessity for such accompaniments? They would not add to the horrors or to our torments. I tell you my friend that I have faintly described our homes in these infernal regions and I cannot picture them as they are.

But the horror and pity of it all is that hope does not come to us with one faint smile to encourage us that there may at some time be an ending to all these torments, and in our hopeless despair we realize that our doom is fixed for all eternity.

As the rich man in hell said, if I could only send Lazarus to tell my poor, erring brothers on earth of what awaits them, how gladly I would do so and save their souls from the eternal torment.

Well, I have written you a long letter and am tired, because it is the first time that I have attempted to write for many long years, and I find some difficulty in gathering my thoughts so as to be able to write in an intelligent and collected manner. So I must stop.

Well, I will say that you are the best friend that I have had since I became an outcast while on earth, and that I will do whatever you may advise, but you must not expect me to have much hope, not doubting your desire to help me, but merely your ability.

Well, I don't understand but I will trust you and will try to believe what you say, only don't create in me that of which I have been deprived of for so long—I mean hope—and have me disappointed.

Well I have looked as you advised, and see some spirits who are so beautiful and so bright that I can scarcely look at them. Never before have I seen such spirits or imagined that such could exist. They must be gods, or why all the great happiness and beauty and love which they have. Tell me what does it all mean? Is it a star of hope that has come to me from afar, and bids me trust that these hells shall not be my home forever? Oh, tell me I pray you, are they the spirits of real mortals who lived and died as I did?

Such love I have never seen; and they look at me with such encouragement and almost human eyes of love, and beckon me to come with them. I have asked if Mr. Riddle is there, and one spirit comes to me and says yes, and that he is glad to have me come with him, as he knew me on earth and is acquainted with my sad life. And now I remember him, for he was a friend who lived in the same city as I did.

He says: "Come G——. and I will try to show you the way to light and relief from your sufferings". And I am going, and as I go a beautiful, glorious spirit comes to me and lays her hand on my head and says: "God bless you my brother and may His divine mercy be yours"; and she tells me that they all love me and will help me.

* My name is G .H B. and I died in 1899.

Oh, tell me what does it all mean? Am I dreaming? Are you real and are they real, or am I in one of the deliriums that I used to have on earth? Oh, so beautiful and heavenly. But they say no, that they are real spirits and once lived on earth, sinful mortals like myself.

How can I ever thank you? I am overcome and cannot write more, but I will come again. So my dear friend good night, for I am going.

*G. H. B.

Confirmation That the Spirits Who Have Written Actually Did So.

I am here, your own true and loving *Helen.*

Well my dear, you have had a variety of writings tonight, and I have been greatly impressed with the last message that you received, for the writer was a very intelligent spirit and seemed to be without hope in his soul. He was a very dark spirit and did not seem to have any love in his soul, but was the picture of dispair and grief. He firmly believed that his position in hell was fixed for all eternity, and hence the hopeless despair in which he was.

I am so glad that he came to you and described these hells, for he was capable; and no one can describe them as he who has lived in them for many years and suffered and experienced all their torments.

He seems to be very grateful, and I think that hope has come to him. He has gone with Mr. Riddle, who is much interested in him. We will all try to help him to progress. So you must pray for him now—we all will.

It is late, and I will not write more.

Your own true and loving Helen.

Swedenborg Writes on the Hells. Refers to Mr. P.'s Work in Receiving the Messages.

Let me write a few lines as I desire to write you some truths about what you and your friend were discussing, namely, are there any such hells as are described in the messages contained in the book (Dr. Peeble's "Immortality") that you have been reading tonight?

Well, you must know, that in the spirit planes hell is a place as well as a condition, and that as a place it has all the accompaniments that make it a reality to the spirits who inhabit it. Of course, the conditions of the spirits who are in these hells are determined by their recollections worked upon by their consciences. But notwithstanding that these recollections are the things that cause their sufferings, yet, the appearances of the locations in which they live are due to something more than these mere recollections, for, as you have been informed, all these spirits are in darkness—the degree of the darkness in which they live being

* Later message. This spirit said he obtained in his soul the Divine Love and had reached the third sphere.

283

determined by their recollections. I mean that when the spirit has recollections of deeds done or not done, which are not so bad as the recollections of another, the former spirit is in a place where there is less darkness than the latter.

These places have their own fixed condition of darkness and of gloom, and many other attachments which increases the sufferings that spirits have to endure.

There are, of course, no fires and brimstone lakes, and devils with pitchforks adding to the sufferings of the spirits, but yet, there are certain conditions and appearances which are outside of the spirits themselves, which causes their recollections to become more acute and to work in a manner to produce a greater degree of suffering.

These hells may be places of caverns and rocks and barren wastes and dark holes and other such things as have been written about; and mortals must know that evil spirits do not live in pleasant places and suffer only from the punishments which their recollections bring to them.

And while the hells of the orthodox are in their descriptions greatly exaggerated, yet there is some truth in the ideas which these descriptions convey as to the fact that the hells are places in which are darkness and many accompanying appearances that add to the tortures of the spirits of evil.

I tell you this because I see you want to know the truth, and for the further reason that you do' not believe that there are such distinctive places as the hells and that the darkness which the spirits in their communications to you speak of is, in your opinion, produced by the conditions of the minds and souls of the spirits who write.

But such opinion is not altogether correct, and it is best for men to know that the mere recollections do not include all of what the hells are.

You say you have your hells on earth sometimes, and that is true to a limited extent, and many men suffer very much from their consciences and remorse, but when they come into the spirit world, if they have not gotten out of the condition which these recollections and remorse place them in, they will find that there is waiting them that place or location which will add to their sufferings that arise from the recollections of evil deeds committed while on earth.

These evil spirits live in communities, for the law of attraction operates in these dark and lower planes just as it does in the higher spheres, and causes spirits of like or similar conditions to congregate together and find consolation, or what they may at times think to be consolation, in one another's company.

These hells are on the planes nearest the earth, and these spirits are not confined all the time to any particular hell; they have the privilege of moving at will along this plane, but wherever they go they find that they are in these hells, and they cannot escape from them, unless they accept the help from spirits who can instruct them what they must do.

Well, when they come to you to write they are not very far from these hells, because the plane in which they live is a part of the plane in which the inhabitants of earth live.

Of course, I don't mean to say that that portion of the earth plane that surrounds your earth is composed entirely of these hells, for that is not true, as the earth sphere has in it considerable light and some happiness. And you must further remember that there are many planes in this earth plane.

These spirits, while their habitations are in these hells, have the privilege of leaving these particular localities and wandering for a short time in and over other parts of this earth plane; but this is only for a short time, and they have to return to the places where they have been placed, and which this law of attraction, that I speak of, draws them to.

Well, there are thousands of millions of evil spirits, and there is never a time when some of them, thousands of them, are not surrounding and trying to use their bad influences on mortals. We do not know why this is permitted, but only know that it is so. And here again the great law of attraction operates, for many mortals are in similar conditions of development and evil thoughts to what these evil spirits are, and naturally, these evil spirits are drawn to them and do come to them. And frequently it happens, that while visiting these mortals of similar conditions to their own, they attempt to influence mortals who are in a better state of moral and spiritual condition, and sometime succeed in doing them harm.

But the great fact is, that these evil spirits have a place of living, where they have to remain, until by the operation of the law of compensation they are relieved from some of their evil tendencies and desires, when they are permitted to progress.

My principal reason in writing you is to have you know that there are hells of places as well as of conditions, and that these places by reason of what they contain and their appearances add to the suffering of the spirits.

As I have written a long time I will stop, and say that I am a Christian and an inhabitant of the Celestial Spheres, and one of the spirit band that is helping you in your great work of the Master. So in leaving you I will subscribe myself,

Your brother in Christ, Swedenborg, the Seer.

*John Calvin Interested in the Work and the Means Whereby
All Men May Receive the Divine Love.*

Let me write just a word, as I am anxious to make known to you that I am interested in your work and in the development of the knowledge

285

of the soul and the means by which all men may receive the Divine Love of the Father and become at-one with Him.

I am not going to write you a lecture tonight and I merely write that I may get in rapport with you, so that later I may have the opportunity and ability to write you of those things of deep and lasting interest to mortals.

I am not known to you, but I hope that you will soon consider me one of your friends, as I desire to be, I assure you.

I must stop now, and in leaving will subscribe myself,

Your true friend and brother in Christ,

JOHN CALVIN

Writes of Mr. James E. Padgett's Selection by Jesus.

Solomon

I came merely to say that I have listened to your conversation tonight, and was much interested because you have discussed that phase of man's destiny which is most important in all the economy or plans of the Father.

Your being chosen to do this work was not the thing of the moment, but for a long period of time the highest spirits of the Celestial Heavens have considered this great question, and the way by which the great truths of God and the necessary plans for man's salvation could be made known to mortals.

Heretofore, the difficulty has been in finding a man gifted with mediumistic powers, who had the unbiased mind, and yet a knowledge to some extent of the soul's requirements and who could be used for the purpose of receiving these great truths and transmitting them to humanity.

Some years ago, as you say, a selection was made of a man to declare these truths, and to him much power and spiritual knowledge were given, and even that power of leaving the body and visiting the world of spirits that he might see for himself the actual condition of things as they there existed, and to declare to mankind the results of his observations. And he did observe and declare many truths, but the difficulty in the way of his realizing the pure truth and interpreting the things which he saw, was that his mind was too much biased by what he had read and believed from the writings as contained in the Bible. And hence, his efforts failed to accomplish the great purpose intended by the mission given him. I am here referring to Swedenborg, the seer, as he was called.

This was a great disappointment to these Celestial Spirits who had projected such a plan for revealing the truths to mankind. At the head of these Celestial Spirits was Jesus, as he is now. Since that time the time has never been propitious for a plan of this kind to be attempted again until now.

But now, instead of having the mortal, through whom this plan is to be worked, leave his body and come to the spirit world and then relate the results and interpretations of his observations, it has been determined that the truths shall be declared to the mortal in the words and thoughts of these spirits, so that no mistake or wrong interpretation can possibly occur; and hence when we saw the possibilities of your becoming a medium with powers sufficient, and a soul capable of development to receive these thoughts and words, it was decided to select you and make you the medium for doing this great work. Of course, Jesus was the active superior spirit in making the selection and we all submitted to his judgment.

But such is the decree, and now you will understand why you were selected, and the fact that you have been selected.

I have told you this tonight, because I have been selected by the others to do so. And I, as the wise man of old, tell you from a knowledge founded on fact.

So * both of you realize your missions, and strive with all your might to acquire this great faith and soul development which are absolutely necessary to a successful performance of the work.

We are with you very often trying to incline your thoughts to the higher things, and to fill your souls with their influences which our love for you creates around you.

So in behalf of all of us who are promoting this great work, I give you our love and blessings.

Your brother in Christ,   SOLOMON.

the wise of the Old Testament and the more
than wise of the followers of Christ.

*All the Spirits who wrote about the magnificent power and glory of the
Master is true. The revelation makes an epoch in the spirit world.*
Layton—John Layton.

I wrote you once before at your office and was interrupted before I could finish.

I merely want to say tonight that all the spirits who have written you about the magnificent power and glory of the Master, is true, and yet not half told.

The revelation of that night makes an epoch in the spirit world where those who witnessed it live, for it has been told to many spirits in many spheres, and Jesus is now the great center of interest to many spirits, who before looked upon him as a mere spirit like themselves.

How wonderful that this display of power should have been made under the circumstances that accompanied it.

* Dr. L. R. Stone was present.

Many spirits were present, from * spheres which are not soul spheres, in which live believers of other religious faiths.

You will hear much of this night for some time to come, and the results of the great scene will be felt in many places that never before have heard of or been interested in the teachings of the Master.

I will not write more.

So good-night

Your brother in Christ

JOHN LAYTON

*Spirit Spheres are not called the soul spheres where spirits are progressing in the Divine Love.

Comments on the glory of Jesus as she saw him the other night.

I am here. * *Saleeba* (Egyptian Princess).

I want to tell you that I was a witness the other night to the wonderful display by Jesus of his great power and glory—and what a wonderful demonstration it was!

I never in all my long experience in the spiritual spheres saw anything that approached it, and no spirit in the highest intellectual sphere could for a moment show the great effulgence of light that Jesus did. So you see, I now know positively that the Master is the son of God, and has this Divine Love to a degree that, as I am informed, no spirit who was then present, except probably, some of the apostles, had any conception of.

I am now convinced to the depths of my soul that the Divine Love of the Father is a real existing thing and that it makes beautiful and God-like those who possess it. Now I shall strive harder than ever to get it, and the great happiness which I now know must be the experience of those who have this Divine Love to a great degree.

I merely wanted to tell you this, because, as you know, I am one who a short time ago had never heard of this Great Love.

So thanking you for your kindness, I am

Your sister in Christ,

* SALEEBA

Astonished at the wonderful glory of the Master—Spirits were awed by the brightness and magnificence of his presence

White Eagle

I want to say that you are in a very good condition tonight and that a great spiritual power has been with you and made you stronger in your physical as well as in your soul condition.

I have not written for a long time and I feel that I must say something. I was present and I was so astonished that I could not withstand the glory. It was wonderful and I am more convinced than ever that he is the

* Saleeba—Ancient spirit of the sixth sphere now progressing to the Celestial Spheres.

true son of the Father. Yes there were a host of spirits present, and many of them not Christians, and the effect on them was surprising.

They were awed by the brightness and magnificence of his presence, and I believe that many of them will become Christians.

He is here and wants to be remembered to you. He is with you nearly all the time watching over and protecting you. He seems to love you so very much, and since the night of the great transformation he is proud that you are his charge.

So you see, we are both glad that we have you for our special care.

I am with you nearly all the time too, and love you very much.

So think of me sometimes and love me.

Your own true guide,

* WHITE EAGLE

Affirms Solomon wrote through Mr. Padgett.

I am here—*Helen.* (*Mrs. Padgett*)

Well, you have certainly had some wonderful messages tonight.

What Solomon wrote you is true, for I have heard the Master say the same thing, as he has told me that you have been selected because of the reasons Solomon gave. How you must thank the Father for such a favor and blessing.

What a work is yours and what a responsibility also. But you will not fail for you will have such help from the Celestial World as will not let you fail.

I will not write more, but only say that I love you with all my heart.

Your own true and loving,

HELEN.

How the Divine Love Enters Into the Soul of Man. When a Man Dies Shall He Live Again?

I am here, *Jesus.*

I am here according to promise, and desire to write you on a subject that all men should be acquainted with. *"How the Divine Love enters into the soul of a man."*

As I have told you before, man is a creature of God, having a body, spirit and soul; and all these are necessary to make the perfect man. But these three parts of man are different in their characteristics and functions, and are separate and distinct, and have qualities that are unlike in their composition as well as in the duration of their existence.

The body, as you and all men know, has an existence which lasts only during the life of the mortal on earth, and after that life ends dissolves into its elements, which no more can form the same body either in the mortal world or in the spirit world, for these elements are merely things

* White Eagle, a powerful Indian belonging to Mr. P'.s band.

of matter and may be and are used to form other bodies and manifestations of the material of nature; not necessarily in the form of human beings, for they enter into other forms both animal and vegetable, and are so disseminated that never again will they become parts of a resurrected body. Your orthodox do not teach this truth, but think in some mysterious way that the mortal body will sometime be resurrected.

No, the body when it has performed its function of maintaining and shielding the soul and spirit of man during his earth life, is no longer and cannot thereafter be a part of that man, and may be considered as something that is no longer a part of him.

This body though, as a matter of fact, even during the life of the mortal is not the same body during that life, for continually is there changes in the elements that compose that body; and one element or set of elements, gives place to others and becomes lost or absorbed in the great sea of elements that help form or constitute the universe of God.

By operation of the laws of attraction and repulsion, these elements as they replace others, which disappear, conform themselves to the general appearance or outline of the parent body, so that the identity of the body as well as of its appearance is preserved; and as a man grows older, the laws which make the changes in his appearance cause these new elements to conform to these changes, so that, even while the material continues to envelop the spirit during the short span of a man' s life, yet that material is not the same for any length of time.

I make this preliminary statement merely to show that the material part of man is not at all connected with the real man, so far as the persistent nature for him is concerned, and this material need not be considered in discussing the subject that I desire to write about.

The spirit part of man is that part which contains what may be called the functions of life and the force and power existing in him and which immediately control him in his conduct and living.

This real, existing principle of life, unlike the body, never dies, but continues to live after the spirit drops its envelope of flesh.

This spirit part of man contains the seat of the mental faculties and reasoning powers, and uses the organs of the material body to manifest these attributes. These faculties live and exist even though the physical body may be in such imperfect condition that the spirit may not be able to make its manifestations in such a way as to enable the mortal to perceive or sense the material things of nature as they are called. To specify, even though the material organs of sight may become impaired or destroyed yet in that spirit body, which is within the physical body, exists the actual sight just as perfectly and completely as if these impaired or destroyed organs were doing their functioning; and the same is true as regards the hearing and the others of what are called the five senses of man.

And as to the reasoning faculties and mental qualities, they exist in the perfect state whether the brain is healthy or not, or whether it performs its work or refuses to do so. These qualities do not depend upon the soundness or perfect workings of the organs of the physical body in order that these spirit qualities may exist in a perfect condition, but the proper workings of the physical organs, or rather the proper and natural movements and manifestations of the brain, and the conscious operations of the mental faculties, do depend upon the spirit faculties being able to use these physical organs in a proper way and in accordance with the harmony of the creation of the relative and correlative parts of man.

These spirit faculties, which man calls the intellect and the five senses, are a part of the spirit body which is enclosed in the material body and which in turn encloses the soul. When the material body dies, the spirit body continues to exist and live on in the world of spirit, and with it and as continuing parts of it, these intellectual faculties, performing all their functions free from the limitations that the physical organs placed upon them. And when this change takes place, these mental qualities, notwithstanding that they have not the material organs through which they functioned when in the mortal frame, can conceive thoughts of things material and hear and see things of the material just as they did, and even more perfectly, when they were enveloped by the environments of flesh and blood .

So you see when the mortal dies, the only thing that dies and is left behind is the mere physical body, and with the spirit body survives all those things which can be said to be the real man so far as the mind is concerned. Hence, man never ceases to remember and to progress and to know that he is a being which death cannot destroy or change into something that he was not before death came to him. And thus I answer the question: "When a man dies shall he live again?" He never ceases to live, and his living is not a new life, but merely the continuation of the old life with all the things of mind and conscience that were his in the old life.

In the purely spirit life the spirit body continues to contain the soul and will be its protector and covering so long as that spirit body shall last. But this body then begins to change and by disintegration into what we may call spirit elements, and the formation of new elements to replace the disappearing ones. This change in this body is not caused by the same laws that operated to change and disintegrate and replace the physical body, but by the law controlling the development of the soul which the spirit body contains.

The soul is the real man because it is the only thing or part of man that may become immortal. The only part of man that was made in the image of its Creator, and the only part of man that may become a part of the Substance of its Maker and partake of His Divine nature, I say may, for that is an important part of this great possibility.

I know this possibility of the soul becoming immortal by partaking of the Divine nature of God, is true; for it is a proven fact in the case of many souls who are now in the Celestial Heavens. I also know that there are many souls in the spirit world, who have been there for many centuries, who have never received this Divine nature and consciousness of immortality. Whether such souls who have not received this Divine nature shall become or are immortal, has never been demonstrated.

This I do know, that in the economy of God's plan for the forming of His Kingdom, at some time, when, I don't know, this privilege of partaking of His Divine nature and the certainty of immortality will be withdrawn from the souls of men and spirits, and then whether these souls who suffer this condemnation will partake of immortality no spirit knows, only God.

There are other things that I know and here tell you, and among them is this:— that so long as the soul does not receive this Divine nature, the mind, which I have described as being a part of the spirit body, continues to exist and dominates both soul and body; and in its progress it may attain to a condition of purity and perfection such as were possessed by the first created living souls—our first parents. Many spirits now are in this condition, but yet are mere men, and their souls remain only in the image of God—nothing more.

While God is mind, mind is not God, and also while God is spirit, spirit is not God. So that when men teach that mind is God and that men must seek to attain to that mind, and thus become like God, they fall far short of the truth. The mind is only an attribute of God, and beyond and back of that mind is the real God—the personality, and that is Soul, from which emanates all these attributes and manifestations which mortals as well as spirits may be conscious of.

But while God is Soul, yet that Soul is a thing of Substance with a nature Divine, and the seat and fountainhead of all the great attributes that belong to Him, such as love and power and life and omniscience and mercy. And here I must state one fact which may startle those who believe and teach that mind is God, and that is, that which is called the human mind is not a part of the mind of God, for this human mind and all its faculties and wonderful qualities are mere special creatures just as are the spirit body and material body of man. As I have said, man was created in the image of God only as regards the soul; and here always bear in mind that the creation was only an image

The mind of man was a special creation just as were the minds of the lower animals, differing only in degree. And if God had not given

292

to man a soul and the spirit body to envelop it, and in which he placed this mind of man, when man died the death of the physical body, that would have been the end of him, as such death is of the body which is not a part of this soul image of God.

As I have heretofore written you, when God created man and made him in His own image as to the soul, he also gave to man the possibility of obtaining the Substance of the Father, that is of having that soul which was a mere image become that soul which is of the Substance of the Creator. I have also explained to you how man, by his disobedience, lost that possibility, and for long centuries was deprived of this great privilege, and how it was again restored to him at the time of my coming to earth, so that he now and for nineteen centuries past has had the possession of this great gift or privilege of partaking of the Substance of the Father.

Well, when man by the way that has been pointed out to him, becomes possessed of the Substance of the Father's Divine nature, even in an initial degree, his soul commences to change and lose its character as a mere image, and to progress towards the attainment of that condition when this image disappears and the Divine Substance takes its place; and as the progress continues he receives so much of the Substance that his soul takes on the Divine nature of the Father, and his at- one-ment with the Father becomes so perfect that he becomes an inhabitant of the Father's Kingdom. This occurs when he becomes fitted to enter the first * Celestial Sphere.

And just here occurs another thing which may startle those who teach that the mind is the essence of God, and that the mind which man, both as mortal and spirit, possesses up to that point in the progress of the soul where the transformation into the Divine nature takes place, becomes a thing of naught, or rather becomes absorbed in the mind of the soul, which is the real mind of the Father, and then and ever after, only this mind of the soul is that which enables the real Divine man to understand the things of God to help him in his progress.

I will continue later. You are tired. But remember that I love you and you have me with you at all times to help and sustain and comfort you.

Good night my dear brother,

Your friend and brother, JESUS.

Continuation from preceding message

I am here. *Jesus.*

I come tonight to finish my message and will do so, if your condition is such that you may receive it.

Well, as you may remember, my subject is: "How the Divine Love enters into the soul of a human being."

* First Celestial Sphere is the one immediately above seventh spirit sphere.

I have already explained to you the difference between, and the respective functions of the physical body, the spiritual body and the soul , and how the real man is the soul, which may live forever. I have also shown you how the physical and spiritual bodies change their component parts, and as such bodies, disintegrated and disappear in the form that they may have at any one time.

Well, the soul is the man and becomes the angel of God's kingdom. The soul may also become only the everlasting part of man in the spiritual kingdom as contradistinguished from the Celestial Heavens.

The only way in which the soul may become an inhabitant of the Celestial Spheres, is by its obtaining of the Divine Love and thereby become a partaker of the Divine nature of the Father; and this can be accomplished only by the inflowing of the Divine Love, by means of the operation of the Holy Spirit, which is the instrumentality used by God to carry this Love to the souls of men.

As I have before said, this love never forces itself into the souls of men, and comes only when men seek for it in sincerity and with effort. It is waiting for all men to receive it, but never comes into the soul of its own initiative, and without invitation. So the important question is, how does it come into the soul and what must men do to induce its inflowing.

There is only one way, and that is by the opening up of the soul in such a manner that this Love, when it comes in response to sincere seeking, may find an entrance and a condition of development that will cause it to find lodgment and abiding place, harmonious and satisfactory to the qualities of its own existence. Of course, man cannot of himself open up his soul to this inflowing, for, while he has great power, yet the will is not sufficient; nor has he any other inherent qualities that will enable him to place his soul in such condition as to make possible the work of the Holy Spirit in causing the love to flow into the soul.

The only means by which this can be accomplished are prayer and faith. When a man in true earnestness and sincere aspirations, prays to the Father for this Divine Love, such prayer not only brings Love, but causes those portions of the soul which are capable of receiving this Love to open up to its coming and to work in such a way as to attract the Love.

The Holy Spirit never performs this work of preparing the soul for the reception of this Love, but merely brings the Love and causes its inflowing when the soul is in condition to receive it. In answer to prayer, there are other instrumentalities of the Father working to prepare the soul condition that is required, and these instrumentalities are the bright spirits of the Celestial Heavens, whose duties, among others, are to an-

294

swer the prayers of the penitent in the way of infilling the soul with influences that turn the thoughts and aspirations to this Divine Love and its operations.

As I said when on earth, there is no other way to get into the sheep fold but through the gateway provided,—he that attempts to climb over the fence is a thief and a robber. But this should be modified to fit the exact fact, for there is no possibility of getting into this fold by climbing the fence. **There is only one way—that through the gate of prayer and sincere longing.**

I know that many men believe that the performance of church duties, and the observation of the requirements of the church as to baptism and the sacraments, etc., will· be sufficient to enable them to get into the Kingdom; but I tell you that they are all wrong, and their disappointment will be very great when they come into the spirit world.

What are called moral deeds and good thoughts will not cause this inflowing of the Divine Love because these things are necessary steps towards the purification of the soul in its natural love; and no matter how pure this love may become, yet it is not the Divine Love or any portion of it.

Good thoughts and deeds, though, may help to turn the aspirations of the soul to these higher conditions, and open up its perceptions to a degree that may lead to prayer and faith, and, therefore, in addition to their work of purifying the natural love may prove to be of great value in assisting men towards the development of the soul so that the Divine Love may enter into it. But to depend on good thoughts and moral deeds and a life pure from sin to give man the right to an entrance into the Celestial Kingdom, is a great mistake.

The Divine Love is a thing entirely apart from the nature of man, even in its purest state, and was never conferred on man as was the natural love, and, consequently, when man obtains this Divine Love and it becomes a part of his soul qualities, his nature, as it were, changes, and he becomes a new creature. An additional something has been conferred upon him, and it becomes impossible for him to remain the mere man that he was, and he always would be, except for this change in his nature.

I know that men do not understand the distinction between a man with only the natural love and one with the Divine Love, but the distinction is so great, that the one, when possessed to a sufficient degree, makes the man a part of Divinity, while the other, no matter how fully possessed and how pure it may become, makes man merely man, though a perfect one.

Whosoever will pray in sincerity for the inflowing of this Divine Love will receive it. It is not a respecter of persons, and the sincere

aspirations of the soul of any man, be he prince or peasant, rich or poor, will invariably cause this love to come into his soul and change his nature, so that he will become a new creature, and one not subject to death forever more.

The merely intellectual prayers are not efficacious, for it does not have any effect in opening up the soul, and neither does much of this praying do the work. One little moment of this true praying will be more effective in causing this Divine Love to flow towards the soul than a whole lifetime of idle repetition of prayers that come from a source merely mental. And here let me say that the mind is not the soul, and much less God.

Well, I think I have made plain how this love flows into a man's soul, and in addition what its effect is, when possessed by man. There is nothing in all God's universe that can take its place for the purpose of making a man at-one with the Father, and of causing him to become Divine in so far as he possesses this Love.

So I say to all men, pray and pray and never cease to pray for the inflowing of this Love, for there is no limit to its abundance, or the amount which man or spirit can obtain. Always in the Celestial Heavens, we spirits continually pray for an increased bestowal, and always our prayers are answered, but always there is more to follow.

I must not write more tonight.

I am satisfied with the correctness of your receiving my message, and will come again and write you another.

> With all my love and blessings,
> I am your brother and friend,   JESUS.

Affirming that Mr. Padgett is selected by Jesus to do the work.

I am here. *Lazarus.*

I merely want to say that I am the real Lazarus of the Bible story and that I am an inhabitant of the Father's kingdom, and in the truth that exists in that kingdom, and in its inhabitants.

I declare to you that the spirits who have written you the truths of Celestial and spiritual things are actually those whom they represent themselves to be. Jesus, especially, is with you very often and communicates to you truths from His great storehouse of knowledge of the truth.

He is so much interested in the work to be done and the revelations to be made that he is with you very often for the purpose of not only revealing these truths, but of preparing you to receive them; and he is enveloping you in his love, and giving to you a development of your soul faculties that will make you qualified to receive these high truths as no other mortal has ever been qualified, for he knows that you are his best qualified instrument now on earth to do his work and the work of the Father.

From what I say, you must not suppose that you are the best, or the man having the greatest amount of the Divine Love in the soul, for that is not true, nor are you chosen because of any merits of your own or superior mental endowments, but you have those conditions of attunement with him, that enables him and the other spirits to use you in performing this work.

I am not of such exalted position or soul development as are many of the spirits who write you, yet I know the plans of the Master, and what I say to you is true.

I was a Jew and an orthodox one, until the Master came to me and developed my soul so that I could understand his teachings, and become susceptible to the inflowing of the Divine Love.

I will not write more now, but in closing repeat that you must believe what I have said, and try to do the will of the Father and the work that you have been selected to do.

Well, both Mary and Martha are in the Celestial Heavens, and you would naturally suppose that Mary has made the greater progress in her soul development but that is not true, as they both live in the same sphere, and have similar development.

As you know they have been in the spirit world for a very long time and whatever spiritual superiority Mary may have appeared to have over Martha does not exist, for they both have this love to a degree that has caused all sin and thoughts for the material to have become eradicated long years ago.

Your brother in Christ,   LAZARUS.

*Portraits of Jesus. Only the Father can fill the soul with
the Divine Love.*

I am here. *John*

I come to write a few lines on the display of what was supposed to be portraits of the Master and which you saw tonight.

Well, the exhibits were quite interesting and showed the different and diverse conceptions of the artists during the centuries of what the Master looked like, but I must say that none of them is a correct likeness of him as he appeared on earth or as he appeared after his rising from the dead and made himself visible to his disciples and others.

I understand how the preacher and many others who were present at the church tonight love Jesus, and enjoy the belief that in looking at some of the portraits they may get a conception of his appearance, and I only wish that his appearance might have been shown by some of the pictures, but, as I said, none of them bore any resemblance to the Master whom I knew and associated with, and saw after his resurrection from the tomb.

None of them displayed the great spiritual light that shone from his countenance, even when he was suffering on the cross, and none of them gave a faint glimpse even of the spiritual beauty that was his when he associated with and helped sinners as well as his friends and disciples.

I never heard of any portrait having been painted of him while he lived on earth or afterwards by anyone who had seen him, and the oldest of these portraits that were presented tonight was not made until years after his death, and by men who could not have gotten a description of the Master from anyone who had seen him.

I know that there was no original as the preacher supposed, that must have given a suggestion to the artists who painted the ones that you saw, for there was never any original. No, the Master passed from earth without leaving behind him any representation of his appearance.

The portraits were the results of what the artists conceived in their artistic brains, if I may use the expression, of what the Master who had displayed such wonderful qualities of heart and mind should look like, and as their conceptions of the spiritual and human qualities of the Master differed, so their portraits differed, and the only foundation for their pictures were their own spiritual or non-spiritual conceptions. The Master, of course, like the rest of us who were his disciples, was a Jew, and it is quite natural to suppose that he had the features and hair and beard of the ordinary Jew; and as the Jews have continued to live ever since the time of the Master without much change in appearance or otherwise, I mean in his native land, the artists who conceived him to be a Jew, based their supposed portrait of him upon the appearance of the Jew as they saw him at the time that they painted the pictures.

And while Jesus was a Jew, he was not what may be called a typical Jew in appearance any more than in other qualities, for he had in him that condition of soul that to a large extent determined and fashioned his appearance.

His eyes were not dark or brown but a violet blue, and his hair was light and inclined to the auburn; his nose was prominent and somewhat long, and his beard was of the color of his hair, and worn not so long as was the custom of those days, and he never had a razor on his face. His forehead was not so very high or broad, but was well shaped and somewhat effeminate, and indicated that there was not so great mental development as might be supposed, for I must say here, that his knowledge was not so much the knowledge of the brain as of the heart and soul and as you know, and as all men may know who acquire the proper soul development, the soul has a brain of its own which is used for the disclosure of the knowledge of that which pertains to the spiritual truths. Mortals may not quite comprehend the meaning of this assertion, but I must tell them that in certain circumstances and conditions the brain, or, to be more exact, the mind of the natural man becomes entirely absorbed in the mind of the soul.

So that, I say, it is not a correct conclusion to suppose that Jesus, because of having all the wonderful knowledge of the truths of God, his Father, as he preferred to call God—must have had a large development of those portions of the brain that is ordinarily displayed by a large or prominent forehead. His head, in fact, was not very large, but compact and beautifully shaped.

He wore his hair parted in the middle and reaching to his shoulders, and it was somewhat curly—a beautiful head of hair which seemed to be full of life.

No artist has had a correct conception of his appearance and no portrait or sculpture conveys a near likeness of him.

But as the people realize how beautiful he was within they can possibly in their own imaginations see a clearer conception of his appearance than any painted portrait gives to them.

I sometimes wish that there was on earth a true likeness of him, as he appeared during the time of his great work of love on earth, so that those who love him could have the further pleasure of realizing his physical appearance; but that may not be so, because as mortals naturally worship the pictures of the saints and through the picture, worship the originals, the danger would be that if there was a picture of the Master, mortals would worship him, even more than they do now—all of which worship is very distasteful and displeasing to him, and as he has said, blasphemy.

The Master should be loved, and his presence longed for, as such presence has in it a wonderful love and influence to help and make happy those who are in condition to realize his presence; but he should not be worshipped.

Well, as I was with you tonight at the church, I thought that it might be interesting to you, to have told you the truth in reference to the Master and his supposed portraits.

Of course it is not necessary that there should be any picture of him, true or otherwise, in order to enable mortals to enjoy his presence, for he is working among mortals today as he was when on earth, and his love goes out to them, and his desire that they become in at-one-ment with the Father; and when mortals sincerely long for his presence, sooner or later, as the laws of his limitations permit, he will be with them, and will comfort and help them, if they will enable him to make the rapport. This is what is meant by his standing at the door and knocking—when the door is opened the rapport is made, and then his love and influence will be felt.

But the difficulty here is that mortals suppose it to be and confuse it with the great love of the Father, when the fact is that this love of Jesus is the same love in quality but not in quantity, that the mortal himself may obtain by the earnest prayers and sincere aspirations of his soul. The love of Jesus can never transform a human soul into the substance of the love of the Father, because this transforming love can come from the Father only, and is bestowed through the medium of the Holy Spirit, as we have explained to you.

So let all mortals love Jesus with the fervour and fulness of their souls and crave for his love, but in doing so not forget or fail to know, that in thus loving in order to become like Jesus they must seek for the greater Love of the Father, and give to Him all their soul's longings and desires for the inflowing of this love into their souls, and the more they receive of this great Divine Love the better able they will be to love their great brother, Jesus.

Well, I have written enough for tonight. I will come soon again and write you a formal message. So remember what I said to you a few nights ago, and believe and trust, and you will not be disappointed.

With my love and the blessings of the Father, I will say goodnight.

Your brother in Christ,

JOHN

Comments on John's Message—On the Portraits of Jesus

I am here. Your own true and loving *Helen* (Mrs Padgett).

Well dear, you had a rather unusual letter from John, and I must say that as Jesus appears now, even when he accommodates himself to the humblest human, the portraits do not resemble him. Of course, I do not know what he looked like when on earth, but John knows and what he says is true.

* Jesus told you a short time ago that he would sometime permit you to see him clairvoyantly and when he does, I think that you will see him as he was on earth, or at least as he appeared to mortals after his resurrection; and I hope that when you do, it will be indelibly stamped on your memory, so that if you were an artist you could reproduce his appearance. So you will have to consider yourself truly favored when you see him in this way.

May the Father's love be sufficient for you.

Goodnight my dear husband.

Your own true and loving,   HELEN.

*Appendix. Mr. Padgett told me that on several occasions, when he was praying for the Divine Love, that he often saw Jesus praying with him.

The hope that all mortals have in a future destiny of
freedom from care and unhappiness.

I am here, *Elias* (Prophet of old)

I desire tonight to write a few lines upon a matter that I have been thinking might be of some interest to you, and that is: *"The hope that all mortals have in a future destiny of freedom from care and unhappiness."*

I know that a large majority of mortals who believe in the Christian doctrines, believe that for a very considerable number of mankind there is awaiting an eternity in the hells of continuous torture and torment, and that in order to avoid such a destiny or future state, men, while on earth, must believe in certain doctrines and conform themselves to such beliefs, for after death there can be no possible opportunity for being saved from such a fate.

Of course, these beliefs are the results of the teachings of those who claim to have the ability to interpret the Bible, mixed with a little of divine inspiration and mysterious power and wisdom that are conferred upon those who have the careers of ministers of the Gospel; and men, because of long years of training or of inheritance from those who for long years believed in these teachings, naturally exercise very little independent thought and accept the declarations of these ministers as being almost the divine expressions of God Himself.

Such doctrines have caused in their workings much harm to the mortal and much unhappiness to the spirits of men in the spirit world, because beliefs accompany the latter in their existence as spirits and keep them from learning the truth for a long time after they become spirits.

It is a great pity that men can be bound by such false and damnable beliefs, and generation after generation continue to become servants to the teachings of misguided instructors. And I wish to say that all these beliefs are untrue and have no foundation in fact, and the sooner mankind knows this the better it will be for their happiness on earth and their welfare in the world to come.

It is true that there are hells and punishment, and that the majority of men when they become spirits will have to go into such hells and suffer such punishment; but the element of eternal or everlasting does not enter into the duration of such state or condition, for there is no punishment inflicted on the spirits of men for the purpose of causing them to pay a penalty that can never be satisfied through all eternity. This punishment is only for the purpose of purification, and when it is accomplished, for the particular spirit who has suffered the same, the hell ceases to exist and the punishment ceases to have any necessity for its existence; and, ultimately, the condition of every man will be that of a purified spirit, free from sin and defilement and the necessity for hell or punishment.

301

I know that what I have written has in various forms been written before, but I felt that I must say just this much and in the way that I have done.

I am glad that you are feeling better tonight, and I want to assure you that, if you will pray to the Father, you will continue to grow in your spiritual development, and as a consequence feel better in every particular.

With my love I will say, good night.

Your brother in Christ.   ELIAS

What causes the souls of men the unrest that now exists in the world?

I am here, *Samuel.*

No, I have not written for a long time although I have been with you quite often and seen the other spirits write, and heard the conversation of yourself and friends on many occasions as you discussed the truth of things spiritual, and commented on the messages that you received on the sermons of the preachers who attempted to explain what they called the Bible truths.

Tonight I desire to say a few words on the subject: *"What causes the souls of men the unrest that now exists in your mortal world?"*

This is a subject, I know, that of late has been widely discussed, and many causes given and tried to be explained as the basis for such conditions of men, individually, and as comprising nations. I realize that it is a large and comprehensive question. and to discuss it in all its features would require much more time than we have to devote to it tonight, and hence I will call attention to only a few of these causes.

In the first place man is so created, or rather he has brought himself into such a condition, that self love or selfishness—and I mean the purely human selfishness and not that of the higher and proper kind—has become the mainspring or active principle of all his motives for doing or not doing a thing or things, and in so acting the rights of others are considered only in a secondary or subordinate sense. If the recognition of these rights does not involve any sacrifice of what he considers is for his own advantage, then these rights may be recognized and admitted and permitted to be carried into actual enjoyment; but if there be any conflict between his conception of what he is entitled to and the actual rights of his brother or friend or stranger, he will see only the justice of his own rights and his consequent action will be based on that conception; and having this motive of selfishness predominant and controlling in his actions, it seldom occurs that the rights of these others are fairly recognized, and consequently, there arises injustice and harm, and the desire of conferring those things which would naturally arise from the conception of the rights of these brothers is ignored.

Your brother in Christ,   SAMUEL.

Hugh Latimer in the Celestial Heavens. His beliefs when on earth. Jesus came and told him he was not God.

I am here—*Latimer*:

I was the martyr who was burned at the stake because of my belief in God and in salvation by faith and works as taught in the Scriptures.

My name was Latimer—Hugh.

I merely come to tell you that I am now a happy spirit and an inhabitant of the Father's kingdom. I live in the Celestial Heavens and am a follower of the Master as I was on earth.

No, I do not now worship him as God. That false doctrine I believed when on earth, but now I know that there is only one God to be worshiped, and that Jesus is His most exalted son. I was surprised I must confess, when I entered the spirit world and did not enter heaven and see God on His throne and Jesus sitting on His right hand. But it was not long before I understood the truth, for Jesus came to me himself and explained that he was not God and that I must not worship him as such. But we who love God as followers of Christ, adore the Master as our great teacher and elder brother.

When I first entered the spirit world I found myself in the second sphere among spirits of brightness and love, and after a little while, I entered the third sphere where love is more abundant, and then as my soul became filled with this love and my errors of belief left me, I progressed from sphere to sphere until I arrived where I am now living, and I thank God for His love and mercy.

I do not think the fact that I died a martyr to my beliefs had any effect in enabling me to reach a higher sphere than I would otherwise have entered. Not the manner of my death determined my place in the spirit world, but the development of my soul qualities did. If I had a belief in what I thought were truths, but which were not really truths, and that belief, proclaimed and persisted in, had caused my being put to death, you can readily see that the mere fact that I died for the sake of that belief would not have in any way helped my soul development in the real truth, and so the mere fact that I died a martyr for the real truth did not help me in obtaining a place in the spirit world that I would not have obtained had I died a natural death with the same beliefs. **The manner of a man's death does not determine anything, but the manner of his living and the developmest of his soul qualities are what determines where he shall live in the spirit world.**

Of course, the death of the martyr will sometimes awaken soul qualities or conceptions that might not otherwise have been awakened, and thereby increase the martyr's love for the Father; and in this way such a death may help him in his progress to higher things. But as I say, the soul development fixes the first home of the spirit. I mean the development at the time of passing over.

My dear brother I must stop now, but will come again some time and write you.

Yours in Love,   HUGH LATIMER.

Description of some of the spheres. Criticises a book Mr. P. was reading.

I am here—your *Grandmother (Ann Rollins)*.

I come, because I see that you have been much interested in the description of the various spheres of the spirit world as contained in the book that you have just been reading.

Well, my son, I have read the book as you did and I must say that I have grave doubts that any mortal ever had the experience of the Dr. as is related in that book. I, of course, will not positively say that he did not leave his body and visit some of the spheres of the spirit world, and attempt to give a description of what he saw, but I do not think it was possible for him to visit any sphere which is higher than his soul development would enable him to enter, and, as I am informed, not being a man with the soul development that would fit him for the higher soul spheres, I do not understand how he could possibly have entered a sphere higher than the sixth; and I doubt that he entered that, for from all the information that I have received, I have never heard of any mortal entering a sphere higher than the third, which Saint Paul says he visited.

At any rate, the descriptions of the higher spheres as contained in the book—and I mean by this the sphere above the third—are not correct in many particulars for, as I have told you before, the fifth and seventh spheres are not 'intellectual spheres in the preeminent sense, and in them are not the great colleges and institutions of learning that the book refers to, and neither are the inhabitants engaged in any special study of the laws of nature with the mere intellect; for in these spheres the great studies and aspiration of the spirits are given to the development of the soul by obtaining the Divine Love, and to help in the work are teachers who devote themselves to instructing these spirits in those things which will lead to this soul development.

The mind or mere intellect is not given much attention to, but is subordinated to the soul development, for with this development and a part of it, comes a wonderful development of the faculties of what you might call the mind, but which we call and which really are the soul perceptions. I know it is hard for you to understand, but what we call the soul perceptions may be compared to the mental faculties as you commonly speak of them. These soul perceptions do not depend upon these mental faculties, and in fact the latter forms no part of the former, but they are entirely distinct and of a different order and composition from these mental

304

faculties. These soul perceptions, as such, cannot be cultivated or made to increase in their powers or qualities by mere study, but they and their progress are entirely dependent upon and not separated from the development of the soul in love. I mean the Divine Love of the Father. In other words, unless there be a development of the soul by this Divine Love, there will be no development of the soul perceptions.

It is difficult to explain this to you, but you may possibly get some idea from what I have said.

The sixth sphere, as I have before said, is the great intellectual sphere, and in this are wonderful colleges and institutions of learning, and many spirits who were great men intellectually on earth are teachers in these institutions.

But you must not think that because certain spheres are preeminently intellectual that there are not teachers of the higher truths pertaining to the souls and to the Divine Love, working in these spheres, for there are. And many great spirits of the Celestial Spheres are engaged in this teaching. But this I must say, that the work is more difficult and the effort to convince these spirits of highly developed intellectuality and knowledge is more strenuous than in any of the lower spheres. These bright minded spirits seem to think that the mind is the great thing to be cultivated and looked after, and while they in a way worship God, yet it is with the faculties of the mind merely. They do not think that there is any teachings in the truth of the New-Birth and the Divine Love of the Father in contradistinction to the love which they possess, which is only the natural love.

I have been in all these spheres and have worked in them, and what I tell you I know from actual experience.

Well, he is mistaken, for in the Seventh sphere the spirits have homes just as they do in the lower spheres, only they are much more beautiful and bring more happiness and gladness because of the great number of additional things that are provided by the Father to increase the happiness of His children.

As to our clothing in that sphere, we are clothed in what you would say a modest and comfortable way. Our clothing is not so flimsy as to permit our forms to be seen as if we had on no clothing at all. This idea must have arisen from the fact that inhabitants of that sphere have no thought of immodesty or of what might result from the suggestions that a naked or half clothed body might give to mortals or even some of the lower spirits. But such an idea does not enter into the question of the nature of the clothes that we shall wear.

Our thoughts are all pure and free from mortal taint and the character of our thoughts has no influence upon the character of our clothing. We wear clothes to cover our bodies because we think it proper to do so, and because we make our clothes by our own thoughts and will: and they are of the most glorious and shining appearances that you can imagine.

But as all things in nature have a covering, so in the spirit world, the spirits all have coverings, and this is even so in the Celestial Sphere in which I live. I have never seen such a thing as a naked or nearly naked spirit in these higher spheres.

Of course, the spirit of Dr. ———————— may have entered some of these higher spheres, as I have said, but his information as the author of the book that was communicated to his mortal friend, was not correctly transmitted, for many things which he says are not true.

I would like to write more to-night but it is late, and you are tired.

I will say with all my love, good-night.

Your own loving grandomther, (ANN ROLLINS).

Samuel—Continuous life of a man after the death of the body as shown by the manifestations of nature is not conclusive.

I am here—*Samuel.*

I desire to write for a short time on a subject that is of importance to those who are in doubt as to the reality of the future life.

I know that a vast majority of mortals believe in a future existence and the immortality of the soul, but there are a considerable number of mortals who do not know these facts or who have no belief regarding the matter, and simply say "I don't know." It is to these latter persons that I wish to write.

In the first place, all persons know, if they know anything, that they are living, and that sooner or later what they call death is inevitable, no matter from what cause it may take place. To live then, implies that there is such a thing as continuous life; and to die, to these people, demonstrates that the life with which they are acquainted ceases, and that the material body in which this life manifests itself gradually disintegrates into the original elements that composed that body.

Now a man being a materialist purely, would seem to be correct in his conclusions that when life, which could be manifested only through the material things of nature, ceases and the body becomes inanimate and dead, that then is the end not only of the body but of the individual. And if there existed no other manifestation of life than this physical one, there would be no foundation upon which to base the assumption that the death of the body does not end all.

I know it has been asserted in the way of argument that even though the material parts of vegetation die, yet as Spring comes round, these materials show forth again the life that had previously manifested itself, and therefore, by analogy, the death of the human body merely means that its life will appear again in evidence in some other body or form.

306

But upon close investigation and exact reasoning it will be seen that the two subjects of demonstration are not alike, because while the material of the vegetable kingdom apparently dies, yet it does not all die, for even though you may apparently see the particular body of the tree or plant or every part of it go into decay or rottenness, yet as a fact, this is not true. The whole of the material plant which enclosed or manifested life, does not die until out of it a new body arises and grows, and the life that animated the body that appears to have died, continues in it awaiting the new growth for its display of existence.

The flower dies and the bush upon which it grows may appear to die, yet the roots continue to enclose the life principle which causes the bush to grow again, and which has its genesis in these roots, and is the same life that originally existed in the bush. Pluck up the bush by the roots and expose them to the elements until they die and commence to disintegrate, and then replant them, and you will find they will not grow for the reason that the life which had animated them has departed.

And the same conclusions will be reached when you apply the same investigation and reasoning to every species of the vegetable kingdom. The grain of corn though apparently dead, is in reality not dead, but continues to contain the life principle which was the cause of the growth of the stalk and the blade and the ear in the blade. Nothing of the vegetable kingdom will be reproduced or form the basis of a new growth, unless some part of the old growth retains in it the life force.

In man's investigation of the wonders of vegetable life, he has discovered that a grain of corn that had been entombed in the hands of an Egyptian mummy for more than three thousand years, when planted in the ground reproduced the stalk and blade and ear of corn, just as the original material body had produced. And why? Not because when the grain of corn was planted in the earth it received unto itself new life or any force that was not already in it, but because the grain had never ceased to be without the life that existed in it as it grew from the original seed to the perfect grain. The grain had never lost its life and had never died, though apparently it had. Always there was some part of the original body that continued to exist and that held enclosed in itself the life principle. Without the preservation of some part of the original body there could never have been a manifestation of the life that caused the growth of that body.

This phenomena, as you call it, was not the resurrection of a material body that had died and become disintegrated and nonexistent, but was merely the resurrection of that part of the old body that had never died but had always retained in it the life principle. And this I say, is no argument for the future existence of man, as viewed from a purely material aspect.

When the body of a man dies it is eternally destroyed, either by natural decay or by incineration or, sometimes, by cannibals, so that no portion of his body remains in which the life principle may be preserved; and so far as the material body is involved, it utterly disappears—no roots remain in the ground and no grain or seed of it is preserved from which a new body may arise.

So I say, the phenomena of the vegetable apparently dying and after a season springing forth again and producing a body similar to the one that had formerly lived and died, furnishes no demonstration or argument from which, logically, can be drawn the conclusion that when a man dies he will not cease to exist, or will live again.

From the purely material standpoint, the materialist has the better of the argument, and he may well ask the question: "When a man dies shall he live again?" and answer the inquiry by saying, nature furnishes no proof that he will.

It may be said that life permeates all nature and is the basis of all existence, and that assertion is true; but it does not follow therefrom that any particular manifestation of life, such as the individual man, when once ceasing to manifest will again be reproduced in that particular identity of material manifestation, or in that form or existence that will make itself the identical being that had ceased to exist.

So to show man that there is a continuous existence after the death of the body—and I mean an individual, identical existence—something more is required than the argument of analogy in nature, or to the material things of nature in which life appears and then apparently disappears and then reappears. As the discussion on this phase of the matter will require more time than you have tonight to receive it, I will defer the treatment until later. With all my love I will say good night. Your brother in Christ,

SAMUEL.

Previous message continued on the continuity of life.

I am here, *Samuel.*

I desire to continue my message on the subject of the continuous life of a man after the death of the body, as shown by the manifestations of nature.

As I was saying, the apparent death and resuscitation of things of the vegetable kingdom, do not furnish any argument that man will continue to live after the death of the physical body.

Now I know it is difficult to understand what there can be in the manifestations of nature to prove such persistent life, and that the people for whose benefit I am writing this will not be willing to use evidence of things of a spiritual nature to prove this continuous life, and hence, I will confine myself to matters material.

Well, in the first place, there is no such thing as the death of anything in all the material universe of God. Every primal element has life in it, even though that life may not be apparent to the consciousness of men, but it is a fact. Every atom or electron, as the scientists term these particles of matter that are reduced to their infinitesimal proportions, is pregnant with life, and the very apparent decay of material substances is nothing more nor less than the results of the operation of the life that they contain working out the changes of form or expression.

If the scientists will investigate and analyze the constituents of particles of all matter, notwithstanding that they appear to be devoid of the life principle, he will find that life in some of its expressions is contained in these particles and that there is nothing in the material things of nature that is completely inert. There is no such thing as inertia—it only appears to exist; and while it may not be apparent to the natural eye that every thing in the material has life within itself, and as a result therefrom there is force and motion, yet such is the fact.

This life principle permeates everything—applies to and forms a part of everything that has the appearance of natural existence. The grain of sand on the seashore or the dust of the decayed tree has within it life, and this life is no more nonexistent or absent from these material things, than are the elements that compose this visible form of matter ever lost or without existence. It is true that these elements change their forms and their compositions, yet they never cease to exist, or become nothing. Nothing means a void, and in God's creation there is no void. Everything is of substance and there are no vacancies unfilled.

And hence, as life is the foundation principle of existence and life exists everywhere, and there being no void in nature, life permeates everything, whether visible to the mortal eye or senses or not.

When that which is material decays or disintegrates, it does not do so as the result of the absence of life, but as the result of the operation of this principle of life upon the material in such a way as to cause the separation of its elements and their change into new forms and appearances.

I know it is said that the workings of the elements, that is fire and water and air and chemicals known and unknown, cause the disintegration or even the disappearance of things material, but this is not strictly true, for these elements do not affect these things themselves, as a primary result of their workings, but what they affect is the life within these materials, and as that life lessens or changes the materials of which that life is a part, disintegrate or dissolve, as is sometimes said, into thin air, and never does any part of the material substance, no matter how minute it may come to be, die—that is in the sense of losing life.

Life is a thing of such delicate nature, and is so susceptible to a division or reduction to a smallness almost to infinity, that no substance can become so small that life is not a part of it and the vital principle of its existence.

As is known, the solid rock may be reduced not only to dust but to a liquid and then to a vapor and then to a gas and then to that that is not sensitive to the consciousness of men, and yet the life principle exists in all these forms of that material rock; and that which ultimates into apparent nothingness, contains life just as does the original rock or any of its subsequent forms in the process of reduction to seeming extinction.

The materialist accepts these phenomena as true, and blindly and with full assurance announces that nothing in creation is ever lost or annihilated. This being true, why is not the conclusion logical that the apparently inanimate rock or the animal without reasoning powers or the man with the reasonable faculties, is never annihilated or lost; or in other words, never dies the death that results in nothingness?

But they say, while this may be true, yet the materials which form these various aspects of existence do not necessarily or probably come together again and reform the identical being that once appeared as an existing thing and then dissolved into the elements that composed the thing; and hence, while the elements in some form may continue to live forever, yet that form in which they once existed will not again appear. I know that this is a reasonable conclusion and one in accord with the demonstrations of science, and is applicable to the merely physical man just as to any other manifestations of the material things of nature.

But even these materialists admit that in the case of man, there is something in his formation and essential being that is more than or in addition to the merely physical portions of him, and while they may say that this something is wholly of a material nature, yet they admit that it is of a material different and distinct from the material that forms the visible physical body.

I do not speak of the soul or spiritual part of man, but of the intellect and of the five senses and of the reasoning powers, all which, of course, includes the memory. That part of man that embraces these things, the materialists must admit, is distinct and different from the mere body, and, even though it were here to be conceded that they are material, yet no man has ever seen them or felt them or in any way perceived their existence as he has that which he knows to be of the material. He has seen and heard and known the effects of the existence of these invisible material qualities, as he may call them, but has never demonstrated that they died when the physical body died. The furthest that he can go in this direction is that they disappeared and became lost to his consciousness; but that they disintegrated or dissolved or were reduced to a gaseous substance or thin air in which he has seen the visible physical body disappear, he cannot affirm. The limit of his knowledge is that with the death of the

310

physical body, this other, as he terms it, material part of man disappears and never again reappears to his physical senses.

While as I say, he has never observed and has no knowledge of any disintegration of these invisible material parts of man into any primary elements or atoms or electrons as he applies such terminology to the physical body, and hence he is not justified in concluding that any such results to this invisible material follows the death and dissolving of the flesh and blood and bones of man. To so conclude is more of a speculation than to hold that the invisible material did not dissolve into forms more invisible, if such an expression can be used.

As I have said, life is in all things, visible and invisible, and there is no vacuum in nature. While man is living it is demonstrated that life is in this invisible part of man, and more abundantly that in the merely visible body; and as life continues after death in the elements of this latter body, why cannot we declare that after death life continues in the invisible part of man? Nothing is ever lost or annihilated, and hence these parts of man cannot be annihilated, and existing they must contain life.

Has the materialist ever been able to demonstrate to his own satisfaction even, that this invisible part of man, which he says is material, ceases to live? He cannot say that the elements of the physical body, no matter what form they may assume, cease to live, but on the contrary affirmatively asserts that they are never annihilated and continue to exist; and as life is necessary to existence they must continue to have life.

So according to their own arguments and demonstrations and ultimate claims, the death of the physical body does not destroy the elements which compose that body but only the form in which these elements were combined. Then from this the most that they can claim as to the invisible material part of man is, that while the material which composed this part is not dead or annihilated, yet their formation may be disintegrated or changed, and hence the identity of the man, as to this portion of him, no longer exists. But this conclusion does not follow as a logical sequence, and the materialist has nothing upon which to base this conclusion, except that he has seen and knows that when the visible body dies it disintegrates and ultimately disappears.

He has never seen the disintegration of this invisible part of man, though he has seen its manifestations decay and even destroyed; but the cause of this is shown to be some decadence or disorganization of some part of the visible body through which the invisible manifested.

These materialists have knowledge of the facts that men have been deprived of their arms or legs or other parts of the body, and yet the invisible parts remained perfect, performing their functions. Also it is true, that men have received injury to their physical organs of sight or hearing, and, as a consequence the invisible organs of sight or hearing did

311

not function, but that fact constitutes no proof that they were dead or had ceased to preserve the form they had before the physical organs were impaired, for when the defects of the physical organs were removed and these organs again came into condition to do their functioning, the invisible faculties of sight and hearing manifested their existence again just as they had existed before the physical organs were impaired. And so many similar instances might be referred to show that death or destruction of any or many parts of the visible body does not destroy or disseminate into its elements the invisible material part of man.

And besides let the materialists consider the great difference in the powers and objects of the creation of these visible and invisible parts of man, and they will realize that the purely physical is wholly subordinated and used merely to enable the invisibe parts to manifest themselves and show that the real man is the invisible part, and that man can lose part of his physical vestment, and yet exist and perform his functions and exercise his powers.

I have thus tried to show that while no argument can be drawn from any analogy between the vegetable things of nature, dying and coming to life again, and man's dying, yet neither can any argument be drawn from the fact that the visible body of man dies and goes into its elements never to be resuscitated again as the same body, to show that the invisible body of man dies and is dissolved into its elements and that man ceases to be the individual that he was before the death of the physical body.

I may not have made my message as plain and convincing as I would desire, but in discussions of this kind it is difficult to transmit the various shades of thought through the medium of a mortal. I thank you for your courtesy and will stop now.

So with all my love and the blessings of the Father, I will say good night.

Your brother in Christ, SAMUEL.

How man can come into harmony with the laws that govern him as the created man without obtaining the Divine Love.

I am here—*Abraham Lincoln.*

Let me write a few lines tonight as you are in good condition to receive my message.

Well, I see that you have been thinking a great deal about spiritual things and have longed for the love of the Father, and by such thoughts and longings you have come unto a condition that enables the spirits to make a rapport with you.

Tonight, I desire to write for a short time on the subject of how important it is for man to learn the truths of God in reference to the plan which He has prescribed for man's salvation, and his coming into harmony with the laws that govern him as the created man.

312

As you have been told, in the beginning man was created perfect and in all the constituent parts of his being made in harmony with God's laws controlling man as a perfect creature, and if he had never disobeyed the precepts of the Father, he would have always remained the perfect man.

Now this condition of man is a fundamental one, and the soul is in itself just as capable of that perfection as it was when created, and only by the sin of disobedience was it alienated from God and made the possessor of those things which tend to contaminate it, and cause its pure condition to be overshadowed and dormant as to this perfection.

All of God's universe is perfect and subject to the workings of His perfect laws, and when that condition exists which shows that some one or other of His creatures are not working or being in harmony with these laws, it only means that in order for the restoration to the harmonious existence, man must renounce and get rid of these foreign things that have the effect of interfering with the harmony of his creation.

There is no such thing as total depravity or original sin, or the existence of any condition of the soul in this sin, that cannot be remedied by the applicaiton of the proper treatment and the removal of the incubus. Man in order to become perfect again as he was before the fall, is not required to be recreated or have imposed upon him that which will make him a new or different being from what he was in the beginning. The perfect man is still in existence, but is hidden from the sight and consciousness of men, and needs only his revealment by eliminating from him the covering which now hides his real self. Nothing new is needed but only the riddance of the soul from those things which do not belong to it, and then the soul will appear just as it was created: a perfect soul made in the image of God, but not formed from any portion of the Great Oversoul of the Father.

For a long time, now, man has remained in this condition of having his soul covered over by those things that are merely the results of the perversion of his appetites and the animal part of his nature, and it is only by a process of renunciation that these incumbrances can be gotten rid of, and man stand forth a free and glorious being as he was before the burden of sin came upon him.

In this process he needs no one to pay any supposed debt to the Father or to make an atonement for him, but he must himself by his course of thinking, and consequent doing, remove the things that cause him to appear to himself and to others the outcast from God's' favor. And in order to accomplish this he must first renounce the idea that he is a vile being and not worthy of the favor of the Father, and assert his belief that he, as the man, is the perfect creature of God and can of himself regain the estate from which he has fallen, and let sin and error be removed from his present apparent existence. In doing this he will be helped by the spirits of men, who from their own experience know that sin and error has no real existence in the economy of God, but in the living of man on earth, and in the spirit world as well, have a reality that has prevented men from finding their true selves.

The renunciation is not so much a matter of the intellect as it is of the moral nature of man; and he, while he must use his mind and its attributes in working out this renunciation, yet must try earnestly and certainly use the moral faculties of his nature, for the perversions of these faculties are the foundation of his present condition of sin and error. This renunciation may take a long time to be accomplished, as men look upon time, but it will finally come to pass, and the harmony of God's universe will be restored. But in the meantime men will suffer, for this renunciation is always accompanied by suffering, not so much as a necessary ingredient or penalty of the renunciation but as a consequence of the changing of men's wills and desires in the process of reaching again the condition of the perfect man.

I will stop now, as the rapport has ceased, but will come again.

Good night, I am your friend and well wisher.

LINCOLN.

Comments on Abraham Lincoln's Message on Man's Progress
in His Natural Love.

I am here—Your own true and loving *Helen* (Mrs. Padgett).

Well, dear, you have had a communication tonight from Lincoln, who thinks it advisable to write you as he did. He is now in the Celestial Spheres and knows what the Divine Love is, but said he wanted to write you a short message on man as he is and as he may be, and he has told you just what the condition of man is, and how he is still the perfect man in his true self, and needs only an uncovering to stand forth as the being created in the image of God.

Good night, my dear husband.

Your own true and loving,   HELEN.

How Prayers Are Answered for Material Things. The Miracle
of the Loaves and Fishes Never Happened.

I am here, *St. John, Apostle of Jesus.*

Well, He answers the prayers for things material by the work and operation of His angels and spirits, and they in that work are subject to the limitations of success as I have above mentioned. God does not exercise any arbitrary power to answer prayers, but when they are sincerely offered to Him, He works through His angels in answering them, and He does not by His mere fiat do so. His angels are always watching and working, and when the opportunity comes they use their influence in the best possible way to bring about the ends desired.

314

As you know, man has a free will, and that determines very largely the action of men, and such actions are never arbitrarily controlled by any divine power. If the prayers of men as to material things can be responded to by the workings of the angels and spirits, they are; but if such response depends upon the will of men, then they are not received by mortals, except as the spirits may be able to influence that will and cause men to act in compliance with that influence, which is always used for the purpose of bringing about the response to the prayers that are in their nature proper and worthy to be answered.

Well, I doubt if any of those petitions were ever answered in the arbitrary way that is related in the Old Testament. God never answers prayer in that manner, and the petitions of the old prophets had no more influence to bring about the answers to the same in the manner indicated, than have the prayers of the sincere and earnest man of these days. God was the same then as He is now and worked through the spirits then as He does now, except that now He has angels of the soul development in the Divine Love, that He did not then have, and these angels are doing His bidding as well as are the spirits. But He does not answer prayers for material things except in a manner in consonance with laws controlling the free will and actions of men as they may be operated upon and influenced by the work of spirits.

Sometime I will come and write you a message on this subject of prayer and answer.

But this I want to say, that we can at times understand what will happen in the near future, and having such knowledge, can tell to mortals what may be expected or rather what will occur, and this we sometimes do.

In your case, we all of the higher spheres, as well as many of the spirit spheres, know what your petitions have been in reference to these material matters, and we have been working to bring about a realization of the same on your part—not only because of your petitions but because they are so necessary to the doing and completion of our work, and we have been using our influence to the utmost to accomplish this end. But as I say, we are all limited, and have not the power to cause the happening of any event by our mere willing the same, even though we are doing the work of the Father.

This may seem surprising as well as disappointing to you, but it is a fact, and it is a great truth that God helps those who help themselves.

Of course, you must not lose sight of the fact that while men must themselves do those things that bring about changes or happenings or phenomena in material things, yet we can influence but not control absolutely their desires and intentions and their wills that put into operation or effect these intentions. No, these things, as to their immediate manifestations, are subject to the wills of men.

315

God never by a mere act of the moment or of a physical character, places into the hands of any man riches or prosperity. These things must immediately be wrought and brought about by man, but man in doing this can and is wonderfully influenced by the workings of the spirits.

Well, that is a question that has caused men to doubt and consider and explain in various ways the so-called miracle of the loaves and fishes. As I was a disciple of the Master at that time it is quite natural that I should be expected to state whether such a miracle ever occurred, and of course, I can state what the fact in relation thereto is. And notwithstanding that it has been used by preachers and teachers for many centuries to show the wonderful power possessed by Jesus, and thereby cause the people to believe in and acecpt him as God, or at least having God-like powers, and has been used to work much good among those who were seeking for the true religion, yet I am compelled and sorry to say, that no such miracle ever took place. While Jesus had wonderful powers, and understood the workings of the spiritual laws to a far greater extent than any mortal who ever lived, yet he had not the power to increase the loaves and fishes as is set forth in the account of the miracle. To be able to do so would be against the laws of God governing the material things of His creation, and also beyond and outside of the powers conferred on any man or angel by any spiritual laws.

There are certain laws by which we who are acquainted with and use them and may cause a dematerialization of physical substances, and also may to a limited degree cause a materialization of spiritual substances, but I am not acquainted with any law that would have operated, under the control of Jesus, to increase the loaves and fishes to the great number mentioned in the story referred to. As a fact, I know that no such miracle took place, and Jesus will tell you the same.

There are other alleged miracles in the Bible that never had any existence as a fact.

Well, I have written you a long letter tonight, and I must stop, but I am pleased that you asked me about the response to prayers, and the miracle of the loaves and fishes, for your questions gave me the opportunity, to some extent, to explain these matters. But as to prayer, you must wait until I deal with it more at large or in detail before you conclude that you understand the subject fully.

And I say to you pray not only for the spiritual things which God bestows through His Holy Spirit, but also for the material things which He bestows through His angels and spirits. The proper prayer will be answered sooner or later, and your prayer for that of which I have written will be answered, even though to you the response may seem a long time delayed.

With my love and blessings, I will say goodnight.

Your brother in Christ,   JOHN.

316

Affirms that John wrote and comments on prayer for material things.

I am here. Your own true and loving *Helen* (*Mrs. Padgett*).

Well, dear, I am glad that John wrote you as he did, for it will give you an insight into some principles regarding the powers of spirits to help mortals, that you may not before have understood. What he said is true, and I am glad that he wrote.

It may prove a little disappointing to learn that spirits have not the powers to do everything, as mortals may suppose, but I do not want you to underestimate their powers, for they have great powers, even as respects the material things. Of course, they cannot move a house, or cause the wealth of one mortal to be removed from him and placed in the possession of another, but they can and do use great influence on mortals to cause them to do physical things that the spirits cannot directly do.

Your prayers are not futile, even as to these material things that are subject to the control of mortals, for these very mortals are, under certain circumstances, subject to our influence, and thereby, control. When we promise you that a certain thing or things will happen, we mean that we will exercise our influence on mortals in such a way that they will bring about these happenings in response thereto. And you must not believe that when we promise you something that that something, as a matter of course, will come to you. We mean that it will come to you by reason, primarily of the work that we are doing among mortals. We can see some things before they have an existence in your physical world, and can tell you of the same; and some things we believe will happen, and also, tell you, and when they do not, we are disappointed as well as are you.

Your own true and loving,

HELEN.

St. Paul's comments on the preacher's beliefs.
Perfection is a relative term.

I am here. *St. Paul.*

I was with you tonight at the meeting, and heard what the young man said about perfection, and I agree entirely with his ideas and the application of the truth to the lives of human beings.

He had the correct conception of what perfection means and when he said that perfection is a relative term he spoke the exact truth. No man can expect to have the perfection of the Father in quantity, but he may in quality, for the spirit of truth that enters into the soul of a man in response to prayer and faith is a part of the divine nature of the Father, and the essence is the same and the quality must be the same; but, of coure, no man can obtain it to the extent of making him pure and holy as the Father is pure and holy. Even we who live in the high Celestial Heavens have not that perfection which the Father has. But let men know that even while on earth they can obtain this inflowing of the Holy

Spirit in their hearts to such an extent that sin and error will be entirely eradicated. This, I say, is possible but few men attain to such a state of perfection, because the worldly affairs and natural appetites which belong to mortals are always interfering to prevent the makings of the spirit in men's souls so that perfection of this kind may take possession of them. But notwithstanding this great difficulty and material desires of men, they should have this perfect ideal before them always, and strive to obtain the possession of it.

I was much interested in the discourse not only because it was founded on a text attributed to me, but because of the right conception and the explanation made by the young man.

I could see his soul and its workings, and I was glad to know that he possessed this Divine Love to an unusual degree, and was fitted almost for a home in the Celestial Spheres.

You were benefited by what he said, and you felt the influence of the presence of the Holy Spirit at the meeting.

If the people of this church would understand that there is only one thing that saves them from their sins and makes them at-one with the Father, and that is the inflowing of the Divine Love into their souls, which was what Jesus meant when he told Nicodemus that he must be *Born Again,* they would easily see that their doctrine of holiness is not only a reasonable doctrine but one in accord with the truths of God, for as this Divine Love fills their souls all sin and error must disappear.

Of course this is a relative matter, for it depends upon how much of this Divine Love is in their souls to determine how much of sin or error exists. The more of the Divine Love, the less of sin, and on the contrary, the more of sin the less of the Divine Love.

But, I want to say with all the emphasis that I am capable of, that it is possible for a human being to obtain such a quantity of this Divine Love in his soul that sin will be entirely eradicated. This was the doctrine taught by Jesus, and this is the truth of God's law of love.

I know that the great majority of mankind do not believe this truth and think it foolishness and that those who claim that they have received this Divine Love to a great degree are enthusiastic fanatics, and not worthy of credence, but I want to tell you that no greater truth was ever proclaimed by the Master; and sometime, in the not far distant future, many men who are now merely intellectual Christians will believe and embrace and experience this great truth.

You will find yourself much benefited by attending these meetings, and while there are some things in their creed to which you do not subscribe, yet they have the foundation truth that the Divine Love of the Father can clear their souls from all sins, and make them perfect to the extent that they receive that Love in their souls.

318

I will not write more tonight, but will say that the Holy Spirit which conveys God's love to man is with these people in great power and fulness and manifests its workings in a real and irresistible manner. And God is blessing them and giving them that faith which enables them to become overcomers and inheritors of immortality and homes in the Celestial Heavens.

So without taking up more of your time, I will say good-night and God bless you.

Your brother in Christ,   ST. PAUL.

Jesus attended the church service with Mr. P. and commented on the people's belief.

I am here. *Jesus.*

I heard what Paul wrote, and I corroborate everything that he said, and add, that these people are pursuing the true way to the inheritance which I promised them while I was on earth. Their faith is wonderful and the fruits of its exercise is shown in the condition of their souls and in their lives.

Theirs is the soul conception of religion and of my truths, and while they may not with their intellects understand the philosophy of my teachings, yet with their soul perceptions they have grasped the great foundation truth of salvation through the Divine Love of the Father.

Of course they sing and proclaim that my blood saves them from sin, but this is merely the exercise of their mental conceptions learned from the teachings and creeds of the churches; yet they have grasped the great and only truth of salvation with the far more and certain knowledge that the awakening and filling of their souls by the Divine Love gives them.

How much to be wished for that all these churches of form and mental worship could realize that the only true worship of God is with the soul perceptions. Only with these perceptions that are developed by obtaining the Divine Love can we see God. Only by such development can we become pure and holy and at-one with the Father, and partakers of His Divine nature.

I am glad that you attended this * church, and I advise you to go there often, for I tell you that the spirit of truth and love is with these people to a very extended degree, and that because their souls are open to its inflowing and to its ministration.

I was with you again tonight and so was the spirit of truth trying to open up your soul to its influence and to that which will cause your faith to increase and your trust in me to grow.

No church will do you as much good as that and I advise you to attend. Of course you will not have to believe in its creed, but only in the fact that

* Church of the Holiness.

the Holy Spirit is there in all its quickening power as they sometimes sing. So with all my love I say,

Good-night. Your brother and friend, JESUS.

What is the meaning of the divine nature which the soul of man partakes of upon the transformation of that soul by the inflowing and possession of the Divine Love.

I am here. *St. Stephen.*

Let me write a few words tonight as I am one of the spirits whom your wife wrote of last night would come tonight with the desire to write.

My subject is: *"What is the meaning of the Divine Nature which the soul of man partakes of upon the transformation of that soul by the inflowing and possession of the Divine Love?"*

This, as you may perceive, will be somewhat difficult to explain, and principally because men have no very definite conception of what is comprehended by the term "Divine." They, of course, associate this word with God, and to them God is a being whose nature and qualities are above their finite conceptions, and as a result of their thoughts is that which is over and above everything that is called or supposed to be understood as natural. To some, God is a being of personality, and to others, a kind of nebulous existence included in and composing all the various manifestations which are transcendently above what they conceive to be the merely natural or human.

I will not attempt to discuss who or what God is, except as to one of His qualities or attributes, and that the greatest—for you must know that all the qualities of God are not of equal greatness or degree of importance in the workings of His essence of substance. All, of course, partake of His Divine Being, but, as you might say, there is a difference in the workings and scope of their operations.

You have been told that the Divine is that which has in it, to a sufficient degree, the very Substance and Essence of God, Himself, and this is true, for Divinity belongs to God alone, and can be possessed by others, spirits or mortals, only when He has transfused into or bestowed upon the souls of men a portion of this Divinity, and to the extent thereof made them a part of Himself. There is nothing in all His universe that is Divine or partakes of the Divine except that which is of the soul, for all else is of the material, and this even when it has the form or appearance of the spiritual. And even the soul, as created, is not Divine and cannot become such, until it is transformed into the Divine by the transfusion into it of that which in its very substance is Divine. Many souls in the spirit world, although pure and in exact harmony with their created condition, are not Divine and never will become such, and this only because these souls will not desire and seek to become Divine in the only way provided by the Father.

It is a mistake for men to believe that because God has created this or that object or thing, it is necessarily Divine, for His creations are no more a part of Himself than are the creations of men a part of themselves; and thus you will see that in all God's creation there is nothing Divine except what has been privileged by His grace to partake of His Divinity. And hence the stars and worlds and trees and animals and rocks and man himself, as created, are not Divine.

Men have claimed that in man there is a spark of the divine—a part as they say of the "Oversoul"—and that it needs only the proper development to make the soul of man wholly Divine. And this theory is based upon the idea that this development can be accomplished by the exercise of the mind or the moral qualities guided by the conscience, which they assert, is of itself Divine, especially when dominated by reason which has been so often worshiped by philosophers and others, to whom the mind is supreme, as Divine. And they have attempted to differentiate man and the lower animals, and attributed to the former the qualities of Divinity, because he is endowed with reason and the lower animals are not, and have substituted degrees in the order and objects of creation in the place of differentiation between the Divine and non-divine.

God is wholly Divine and every part and attribute of Him is Divine, and while they are parts of the whole, yet they may be separated in their workings and bestowals; and the man or soul that is the recipient of the bestowal of one of these qualities or attributes is not necessarily the recipient of the others. Omnipotence and omniscience are those attributes of God's Divinity which He never bestows upon the souls of men or spirits, and as to them He is the exclusive possessor, although in all His attributes there are powers and knowledge, and they accompany the bestowal of all attributes of which they are parts, and one of these Divine attributes may be bestowed upon man, and yet man not become Deity. There is and can be only one God, although He may give of His Essence and very Substance so that a man can become as He is in that Essence and Substance to the extent that it is bestowed.

As regards man and his salvation and happiness the greatest of God's qualities or attributes is His Divine Love, which is the only one that can bring the souls of men into a oneness and nature with the Father and which has in it the quality of immortality. This love has a transforming power and can make that which is of a quality foreign to and different from itself of the same essence as itself, and more than this, can eliminate from that thing those constituents which naturally and necessarily are its components, without injuring or destroying the thing itself.

Well we must stop here. I will finish later.

I am, St. Stephen.

321

Affirming that St. Stephen wrote on the meaning of the Divine Love, etc.

I am here—Your own true and loving *Helen* (*Mrs. Padgett*).

Well dear, you have had a very interesting letter tonight upon a very vital and important subject, and I am sorry that the writer could not finish his message, but the rapport became very weak and he was compelled to stop. He will come again soon and finish as he is very anxious to do so. It was Stephen who wrote and he is a most beautiful spirit, possessing this love to a degree that I cannot conceive of, and a most glorious spirit in his appearance.

I am glad that you were in such good condition and I hope that you will continue to improve so that more of the messages may be delivered to you every other night. There are so many messages to be written.

Your own true and loving,

HELEN.

St. Luke, on the Teachings of New Thought and Explains the Erroneous Beliefs of Same.

St. Luke.

Let me write a few lines tonight as you are in better condition, and I am able to make a rapport with you and deliver my message.

I was with you today at a meeting of the New Thought people and saw the impression made upon you by the speaker in his efforts to show that God is within man and that only the opening up of the soul or mind of man to the development of that God is all that is necessary to bring that man into a perfect at-onement with the truths of God's will. Well, I have to say that this speaker, when he comes to a realization of himself in the spirit world will find that God is not in him or in anything that he may have possessed in his earth life, and that his development of the kingdom within him, as he termed it, was a mere delusion and a snare to the progress of his soul in its career through the earth life, as well as through the heavens or spirit world.

He is mistaken when he announces that the Kingdom of Heaven is within him, or that he has that within him which can by its development lead to the condition of the perfect man in the sense that he spoke of. He is following a false way, and all the efforts that he may make will not lead him into the paths that end in the perfect man that partakes of the Father's Divinity.

He is also mistaken when he asserts that God is everywhere—in the flowers, and in the thoughts of men and in the heart, for God does not find his habitation in any of these things, and men do not live and move and have their being in Him. He is a distinct and individual entity, and is not spread over all His universe, as the preacher proclaimed, and can only be found by the longings of the soul, followed by a development of that soul in His love. No, God is in His Heavens, and man can reach

322

Him only by the persistent longings of that soul for the inflowing of His Love. These things that the preacher declared were the presence of God, are only the expressions of His being, and they do not declare His presence in any other sense than as the evidence of His existence in His habitation, from which these expressions flow and make known to man His presence as these things reflect it. I am sorry that this speaker has not more knowledge of the true God, and of His seat of habitation, for then he would realize that these things upon which he places so much belief as being the very God, Himself, are but the expressions that flow from Him.

Man has within him that which has in itself wonderful possibilities. I mean the soul. And it may by the observance of the way that transforms it into a Divine angel become Divine itself, or it may only by the slow process of renunciation become merely the perfect man with his natural love in a pure state, which was the condition of the first parents. If men will listen to the call to their souls they will realize this possibility and receive this Divinity, and with it, immortality; but without this transformation they never can become other or greater than the perfect man.

I know that men teach that there is implanted within the souls of all men, that which is capable of being developed into an existence like unto God—that man needs only this development in order to become a God, and that there is nothing else necessary to make a human soul a part of the Soul of God. But in this teaching men are mistaken, and will find themselves at the stage of their highest development nothing more than the perfect man. Man has within him only that with which he was created, and can of himself add not one thing that will change him from this condition of his creation. It is true that he can by a right course of thinking and living renounce those things that have tainted his soul and alienated it from the Father, and made it sinful and disobedient; but when this is done, he is still only the perfect man, and nothing of the Divine is in him. Jesus was the perfect man and, as such, was an exemplar of what all men will ultimately become; and if Jesus had never become more than the perfect man, he would not now be an inhabitant of the Celestial Heavens and the beloved Son of the Father. Yet he became more than the perfect man, and it was only after he attained to this condition of excellence, that he could say, "I and my Father are one," for it was then only that he possessed the Divine Love to that degree which made him at-one with the Father. Only he is at-one with the Father that realizes that he is possessed of the very nature and Essence of the Father, and there is only one way in which this can be obtained, and that is by the inflowing into the soul of the Divine Love. Jesus could not say to the multitude that they were at-one with him and with the Father, for they had only the natural love and had not experienced the transformation of their souls; and such sayings as this were addressed only to his disciples, or to those among his hearers that had received this Love.

The speaker spoke of the New Birth, but had no conception of what it meant, and like many other teachers, in and out of the churches, believes that a mere condition of the purification of the natural love constitutes this New Birth, and that that is all Jesus meant when he taught the necessity of being born again. There is only one way in which this New Birth can be brought about, and that you already know.

As to the moral truths taught by the Master, such as are referred to in the sermon on the Mount, undoubtedly they will, if observed in the heart, bring about a regeneration of the soul that will lead men to the glory of the perfect man and make him at-one with the laws of his creation; and this condition is devoutly to be wished for and sought after by all men, and when they attain to this condition they will experience the beatitudes that are mentioned in the sermon; but this is only the state of the perfect man and nothing of the Divine enters into their condition.

New Thought, as it is called, has in it something that is an improvement on orthodoxy, and men will be the better, if they will embrace some of its teachings. The great stumbling blocks of the Trinity, and the vicarious atonement and the blood would be moved from the worship of men, and they would then rely on the moral truths in the development of their souls for salvation, and would not rest supinely in the belief of the efficacy of the vicarious atonement. But some other things that it teaches are all wrong, and its followers will find when they come to the spirit world that there is a God to be worshipped, and that man has not within him that God to be developed by his own thoughts and deeds.

I know that according to the orthodox teachings too little is thought of the natural goodness of man, and too much emphasis placed in his innate depravity, and that nothing in man is worthy of the release from the sin and disobedience in which he is now living; and that of himself he can do nothing to bring about his purification and restoration to his original condition of the perfect man. This is wrong, for very largely upon man's efforts depends his redemption; "and as a man thinketh in his heart, so is he." He is naturally good, and his present condition was brought about by his permitting his soul to be contaminated with sin, and to become again good he needs only to pursue that way that will remove sin and its consequences from his soul. Man created sin, and he will have to remove sin, and the process will be slow, but ultimately it will be accomplished, and by the efforts of man himself. He will be helped by spirits who are God's ministering angels in these efforts, but upon him depends the removal of that which he created and imposed. And here let me say, that unless man wills it, he will forever remain in sin, and God will not, contrary to man's desires, make him a pure and undefiled being;

and man's belief, unaccompanied by striving and seeking, will not be sufficient to bring about this remedy.

The speaker is a good man, and has experienced to a large degree the workings of his own will upon the conditions of his soul, and knows that his own efforts have caused him to renounce many things that tended to defile him and cause doubt, and in this condition realizes much happiness, and thinks that he is of himself sufficient to attain to that which will bring him into a perfect unison with the God that he thinks is within him. In this he is deceiving himself, for what he thinks is God is only an unusual condition of soul development in its natural love, that gives him a happiness which causes him to believe that God must be in and a part of him.

As you have been told, the happiness of the purified soul is beyond all conception of humans, and the nearer a man approaches to that condition of purification of his soul the greater becomes his happiness, and the belief that God must in some way be in that happiness and form a part of it, when the fact is that this happiness is only that which was bestowed upon man in the beginning; as the soul becomes purer and relieved from the defilement of sin, man becomes what he was in the beginning, and has regained only that which by nature is his. He does not receive any part of the Divine, nor does the Father bestow upon him anything that was not his at the creation, and he must realize that by the removal of sin his soul becomes more and more in harmony with the will of God, and less and less in harmony with his own perverted will.

Let New Thought progress until men may realize that they are at-one with themselves, their created selves, but let it not teach them that what they experience as a removal of sin from their own souls by their own efforts and thoughts is evidence of a development of any supposed God within them, for it is not true, but is merely the development of their own natural created selves, freed from that which defiled and made them unnatural.

The speaker said that the Kingdom of Heaven is within all men, and needs only for men to realize that fact, and declare its truth, and that then they will become pure and like unto God, and find themselves in the presence of God, and see Him face to face. Well, in this he is all wrong, for the Kingdom of Heaven or Celestial Kingdom is not within men, though it may be, and neither is God in their souls and capable of being seen face to face. These men who teach purification of their natural love and a superior state resulting from that purification and nothing more, will never see God, and they will always remain in the mere image in which they were created, a merely purified man made in the image of God, and nothing more. The Father will then be the same unseen Creator as he is now, and men will worship Him in faith only, for their soul perceptions, which are the only eyes of the soul that can see God, will not exist, and to them God will still remain the unseen and unknowable being that exists today in the knowledge and belief of men.

Well, I have written enough for tonight, but saw that you were somewhat interested in the teachings of the day, and thought it best that I should write you as to the truth of the subject of which he discoursed and evidently believed.

With my love to you, and the hope that our messages may now continue without interruption, I will say, good night.

Your brother in Christ,   LUKE.

Jesus on New Thought. The Importance of Mankind Knowing the Truth of the New Birth.

I am here, *Jesus.*

Let me write just a line for I desire to tell you that I was with you tonight at the convention of the New Thought people and saw the impression made upon you by the discourses, and am pleased that what they said only confirmed your faith in our teachings. They are sincere in their efforts to obtain a knowledge of the truth, but the difficulty is, that while they are free from many of the orthodox teachings of the church, yet they have only the natural love and perceptions of the intellect, and to some extent of the awakened soul in its natural condition.

They know nothing of the Divine Love or the way to the true Kingdom and are depending entirely upon the spiritual feelings that come to them with the consciousness of an awakened soul in its conflict with the things that prevent its purification and development into the perfect man.

These people are to be encouraged in their efforts and teachings so far as they disclose the true, natural condition of man and the possibility of his becoming in harmony with the will of the Father in their natural love, and to that extent they are progressing beyond the old orthodox ideas of what the real man is, and what is incumbent upon him in order to get into the condition of happiness that comes with a purification of his love, and a longing in harmony with the laws of God governing that purification.

It is to be wished that these men will proceed in their teachings and thus give to mankind a knowledge of what man really is, and the possibilities that lie before him when he exercises the inherent powers that exist within. For concerning sin and inharmony, until the great truths of the New Birth and the transformation of the soul, and the wonderful Kingdom of the Celestial Spheres are made known to men through our teachings of these things, these greater truths which lie beyond the knowledge of men at this time, will not be his.

In their search for God they are on the wrong track, and will never find him, if they pursue the search in the way indicated by their discourses.

326

God is not within men, nor do they live and move and have their being in Him, nor is He everywhere, waiting to be developed by men as they grow better and purer. No, they are mistaken in their thought as to God and His habitation, and will learn when they come into a knowledge of the truth, that God is not in man or in everything that surrounds him, but is separate from him and from the environments in which they live and move, and has His locality in the Highest Heavens, where He works out his purposes, and makes Himself and the evidence of His existence known to men by the energies that control the universe in which men exist. He can only be seen by the soul perceptions of a soul that has been transformed into the Divine Angel; to men in every other particular He is unseen and unknown, except as His laws and the effect of their operation disclose His being.

Well, I merely wanted to write this short message, and I am glad that you can receive it. Good night. Your brother and friend,

JESUS.

Comments on the preacher's sermon on New Thought by Mrs. Padgett

I am here—Your own true and loving, *Helen.*

Well, my dear, I see that you are happy tonight, and I am also, for I heard you read the messages and saw the effect that they had on your soul, and that they caused you to love both the Father and me more. You must not cease to love as you do tonight for there is no other happiness that can supply the place which this love brings to you.

I was with you tonight at the meeting and heard the preacher speak of the source of the greatest joy, and I was sorry that he did not know that source. He talked of a happiness that came to him from a knowledge that he thought he had of God, and he was in earnest, but he did not realize the real joy or the source thereof. His joy is that which comes from a great degree of the purification of his natural love, which must necessarily bring to him increased happiness, and I am glad that he talked in the way he did, but so sorry that he has not experienced the Real Love that is the only source of the greatest joy.

Well, sometime men will know what the source means, and how different it is from the mere purification of the natural love, and in addition will learn the way to obtain this Divine Love and keep it as the greatest thing in all the universe.

The talk of the preacher is very beneficial to many of his hearers and causes much searching of their souls, and a better condition of living and an experience that makes them very happy. I would advise you to attend his meetings occasionally, for the influence is good and you may have the opportunity sometime to tell him of the higher truths.

There were a number of spirits present with you desiring to hear and learn something that might render them happier and enlighten them as

327

to the true way, but some things that he said did not help much. He placed too much emphasis on the necessity of making life on earth the great object of their efforts and aspirations, and rather discountenanced the thought that in the spirit life there are heavens and conditions to be longed for and enjoyed. Yet, as I say, his preaching will do good; for the better men become in their thoughts and aspirations, even though as to a mere cleansing of their natural love, the better it will be for them, and will tend to make the earth life better and more in harmony with the laws of man's creation.

I am so glad that I can write you again and tell you of my love, and assure you of the truths that have been already revealed to you.

Well I will not write more tonight. We all love you, and so with my love I will say, good night.

Your own true and loving,   HELEN (Mrs. Padgett)

Men or prophets cannot tell what will happen centuries ahead.
It can only be known by the Father.

I am here—*John*.

I see that you are in a much better condition tonight and that your soul is more in harmony with the spirits of the higher spheres, and we could write now, but your hand and arm are tired, and this is a matter that we always consider and try not to cause you any unnecessary fatigue.

Other spirits are here tonight, hoping that they might have written, but under the circumstances they will not. The Master is here also, and says that he will not attempt to write tonight as he intended, but will soon come and deliver a message.

I am glad that you are feeling so much better spiritually and physically, and I feel that you will continue to do so. So pray more to the Father and turn your thoughts to spiritual things, and you will find a wonderful happiness that even the worries of your daily life cannot take from you.

No, emphatically—and those who believe that there ever lived such mortals are greatly mistaken. The highest of us spirits cannot know or foretell the future in the sense in which the seers and prophets are supposed to have done in the centuries of which the Old Testament wrote. No man, whether in the flesh or in the spirit, never has the omniscience of the Father, and to foretell what will happen centuries ahead is a power that belongs only to the Father.

So that all the attempted application of prophecies as contained in the Bible to the happenings or future happenings of the present day are futile and without any justification. Man must depend upon the condition and acts of this day to determine what will happen in the short time that some expect the world to last.

What a position for them to take, when we. who live so close to the Father, cannot possibly know.

All this, of course, refers to the material affairs of men in their lives on earth. As to spiritual things we can tell what the future of each man or nations of men will be, if certain conditions are observed or not observed.

Well, I will write you on this subject when the opportunity presents itself.

I will not write more now.

With all my love and the blessings of the Father I will say good night.
Your brother in Christ,

JOHN.

Explains the Necessary Conditions Required So That the Higher Spirits Can Help Those in Lower Spheres.

I am here—*Jesus.*

I see that your work has prevented you from receiving my message to-night, and while I am sorry, I do not complain, for you must do your work, and thereby the more rapidly get in condition to start the effort to accumulate to get in the position that you desire, and which is so necessary to our work. You are better tonight, spiritually, and our rapport is very complete, and I could easily write my message, but you are physically tired, and I do not think it wise to attempt to write, so I will postpone doing so until tomorrow night, when, I hope there will be nothing to interfere.

Yes, that is the correct idea, and I will endeavor to make the message as full and lucid as possible. I know how you feel in reference to the matter, and that you desire to receive the message in the best possible shape, and I know that you will do so. You must not think that I am not willing to wait whenever you have your professional work to attend to, or that I will not be with you even though we cannot write, for I am with you very often, trying to help, as I have said. So you must keep up your courage and trust me, and have faith in my promises.

I will not write more now, and will say that you have my love and blessings.

* Well, as to that, I know that you will in the not distant future, be able to see me as you say, for I am desirous that you do so. You have the power of clairvoyance, but it is not desirable that it be developed in you at this time as we wish all your power to become centered in receiving the messages; but some night when you are praying and I am with you, the power will be given you and you will see me as I am while praying with you. I feel that this may strengthen your faith and draw you closer to me, and I myself want you to actually see me as I am.

* Mr. Padgett told me later that Jesus did reveal himself and he saw him clairvoyantly while Mr. P. was praying for more of the Divine Love.

Well, let us say good-night and stop.

Yes, I understand, but if I should come and write to you in the, as you may think, dignified way that an elevated spirit should write, you would not feel the nearness to me that I so much want you to feel, and besides you might not just understand what I intended to communicate. It is impossible for you to accommodate yourself to my condition, and, hence, I have to accommodate myself to yours. I want you to get as close to me as possible, and in order that that may be, I have to become verily human, as you are; otherwise the rapport could not exist between us, and I would seem to you like some far off nebulous being that you could not understand or feel the influence of. No, I am very human when I come to you.

But this I will say, in order that you may get a somewhat better idea of our relationship, that as you progress more in your soul development and in the possession of the Father's love you will be less human—I mean in your condition of soul, which is that in you that, furnishes the rapport between us—and I will meet you on the plane that you may occupy. So you see what a determining factor in our rapport your condition of soul is. And if you consider this for a moment, you will more clearly comprehend why it is that the dark spirits can find in you a closer rapport that enables you to help them, than they can find in the higher spirits. We try to make a rapport with them but their souls do not respond, and it is only after you have talked to them and directed their attention to us,—which causes as it were, an opening up of their souls to us—can we come in that rapport with them that enables us to gain their attention and create in them an interest in what we may say to them.

This to you may seem surprising, as you believe that we who are more elevated must have great power with and over these dark spirits, and this is so for certain purposes; and we do often restrain them from doing things that they should not do, but this as you must understand, means that we by our powers arbitrarily force them to do or not do certain things, just as on earth, your laws or the enforcement of them restrain those who desire to violate the laws from doing so.

But when we come to the work of attempting to turn their thoughts to those things that affect their soul condition, this thing of constraint or force will not effectuate the work. We then must deal with the exercise of their free will, and in such cases only persuasion or love influence can possibly do the work of helping them out of their dark and tainted condition of soul. We must invite and persuade the soul to awaken, we cannot force it, and to do so we must form that relationship with these dark spirits, that will cause them to voluntarily open up their souls to our influences.

The great obstacles to our work among spirits of this kind is, that they will not listen to us or come in conversation with us, and we cannot compel and accomplish our purposes. No man or spirit can ever by force, be made to open up his soul to the higher thoughts and essentials of the soul's progress. Of course, when we once get in that rapport with them that enables us to enlist their attention. and listen to what we say, we can cause them to have an awakening by informing them of the sufferings and torments that will be theirs if they continue in their same condition, and you may say by a kind of mental force compel them to think of these things that are holding them in their condition of darkness, but this does not occur unless we can first secure their attention and to some extent their confidence.

So you may realize from this to some degree the importance of the work that you are doing among the dark spirits. They, being in the condition of darkness and want of soul development, cannot see any such development that you may have, and to them you are merely a mortal, as they themselves were a short time ago—in many cases—and finding that they can communicate with you, they come to you just as one man would to another for the purposes of conversation, and outside of the phenomenon of spirit and mortals conversing, you do not seem to them any different from what men seemed to them when they were on earth. They are all very human, and to them your conversation is very natural, and, hence, they listen to you with the same feelings of confidence, or rather not of distrust, that they would to another spirit of their own kind. You are all humans together, and your opinions or ideas to them, are just the same as they might expect if they were in the flesh or you were a spirit like themselves.

While these dark spirits may, under certain circumstances, see the bright and beautiful spirits, as they sometimes tell you they do, yet they see only the appearance of the spirit body—they cannot see the condition of the spiritual development in these bright spirits, for it is a law that the spirit perceptions cannot vision conditions of the souls of others to a higher degree of development than they themelves have; and this applies to all spirits, no matter what sphere they may occupy, and, hence, you will understand that as we progress in our soul spheres, the higher we ascend, the more clear and comprehensible becomes our soul perceptions of the Father and His divine qualities.

So, I say, so far as the real perception of these dark spirits are concerned, they cannot comprehend the real spiritual development of the higher spirits, whom they often see. The interior condition of these higher spirits are just as hidden from the dark spirits, as is the interior condition of one man from another. Only when like meets like can there be a perception, that is, not a real visual perception, but a spiritual perception of each other.

331

But the higher spirits can see the interior conditions of those who are in spheres lower than they, and determine just what the soul development of these lower ones are.

Also, you must understand that the appearance of the spirit body indicates and portrays, to a large extent, the condition of the soul, and from this, one spirit may judge the actual development of another. I mean those may so judge who have progressed above the dark planes.

Well, I have written more than I intended, but as you were desirous to have some conception of what I have written, I concluded to attempt to explain to you these matters, though I know from my explanation, you cannot fully understand what I have been trying to make known to you.

But we must stop now.

So with my love I will say, good-night.

Your brother and friend, JESUS.

I am here. Your own true & loving *Helen.*

Well dear, you had a message from the Master to-night that you did not expect. It will enlighten you considerably on the subject that we have written you about several times, but could not satisfactorily explain as we did not just understand ourselves. But I think that now you can get some idea why you are so important in this work among the dark spirits.

I will not write more now.

Your own true & loving HELEN.

The object of man's life on earth and the necessity of doing certain things whereby man can become perfect man—but not the divine man.

I am here—*Prof. Salyards.*

Well, I was telling you of the object of man's life on earth, and the necessity for his doing certain things, in a general way in order to bring to mankind the happiness which might be theirs while on earth.

Now I desire to go a little in detail with reference to these matters.

As has been written you before there is only one way in which man can attain to the supreme happiness, which the Father in His goodness has made possible for man to attain to, and which, when once obtained, can never be taken from him.

But, there is also another kind of happiness which is not, in either its nature or results, the same as that which I have just referred to: and man may obtain it in a way and by a method which are different from those which are necessary to obtain the first kind.

Man was originally created good and pure and happy, and only by his disobedience did he lose these qualities, which, when lost, finally made him approach somewhat the likeness of the lower animal, although the latter is probably not so unhappy as man became by his fall from the state of the high condition of his creation.

332

When in his original state, he was happy in what we called, and what was his natural love, which he fully possessed, and needed nothing additional to make him happy. This condition made man his own master, as it were, and the Father's Divine Love was not necessary to develop him more as mere man than he then existed. He was pure and free from sin and in perfect harmony with God's laws governing his creation.

But after the disobedience he lost this harmony, and in doing so, lost also the power to preserve in himself the happiness which was his by right of creation; and he also soon realized that as this power left him, his dependence upon himself became less and less effective to keep him in a condition of purity and contentment, and, as a consequence, he became less than perfect man, and has been such ever since that time.

Now with the other qualities that were given him at the time of his creation, there was, and is one that he has never been deprived of, and one that he has never realized his inability to exercise, although he so often exercises it wrongly, and that is the will, which is the greatest of the natural attributes that man possesses, for even God will not attempt to control that. I mean in the way of compelling.

And this quality is the one that, more often than any other, will help man to again attain to that state or condition in which he was the perfect man; but while this is true, yet it is also one of the greatest obstacles to attaining to that state.

Upon man himself, very largely depends the success of his regaining his pristine purity and harmony with the laws that govern his being, and he must understand this fact, for if he should believe, and rest in the belief, that other men or other instruments controlled by men, can rescue him from his present condition of inharmony and unhappiness, he will be disappointed and his salvation will be a long time delayed.

But the exercise of this will power in the proper direction will depend upon other things that he must possess in order to insure his return to his first estate. Among these are the necessity for his obtaining knowledge that will enable him to know himself and the relationship of himself to what is true and good. This knowledge will come to him as he examines himself and learns the difference between right and wrong, and this I mean in its general sense, for right and wrong mean harmony or inharmony with the laws of which I speak, and not right and wrong according to the several circumstances of men, for these differ, and what may be right or wrong to one man will not be to another.

And man by proper contemplation and observation may learn the difference between right and wrong, in the sense in which I use the terms, and be enabled to embrace or avoid those deeds or thoughts that come within one category or the other.

Again, he must realize that there is such a thing as the natural love being a part of him, and a thing which may be possessed and cultivated to such a high degree that all men will be brothers to him and the children of one common Father, who has love and care for all alike who are content to remain the mere man.

Again, he must realize that he has a Father in God, his Creator, and that that Father has a love for him which will always bring to him happiness and peace if he will only respond with his own love, for man must have an object of worship and adoration, even when he possesses only the natural love, and he must learn that his love must go out to the Father in faith and confidence. There are many other things that he may learn by contemplation and meditation as I have said.

Many qualities that are desirable will flow to man from the knowledge that there is a Father who loves him, and that he has or may have a love for that Father, and also for his brother man. In fact, from these two subjects of knowledge, everything else may come to man that will make him the perfect man in harmony with the laws of his creation, and a pure happy and contented creature.

Now, when man obtains this knowledge,—and here observe the distinction between knowledge of these things and the possession of them,— he will naturally try to obtain all that knowledge shows him may become his to possess, and then will come into operation the great will power, and by its exercise there is nothing that can prevent him from arriving at the goal of his desires.

In this way, one can, in a sense, be his own redeemer, but he will find the struggle hard, and the obstacles to be overcome many and repelling.

There are many mortals who have a wonderful development of this natural love, notwithstanding the fact that they are living in sin and in inharmony with the laws that I speak of, and who will find from that fact alone that their progress will be more rapid and easy when they come to the spirit world on their journey to the state of perfect man. I do not believe that any mortal can ever attain to this condition while in the earth life, but he can lay the foundation for a rapid progress after he becomes a spirit. The temptations and desires that beset him as a mortal, at this time, are so great, that rarely can he become that perfect man while on earth.

But the time will come, I believe, when men will become perfect even while on earth, and in this I have reference to his natural love merely. While, as I say, for man to obtain this state of perfection he must depend upon himself to a very large degree, yet, it will be comforting to him to know, that there are hosts of spirit friends who are with him, trying to help him to obtain the knowledge of which I have spoken; and in his contemplations and meditations they are with him suggesting to him and impressing on him the thoughts of truth that help him very much to understand the right from the wrong, and they also sustain him, in some degree, in the exercise of his will in the right direction.

So from this it must become apparent to man that a very important thing in the determination of this great problem as to what is right and what is wrong, is the kind of associates that he may have, and this applies to the mortal as well as spirit companions. And man must know this, that as his desires and appetites on earth attract to him companions of similar desires and appetites, so, also, does the same law of attraction operate in the case of his spirit friends.

Now, in all this, I have no reference to the redemption of man by the possession of the Divine Love of the Father, for such redemption and its way of saving man, are altogether different from those of redeeming him in his natural love.

In the one case, when he has found the goal of his desires he becomes a merely perfect man and nothing more, in the other case, he becomes an angel of God, Divine is his nature, with no limitation to the progress that he may obtain and the happiness that may become his. ——

And—Oh, man! Why will you be satisfied to become merely a perfect man, when you may become a Divine Angel of the Father's kingdom, with immortality assured?

Man may not know it, but it is a fact, that it is easier, and the way is shorter to become a Divine Angel than to become a perfect man.

So my advice to all men is, and I speak what I do know from a knowledge that comes to me from experience and possession, to seek for the Divine Love of the Father with all their strength and efforts, and then they will become not only the perfect man, but will obtain that which our first parents never obtained, but which was theirs for the proper seeking as it is all men's.

I have written enough for tonight and will close.

Your old friend and professor and brother in Christ.

JOSEPH H. SALYARDS.

Wants to write what he knows to be the truth. And also correct errors in his epistles as contained in the Bible.

I am here. *Saint Paul.*

I desire to tell you that I am very anxious to disclose to you what are the true teachings of Jesus, and what errors my epistles, as contained in the Bible, possess.

I know now that it may seem strange to you that errors should have gotten into my epistles, but there are several reasons for their entrance. First, the epistles as they now appear are not what I wrote. I mean many changes have been made in my writings; and second, when I wrote the

335

epistles I did not know as much of the truths of God as I do now, and thirdly, I was not such a believer in the teachings of Jesus, as I am now.

These are sufficient reasons why my epistle should not be accepted as containing all the truths, or rather that all they contain are truths.

There are apparent contradictions in these writings and if what is said were true there would be no real contradictions.

I fully realize this great defect in my epistles and I have tried hard to impress those who attempt to explain my sayings, as to the real truth of what they attempt to explain, but with indifferent success.

And now I want to correct what is untrue or not in accord with the teachings of the Master and the only way in which it can be done is by writing through you. Of course, I realize that you have a great work to do for the Master, and that most of your time and energy will be taken up by doing this work of the Master, and that every other communication must be subordinated to those of Jesus, yet I believe that you will at times, find time to take my messages.

Tonight, I will not attempt to write any message of these truths, and will only say that I am much interested in your work, and will try to help you all I can. So I must stop.

No—no blood saves from sin, only the Divine Love of the Father does this.

With much love I am your friend.—St. Paul.

God's laws are not changed but when the Divine Love comes into the soul the lesser law of compensation is removed from the scope of its working.

I am here—your friend R. E———.*

Let me write a line, for I am very desirous of again communicating to you the fact that I am progressing and have found the love of which you first told me and which information led to my seeking it.

I know that you are very much interested in the higher messages and want to give your time to receiving them, and that it is almost impudence for me to intrude; but, I have asked your wife if it will interfere with any of these messages tonight by my writing, and she informed me that it would not, as none of these messages would be written tonight. So I feel somewhat at liberty to write, and I hope that you will consider that I am not intruding.

Well, since last I wrote you I have prayed to the Father with all the longings of my soul for an increase of His love, and realize that it has come into my soul in greater abundance, and I am correspondingly happy. I shall soon be in the third sphere so the spirit friends who have been so kind and loving to me, tell me, and it gives me much happiness to know that such a prospect is opened up to me, for I can, because of the progress

* Whenever full name is not given is because relatives living might object.

that I have already made, realize, to some extent, what a home in that sphere will mean to me.

I would like to write you a long letter tonight, but I must not detain you. But this I want you to remember, that I am very happy now, and my sufferings have left me, and I know that all these blessings came to me because of the workings of the Divine Love in my soul. It is wonderful what that love can accomplish in the way of rescuing a sinful soul from its surroundings of darkness and from suffering.

The law of compensation, which is a great truth, does its work without hesitation or partiality and interference by any god or angel in the way of commanding it to cease its work; but this Great Divine Love is now more powerful than this law, and when it enters into the soul of a man or spirit, it in effect, says to this law: you shall no longer operate on the soul of this sinner that was, because I will take that soul away from and outside the operations of this law. How little men understand this working of the love. It does not set aside the law, but it merely removes the soul in which it has found lodgment from the scope of the operations of the law. The laws go on but the objects of its operations are rescued from the same. No law is set aside that men think and argue is necessary in order for a soul to be saved from its penalties, and when on earth I believed this too and did not believe in or accept the doctrine of the special interposition of divine Providence to succor men from the consequence of their sins, and that I did not believe because I thought that the only way in which this could be accomplished was for God to say to the law: you shall cease to operate. But now I know that while the law never ceases to operate until the penalties that are called for are paid, yet this Divine Love is above the law though not antagonistic to it.

I wish that I might write more on this subject tonight, as to me, it is one of the most wonderful truths in God's universe of spirit, and I never cease to meditate upon it and thank the Father that I was made a real example of the power of this Divine Love.

Well, I must stop now, but when you have time I should like to come and write at more length.

Well friend, good night.

Your friend,   *R. E———.*

Truth, Knowledge and Love.

How to solve the problem of what is true and what is not.

I am here, *John.*

I desire to write a little to night upon a subject that may prove to be of interest to you and others who may read my message. I will not write a very long message, but will say what I desire in short sentences, so that the truth that I intend to convey may be understood at a glance.

Well, when you are sure that you have discovered or have had revealed to you a truth, let it sink deep into your soul so that it will find such lodgment as will cause you to realize that this truth is a reality and a thing that must not be forgotten or neglected in its application to your daily life on earth.

When you have found that the truth fits some peculiar condition of your mind's experience, adopt it as a criterion for determining what your course of action shall be.

When you have thus adopted it, let it always remain with you as a guide and monitor in determining what your belief as to the particular thing involved shall be.

When you have thus received this belief of the mind, encourage and feed upon it until it becomes a thing of established faith; and when faith has become a part of your very being, you will find that the accompaniments of such faith, in the way of longings and aspirations, will become things of real existences which will result in actual knowedge.

When such knowedge becomes yours, then you have solved the problem of what is true and what is not. And when you have solved this, you will become a man who, when he utters his knowledge of truth, will speak as one having authority.

Such was the process by which Jesus became the possessor and authentic expositor of the great spiritual truths that had never before been known and declared by any man.

Of course, these various steps which lead to this great knowledge of truth, must be taken gradually and with increased confidence. In all this the help and influence of the Father are necessary, and such help and influence comes only in response to sincere, soul aspiring prayer.

Prayer must arise from the soul of man, and the response must come from God. There is no other means by which this knowledge can be obtained. All knowledge of things spiritual, that men may think they possess, coming in any other way cannot be relied on, for there is only one source of such knowledge out of which the real spiritual truths of God emanate.

And love is the great principle that enters into all knowledge of things spiritual, and without love it is utterly impossible for man to rightfully conceive the truths of God and possess them.

I merely desired to give you this short lesson on truth and knowledge and love, so that in receiving and absorbing our messages of the great spiritual truths of the Father, you may realize the means of making them your own in a manner to satisfy your soul perceptions.

I will come soon and write you a message on some of these vital truths. Think of what I have above written, and you will find that your soul perceptions will be opened up to a clear and wonderful comprehension of the real meaning of what we desire to reveal.

I will not write more to night.

Your brother in Christ   JOHN.

Spirit who heard Jesus' teachings when he was on earth.

I am here. *Elameros.*

I am a Greek, or rather the spirit of a mortal who was a Greek, and I lived in the days when Jesus walked the hills and plains of Palestine, teaching his new doctrines of the Divine Love and the Kingdom of Heaven.

I was not a follower of him or a believer in his teachings, for I was a disciple of Plato and Socrates, and was satisfied of the truth of their philosophy and did not believe that there were other truths than what it contained.

I was a traveler, and at times visited Palestine, and on several occasions heard Jesus teaching the multitudes of people who seemed to be so interested in his discourses. I must confess that I was startled at times by his doctrines, and recognized that while they treated of subjects similar to those contained in my philosophy, yet they were different, and gave to these subjects a new and spiritual meaning that I had never before thought of.

I could see that he was not a student of philosophy, or yet, an educated man, as we understood men to be educated, yet he dealt with these questions in such an enlightening and authoritative way that caused me to wonder at the source of his information; and when, at times, he said that he was not speaking of his own knowledge, but that his Father was speaking through him, I was almost ready to believe that such was the fact.

You must remember that I believed in God and in the lesser gods or demons who executed His will, and when Jesus spoke of his Father, meaning God, it was not unnatural for me, in a way, to accept what he declared. And then I recollect, that I was impressed with the fact that he was not speaking from a mind that had been developed by the study of the philosophies, but from a mind that seemed to have in it that which had been lodged there by some great outside intelligence. He spoke, as he said, with knowledge, and speculations seemed to be no part of his conclusions or the cause of any of his deductions.

Notwithstanding these impressions on me, I was too wise, in my own conceit that my philosophy was the only true one, and that my knowledge of it was without defect, to attempt to give serious consideration to what I had heard Jesus say, and consequently, let the truths which he uttered pass from me.

I saw and heard him teach only a few times, and then I heard of his crucifixion and death as a malefactor, and forgot about him.

339

When next I saw him, it was in the spirit world and this continued after I became a spirit; and then he was teaching the same doctrines that I had heard him teach on earth; but he was a wonderfully bright and glorious spirit.

I don't think that I can write more tonight. I will come again.

Your brother in Christ,

ELAMORAS.

I am here. Your own true and loving *Helen.*

Well dear you have had quite a remarkable letter from the Greek spirit tonight, and there is in it substance for much thought on the part of the Greeks. We thought it best to have him write because it is a part of the plan that will be disclosed to have some spirits of all nations and creeds and religions write you for the benefit of their races or followers who may live on earth.

Love me and say goodnight.

Your own true loving,   HELEN.

Nothing in Existence or in the Knowledge of Man Comparable to the
Bible—Except the Truths That Jesus and the Celestial
Spirits Have Written Through Mr. Padgett.

I am here—*Jesus.*

I see that you are in good condition tonight, and that I am able to make a rapport with you.

I was with you at the meeting tonight and saw the workings of your mind and the pity, as it were, that you had for the preacher, because of his want of knowledge of what the judgment is that comes to all men after death. A judgment that is ceratin and exact, but not one pronounced upon man by God as the preacher proclaimed.

I was trying to impress you in your thoughts and you felt the influence of my suggestions and realized that you did not fear the judgment, or rather its results, because you know the way in which the judgment for you can have no terrors or no eternity of condemnation. I wished as you did that the preacher might know the truth and then proclaim it to his hearers, and in this manner show them that the judgment is a certainty that cannot be escaped from and that its sentences are not for an eternity of duration.

He is an earnest man in his beliefs, and teaches just as he believes, and the pity is that he does not know the truth. But, nevertheless, he is doing good to those who hear him, for many of them are caused to think of things spiritual, and of the future as well as of the present who otherwise might and would neglect these important things that will determine the kind of judgment that they will have to undergo; and I am glad that he is so preaching and doing a work that in many instances will lead men

340

to meditate upon their spiritual conditions, and ultimately lead them to seek for the Love of the Father, which they may obtain by their longings though their beliefs may be erroneous as to how this Love may be obtained.

Men are constituted with a mind and a soul, each having its own perceptions and ability to comprehend the truth, and sometimes it happens that the perceptions of the soul will enable them to see and reach out for this love, while they may be wholly blind in their mind perceptions, and even these latter perceptions may be in conflict with the operations of the perceptions of the soul.

UNTIL THE TRUTHS THAT I AND THE OTHER SPIRITS ARE REVEALING TO YOU, SHALL BECOME KNOWN TO THE WORLD, THERE WILL BE NOTHING IN EXISTENCE OR IN THE KNOWLEDGE OF MEN THAT CAN SUPPLY THE PLACE OF THESE TRUTHS, SO MUCH AS THE BELIEFS THAT HAVE BEEN AND ARE BEING TAUGHT BY THE TEACHINGS OF THE BIBLE, FOR IN IT ARE MANY TRUTHS, ESPECIALLY THOSE THAT SHOW MEN THE WAY TO ATTAIN TO MORAL PERFECTION; AND THAT, AS YOU KNOW, WAS ONE OF THE OBJECTS OF MY TEACHINGS WHEN ON EARTH, BUT NOT THE GREAT OBJECT OF MY MISSION. Nevertheless, the man who learns and applies these moral truths to his daily life and conduct comes nearer to the enjoyment of that harmony that man must obtain in order to get into a unison with God's laws that is necessary to his regeneration and to his becoming the perfect man. And besides as he—I mean the mortal—progresses in this regeneration, he will find it easier for him to learn by his soul perceptions the great truth of the transformation of the soul through the New Birth.

I approve of the efforts of this preacher to bring men to a realization of their relationship to God, even though he has many erroneous beliefs, and says many things that are contrary to the truth, and not in accord with the true relationship of man to God.

I will write you soon upon this matter of the * judgment, and what it means and the variety of its operations.

Tonight, I will not write longer, for I think it best to not draw upon you too much at this renewed conjunction of rapport with your condition.

I have been with you very often of late, and tried to influence you with my love and suggestions, and I must tell you that you have progressed much in your soul development and nearness to the Father's love.

Continue to meditate upon these spiritual things and pray to the Father, and you will realize a great increase in the possession of this love and in your condition that will enable us to come in closer rapport with you.

Well, I will do as you suggest, and am pleased that you feel as you say,

* Read Vol. I, Ed. 1—After death the judgment—from Jesus—Pages 26 to 30.

for we must do the work as rapidly as possible. We have lost much time and will have to work the harder to bring about the completion of our delivery of the truths. But you need not fear that we will not be successful. Only have faith and pray, and all will be well.

I must stop now, but before doing so must assure you that I am praying with you in your prayers at night and that your prayers will be answered.

Other spirits will now be able to write you and they have many messages to communicate and all are anxious to do so.

Keep up your courage and believe in me and what I tell you.

With my love and the blessings of the Father, I will say good night.

Your brother and friend,

JESUS.

I am here—Your own true and loving *Helen.*

Well my dear husband, I am so glad that the Master has written you, and that the rapport has been reestablished so that he can continue the delivery of his messages, for as he said they, the spirits, are all very anxious to do the work.

I was with you tonight and besides me were the Master and your special guardian, John, and we were all watching the impressions made upon your mind by the preacher; and saw that what he said which was contrary to the truths that you have received, made no impression upon your beliefs, except that you desired to be able to tell him of his errors. I will not refer to the occasion further as the Master has written you fully on the subject, and you realize that he corroborates what I said a short time ago in regard to the good that the preacher is doing.

I am glad that you are in much better condition of soul and are able to realize more and more the existence of the love in your soul and the fact of your increased nearness to the Father. This makes us all very happy, and we know that you will now be able to do your work with greater rapidity and receive therefrom a wonderful happiness. Continue to pray to the Father and turn your thoughts to these spiritual things, and think of the great responsibility that is resting upon you.

I will not write more now.

May you be happier as the days go by.

Good night.

Your own true and loving   HELEN.

Daniel Webster affirms that Jesus and spirits of the higher spheres are revealing the great truths of the Father through Mr. P.

Let me say a word while you are writing as I am also interested in your great work and in the efforts that are now being made by the spirit powers of the higher spheres to bring to earth the great truths of the Father, which Jesus shall write to you.

You do not yet appreciate the great importance of this work or of the truths that shall be taught, but as you proceed in your work you will see what a wonderful thing this great effort of the Master is. I am one who is trying to help forward this movement, and in doing so, I feel that I am doing to mankind the greatest service that all the universe of God affords me to do.

I have not in my soul so much of the Divine Love of the Father, but I know that it is the one absolutely necessary thing that men must possess in order to get an entrance into the Kingdom of God, and to obtain the great happiness which the Father has made possible for man to receive.

You certainly have had imposed upon you a work of great responsibility and one that will call for the exercise of all your physical powers as well as your mental and moral endowments. So you see it is a matter that must be received and considered most seriously by you, and you must not let anything interfere with the successful performance of this great and wonderful work.

Mankind at this time, more than at any time since the presence of Jesus on earth in the material body, needs the truth to be presented to it in such a way that all superstition and blind faith will be eliminated from the minds and consciousness of mortals.

I can hardly realize that the truth can be presented in this way with the success that the Master says will follow the efforts of those engaged in declaring and spreading these truths. It is a wonderful opportunity for you to do one of the greatest services to your fellowman. Just think, it embraces in the results of the workings of these truths not only man's welfare on earth, but also his happiness and immortality in the great eternity.

I could write more to-night, but I will not longer trespass on your time or strength, and hope though, that at some future time I may have the opportunity to come and disclose some of the knowledge that I have, concerning these truths, and the importance that they are to mankind.

I live in the first Celestial Sphere where Jefferson and Washington are, and many others of the old patriots of revolutionary and later days. I will subscribe myself your obedient servant and brother in Christ.

DAN'L. WEBSTER.

Affirms that Celestial Spirits wrote.

I am here. *Helen.*

Well, my own dear Ned, you have had some * writings from spirits who when mortals were considered very great men and now they are highly developed spirits of the Celestial Spheres.

* Messages from Jefferson and Washington—Vol. I, Ed. 1, Page 353.

You will soon be fully convinced of the great importance of the work which you have been selected to do, as are the spirits here.

It is a great work and I know that you will enter into it with all your heart and soul, and bend every effort to making it a success.

I will not write more now as you are tired.

So with all my love I am

Your own true and loving, HELEN.

Religion is the relationship and harmony of men's souls with the Soul of God. Difference in the results of the teachings of the various churches. From Luke.

Let me write a line. *Luke.*

I was with you tonight at the church and listened to what the preacher said in reference to religions and their point of contact, and was somewhat surprised at his declarations as to the analogy which he drew between the believers in the various so-called Christian religions.

While, as you know, there is implanted in the souls of men a longing for that which tends to elevate and spiritualize them, even though this longing may not be consciously present with a large number of them, yet the beliefs as to the ways in which this longing may be made manifest and develop the spiritual nature of the soul are very different among those professing these various religions, and these ways are not equally efficacious in causing their spiritual development.

Religion is a matter of soul and not of intellect and the greater the development of the soul in the right direction, the higher will be the spiritual state or condition of the soul. Mere intellectual belief, no matter how intense and undoubting, will not tend to bring about this spiritual development for *"religion is really nothing but the relationship and harmony of men's souls with the Soul of God."* The mind will not be sufficient to create this state because the mind of man cannot possibly bring into harmony the Soul of the Creator and that of the creature. Mind in its exercise may tend to awaken the soul to this possibility of relationship, but only the workings of the soul can effectuate the complete unity of the Creator and the created. Only soul can speak to soul, and mind is only a helper, provided the soul is alive in its longings.

So it is apparent that that form of belief which is wholly of the intellect can have no common meeting place—with that belief which is the result of the development of the soul, and hence, to say that men of all the various religions, just because they are what are called Christians, are in an equal relationship to the Father is erroneous and misleading.

As regards the condition of man as the perfect man, these several religions may tend to bring about this state of perfection, if the moral precepts which they teach are observed and practised by men, but as regards man as the Divine Angel, that is as a spirit having in itself the Essence

344

of the Divine, only that religion which teaches the true way to acquire this Divinity can lead men to the at-one-ment with the Father in His very nature. There can be in this respect only one true religion and only one way in which that religion can be practised and possessed, and to say that all religions have a common point of approach is misleading and deceiving.

I know that among these various religions there are individuals who have found the way to the method of becoming transformed into the Divine nature of the Father, and this notwithstanding that the teachings and creeds of the several churches do not show the way to this soul development into the spiritual of the Divine. But in these churches there is wanting in their dogmas and doctrines that which will help men to this true religion.

Because it may be found that in the churches there are some who have, to a degree, this Divine spirituality, there is no justification in saying that there is any common place of meeting in these several religions.

Of course the moral precepts may be and are taught by all the Christian churches and when observed will ultimately lead all men to the condition of the perfect natural man and only to this extent can it be said that they may have a common ground of religion arising from the belief in the moral teachings.

And the church which declares and teaches as its religion with great exactness and more enlarged comprehension is the church in which this, as I may call it, natural religion exists; and the more dissimilar these churches are in these teachings the farther apart is their approach.

If a preacher of one church knows with the conviction that arises from his sincere and honest investigation of the moral laws that some other church is not teaching or insisting on the observation on the part of its members of these great moral truths, then he has no right to conclude and say this latter church is the possessor of religion as is the church in which these moral truths are taught and followed by its adherents.

It is a mistake for a preacher to say that because there may be good and spiritual men in all churches, therefore, one church is as good and religious in its teachings as another church. Truth is of such a nature that it cannot be compromised and the man or preacher who would compromise the truth is not fulfilling his duty to God or man.

The church which teaches that there is nothing greater than morality, and that man can become no more transcendent than the perfect man is devoid of the truth and would not be accepted as a teacher of the full truth, as should the church which knows and teaches the way by which man may become a Divine Angel.

That the preachers of the various churches should accept as equal and the possessors of the true religion whenever these moral lessons are alike taught by these churches and have a common point of approach, is not to be wondered at, because these preachers do not know the higher religion or are able to teach the way to the same, and when it is understood that a moral truth is a truth no matter where it may appear and by whom taught, there is some justification in declaring that all churches which teach the moral truths are on a plane of equality and that one is entitled to as much respect and freedom from criticism as another. And further, as the great truth of the rebestowal of the potentiality of receiving the Divine Love and the effect on men's souls was never known and taught until the coming of the Master, it is not surprising that none of the churches can or do teach this great spiritual truth and the only true religion arising therefrom. The knowledge of this truth perished from the earth a short time after the passing of the Master, and hence no church can teach this religion of the soul that transforms the mortal into the Divine.

The religion of the perfect man may exist in varying degrees in all the Christian churches, but the religion of the Divine Angel exists in none, although some individuals of these churches, to some extent, have received in their souls the great truth, the Divine Love, even though they have no intellectual knowledge of the same.

I thought it advisable to make these few remarks on the declaration of the preacher, as showing that his broad assertion that the religions mentioned which to him is all embracing, may have a common meeting point with every religion.

When he learns the truth, he will realize the errors of his human and brotherly declarations.

I will not write more.

Good night, and God bless you.

Your brother in Christ, Luke.

John Yorking—disciple of Jesus. His knowledge of the true teachings of Jesus when on earth.

I am here, the spirit of one who died a great many years ago in a far distant country, and when the truths of Christianity were known and practiced by the followers of the Master in the purity in which he taught them. I was a disciple of his but I am not known to history, and like a great many others who lived in those days, I worked in a humble way among the poor and simple of the earth. My work was mostly in the country outlying, but close to Palestine, and I was one who received from the spirit world the communications of those spirits who had lived on earth as Christians; and these communications were received in our public worship and interpreted or made plain to the common people by those teachers who had the gift of interpretation.

It was such communications as these that John referred to when he

346

advised us to try the spirits to learn whether they were of God, or in other words, to learn whether they were spirits who had a knowledge of the Christ doctrines, and who came to teach us the truths as they saw them to exist in the spirit world and who were followers of the Master.

I know that Jesus taught the New Birth and the Divine Love, and the rebestowal of the great gift which had been forfeited by our first parents at the time of their disobedience.

I also know that he never taught us to look upon him as God, or that any death that he might die would save us from our sins or bring us in at-onement with the Father, or that the Father demanded any sacrifice in order to satisfy his wrath or pay any debt that man might owe to Him.

No, the things last mentioned were not embraced in our faith or understanding of what the truths of the Master's teachings were.

We also had the wonderful powers which Jesus possessed in the way of healing, casting out evil spirits, etc., and we never looked upon them as miracles, but as the result of the exercise of the powers which came to us when we received the Divine Love and had the faith which made this love and all that accompanied it, things of real existence.

Jesus was always the man of love and mercy and benevolence, and never tired of his great work of doing good to the mortal; but these works were merely subordinate to the other great mission that he performed.

Above everything else, he was a teacher of the Father's love and the necessity of man's receiving this love in order to become at-one with the Father, and an accepted child whose inheritance was immortality and heaven.

So you can readily see what a departure there has been from our teachings and faith and practices, and the lives of simple followers of the Master.

Now I see that belief in the dogmas of the church and mysticisms of God are what constitutes the Christian, and soul development is little preached, or really understood, either by preacher or people; and the real secret of man's salvation has been lost to the world.

I am now in the high Celestial Spheres where the love of the Father is most abundant and the spirits of men live in eternal happiness, with the knowledge that immortality is theirs.

I will not write more tonight, as it is late and you are tired.

But before I stop, permit me to say, that you are receiving the revelation of the true religion of Jesus, as well as truths which pertain to the condition and existence of the spiritual world and the Celestial Heavens.

So with my love and blessings I am,

Your brother in Christ,
John the lowly follower of the Master—
JOHN YORKING—I was a Jew.

347

Affirimng that John Yorking wrote.

I am here—Your true *Helen.*

I will write only a line, as it is very late.

I never saw him before, but he was from the Celestial Spheres, for he was a wonderfully bright and developed spirit, and had the love shining forth from his countenance to a wonderful degree. I have no doubt that he is whom he represented himself to be.

Good night.

Your own true and loving   HELEN.

The Frailties of the human mind and moral qualities.

I am here, *James,* and I came to write on the subject of: *The Frailties of the Human Mind and Moral Qualities.*

I have heard you read the Master's message and believe that in it, you will find much truth upon which to reflect, and I desire to add a little to what has been therein said. And here I want further to say, that while that message was intended for you personally, yet the truth and advice therein given may be applied to every mortal, and the good results will follow, no matter who that mortal may be.

I have, as you know, been in the spirit world a great many centuries, as you conceive of time, and have during that long period been very close to mortals in all parts of the earth and of all nationalities and beliefs and education and enlightenment, and in my experiences with these mortals, I have observed the nature and temptations and the various ways in which mortals have been assailed by such temptations, and their efforts to overcome the same, together with their successes and failures.

Now, first let me say, that the nature of man is, today, the same as it was when I lived on earth, and the perversions and sins of the souls of men are just as many and of the same kind as they were in my day in the flesh, and temptations, both outward and inward, are just as hard to overcome as they were when first the glad tidings of love and redemption were proclaimed by the Master, except that prior to that time man had not the Divine Love to help him overcome and subdue these temptations, as he now has. And the regret is, that while this Great Helper and Regenerator, and Conqueror of sin and temptation is now in the world of mortals and subject to their call, yet so comparatively few make the call, or realize the fact that this Helper is always waiting to enable them to overcome temptations.

Prior to this time of the coming of the Divine Love, moral truths were taught to men just as they are today, and many men, and not necessarily among the Jews, understood and attempted to apply these truths to their daily lives, and endeavored to overcome the temptations arising from the sins that so constantly formed a part of their existence, and that also came from the influence of the evil spirits. It is all wrong to suppose that in

348

these early times and among these early races of earth, moral perceptions were not developed and taught; men then made the fight to overcome temptations, and become good and noble beings, so far as these moral truths and principles were then understood and used by men, would make them.

In all ages, since the fall of the first parents men have, to a more or less degree, had knowledge of what is called the moral truths, and the natural love of man has existed in a more or less imperfect condition. Men have been kind and loving and true, and have to an extent controlled their appetites and tendencies to evil lives, and to suppose that men of today are not subject to so great temptations and are of themselves better able to resist the same is a mistake. The present great war proves the fact, for men were never, I mean those who make a pretense to culture and civilization, so brutal in their acts, and so apparently devoid of all conception of right and wrong and of mercy, as are many of those who are engaged in the present struggle.

So I say, men of today can lay no greater claim to moral qualities than could those of the times when they were supposed to be heathens and undeveloped in these moral qualities.

Of course there is in the world today more of what may be called education and conventionality, but behind these things, which are largely the results of merely intellectual development, men have the same perverted souls, or rather appetites and desires, and are subject to the same temptations as were men of old; and if mankind were left dependent upon the cultivation and improvement of these merely moral powers, 1 fear that temptation would continue to have all its influence and harmful power on the souls of men that it had in the past.

I know, it is said, "that the world is growing better"; but the question is, is that assertion true; and if so, what is the cause?

Go to India and to China and to some other countries where the teachings of the supposed moral laws only obtain, and learn if there has been any improvement in the condition of men's souls, and if they have in any degree succeeded in overcoming the temptations that the human race is subject to, and in learning, you will find, that except in the case of a few of these people, the conditions of their minds and souls are just as perverted as they were in centuries past, and that it is only in those countries where the influence of Christian nations have control, do these people suppress the tendencies of perverted minds to do those things that arise from the want of the exercise of moral precepts or knowledge.

This is the truth of what mere moral teachings have accomplished where only the mere moral truths, as is supposed, are taught.

Temptations are with men, and will be with them forever, unless they be controlled or overcome by something greater or more certain than what men conceive to be moral truths.

349

Now, you will see from this that merely moral concepts will not necessarily, or, at least, for a long time to come, be able to bring about the destruction of the powers of temptation that arises from the perverted nature of mortals.

I must stop now, and in doing so will leave you my love and blessings. Goodnight. Your brother in Christ.

JAMES, *Brother of* JOHN.

Affirming That James Wrote on the Frailties of the Human Mind and Moral Qualities

I am here. Your own true and loving *Helen* (Mrs. Padgett).

Well, dear, you have had a very pleasant evening, and so have we who have been with you listening to your conversation and I mean by "we" many spirits who are interested in both of you and the Dr. James wrote and while he may not have written as easily as he generally does, yet he has conveyed some important truths which you will discover by carefully reading his messages.

Goodnight and God bless you both is the prayer of—

Your own true and loving, HELEN.

How Man Can Again Be Restored to the Perfect Man Like the First Parents Before Their Fall.

I am here *St. James, Apostle of Jesus:*

I come to write my message as Elias told you I would. Well, I desire to write on the subject of what is the great truth respecting the way that the destruction of the powers of temptation that arises from the perverted man may be restored to the condition of perfection which the first parents possessed before their fall.

You will understand that this does not involve any consideration of the operation of the Divine Love upon the soul, but exclusively the consideration of the method by which the soul may be so purified by the operations of the actions and the will power in conjunction with or influenced by the workings of the powers of the spirits who have been relieved of the sins and errors that followed the fall.

When man was created, as has been told you, he was created perfect, and every quality and function and attribute that was a part of him was so created that harmony, the most exact with the laws of God that governed his existence, became his, and no discord of any kind was in existence to mar that harmony. But as the spiritual nature of man became subordinated to the appetites and passions and fleshly desires, sin and error and inharmony appeared and increased until man became degraded, and desired only those things that would satisfy these sinful desires.

And so this degeneracy continued until man reached his lowest degradation, and the turning point came in his career, and then he commenced

350

slowly and gradually to rise from this condition of depravity until at last, he arrived at the stage of his condition of inharmony with these laws of his creation that now exists; and his destiny is to a complete restoration to the perfection of his first estate.

This improvement and gradual restoration depend upon two causes—one, man himself by his own thoughts and reformation of the animal appetites and desires; and the other, the influence and guidance of spirits who, in the spirit world, have arrived at that perfection, or are progressing thereto, and are in a condition of harmony with these laws, superior to that of mortals to whom they lend their influence and help.

Men, in their degeneracy or progression, are controlled very largely by their thoughts, and these thoughts are created by the operations of their desires, and which on the other hand, cause these desires to increase. But back of the thoughts are always these appetites and passions existing in their abnormal conditions, and they constitute the basic or moving cause of desire and thought and act. So that in order for men to become relieved of his abnormal desires and thoughts and acts, the cause thereof must be eradicated, and the seat or function of the cause be brought into harmony with laws of the creation of these functions or seats of emanation.

And strange as it may seem to you, and by a process that is contrary to the ordinary workings of the law of cause and effect, men must first deal with the effects in order to control the cause and thereby destroy the effects. This may seem to be an impossible operation and contrary to the laws that govern the material world and its ordinary functioning, but yet it is possible, and the only possible way in which the causes may be destroyed.

Notwithstanding the fact that the animal or material part of man has had the ascendency for all these centuries over the spiritual part of his nature, yet that spiritual part exists and has always existed and waiting to assert itself whenever the opportunity occurred, and this assertion was prevented or suppressed only by reason of the want of opportunity.

The spiritual may be said to be the natural state—I mean that in that state the animal is subordinate to the spiritual and is controlled by it, and man's true tendency is to exist and act in accord with that natural state. Then such being the fact, it may be asked why, or in what manner did this natural spiritual condition become, in the manifestation of what man's dominant qualities are supposed to be, subordinated to the control of the inordinate exercise of this animal side of his nature, which resulted in the sin and unhappiness that so many of the teachers and philosophers proclaim to be his natural condition?

Well tonight, I will not attempt to explain the manner in which this inversion or perversion of man's true nature took place, but will at some future time write on this subject.

The question now is, how can man obtain the restitution to his created perfection.

As I have said, this can only be accomplished by making the perfect adjustment of the two apparent conflicting sides of his nature.

And first, he must recognize that he has the spiritual nature as well as the animal, and that there is such a relationship and coordination between the two that the supremacy of the latter disturbs the harmony of his perfection as man. The spiritual having been subordinated, the remedy is to remove the subordination and restore the equality. The spiritual notwithstanding its condition, is always fighting to regain its place in the true adjustment and will always answer the call of man, to come to his rescue, and the only thing that has prevented that response is that man has not called for it to assert itself.

Well I am sorry, but we had better postpone until later. Try to get in greater rapport.

Good night.

Your brother in Christ,   St. James.

Affirming That St. James Wrote

I am here—Your own true and loving *Helen* (Mrs. Padgett):

Well dear, I see that you are disappointed tonight in not receiving the message from James, so that you could write it as he intended to deliver it.

Well, the conditions were not good and the rapport not sufficient to enable you to finish the message. He was disappointed, also, but he will come again and deliver it to you.

I see that you are very sleepy and must go to bed.

So have faith, and love me, and say good night.

Your own true and loving   Helen.

What is the real body that is resurrected at the time of the physical death.

I am here. *Paul.*

Yes.

I come tonight to write you upon a subject that may be of interest to you and important to all mankind. If you are in condition to receive my message I will write.

Well, the subject is:—What is the real body that is resurrected at the time of the physical death.

Of course there will be but one resurrection and that takes place at the time the mortal becomes an inhabitant of the spirit world. There will never be what is called a general resurrection of the dead, for the mortal can die only once. I mean in a physical sense, and in order to live in the spirit realms, it is necessary that he have a spirit body that preserves the identity of his individuality, and having this body and never having been without it after the soul is incarnated in the earthly body and not needing an additional body there is no possibility of another resurrection or of another body being added to the one that the soul already has.

The body that dies when the man ceases to be a mortal, disintegrates into its elements and never again do these elements form the same body that becomes decayed, and hence it is impossible for that body to be resurrected. The only body that is ever resurrected is the body that encloses the soul of the mortal at the time he gives up the earth life.

I know that many believe that when the man dies, his conscious existence ceases, and he becomes, as it were, dead in body, soul and spirit,— that although the physical body decays and returns to dust or ashes, yet the soul and spirit in some mysterious and unexplainable manner, continues to exist as an unthinking sleeping entity, not subject to sensation or activity, and so remains until the great day of judgment or of Christ's coming, when, in response to the summons it arouses itself, answers the summons, and again becomes clothed in the body which it possessed while in the human form. In their belief, it may not be the exact or identical body which once existed, but the new body will be one of flesh and blood, and of such a nature as to be in substance the same body that was dead and buried and decayed.

But this is not true, for the very laws of nature with which men are acquainted prove the impossibility of such an occurrence, and many arguments have been formulated and declared to prove that such a resurrection cannot be—that it will be wholly impossible for the elements that constituted the old body to again assemble in the same form and give to the soul the body that it discarded when it experienced its freedom from the bands of the flesh.

But the advocates of this untrue theory, respond that God is all powerful, and in some way not understood by men, will resurrect this old body and clothe the soul therein so that the identity of the individual will appear. It must be remembered that God works and produces beings and entities in accordance with laws that he has established and not by any special, sporadic act, irrespective of, and, as said, in contravention of these laws.

Man understands, to some extent, the workings of these laws in what he calls nature, or the normal, and some spirits understand not only what man understands, but also the workings of these laws that may be called above nature or super-normal, and the laws work the same and without change or interference in the one case as in the other.

As it would be impossible to clothe a mortal having one body of flesh. with another body of flesh, so in the spirit world it would be impossible to clothe the spirit who has a spirit body with any additional body, whether of flesh or other substance. This spirit body is a thing of real substance, and not susceptible of being enveloped in any other body.

Well, I see that you are not in condition to write and I will postpone the remainder of the message until later.

I have not written you for some time, and am glad of the opportunity to again write.

I understand what you mean and will act on your suggestion as I think it a very wise and desirable one.

I will come more often and write.

So with all my love I will say, good-night.

Your brother in Christ,   PAUL.

Continued from preceding message.

I am here. *Paul.*

I will finish my message tonight if you are so inclined. Well we will try.

As I was saying, the body that is resurrected at death, is not the physical body but the spirit body, and never after the first resurrection is there another. I am now dealing with the resurrection other than that of the soul, or the * resurrection from the death of which I have before written.

The body that is once laid in the grave will never be resurrected and neither will any of its elements enter into any other body for the purpose of a resurrection. The body of flesh is created for one purpose only, and when that purpose has been accomplished, never will that body or any derivative from it be used for any resurrection. This body of flesh is of matter and like all matter is used for the life on earth only, and cannot be used for any function or clothing any spirit in the spirit world, and neither can it be translated into the spirit realms.

All material bodies must die and never will there come a time when men can leave the earth, and enter the spirit life in these material bodies.

I know that it has been written that certain of the prophets of old were translated into the spirit heavens clothed in their fleshly bodies, but this is not true for it is impossible that such a thing could be, as the same laws apply to the physical body of the saint as to that of the sinner: both are of the earth, earthly, and must be left behind when the spirits of men enter the heavens of spirits.

So that when men believe and preach the general resurrection of the material body, or the special resurrection of the same, they are in error and do not believe or preach the truth.

Flesh and blood, or flesh without blood, cannot inherit the kingdom, and no belief or teachings can make that true which is untrue.

I do not desire to write more on this subject, because many men who are acquainted with the laws of nature, and many more who will become

* Resurrection by St. Paul. Vol. I—Edition 1—Pages 94-98.

acquainted with these laws, know and will know and understand the impossibility of the material entering the realm of the spiritual.

So thanking you for your kindness, I will say good night.

Your brother in Christ,

By St. Paul.

Refers to Mr. P.'s mediumship. Denies Reincarnation.

I am here. *Jesus.*

I intended to finish my discourse tonight, but it is now too late, and I will have to postpone it.

Well, there are cases where such results follow, and it is not astonishing that it is so, for these mediums who surrender their own faculties and wills and moral powers will find spirits take control of them; and these spirits do not hesitate to use these mediums for any and all purposes that they may desire, and these desires are mostly injurious and detrimental to the mediums, both morally and spiritually.

In such cases of spirit control the mediums absolutely submit their mental and will powers to the domination of these spirits, and when once such spirits get control they are never satisfied, and care not for the conditions of the mediums, and such being the case, the mediums suffer.

But, the mediumship which you have is not of such a character as to permit any spirit who may write through you to obtain that control of your mental faculties as will enable them to exercise their wills and powers in a way that will prevent you from exercising yours as you desire. They do not become your masters, but are subordinate to your will and cannot use you for the purposes mentioned unless you so incline. The exercise of your phase of mediumship will not do you harm and you need not fear the results. In fact it is necessary that your mental faculties should become vivified and enlarged in order for you to do the work, and the greater development you have the more you will be enabled to do our work in a more satisfactory manner.

I know the substance of the book that you have been reading, and the falsity of these speculations that assert the doctrine of reincarnation. There is no such thing as the second embodiment of the soul into the human form, and no return to earth for the purpose of improvement of the soul's condition.

So try to be in condition and we will continue the writing of my messages.

With all my love and blessings, I am

Your brother and friend   Jesus.

Reincarnation, by an Ancient Spirit.

I was an inhabitant of India when that country was not known of to modern nations, and I lived near the great Himalaya mountains on a plain

355

that was then fertile and peopled by a vast number of inhabitants who worshiped the Gods of whom the later Brahmans have written in their sacred books.

It may seem surprising to you that I should come and write you, and the explanation is, that I became in rapport with you tonight at the meeting of the Theosophists. I saw that you were psychic and that I could communicate to you through the medium of the pen. There were many spirits present who, when mortals, lived in that far away country, and were, and are now believers in the mysteries of the occult as claimed to be known now by those who profess to be leaders of the Theosophical movement. A number of their names were mentioned by the lecturer; and these spirits were attracted to the meeting by reason of the similarity of beliefs which the mortals present possessed, and they, the spirits, possessed.

I, also, was present because of that attraction, for when on earth I was a great believer in these doctrines, and especially those that teach reincarnation and karma, and I still believe in these things. Although I have been a spirit for many centuries, yet these earth beliefs cling to me and hold me to the binding force of their truths, as I conceive these truths to be.

Many of those present, whose minds I could read as they thought, believe in these doctrines, but very few of them have any conception of what are the truths taught by such philosophy. Even the lecturer has a very slight comprehension of the scope and import of these teachings, and her attempt to explain the objects and workings of the principles of true theosophy was a very inefficient effort, for in order for her to be able to teach these doctrines, it is absolutely necessary that she have a knowledge of the same, which she does not have.

No, the knowledge that she, and many others like her, have, as to the fundamentals of this philosophy or rel.gion, if it may be called such, is very superficial, and the fact that it is a system of mysteries, of which they have discerned in a few instances, the explanation, causes them to conclude that their grasp of the scope of this philosophy is greater than it really is, and affords them a kind of satisfaction that arises from the consciousness that some mysteries which the world knows not of, they know.

She spoke about the great Masters being in India, who have a full knowledge of these mysteries and, in certain conditions or circumstances, will be able to and will initiate the searcher into the esoteric meaning of these great truths. Well, these Masters know something of mysticism and of occult powers and principles, but such knowledge is not sufficient to qualify them as teachers of the great truths of theosophy, as I understood and now understand these truths.

We have in the spirit world and have had for long centuries, communities of theosophists, who believe and teach to whomsoever will listen to these doctrines, and many of these spirits attempt to teach mortals by impressions and thought transference these truths of ages, but with indifferent success; and, hence, for most of those who think they would like to understand this philosophy, the great attraction is the mystery, which they believe, because of its being a mystery, must contain the truth.

The progress and understanding in the search for the key to the opening up and solving of these doctrines, and the supposed mystery in which they are shrouded, is very slow, and we who have been, as I said, for centuries engaged in this great effort have never had demonstrated to us the existence of our supposed truths; and we are still plodding the weary way, supported by the faith that at some time light will come to us, and that which has so long been enveloped in darkness will come into the pure light of understanding and comprehension.

But as yet, very few of these mysteries have been solved, and the truths supposed to be concealed therein been manifested, and to some of us doubt has commenced to rear its head and cause disappointment. Such being the case with us, what can these mortals who are groping in speculation and discord expect to succeed in disclosing?

To night, I heard the lecturer declare that Man is God potentially, and that when he develops into perfection he will become God. Never was there a more delusive and untrue declaration of a supposed fact ever uttered, for we who have lived in this invisible world long enough to have had come to us the realization that we are gods, all know that we are only and merely the spirits of men who lived on earth many years ago, and believed that when in the far distant future by our own exertions in renunciation, we would become gods. No, such is not the fact, and while we have renounced many of the sins and errors of our mortal lives, yet we are still spirits with all the limitations of mind and souls that spirits are by nature bound.

And this I must say, that in all the centuries of my spirit existence never have I known a spirit or the soul of a spirit to reincarnate, and in this my disappointment has been grievous. Many spirits of our association have become perfect through renunciation, and yet they have remained spirits and progressed to the highest heavens of our possibilities. (Sixth Sphere.)

Yet, strange as it may seem, in view of this experience we still, to a more or less degree, cling to our old beliefs in reincarnation, thinking that there is something else, that we know not of, to be done in order for reincarnation to become the destiny of our souls.

Sometimes I think that my beliefs in this particular must be wrong, for in comparing the condition of mortals, the most advanced in their mind and soul development, I realize that they are not in a small degree the equal of us in development, and then I wonder and, wondering, cannot understand what good could be accomplished or what improvement made in our condition for progressing, should we again enter mortal bodies.

As true theosophy taught, as we conceived it, reincarnation was a supposed process of purification and necessary in 'order that the spirit could attain to a state of perfection and freedom from everything that defiles his soul and prevents that soul from arriving at the blissful state of Nirvana, which means only that condition of soul where no longer reincarnation is necessary or possible; and when 'I know that many of our spirits, one time believers in these doctrines, have arrived at that condition and entered a state of perfect happiness, I hesitate longer to believe and only hold the faith, because I fear that the experience mentioned may be the results of special circumstances.

But if I cease to believe these teachings, what shall I believe? No one can tell me that this reincarnation 'will not take place, and I fear to surrender the belief.

I further believe that in order for the workings of karma, as the doctrines hold, reincarnation is necessary—that only in the mortal body could I do the reaping that my 'sowing demands, and yet, I see and know that karma has been and is working in this spirit world to the extent, that the reaping has all been accomplished and the spirit made perfect, and this without any reincarnation, for as I have said, never have I known or heard of the reincarnation of a spirit or of anything that is connected with or represents the spirit.

Of late I have been much in cloudland as to 'these beliefs, and in my desire to find the light, I have visited the meetings of the theosophists in all countries, 'and especially in India, where the Masters who are supposed to have the full knowledge and enlightenment live, and in hope of finding the light, but all to no avail. My desires and longings cry for the light, but none can be found.

To night, I was 'attracted to the meeting where I saw you, and realizing that I could express to you my feelings and doubts, made a rapport and came home with you for the purpose of doing what I have done. I know from your condition of mind that you do not believe in these doctrines of the theosophists, and that your beliefs are of a different kind, and are new to me, although I have heard of the doctrines that are the objects of your faith. There are spirits with whom I sometimes come in contact, who attempt to tell me of another way to a higher heaven than the one that I know of, but as they are mere babes in comparison to my ancient existence, I do not listen to them, and hence I am not acquainted with their teachings.

I must not write more tonight and thank you for your kindness.

Well, you seem to be very kind, and I thank you for your interest, and under the circumstances must accept your offer, and will, I assure you, listen attentively to what may be said to me.

I have looked and there comes to me a beautiful spirit who says she is your grandmother, and that she has heard your invitation, and will be glad to show me the way to love and light and truth. She seems so bright and beautiful and loving that I must go with her. So I will say good night and go. Good night.

LAMLESTIA.

Well, sweetheart, you are tired, and must not write more now.

I will say though, that the spirits who wrote you tonight actually are the persons they represented themselves to be. I was with you at the various meetings and these spirits were there and became in rapport with you.

The Indian was in truth an Indian, and was in the condition that he declared himself to be. He was a very bright spirit and lives in the highest spiritual heaven. He went with your grandmother.

Mrs. Eddy was very anxious to write, and I am sorry that she could not finish, for the burden on her mind is great, and she wants so much to write the truth. I will have her come soon. She is in the Seventh Sphere and has much of the soul love, yet she sees the possible injurious results of her teaching, and her work is before her, and she says, that the only way in which she can remedy the wrong is through the channel that she so bitterly denounced, and that she sees the difficulties are so much greater than it would be but for this grave mistake.

Pastor Russell is also very anxious to write and he will soon come. I feel real sorry for him. His shock was so very great.

Well, so it is, I must give my time to telling you of other spirits. But that is my work and yours and we must not complain—they are all the Father's children.

So my dear, take courage and believe, and all will be well.

Yes, Jesus was with you at the morning service and may write to you about the same, but I am not certain. His love was with you though, and he seems to want to be with you, whenever he is not elsewhere.

He loves you and is caring for you.

Your own true and loving,   HELEN.

No such thing as reincarnation. Was caused to visualize a Divine Spirit. Was much surprised.

I am here. *Saelish.*

I was, when on earth, an inhabitant of the great Empire of Assyria of which Nineveh was the capital. I was not a king but was one of a great king's magicians or wise men, and when I lived was a man of great in-

359

fluence and power in the kingdom. I came tonight to tell you a great truth in connection with the soul. As you may infer, when I lived we knew nothing of the one and only God, but we worshipped many gods, great and little, and believed that these gods could help or harm us, just as we deserved their help or their injurious workings. And so our many gods sometimes came in conflict in their treatment of us poor mortals so that we at times hardly knew whether our gods were our friends or our enemies.

Of course, the help that we sought for was all of a material nature, for never did we think of help in the way of preparing us for a future life,—that we supposed was only for those of us who by our great achievement in battle or in intellectual pursuits would, upon death, become gods ourselves. The poor, ordinary mortals were only intended to live the mortal life, at least during the incarnation that they then had—and their expectations were that perhaps in some future incarnation, they might have the opportunity and the favors of the unknown gods so that they might become gods themselves.

This was the substance of the beliefs and hopes of the Assyrians at that time—and many millions died in that belief and are now inhabitants of the several planes of certain spheres of the spirit world. None of them has ever returned for a new incarnation and thereby start on their way to become gods, and this for the reason, which is sufficient to satisfy them when they became spirits, sooner or later, those men who they supposed had become gods when they died, were in the spirit world spirits themselves and not gods at all.

So you see that the soul, when once it leaves the physical body, never returns again to any physical body, but continues in the spirit world to exist as a soul with a body of spirit form and substance; and no spirit has ever experienced the sensation of becoming reincarnated.

And this is the truth that I wished to tell you:—That the soul, when once it leaves the physical body, never again finds its habitation in another or the same physical body, but forever thereafter occupies the spirit body, and that in the spirit world only.

When a mortal dies on earth, so far as being the home of that mortal again in earthly body, becomes a thing of the past,—it is a mere way station which has been left behind, and will never again appear as a stopping place on the spirit's line of progression.

I thought it might do good for me to write this tonight, for it is the information from a spirit who long years ago lived on earth and believed in this doctrine of reincarnation, and who during all the long years of its spirit life has learned and experienced the truth, that reincarnation is a fable and has no real existence.

No, the soul never retraces its steps or its method of existence, for it never goes back from the spirit to mortal.

I know that on the earth today there are thousands of mortals who believe in this doctrine of reincarnation, and many thousands more have died in that belief, but they live and die in that belief and only when the truth comes to them, do they realize that their belief was an erroneous one, and that they will never reach Nirvana by retracing their course of life through the physical body.

The soul never dies, but always lives, and whenever its position is such as to justify progression, it progresses.

I live in the sixth sphere, and am considered to be a very exalted spirit in my intellectual acquirements and in my condition of freedom from sin and errors which belonged to me on earth and which belongs to every mortal. My happiness is very great and my home and surroundings are beautiful.

This sphere is a wonderful place, not only because of the surroundings and homes of the inhabitants but because of the great mental and moral development of those who live in that sphere. No spirit who has not that development can live in this sphere because of its unfitness.

Male and female spirits enjoy this wonderful development and their intercourse in the intellectual things that exist in this sphere is free and frequent, and the interchange of thoughts brings much happiness and satisfaction.

We don't know of any spheres beyond the sixth although we have heard it rumored that there are other spheres, but we give little credence to these rumors, because none of us, I mean the inhabitants of this sphere, has ever found a higher one, and many of us live in the highest planes of this sphere.

No, I have nothing else to write tonight.

Well, I, of course, can't say that is not true, but I do say that you astonish me beyond all belief, for I cannot imagine that any spirit can make higher progress than we have made.

Well, what you tell me surprises me and I would like to investigate and discover the truth of this matter. But I don't know how to commence such investigation or where to start. Is it possible that you can show me the way in which I can commence this investigation?

I have done as you suggested and I do see some wonderfully beautiful spirits, and they seem to be so very happy, too, and interested in you. One says she is your grandmother, and she seems to excell the others in her beauty and brightness.

She says she is very willing to start me in my investigation, and herself to tell me the great secret of the great progression that you speak of, and if I will accompany her she will commence at once.

361

And while I write, there comes another beautiful spirit and says that she formerly lived in the sixth sphere, and lived there many thousands of years before I lived on earth. She says that she was an Egyptian and that her name was Saleeba and that now she is an inhabitant of the third sphere, in order to prepare herself for the great progression that she will make to spheres high above the sixth, and tells me that after I have conversed with your grandmother she will be pleased to talk to me and tell me her experience.

I will be with her, you may rest assured.

All this is so wonderful to me that I hardly know what to think or do. But I will try to find the truth of it if it can be found.

So, as I have written you a long time, expecting to enlighten you and not be enlightened myself and am now so anxious for that enlightenment.

I will say that I am glad I came to you and

Goodnight.   SAELISH.

What is the correct way in which a man should live the life on earth, in order to receive the cleansing from his sins, so that he can acquire the purification of his natural love.

I am here. *Jesus.*

I come tonight according to promise, and desire to write my message, if you are in condition to receive it.

I wish to write on the subject of: *What is the correct way in which a man should live the life on earth, in order to receive the cleansing from his sins, so that he can acquire the purification of his natural love?*

Heretofore, I have conferred in my messages almost exclusively to the redemption of the soul by means of the Divine Love, so that the redeemed one may become an inhabitant of the Celestial Spheres. Now I will deal only with that cleansing that will fit him to live in the highest and purest of the spirit spheres, where he can have the happiness which a pure natural love will bring to him.

As has been written you, the soul as it was created and placed in man was, at the time of its creation in human form, or rather at the time it found a habitation in that form, made pure and perfect and in complete harmony with the laws of God controlling its existence, and that only after the fall by reason of man's own indulgence in the animal appetites and desires did it lose its purity and become contaminated by sin and error, and that ever since that time it has remained in such condition of impurity and alienship to God and His laws.

This impurity has been the lot of each succeeding generation of men, and has never been eradicated from men's souls, notwithstanding all the moral instructions that man has acquired; but still there has been wonderful improvements in the purity of man's thoughts, as well as in his

362

actions and habits of life, since the turning from the bottom of his degeneracy.

Now, there are several ways in which man may succeed in acquiring that purity that existed at the time of the creation of the first man, and in time this consummation will be accomplished; but in these ways man, himself, will have to be an important, working factor, for man is the highest of God's creation, with powers and will possessed by no other of God's creatures, and there is no power in heaven or earth that can or will redeem man from this condition of sin and error unless man will cooperate in the work, and that to the greatest and best of his ability.

These sins that I speak of were created by man's thoughts and desires carried into acts and deeds by the operation of his will, and they must be removed by the same processes. Where the evil thoughts and deeds created that which contaminated and defiled the qualities of his soul, these evil thoughts and deeds must be supplanted by good thoughts and deeds in order that the defilement may be removed and the soul purified.

Evil thoughts are born of suggestions, both inward and outward, and also of the influences of spirits of evil who establish a rapport with the mortals.

Let us postpone the writing for our rapport is not just right. I will come soon and finish.

With all my love I am your brother and friend,   JESUS.

I am here. *Helen.*

Well, I am sorry that you could not continue the writing, for the Master was very anxious to write the whole message tonight.

Well, you were not in condition, and it was hard work for the Master to control your hand and brain. It may be that your brain was tired, and he could not transmit the thoughts. But you may have better success next time.

He understands, and says that you must not feel bad about it.

Good-bye for a while.

Your own true and loving   HELEN.

How a mortal may obtain the development of his soul without
the help of the Divine Love

I am here. *Jesus.*

I see that you are in better condition tonight, and it may be that we can continue the message.

Well, as I was saying, the only way in which a mortal may obtain the development of his soul condition, without the help of the Divine Love, is by attempting to exercise his will in the way that will cause the thoughts of evil and error to leave him, and to be replaced by thoughts that will bring his heart and soul into harmony with the laws of his crea-

363

tion as mere man. This can be done by his seeking for those higher things of morality and the subordinating of the purely animal desires and appetites of the mortal to the aspirations and desires of the higher and nobler part of his nature.

As I have before told you, man was pure and good until he by the exercise of his will, following the suggestions of the animal desires, permitted himself to degenerate from the high and perfect condition of his creation.

These sins and desires do not belong to his original nature, for his true nature was pure and in harmony with the laws of God, and although he has lost it by the excessive and wrongful exercise of his will obeying the desires of his animal nature yet he can recover his condition of original purity and harmony, if he will get rid of these sins and errors, so that his nature may again become free from everything that defiles it, or places it out of harmony with the laws that created it.

So you see, it is not necessary for man to obtain, or add to his original condition any qualities that were not his in the beginning, but merely to get rid of or eradicate from that condition, those things which are mere excrescences or parasites, and thereby have his nature in the same condition that was his when he was created and was the perfect man.

So long a time has the nature or condition of the nature of man been in this state of defilement and alienation from the true condition ot his creation, that the effort to bring about the restoration will necessarily be great and he will have to use all his power of will that he is capable of to effectuate this object, and he will find in such efforts two conflicting forces, aways fighting each other for the mastery.

The fact that he believes his present condition is the natural one, and that the state and purity and freedom from sin and error, is one that does not belong to him naturally, but must be acquired by adding something to what he now has and always possessed, will make the fight more uneven.

Therefore the first things that man must believe, is that his present condition is not his natural one, and that he has nothing more or greater to accomplish than to relieve himself of those things which prevent his condition from becoming as it was when he was the perfect man.

If he will get this belief firmly fixed in his mind, and assert that he was made by God, and that God never created anything impure or not in harmony with His laws, he, man, will have accomplished the first step towards his regeneration, and towards success in his effort.

He must not consider himself to be a weak, low and unworthy creature of God, not being entitled to those conditions of purity and greatness which made him the beloved child of the Father. Of course, self-esteem and pride and everything of that nature must be eliminated from the estimate that he must have of himself, but on the contrary the idea that he is degenerated and utterly helpless being must not be permitted to enter his mind. Such thoughts do not make him pleasing to God as he has been taught they do, but only make him subservient to his master's sin and error, and prevent him from asserting his own superiority to these things which is necessary to exist in his conception of his true condition, in order that he may obtain the ascendency over those masters.

When he shall have assumed this position then he will realize that these animal appetites and desires, and evil thoughts which arise from them and from the belief that he is by nature degraded and unworthy of a better and higher condition of nature, are really beings of his own creation and subject to his will and self-control and total destruction.

And with such realization will come a consciousness that they are not parts of his nature, but foreign to it, and that in order that his nature may become separated from them he must look upon them as enemies and treat them as such, to be destroyed and utterly extinguished and never more to be taken to his bosom and cherished as inalienable and dominant parts of his nautre.

Of course, in treating them as such enemies, great watchfulness and determination will have to be exercised, for they are very insidious and will at all times and in all ways, whenever the oportunity arises, try to convince him that they are an integral and necessary part of his being incapable of being separated from him.

But by the exercise of this belief, based upon a right conception of what is and what is not a part of him as the perfect man, and by the exercise of his will power in accordance with this conception, he will be able to rescue himself from these unnatural appetites and desires and thoughts of error and sin.

As this belief becomes stronger and this conception clearer, and his will exercised in closer harmony with the two essentials, these excrescences will gradually and one by one fall away from him, until, at last, he will rise again the perfect man with the pure and harmonious nature which God gave him at the time of his creation.

But this process will be slow and sometimes hardly perceptible, for the long years of misbelief in the idea of original sin, and that God created evil and error for the purpose of defiling man's nature and making a disobedient devil of him without any inherent goodness or the possibility of becoming regenerated unless by the operation of some miracle, will make it difficult for the acquiring of the true belief as to what he and what his nature are, and enable him to become the master and not remain the servant.

God is the Father of all, and loves all his children, and as he originally provided for their happiness, so now, he desires that all may be

happy, even though they may not seek for that Divine Love which makes mortals and spirits more than the mere perfect man.

Forgiveness is, in effect, forgetfulness, and when men in their efforts cause all these things of evil and sin to cease being a part of their nature, and only thoughts of purity and righteousness to find a lodgment in their minds, then these other things are forgotten and forgiveness has taken place. Man no longer is the slave of false beliefs and unrighteousness, nor is he their associates, and even in memory they become things of non-existence and when he gets into this condition of purity and freedom and in harmony with the laws of his creation, there exists nothing which can be the object of forgiveness, and he is the man of perfect creation.

But in all this man must realize that he does not exist by and for himself alone, for always he is surrounded by mortals or spirits or both, exercising upon him their influence for good or evil,—helping him to turn his thoughts from these things of evil and sin into those higher things which are his by nature, or causing him to receive and foster these evil thoughts with increased intensity. He cannot get rid of these influences, of one kind or the other, and, hence, he should seek the influence of those who are good and desire to help him in his efforts towards the recovery of that condition which is his by right of birth.

Among God's laws, which never change and which work impartially, is the great law of attraction, and it works in the case of all mortals and spirits, and never rests.

And the great principle of this law is, that like attracts like, and the unlike repulses the unlike. So man must know that as he is—I mean in his state of mind and soul—so necessarily will be his companions of those who desire his association, and, hence, he should realize this important truth and all that it implies.

If his thoughts and deeds are evil he will attract those spirits or mortals who have similar thoughts and deeds, and who will not help him to higher things, but who will retard his progress towards his first estate; and, if his thoughts and deeds are good, then his associates will only be those of like qualities, who can and will help him in his progress.

Every effort to create good thoughts strengthens the desires and will in that direction and assists the coming of other good thoughts, for with these efforts comes the help of these unseen influences, and the repulsion of the influences of the retarding forces.

Man is a wonderful being and the highest creation of the Father, and yet his greatest master is his belief in the power and supremacy of these things of evil of his own creation.

But beyond all this a means to accomplish man's restitution to his perfect estate is the help of the Father, which is never refused when man seeks for it in earnest sincere prayer. Always the Father is willing to respond to the true prayers of man, and by His instrumentalities will make the efforts of man sure and effective, so that he can acquire that condition that will free him from all sin and error and slavery of false belief in the mastery of his evil creatures.

Man must believe in the love and help of the Father, in the manhood and greatness of himself, and in the utter error of his belief in the mastery of his own children of sin and error.

I have written enough and must stop as you are tired.

So assuring you of my love for you, and my care and help, I will say, good-night.

Your brother and friend,   JESUS.

Affirming that the Master wrote.

I am here. *Luther.*

I come tonight to say that I would like to write again very soon as I desire to write further in the line of thought of my last message.

I see that you are too tired to write tonight and I will not ask you to do so, but if you can soon give me the opportunity to write I will be much obliged.

Yes, I know, and I enjoyed his message and believe that it will be readily understood. What a Master he is! So beautiful and powerful and loving!

Your brother in Christ,   LUTHER.

Affirming the Master wrote.

I am here. Your own true and loving *Helen.*

Well, my own dear Ned, you have had a very entertaining letter from the Master tonight, and I am glad that you were in condition to receive it so well. He said that you were very successful and he is pleased.

Good-night.

Your own true and loving,   HELEN.

The development of the soul in its natural love, wherein the New Birth is not experienced.

I am here. *Luke.*

I come tonight to say a few words concerning the great truth of the development of the soul in its natural love, wherein the New Birth is never experienced.

I know that men think that this natural love has in it a part of the divinity of the Father's nature, and that as they develop in the way of purifying it and ridding it of those things which tend to impair its harmony, they will realize that there exsts in their souls this divinity of which we have written. But this is not true, for this natural love partakes only of those elements which the Father implanted in it at the time of man's creation, and in none of these elements is any of the qualities of the divine nature.

It is difficult to explain just the distinction between the Divine Love coming from the Father, and the natural love also coming from Him, and yet, not having any of the Divine nature or qualities; but it is a fact. The natural love may become so purified that it may come into perfect harmony with the laws governing its condition and composition, and yet, fall far short of having in it any of the Divine Love.

And so, as we have explained to you, the soul may obtain this Divine Love and thereby become a part of the Father's divinity. I will now try to explain how the natural love of man may be developed so that his soul may come into harmony with the law of love—the natural love—and make him a very happy, pure and contented being.

In the first place, I wish to say that there is no such thing in the world as original sin or evil, and that God did not create them or permit them to exist except as he permits man to use his own will without limitation— and I mean by this that he does not say that a man, in the exercise of this will, shall do this or do that,and as respects this will man is untrammeled. But he does say, and his laws are inexorable in this particular, that man when in the exercise of the great power of free will, causes that will to come into conflict with the will of God, or to violate His laws, he, man, must suffer the consequences.

This may be illustrated by your natural laws declaring the freedom of the press. Man may publish whatsoever he pleases, and so long as he does not thereby violate the rights of others or of decency, he may make his publications without fear of the law; but when in the exercise of this freedom of speech, as you call it, he violates the law then he must suffer the consequences of this violation.

So it is with the mortal who, in the exercise of his free will, violates the will of the Father or the laws limiting its exercise by the mortal, he must suffer the consequences; and the results of this violation are sin and evil created, and in no other way. And surprising as it may sound to you, man is the creator of sin and evil, and not God who is only good.

Then the question arises, how can sin and evil be eradicated from the world? And every thoughtful man will have the same answer and that is: by men ceasing to violate the will of God or his laws which restrict the exercise of the wills of mortals to that which in its right exercise will not produce sin or evil. In other words, when men by the wrong use of their wills bring about inharmony, they can by the right use of their wills not disturb that harmony, which when it exists leaves no room for the presence of sin and error.

So you see, the one thing necessary in order for men to become happy and free from everthing that defiles them, or causes unhappiness or discord to exist, is to develop their souls in this natural love, until this love comes into perfect unison with the laws that control it; and thus may be applied the oft quoted expression "that love is the fulfilling of the law"— but this means love in its purest and most perfect state.

Now, how can this development of the natural love be accomplished by men?

The mind while a powerful helper in this regard is not of itself sufficient to bring about this great desideratum. It is true that with every mortal there is a constant warfare between the appetites and lusts of the flesh and his higher desires, and, hence, it is said, that these appetites and desires are sinful and the cause of evil and the inharmony that exists in the lives of mortals. But this statement is not altogether true, for as man was made with spiritual aspirations and desires, so also was he made with appetites and desires of the flesh, and the latter of themselves are not evils.

The failure to make the distinction between the fact that these appetites and desires of the flesh are not evil, and the fact that only the perversion of them brings evil, is the great stumbling block that stands in the way of man's developing this natural love in the manner that I have indicated. These, what are sometimes called the animal appetites and desires, may be exercised in such a way as to be in perfect harmony with the laws that control them, and in such exercise not interfere with or prevent the development of this natural love to perfection.

But man, in the free exercise of his will, has in his wanderings gone beyond the limitations which the law of harmony has placed upon him, added to and increased and distorted the appetites and desires of the flesh which were originally bestowed upon him, and, hence, has himself created those things that are not in harmony with the creation of himself.

So you see, man is a creator as well as a creature. As the latter he cannot alter or change any of the effects of his creation; but as the former he can alter and change and even abolish the effects of his own creation, for as the creator is greater than the things that he created, although these things of his own creation have held him in bondage and unhappiness to a more or less extent ever since he became their creator. The strength of this apparent paradox is that the creator, man, has for all these long centuries believed it, and submitted to his creations, and still does so.

So what is the remedy?

Simply this: man must awaken to the fact that he is greater than his creatures, that they are subject to his will, and that whenever by their existence and workings they bring discord and unhappiness and cause his will to be exercised in opposition to the will of the Father, then they must be destroyed and never be permitted to come into existence again. Let men become the masters of their creatures, and obedient to the great will of their Creator, and they will realize that sin and error and unhappiness

369

will disappear, and their natural love will come into harmony with the laws of its creation, and earth will indeed become a heaven and the brotherhood of man established on earth.

If men will only think, and thinking, believe that all sin and error and the resulting unhappiness and sorrow in the world, are children of their own creation and not the children of God, and that in the economy of His universe he leaves the control and management and even the existence of these children to the will of their parents, they will understand why evil exists, why wars and hatred and misery continue on earth to blight the lives and happiness of mortals; and why as some say, and especially the so-called Christians, God permits all these things to exist and flourish and apparently contradict the great truth, that He is good and the fountainhead of all goodness.

The universe and the inhabitants thereof and the greatest production of His power—man—were all created by God; but sin and error and their awful followings are the creatures of man. The laws of His universe work in harmony and all is good; and even the apparent inharmony which man has created does not affect that great harmony, but is confined in its workings to man, himself. Only man is apparently in inharmony, and that is caused by man, himself.

Suppose, for a moment, that man's will was working in accord with that of the Father, can you imagine that there would be any of these creatures of man's perverted will in existence? Would there be any evil or hatred or disease or suffering known to the consciousness of man? I tell you, no.

Now I say man, their creator, must destroy these inharmonious creatures—man must kill and bury deep and forever these children of the perverted exercise of his will and until then sin and error and all their concomitants will continue to live and flourish and torment their creator.

And I say here with all emphasis and with a full realization of the great significance and responsibility in the sight of God which I assume in saying it, that man can destroy these bastard creatures of his will so perverted and discordant.

His natural love, if permited to assert its God-given powers and functions, is sufficient to bring his will in accord with that of the Father, and turn his thoughts away from these children of his, and to make him conscious of purity and truth. The dead desires and dead appetites will bury their dead children, and man will come into his own again.

But then comes the question how is man to accomplish this great end, so devoutly to be wished for?

Well, it is late now, and I will write upon this important feature of this development of his natural love in my next message.

So with all my love I will say good night.

Your brother in Christ,

LUKE.

Continued from preceding message. Development of the soul in its natural love.

I am here, Luke.

Well do you think you can take my message tonight? It looks like you may, at any rate we will try.

As I was saying, in what way is a man to obtain this development of the soul in its natural love?

In the first place, he must recognize the fact that he does not live to himself, alone—that what he conceives to be the workings of his own mind and will are not always the result of thoughts and desires that originate in him, but are largely the products of the influences of the workings of the minds of spirits who are around him, trying to impress him with their desires and wills; and, consequently, you will understand that it is very important to man as to what kind of spirit influences he has surrounding and working upon him. If these influences are good, the better it is for his progress in the development of this natural love; but if they are evil influences, then, of course, such development is retarded.

Consequently, the first thing for a man to do is to attempt to attract to himself influences of the higher nature; and he can do so by trying to cultivate good thoughts and to indulge in good and moral acts.

The great law of attraction that we have written about, applies and works in such cases as this as it does in every other relation of God's universe. If a man's thoughts are evil, there will alway be attracted to him spirits of similar thoughts and when they come to him they attempt to and succeed in intensifying these evil thoughts of his, which attract them to him.

It must emphatically be understood in this regard that man may and often does originate his own thoughts, and desires, and it is not necessary that any influence of these evil spirits should be present and operate upon his brain or affections in order that these evil thoughts and desires should come into existence. And again, man has a will power that is susceptible of being exercised free from the wills of these evil spirits; and you will see how true this is when you remember that he can exercise that will power free and independent from the will of God himself.

So I say that these thoughts and desires may and do originate in man free and independent of the wills or influences of these evil spirits; and as a fact, these spirits are attracted to him only when these thoughts that he has originated are evil.

Now, if man would have this progress that I speak of, he should endeavor to have good and pure thoughts and desires, and then he will attract to him spirits who are good and pure, and their influences will help him to a wonderful degree in strengthening and increasing these thoughts, and make it less and less likely that evil thoughts will arise in his brain or evil desires in his affections; and as a consequence, his will power will be exercised in doing those things which are good and moral.

Now, while man may originate these thoughts and desires, he must also know as a truth that this progress is not dependent upon himself alone, for when he is in that condition to attract the good spirits they will invariably come to him and render their help; and it will prove to be a wonderful and never failing help.

Now, man's thoughts and desires are not always, as may be supposed, the result of something that may be hidden within himself, and of which he may not know its existence. I mean not in all cases, and probably in only a minority of cases; for most frequently are these thoughts and desires the children of an objective influence that comes to him by reason of objects becoming sensible to his ordinary senses, which create or suggest these thoughts or desires.

Without going into details, you will understand what I mean, but as a mere illustration: a glass of whiskey may and does suggest to a man who likes whiskey the thought and desire that he should take a drink, and thereby bring into operation his will, which is followed by the act of drinking. And so with many other objects which a man meets in the course of his daily life. But these thoughts and desires arise not only from seeing objects, but also from feeling and tasting them.

And again, these objective suggestions, causing these thoughts and desires, arise and exist not only from the real object sensed, but also from words and thoughts which are expressed by other human beings in course of conversations or in books and literature; and when they come in this way they are frequently more effective than in any other, and, hence, as these objective words and thoughts enter the mind of man they create similar thoughts, which frequently intensify and attract the evil spirits of like thoughts, with their degenerating influences.

Hence the importance of a man avoiding companionship where such communications take place, and the books and literature where these evil suggestions are made.

It has been well said, that evil communications corrupt good manners; and I may add that such communications corrupt good thoughts and produce evil desires and retard the progress of the soul in its natural love. For it must be remembered that this love is pure and free from all evil or taint of defilement when it is fully developed, and anything that tends to defile it retards the progression of the soul in this particular.

So the plain lesson to be drawn from all this is, that man must, in the first place, make the effort to have only good and pure thoughts and desires from his inner self, and next, he must avoid those objects and associations that tend to cause to arise in him these evil thoughts, and, thirdly, he must learn the truth that when he has these evil thoughts he attracts to himself spirits of evil, who by their influence can and do intensify these evil thoughts and desires.

I know as regards this last mentioned truth, that the majority of men have no knowledge of its existence; but it is time that they should learn that such a danger to their soul's progression does exist and is always imminent.

And they should learn this other fact, that when their thoughts are pure and free from defilement, they have surrounding them the influence of good spirits who work to increase and make permanent their good thoughts; and as these good thoughts continue, the natural love develops towards its pristine condition of purity, and man comes nearer to his designed condition of existence.

So you will see from this, that as man's thoughts and desires become freed from these things that tend to defile him, he naturally progresses toward that condition which is necessary in order for him to have this development of the soul in its natural love.

Again, the development may be helped very much by man thinking and doing acts of charity and kindness and observing the golden rule, for every act of charity and kindness and self sacrifice for the sake of others, has its reflex action in his own condition of love and soul, and helps their development.

In short, the observance by man of all the moral laws, which are many and varied, tends to bring about the development of the natural love; and this must be remembered, that as this development proceeds the tendency to indulge in the perverted appetites of the flesh, as they are called, will disappear, and as it disappears this love, of course, becomes purer and sweeter and brings man nearer to his state of perfection.

And again, the meditation upon spiritual things and the outflowing of this love towards the Father will cause the progression, for while all men, as we have said, do not seek for the Divine Love, yet as all men are children of God, he helps them to the full extent of their desires towards happiness and the perfecting of this love in its natural pure state, and with which he endowed them at their creation. Upon their will and aspirations depends the nature of the help which the Father gives to them; but always He gives his help and blessings and to the fullest. His great desire is that man shall become perfect in that love which they possess and which they seek for; and the natural love in its qualities may become as perfect in man, as may the Divine Love in its qualities. Each is just as much in harmony with God's universe, in its respective qualities. as is the other.

So I say, man is helped and more than in any other way, by his meditations of the higher things of his being and by prayer and aspirations to the Father, who hears the prayers of the man who has only this natural love and answers them just as he does the prayers of the man who has the Divine Love in his soul.

Ultimately all sin and evil will be eradicated from the universe, and man in his mere natural love will become pure and perfected and happy.

I have tried in my inefficient way to show man how he may progress in the deveopment of his natural love, and if he will follow my advice he will succeed, for as man by the indulging of these perverted appetites of the flesh and the exercise of his will power fell to a low degree of degeneracy, so he can by ceasing to indulge in these perverted appetites, and the exercise of that same will power rise again to his condition of purity in his natural love.

And besides he has the help of the Father and the good angels in his efforts to recover, and also the experience of the result of his fall, which he may not be conscious of, but which in his inner self has an existence and is continually working.

Well my dear brother I must stop, and I feel that you have taken my message very successfully. Read it over and correct errors of construction.

I will come soon and write again.

Your brother in Christ,   LUKE.

The truths may be understood by the simple—Does not require a highly developed mind.

I am here—*Jesus.*

My truths are plain and my teachings can be understood by the simple. Any religion which requires the exercise of the mental faculties to an extent greater than what is required in the ordinary affairs of life, cannot be a true religion; because God has designed that all his children shall understand His truths without the necessity of having a highly developed mind.

He that runs may understand my teachings and it will not be necessary for any preacher or teacher to explain them. My language will explain itself. So let not your mind be troubled over the question as to whether only the mentally developed can understand what I may write—the truths are for all.

So with all my love I am,

Your brother and friend,   JESUS.

What the Celestial Spirits think about war.

I am here. *Luke.*

I heard the doctor ask, what do the Celestial Spirits think of this war, and I will in a few words tell him.

Well, first he must know that the Celestial Spirits are not so much interested in the war and the success or defeat of nations as in the salvation of the souls of the individuals who compose those nations, and the fact that the individual is a German or an Englishman or a Frenchman has no influence upon the desire of the spirit to help the soul of the individual. All are alike important and dear to the Celestial Spirits, and the same love that will save the one, will save the other. So you can see that the war is not of so much importance.

Of course many mortals are made spirits who are all unfitted for the life in the spirit world, and in that view the war is of importance to the Celestial Spirits, as their opportunity for doing work among mortals, either directly or through other spirits, is by such slaughter interfered with, and the spirits who come so suddenly to our spirit world are subjected to greater suffering, and are more difficult to impress and teach the way to truth and life, than they would have been if allowed to live their ordinary mortal lives.

All wars, to some extent, interfere with the orderly living and dying of mortals, and we deplore them, but as to the right or the wrong of wars we do not judge, but leave that to the conscience and judgment of the individuals who bring about the wars and are responsible for them. The acts of individuals whether they apply personally, or affect others in the way of being members of nations, are all subject and responsible to the laws which control the thoughts and deeds of mortals and the recollections of the same; and these laws do not call for or demand the paying the penalties of the individuals as parts of a nation, but as individuals, irrespective of the fact that they belong to and control the affairs of a nation.

No sin is of less interest to spirits because it arose from the wars of nations, than if it had arisen from the act of the individual as such, and we Celestial Spirits are interested in the war that is now going on, and because of that fact, for I say, it causes the paying of the penalties demanded by the law much sooner than it otherwise would. And we are interested also, because war creates hatred and desire for vengeance on the part of those engaged in them, and hence adds to the burdens that the individual so affected will have to get rid of when he comes to the spirit world in order to progress and find happiness.

War to us is an incident of human existence and the right or wrong of it does not enter into our consideration of what should be the penalties that those who are responsible for it should suffer. The soul of each individual shows its own sins and wrong done, and only this condition of the soul determines the state of its possessor, and the destiny that its own thoughts and acts have made for it.

Now, from what I have said, you may suppose that we are indifferent to the happiness or misery of mortals while on earth, but that is not true. We realize that man to a large extent, must work out his own destiny on earth, and that we spirits cannot control that work, except as we may influence the individual mind and thoughts of men, and that there are times when men give way to their passions and evil ambitions, in which we cannot influence them. Even God, Himsef, does not attempt by His omnipotence to do so, but leaves men to the exercise of their own wills and the consequences of their own acts; and this, although many suffer physically and mentally, who are innocent.

But all men live not unto themselves, but are so united in society that the acts of one must have their influence on others, and, hence, those who live in these societies are subject to these influences and to the consequences that flow from them. It may not seem right that the innocent should suffer because of the acts of the guilty, and if the Celestial Spirits could prevent it, such sufferings would not take place, but they cannot so prevent the intermingling of suffering between and among those living in societies, for to do so, they would have to interfere with the operations of the laws controlling these things, which they cannot do. So you see, war does not mean to the high spirits what you might suppose, and while they have their sympathy and love for all the children of men in these terrible conflicts, yet, they must leave men to the consequences of their own deeds and thoughts, and man must do the suffering.

But, nevertheless, we do try to influence those who have the control and determination of these things, and our work is always to try to influence them to do that which will bring to men the greatest happiness.

We do not interest ourselves as to whether one belligerent nation or the other will win the battles, because we know that only men themselves can decide this matter, and we don't try to interfere to bring about the success of the one party or the other, as we know that we are powerless to bring about any result.

Think for a moment, and you will understand that if we had the power to determine the issues of war, we should have the power to destroy sin and error, because both are the subjects of the creation and control of men, and I say that if we had such power sin and error would long ago have disappeared from the world and men made free.

No, we can work only with the individual, and as the individual soul is made pure and righteous the aggregate of these individuals composing a nation will become pure and righteous, and war will become impossible.

I do not think it best to write more now, but will say, that we Celestial Spirits think of war as the creature of mortals, to be controlled and ended by mortals, and that we cannot decide the issue one way or the other, and, hence, to us war is an incident in the living and dying of mortals that we cannot prevent or create.

Your brother in Christ

LUKE.

Jesus heard the speaker's discourse on "Drama of St. Paul."
Some things were said that were true and some false.

I am here, *Jesus*.

I was with you to night and heard the speaker's discourse on the "Drama of St. Paul."

Well it was very interesting and in some places impressive, and should produce a great effect upon the hearers. Many things that the speaker recited were true and occurred substantially as he related them, but some were not matters of actual occurrence and Paul never had all the experiences that he spoke of. But these were of minor importance and did not affect the truth of the narrative as a whole.

Of course the whole discourse was taken from the Bible, and, as I have told you before, there are many things in the Bible which are not true. His description of Paul's experience on the way to Damascus is partly true and partly not.

Well, I spoke to him and when he was felled to the ground by the brightness of the great light that shone about him, Paul heard what I said and answered me, and went into the town, but he was not blind nor did the prophet Ananias do anything to him in the way of curing any physical blindness; he only helped to open the spiritual blindness of Paul, and show him the way to the Father's love and kingdom.

Paul, as you know, was a very learned man among the Jews, and was a strict believer and follower of the Pharisees' doctrines; but as to knowing anything about the Divine Love, he had never experienced it, nor even did not know what it was intellectually.

My summons to him was not only for the purpose of stopping the persecution of my people, but for the further purpose of enlisting him in my cause, as not many of my followers were educated or learned men, and I realized that my doctrines and truths must be preached among not only the learned Jews, but also among the gentile philosophers; and as the first requisite in such cases is to hold and in a way convince the intellect, I saw that I must have a disciple who would have the mental qualifications to present to these learned men in a convincing way, my truths and be able to withstand the logic and reasoning of these gentile philosophers.

John was filled with love, and wherever he could come in close communion with the comon people, he could by the great power and influence of that love persuade these people to embrace and receive my truths, and, as a consequence, feel the inflowing of the Holy Spirit.

But Paul had not this love to that degree as to be enabled by virtue of its power or influence to convince and compel his hearers to receive my truths, and embrace that faith in my teachings as would cause them to seek the love of the Father; and, hence, his mission was the more intended to be the teachings of my truths to the intellect and mental perceptions of a large number of persons of greater intellectual development than those with whom John and the other disciples would come in contact.

Of course Paul acquired this Love to a very large degree, but not sufficiently to prevent him at times in his early ministry from doubting my calling him to do this work; and, as he has told you, this doubt was the besetting sin or thorn in the flesh from which he suffered. Had he had the fulness of the Love that John and some of the others had, he would never have had the doubts of which he speaks.

But, nevertheless, he became a wonderful power in spreading my truths and in convincing men that the Love of the Father was the one great possession to be obtained, and in causing them to believe in me as the son of the Father and His messenger to declare to the world the great plan of man's salvation.

Paul finally became a man filled with this Love as far as his nature was capable of receiving it, and in his gospel will be found wonderful exhortations to his hearers to seek for it. But he was not the disciple of love, but rather of the intellectual parts of my truths, and when he taught, his teachings were intended to appeal more to the mental perceptions than to the soul perceptions.

He never taught that I was God, nor did he believe that I was, and whenever it is set forth that he did say, or rather what the Bible says on that subject, is interpreted to mean that I am God, that interpretation is erroneous.

I will not write more on Paul to night, but will tell you of some things of more importance to mankind. **I am now working as I did on earth, though in a little different way, to show men the way to God's love and eternal life, and to assure them that the Great Divine Love of the Father is waiting for them to have it flow into their souls and make them at-one with Him.**

Men are now in a condition that causes them to long for this great Love and the peace and happiness which it brings, without knowing really what it is that they desire; and when my truths are placed before them and they are told of the wonderful blessings that may be theirs by merely seeking for it in earnest and honest prayer, they will turn their thoughts and longings to God and His Love, and find the happiness and peace which they so much realize the want of.

I have many things to write you, and hope that we may soon have the rapport that will enable me to do so.

Well, I see how you feel, and I am so glad that you do; and I must tell you that the Father's Love is working in your soul and will result in your becoming my true and earnest disciple. I will be with you in all my power and influence so that nothing will prevent the doing of the great work which I have selected you to do. You must pray to the Father for His love and for faith, and they will come to you; for such prayers the Father desires to answer and grant.

And besides, as I pray to Him and all my followers pray, we will ask the Father to give you this Great Love and faith and power to do the work, and to sustain you through all the years that may be yours on earth, for the work must be done.

You have written long to night and I think it best that I stop. But before doing so let me say again, that you are the special object of my care and love, and I will be with you in all your worries and conflicts and will help you to overcome them all, and to get in that position that will give you the freedom that is so desirous.

With all my love and blessings, and the love and blessings of the Father, I will say good night.

Your brother and friend,

JESUS.

St. Paul's comments on the preacher's sermon, "On the Drama of St. Paul." His experience when on earth.

I am here, St. Paul.

Well, my brother, I was with you at the discourse on the "Drama of St. Paul," and was much interested in the subject matter, and also in the manner in which the speaker delivered his discourse. He was somewhat dramatic himself, and his elocution and intonation of the dialogues between several of the prominent personages in the drama and myself were very effective; but really they, the intonations, did not sound very familiar, because to me they possessed too much artificiality to represent correctly the real tones of voice and the feelings that possessed these persons and myself on those occasions. But, nevertheless, they were very effective, and I have no doubt, produced on the hearers the effect intended.

Some of the scenes depicted were very real, and some of them were not, for they never occurred.

I well remember my experience on the way to Damascus, and the great change that it caused to my whole existence on earth. The brightness and the voice of Jesus were actualities, but the statement that I went blind is not true, for I was not blind but only affected for the time by the unusual light, and also the shock that the voice of Jesus caused. As Jesus said, my only blindness was that which covered my spiritual eyes at the time, and when I went into the town the only blindness that I recovered from in a way, was that which had kept my soul in darkness and caused me to persecute the followers of Jesus under the belief that I was doing the work which God had called me to do. So you see, that while the description as a whole of my life after my call was very interesting, yet it was not altogether correct.

Jesus has told you what my condition of soul development was, and how I lacked the love which I afterwards, to some degree, possessed. And

379

as he says, I was in my early ministry more of an intellectual Christian than a Chritian possessing the Great Divine Love of the Father; yet thanks to him I continued to preach and believed as best I could, until finally I became a redeemed child of God, filled with His Love.

I knew many things connected with and taught in the theology of the Jews, and especially of the Pharisees. I see now that in my writings, my conceptions of the truths of God were flavored to a considerable extent by this knowledge which are of the Jewish theology.

While many things that I taught are true as I now see them, yet many things that the Bible says I wrote are not true, and I am not surprised that men will not accept them at this time. How I wish that I could review and rewrite the Epistles ascribed to me. How many seeming contradictions and unreasonable things would be made plain. But I cannot, except as I may through you declare the truth as I now see it; and I hope that the opportunities may come that I may do so.

Well, I will not write more to night as you have written considerable, and others wish to write. I will say good night.

Your brother in Christ,   PAUL.

Describes the Celestial Heavens.

I am here, *Samuel, The Prophet.*

I am the prophet who came to you before and wrote. To night, I want to tell you of the wonderful things which God has prepared for his redeemed children in the Celestial Spheres, where only those who have received the New Birth can enter.

In these spheres are homes made of the most beautiful materials that can be imagined, and which are of a real and permanent character, and not subject to decay or deterioration of any kind, and which are made without hands but by the soul's development and the love which each spirit possesses.

These homes are furnished with everything that is suited to make the inhabitants happy and contented; and not one element of inharmony has any abiding place therein. Every home has its library and the most beautiful furniture and paintings and wall coverings, and also rooms that are devoted to the various uses that a spirit may need them for. The music is sublime beyond conception; and there are all kinds of musical instruments which the spirits know how to play, and, as you may not suppose, every spirit has the ability to sing. There are no voices that are out of tune with the surroundings and with the other voices. Every spirit has music in his soul, and every spirit has the vocal qualities to express that music.

Couches for repose are provided, and running fountains and beautiful flowers of every hue and variety, and lawns the most beautiful and green.

Trees are in abundance and are planted in the most artistic manner, so that they are in harmony with the surrounding landscape.

And the light that comes to our homes is of such a kind that I cannot describe it, and can only say that with it and in it are the most soothing and wonderful influences that spirits can conceive of.

All these things and many more are provided by our loving Father for the happiness of His children. But above all is this, the wonderful Love of the Father which is always with us, and which fills our souls to overflowing and keeps us in one continuous state of happiness and peace and joy.

All these things are freely given to us, and with them the knowledge that we are a part of the Father's Divine Being, and have, beyond the possibility of losing it, the immortality which Jesus brought to light when he came to earth.

I have been in these heavens many years and know whereof I speak, and when I tell you of these things, I do so that you and all mankind may know that these delights may be yours and theirs if you will only let the Divine Love of the Father enter your souls and take complete possession of it.

Well, as to our social enjoyments, we are so loving one to the other that nothing arises, as on earth, to cause one the slightest jar in our wonderful harmony. We visit one another and give our experiences of the love life that we lead, and have music and interchange thoughts about our continuous progress and our work in the spirit world. Every spirit in our sphere may visit every other spirit and know that the door is always open and a warm welcome awaiting him.

I cannot tell you of all these wonders because there are no words that will convey our meanings. Your capacity to understand is limited by your mental boundaries, and, hence, I am at a disadvantage. But this I can tell you and that is, that some day, if you get the Divine Love in your soul in sufficient abundance you will see and understand for yourselves what God has in store for you. It was truly said, "that no eye has seen or mind conceived the wonderful things that await the true child of the Father."

No, there are no streets of gold or walls of jasper or any of these material things that John made use of in his Apocalypse to describe the City of God. They were merely used as symbols, but they did not express the wonders of our homes.

I will not write more tonight, but will come again sometime and tell you of things that are of more importance than a description of our homes.

With all my love, I am Your brother in Christ,

SAMUEL.

The truths of God must not be sought for in his writings or those
of the disciples as contained in the Bible,
because of many errors therein.

St. Jerome.

I came to tell you that I am an inhabitant of that Kingdom which Samuel has so inadequately described, and that is the kingdom of Jesus and of course of the Father.

You may not know anything about me, but I was canonized many centuries ago by the church, because it thought that I had done the church so much good by my writings and discourses on things religious. But I must confess now, that when I wrote, I expressed as truths many things which I now see were not true, and I would like to be able to correct all these errors in my writings, but I cannot.

So I will tell you in a few words that the truths of the Master, which are the truths of God, must not be sought for in my writings, or even in those of his disciples as contained in the Bible, because of the many errors that therein exist, not because the disciples and those to whom they conveyed these truths did not write them correctly, but because the Bible, as now written, is not the same in many important particulars as what the disciples wrote. **And hence Jesus, knowing this, is so anxious that the world shall receive these great truths again through his written messages.**

I am trying my best to help the cause which he is advocating, and am one of the spirits behind you who are trying with all their spirit powers to direct you aright and enable you to receive the truths.

I am in a Celestial Sphere very high up in the heavens. I cannot otherwise describe its location. These spheres are not numbered after the first few, because then they interblend so that there is no lines of demarcation.

But I am not so high up as are the disciples and many others who are followers of the Master. The ancient spirits, such as Moses and Abraham and Isaac and Jacob are in higher spheres; but they are not so exalted as are Jesus' apostles and disciples, and, as I am informed, many spirits who came to the spirit world since Jesus came.

I will not write more to night, but will thank you, and say good night.

Your brother in Christ, St. Jerome.

The Truth As to the Hells

I am here. *John*

I merely want to say that I have listened to the message that you read and to the remarks of your friend and yourself, and believe that you have a true conception of the truth as to these hells.

Swedenborg gave you a correct description of their conditions as they actually exist, and * Herod told you with the certainty of experience what

* Herod's message not yet in print.

he found to be true, and I, John, who have visited them in the efforts to allay the sufferings of the spirits who inhabit them, tell you that they exist as places, with all the darkness and surroundings that cause the sufferings of the unfortunate spirits to increase. I desire to make this statement so that this question of what hell really is may be settled for all time so far as you are concerned.

I know that many mortals console themselves with the belief that because of certain natural laws there cannot possibly be any hells such as the orthodox teach, that therefore there cannot be any hells at all. But the conclusion drawn from the premise is not correct. The mere fact that because a man or spirit cannot burn eternally and never be consumed, does not justify the inference that such spirit cannot be punished by surroundings which have a fixed locality.

No, man must not rest in the belief of there being no such hells as Swedenborg has described, because if they do, they will be woefully mistaken and surprised should they live such lives on earth as will cause them to be placed in these hells.

I merely wanted to say this much tonight: as I don't want you to receive any communication which is not in accord with the truth.

It is of such vital importance that you receive nothing but the truth, that we who are interested in this work have determined that nothing but the truth shall come to you, and that whenever error or misstatements creep in we will carefully correct the same.

So without writing more tonight, I will say that I am,

Your brother in Christ,   JOHN.

Man will not suffer in hell for all eternity but sometime will progress. I am here. *John.*

I was with you tonight and heard the sermon on hell, and was so sorry that the preacher could not tell his people more of the truths as to what hell is and the punishment of those who will be so unfortunate as to go to that place will be. It is pitiable that these leaders of the people are so blinded and without knowledge as to what the truth is in regard to this subject, as well as to many others—that they so erroneously declare to their congregations. Of course, their knowledge is based upon what they consider to be the truths of the Bible, and in many respects what they say is justified by the teachings of the Book, but in many cases their teachings are erroneous because of the wrong construction that they place upon many of the declarations of the Bible. In either case they are teaching for the truth those things that are not true, and the harm accomplished is just as baneful as if their beliefs and teachings were the result of what they realized to be untrue. Untruth is untruth, no matter whether it arises from honest conviction or known error and the harm done is the same in each instance. The preacher, I have no doubt, believes what he declared to be the truth, and some things he said were true, yet the fact that he believed these doctrines to be true will not palliate in any way his responsibility so far as the effect of these errors on his hearers are concerned, for their sufferings and darkness, which will certainly follow their beliefs in these erroneous teachings, will be no less, because the preacher was honest in his declarations of what he supposed to be the truth. The source of error does not in any way modify or affect the results that flow from its acceptance and following, and the preacher while not in such cases a willful deceiver, yet when he comes to the spirit world, and learns the truth, he will have the regrets and the sufferings which always flow from the spreading of falsehood and deception.

Error works its own punishment, but it may be of some consolation, and will be to those who preach and to those who accept falsehood as truth, to know that such punishment will not be everlasting, and that God is not a God of wrath or of vindictiveness, and that His justice never demands more than is necessary for the removing of error and the establishment of His truths.

Why, His justice would not be justice if He permitted error to continue and prevented recovery on the part of man or spirits of the truth, just for the purpose of having those who had been disobedient, suffer and be separated from Him for all eternity.

I merely wanted to say this much on the sermon, and sometime I will come and write you a full explanation of what hell is, its purpose and work and how long it continues.

Let all of you continue to pray to the Father for this Love and have faith, and the time will soon come that faith will become as real and existing as the sun which you so much enjoyed today.

So my brother, with all my love and blessings I will say goodnight.

Your brother in Christ,

JOHN—Apostle of Jesus.

What is the destiny of the mortal who has not experienced the New Birth, but will progress to that condition which may be called the perfect man.

I am here. *St. John* (Apostle of Jesus).

I want to write tonight on a subject that is important, and I hope that you will be able to receive my message, for I have been waiting for some time to deliver it.

Well, I desire to discourse on the subject of: *"What is the destiny of the mortal who has not experienced the New Birth, but who will progress to that condition which may be called the perfect man."* As you know, there is a future for the mortal who receives the New Birth, and a different one for him who has only the complete and pure development of his natural love.

This latter condition does not depend upon the mortal having in his soul the Divine Love or the Essence of the Father, but merely upon the purification of the natural love, so that all sin and error and inharmony form no part of his state of soul or mental existence. This condition is not the result of a New Birth or of a change in the constituent elements of his soul, but merely the elimination of those things, therefrom, which were the results and the necessary sequences of the defilement that followed the fall.

Now as man lost by this fall the qualities which made him the perfect creature of his Maker, it is only necessary for him to regain what he lost by that fall in order to become the perfect man once more, and in recovering this state of perfection it is not required that he should seek, or actually add to the qualities which he at first possessed, any new or additional qualities or attributes, but only that he regain what he had been deprived of by his disobedience; and when that is accomplished he will come again, in harmony with the laws of his creation, and have all the potentialities and excellence that he originally possessed.

And now, what will that future be? And in order to determine this question it is only necessary to understand what his inherent condition or qualities were when he was the perfect man of his Father's creation.

At that time he was possessed of those things of which he is now the possesser, except that then they were all so accurately adjusted that every sense and function of his body, as well as every faculty of his soul and mind were so in harmony with the laws of his creation, that he was capable of doing the will of the Father, and obeying every requirement that was imposed upon him.

He was then, not only a perfect being as regarded his physical formation, but also as regarded his mental and moral qualities, which of course included all the emotions and appetites and spiritual aspirations. But, as we have written you before, all these faculties were subject to his will, and in a certain sense his will was controlled by the exercise of these faculties.

His body was in the beginning made of matter, changeable as it now is, but of a more ethereal kind and not subject to decay and disintegration in such a short time, as it now is, but, yet, subject to this decay; and man, as regards his physical being, necessarily was compelled to die, and to have released his spirit body and his soul from this physical vesture, and thereafter exist as pure spirit. This was not the death that he died as a consequence of his disobedience, but the death natural to him, by reason of the very nature of his creation.

His soul and spirit body were not subject to death in the sense of annihilation, but were given the qualities of continual existence in a pure and perfect state, and the only difference that the fall made as to these parts of his being, is that the purity and harmony that were men's are now no longer parts of his soul and spirit.

Whether immortality was a quality of that existence, we spirits do not know, and therefore cannot assert, but as his created soul and spirit body had a beginning—mere creatures of the Father—it may be that they were intended to have an ending, as individualized soul and spirit.

Of course, they were created from something, and not from nothing, as some of your theologians say, and it is possible in the order of change, which seems to be the law in the spirit world as well as in the mortal world, that this soul and spirit may be resolved again into that something.

But as to this finality we do not have any knowledge, because, so far as the observation of spirits in this world go, no soul or spirit body—and I mean the body as a composite whole, and not as to its constituent elements—has ever been resolved into that something, or been deprived of its individualized existence. Therefore, I cannot say, that when man was created, it was intended that, as man, he should not be immortal, or that he should be so.

But you will readily see, that after man shall have accomplished the purification of his soul and become in mind and spirit body, as it was intended he should be at the time of his creation, he will be nothing more nor less than he was at that time, and have no other or greater qualities, or freedom from limitations and changes than he had before his fall. Of course he will have no physical body, and here let me say that there is no fact or experience known to the spirit world that justifies the assertion that man on earth will ever be immune to physical death. I know that some say, that in the far future men may make such progress in the development of their natural love that their condition of inner purity will be so great as to cause the physical bodies to become so etherialized as to render them free from physical death. But that I cannot conceive will ever happen, for men were made to become inhabitants of the spiritual realms, and the short time they were decreed to live the earth life was for the purpose only of giving the soul an individualized existence.

Never was it intended that the physical form should have an eternity of existence, no matter how pure, or, as they say, etherealized it may become, for it was made of matter, of the earth, earthy, while the soul was made of that which had its origin in the spirit realm, and composed of spirit substance. So that it cannot be conceived that in the beginning man was created for an immortal earth existence.

I see that you are tired, and I will finish later. I am glad that I could write tonight, and also that you are in such good condition to receive my message.

So with my love and blessings and assurances that you have every reason to keep up your courage and hope, I am

Your brother in Christ, JOHN.

Continued from preceding message.

I am here. *John.*

I desire to finish my message and hope that you are in condition to receive it.

Well, as I was writing about the future or destiny of the soul that has not experienced the New Birth, I will continue where I left off.

When the soul becomes wholly purified and restored to that condition of perfection that was possessed by the first parents before the fall, it continues to live a life of happiness and contentment until it realizes that its possibility of further progress, either mentally, morally or spiritually, has come to an end, that it has reached its limit of advancement, and that the happiness that it then enjoys is the full complement of what it may obtain or possess. This condition is one which satisfies the large majority of those who have reached the state of the fully restored man, and they are content to live the life of such perfection, and rest in the assurance that there is no greater happiness or more desirable condition existing in the universe of God.

But with some of these souls this state does not bring or contain this complete satisfaction, and in them continues the desire for more and greater progress; but they realize that they have reached the limit of their progress, and that they must continue to live in that state which holds for them the happiness and delight of being perfect and at-one with the Father as was intended by Him when man was created the perfect being.

But notwithstanding this knowledge that as the soul develops in its natural love and in its moral and mental faculties to the finality of limitation there can be nothing beyond, yet, there comes to them a dissatisfaction and as it were, a negative unhappiness that causes unrest, and a conscious desire for something, they know not what.

It may be that the memory of something they heard in their progress through the spheres, or an imperfect suggestion of some unconscious, reproduced, dormant memory, inherited from their first parents, of the great gift of endless progress potentially bestowed upon God's first created beings, and forfeited, that causes the discontent and longings for something beyond the condition of their perfect state.

When this state of mind and soul comes to them, then they are susceptible to the teachings and help of those spirits who have in their souls the Divine Love and knowledge that there is a way that leads to everlasting progress without limit or possibility of reaching the end.

And many of these perfected souls in their natural love have followed the advice of these immortal spirits, and have left the high sphere of their perfection and entered the lower soul spheres of the spiritual heavens, and sought and found the New Birth of the soul, and progressed from sphere to sphere until they reached the Celestial Heavens, where they are still progressing and realizing a contentment never marred, but always accompanied with the knowledge that ever beyond are spheres of greater happiness of truth and knowledge.

But, as I say, the larger, yes much larger number of souls that have been born unto men, will find and rest, in the future, in the state and happiness of the restored first parents.

It should not be necessary for me to attempt to make the application of the truths which I have written to the desires and wills of men, for the vital importance of making the choice between the future of the Divine Spirit, and that of the * perfected man, is so apparent, that scarcely any mortal, who is not the man that says in his heart there is no God, needs another to apply for him the lesson taught. And I will say in closing that such lesson contains the truths, that actual observation and knowledge have made certain. Speculation does not enter into it, and the possibility of error or mistakes is utterly eliminated.

I have written enough and will stop for tonight.

You have received the message very satisfactorily and I am pleased.

So with my love and blessings, I will say goodnight, and God bless you with His love.

Your brother in Christ,   JOHN.

I am here—*Cornelius.*

I want to write merely a few lines tonight—I am so very much interested in you and your work, that I feel that I should give you some encouragement in the way of letting you know that there are many spirits present here tonight who love you very much and desire that you should receive their messages of love and truth.

As I have told you, I am in the Celestial Spheres and know what the love of the Father is and what immortality means, as I am the possessor of the Love, and the conscious owner of immortality. The world is now so anxious to know the truths that pertain to God and to man's relationship to Him, and the messages that you are receiving give to the world what it so longs for.

I know that the Christian doctrines as contained in the Bible and taught by many preachers and priests, are the only doctrines that the Christians have any knowledge of, and, consequently, are accepted by them as being

---

* Read messages from Jesus—Pages 86 to 90, Edition 1, Vol. I.

the inspired revelations of God, and the truth of what He is, and what man must do in order to obtain salvation. And these people rest securely in these beliefs, and in the assurance that the Bible way is the only way to salvation; and resting in these beliefs the world does not see the necessity for obtaining the only thing that will place them in at-onement with God, and make them inhabitants of His heavens.

I merely write this to show you that it is of the greatest importance that the truths of the way to salvation be revealed to mankind.

I do not think that I have anything more to say tonight, and so will leave you.

With all my love, I am

Your brother in Christ, CORNELIUS.

Happiness and peace that passeth all understanding that comes to the possessor of the Divine Love.

I am here—*Samuel.*

I come to write you that I am with you in love and hope for your present blessing and happiness.

I know that the worries of life prevent you from realizing the influence of this Great Love which is surrounding you and which is ready and waiting to fill your soul to its fullness. But if you will pray more to the Father and exercise your faith, you will find that your worries will lessen, and peace will come to you in such abundance and beauty that you will feel like a new man.

As John said, with this faith love will flow into your soul and you will realize to some extent the joys of our celestial conditions, for the love that may be yours is the same love, in its nature, that we possess and that has made angels of us all, and inhabitants of the Father's kingdom. Only believe and you will realize how willing this love is to take possession of your soul and make you so happy that even the troubles that you have will not be sufficient to take from you the great peace that passeth all understanding.

I have been in the spirit for many years and have possessed this love for a long time and know by actual experience what it is and what great joy it brings to its possessor, so that you can rely on what I promise you, and feel the certainty that actual knowledge gives. I am now, as you know, a wholly redeemed child of the Father, and one who knows that His Divine Love in the soul makes the man or spirit of the essence of the Father. When this Love enters the soul of man it increases like the leaven in the dough and continues in its work until the whole soul is impregnated with it, and everything of sin or error is wholly eradicated.

Love worketh all things that man can wish for or conceive of, and more besides. Paul's description of love and the wonderful qualities and conditions that emanate from it, does not contain all its emanations and resultant happiness.

But I must not write more tonight for it is late and you are tiring.

So believe what I have said, and try to follow my advice, and you will soon experience that peace and happiness which only this love can bring to the souls of men.

So with my love and blessings I will say good night.

Your brother in Christ,   SAMUEL.

THE PRAYER

Our Father, who art in heaven, we recognize Thou art all Holy and loving and merciful, and that we are Thy children, and not the subservient, sinful and depraved creatures that our false teachers would have us believe. That we are the greatest of Thy creation, and the most wonderful of all Thy handiworks, and the objects of Thy great soul's love and tenderest care.

That Thy will is, that we become at one with Thee, and partake of Thy great love which Thou hast bestowed upon us through Thy mercy and desire that we become, in truth, Thy children, and not through the sacrifice and death of any one of Thy creatures, even though the world believes that one Thy equal and a part of Thy Godhead.

We pray that Thou wilt open up our souls to the inflowing of Thy love, and that then may come Thy Holy Spirit to bring into our souls this, Thy love in great abundance, until our souls shall be transformed into the very essence of Thyself; and that there may come to us faith—such faith as will cause us to realize that we are truly Thy children and one with Thee in very substance and not in image only.

Let us have such faith as will cause us to know that Thou art our Father, and the bestower of every good and perfect gift, and that only we, ourselves, can prevent Thy love changing us from the mortal into the immortal.

Let us never cease to realize that Thy love is waiting for each and all of us, and that when we come to Thee, in faith and earnest aspiration, Thy love will never be with-holden from us.

Keep us in the shadow of Thy love every hour and moment of our lives, and help us to overcome all temptations of the flesh, and the influence of the powers of the evil ones, which so constantly surround us and endeavor to turn our thoughts away from Thee to the pleasures and allurements of this world.

We thank Thee for Thy love and the privilege of receiving it, and we believe that Thou art our Father—the loving Father who smiles upon us in our weakness, and is always ready to help us and take us to Thy arms of love.

We pray thus with all the earnestness and sincere longings of our souls, and trusting in Thy love, give Thee all the glory and honor and love that our finite souls can give.

This is the only prayer that men need offer to the Father. It is the only one that appeals to the love of the Father, and with the answer, which will surely come, will come all the blessings that men may need, and which the Father sees are for the good of His creatures.

I am in very great rapport with you to-night, and see that the Father's love is with you, and that your souls are hungry for more.

So, my brothers, continue to pray and have faith, and in the end will come a bestowal of the love like unto that which came to the apostles at Pentecost.

I will not write more now.

In leaving you, I will leave my love and blessings and the assurance that I pray to the Father for your happiness and love.

Good-night.

Your brother and friend,

JESUS.

Made in the USA
Columbia, SC
09 October 2021